GRANDPA'S RIB-TICKLERS and KNEE-SLAPPERS

JOKES AND STORIES
(some bawdy)
FROM AMERICA'S PAST.

Collected, edited and annotated by

JAMES E. MYERS

Lincoln-Herndon Press, Inc.
#1 West Old State Capitol Plaza
Springfield, Illinois 62701

First Edition
Manufactured in the United States of America.

For information write to:
LINCOLN-HERNDON PRESS, INC.
#1 West Old State Capitol Plaza
Springfield, Illinois 62701

Library of Congress Cataloguing in Publication Data.

Library of Congress Catalog Card Number: 84-81155.

ISBN 0-942936-03-5 (Softcover).
ISBN 0-942936-02-7 (Casebound).

Contents

"Genuine laffing iz the vent of the soul, the nostrils of the heart, and iz jist az necessary for the helth and happiness as spring water iz fer a trout. It iz the language of infancy—the eloquence of childhood—and the power to laugh iz the power to be happy."

Josh Billings

Acknowledgements.. ii
Introduction... iv
  I. Tall Tales, Windies and Whoppers............................ 1
  II. Jokes from 1842-1912... 37
  III. Colonial and Frontier Humor, a Rare Vintage............ 73
  IV. A Gallery of Fearsome Critters.................................136
  V. Oh, Those Phunny Phellows!....................................183
  VI. Abraham Lincoln's Stories.......................................234
  VII. Humor after the Civil War.......................................285
  VIII. The Bawdy Part..351
A Selected List for Further Reading.................................402

Illustrations by Matt Hylton

To my wife, Edith Sarah:

> Strength and dignity are her
> clothing;
> And she laugheth at the time to
> come.
> She openeth her mouth with
> wisdom;
> And the law of kindness is on
> her tongue.

Proverbs, 31:25, 26

Acknowledgments

The author is grateful above all to our national system of public libraries, without which this book could not have been written. The Interlibrary Service provides a national pool of books from which all member libraries may draw, thus making available to all citizens a cornucopia/reservoir of books. The value of this Service to the researcher is incalculable.

The staff of the Springfield, Illinois, Lincoln Library—especially its reference staff—earned our gratitude. Of particular help were Naomi Downing, Mary Cartwright, Marie E. Halcli, Alice Lanich, Peggy Sleeth, and Geri Whitaker. In that same city, valued assistance was given by the reference staff of the Illinois State Library: Garnetta Cook, David Morse, Rolla Truesdale, and Larry Weyrich. Further, the resources of the Illinois State Historical Library were invaluable, especially the help of Roger D. Bridges, Head Librarian and Director of Research.

The Institute for Research in Sex, Gender, and Reproduction, at Indiana University, Bloomington, provided their library as a prime source for scarce, early bawdy material. We are very grateful to Jan Scherer Brewer, Information Services Officer, for her unselfish aid. Also at Indiana University Folklore Institute, the author was signally aided by Jean Harrar-Conforth, Archivist and Prof. Linda Degh.

Mrs. Jan Anderson, Folklore Archivist at Western Kentucky University was most helpful with that University's resources in its Folklore and Oral History Archives.

Dr. Clyde C. Walton, Director of Libraries, University of Colorado, provided exceptional insight to resources at the facilities under his direction.

One of the great sources for American humor of the last century is the Meine Collection at the University of Illinois library, in its Rare Books Collection. Indispensable there for purposes of this book were N. Frederick Nash, Mary S. Ceibert, and Louis Fitton.

Professor Charles Strozier, eminent historian, biographer and teacher at Sangamon State University, Springfield, Illinois, served as the competent editor, bringing his astute observations and broad experience to bear on the selection and arrangement of material.

Walter Blair, Professor Emeritus at the University of Chicago, gave rare insight to the humor available, and its sources. His knowledge and enthusiasm for early American humor was a stimulus to look ever further and deeper into the endless delight of that humor, and to seek the special insight to the nuances, the *geist* of American history that our early humor can reveal.

We are indebted to the following publishers and authors for permission to print from earlier books and articles.

Frank L. DuMond. *Tall Tales of the Catskills.* Atheneum Publishers. New York. 1968.

Harold W. Felton. *The World's Most Truthful Man.* Dodd, Mead & Co., Inc. New York. 1961.

James R. Masterson. *Tall Tales of Arkansas.* The Rose Publishing Co. Little Rock. 1942.

Vance Randolph. *Pissing in the Snow.* University of Illinois Press. Champaign. 1976. Note: All selections from this anthology are in Chapter VIII and are indicated by an asterisk ending the title of the story.

Benjamin Thomas. *Lincoln's Humor, an Analysis.* Abraham Lincoln Association. Springfield. 1935.

Lowell Thomas. *Tall Stories.* Harper and Row. New York. 1931.

Mark Twain. *Letters from the Earth.* Bernard De Voto, Ed. New York. 1974.

Roger Welsch. *Shingling the Fog & Other Plains Lies.* U. of Nebraska Press. Lincoln. 1980.

Introduction

The American inventive genius has been apparent in the production of humor as it has in the production of other wonders like baseball, the automobile, Coca-Cola, and jazz. We are forever laughing or joking at all aspects of American life. Back in 1915, the critic F. L. Partee wrote: "The incongruities of the new world — the Cavaliers, the Dutch, the Negroes and the later immigrants; the makeshifts of the frontier, the vastness and richness of the land, the levelling effects of democracy, the freedom of life, and the independence of spirit — all have tended to produce a laughing people."

Andrew Lang, an Englishman traveling in America toward the close of the last century, wrote: "All over the land of America men are eternally 'swapping stories' at bars, and in the long endless journeys by railway and steamer. How little, comparatively, the English 'swap stories'." But from Ben Franklin to Ronald Reagan, jokes and stories have been as American as fried chicken and mashed potatoes. Described variously as bawdy, irreverent, exuberant, zestful, gusty, earthy, rib-tickling, knee-slapping and gut-busting, the people of America have created out of their grass roots, branches, and leaves a wonderful way of looking at and accepting the joy, fulfillment, and the terror of life in the ongoing generations.

There is a bonus — over and above joy — to be found in earlier American humor, and that comes with the opening of a window on our past, an opening that gives us a feeling for the *geist*, the way things truly were with our forebears, as they built America.

For example, there comes a new understanding of that most fateful event in our history, the Civil War, as you read the funny letters to President Lincoln written by Artemus Ward, Petroleum V. Nasby and, for the Confederacy, Bill Arp. Other humorous stories reveal the churches of bygone days, and the courting, trade, amusements, agriculture, and family life in ways that give us an intuitive vision of our past that no formal, factual history of the times could do.

But just what is the nub, the essence of American humor? There have been many attempts to analyze it, pin it down to an apple pie order, but all fall short of precision. As humorist E. B. White says: "Humor can be dissected as a frog can, but the thing dies in the process, and the innards are discouraging to any but the pure scientific mind." And yet there is one element that most analysts agree is most characteristic of American humor, something that distinguishes it from the humor of other nations: exaggeration! And that tells us that when it comes to humor, Americans are the most artful, delightful, and amusing liars in the world! This being so, and given our naturally extraordinary and debilitating droughts, woeful winds, fearsome critters, and super soils, we Americans have made of our environment a funny, laughable — hence bearable — matrix for a superb and unique humor. The tall tales, more intimately known as whoppers or windies, those mad and wonderfully inventive, witty, and shameless lies that convulsed our fathers, are a superb and special gift to the humor of the world. Van Wyck Brooks writes: "The West possessed the largest rivers; and were not the storms more terrible than anywhere else? No tales about the West could ever seem tall to anyone who saw the frontiersman with a rifle. He could perforate a milk pail half a mile away, he could enlarge the tin eye of the cock on the steeple, he could split a bullet on a razor at a hundred yards."

Even Ben Franklin told whoppers: "The very tails of American sheep are so laden with wool that each has a little cart or wagon on four little wheels, to support and keep it from trailing on the ground."

Or listen to a newspaper account in the *Spirit of the Times*, July 28, 1851, about a frontier town: "Out west is certainly a great country . . . there is a little town in them diggins which is all sorts of a stirring place. In one day, they recently had two street fights, hung a man, rode three men out of town on a rail, got up a quarter race, a turkey shooting, a gander pulling, a match dog fight, had a preaching by a circus [circuit?] rider who afterwards ran a foot race for apple jack all around, and, as if this was not enough, the judge of the court, after losing his year's salary at single-handed poker, and licking a person who said he didn't understand the game, went out and helped to lynch his grandfather for hog stealing." True story? Well . . . why not?

A large part of the fun was in the dialect used in the descriptive language of the time. James Russell Lowell said of it: "Language is the soil of thought; and our own especially is a rich leaf-mould, the slow growth of ages . . ." He further suggests that "for directness, precision, and force" writers should turn to the language of the "divinely illiterate" for "our popular idiom is racey with life and vigor and originality, bucksome . . . to our new occasions, and proves itself no new graft by sending up new suckers from the old root in spite of us." Much of our early humor was in dialect, so that if you, the reader, will only stay with it, the American language as then spoken will provide a special pleasure because of its original ways, and the funny, appealing quality of its fractured grammar and phonetic spelling. As Ben Franklin suggested, American dialect is merely the simple, honest way to write the language.

Nearly a century after Ben Franklin's observation, James Russell Lowell has his hero, Hosea Bigelow, say: "You kin spall an punctuooate thet as you please. I allus do, it kind of puts a noo soot of close onto a word, thisere funatick spellin' doos, an' takes 'em out of the prisen dress they wair in the Dixionary." Later, Josh Billings added: "That iz jist az mutch joke in bad spelling, az thar iz in looking Kross-eyed, and no more."

The spelling at first is not easy to read, but if the reader tries, persists, the "noo soot of close" becomes a very sensible and natural and easy thing to read, and is sure to bring on a kind of appreciative smile, a grin that says, "Well, all right now . . ." As you wade into it, begin to master and enjoy it, you'll find that the eye dialect, all this spavined language, will add a new dimension to your own correspondence as you adopt bits and pieces of it to bring a new kind of humor to your own business or personal writing.

Ethics? There were fictional characters of those times who titillated Americans with their picaresque reflections on the morality of their day. Johnson J. Hooper's unforgettable fictional character, Simon Suggs, was considered "a downright rascal," who lived by his wits. His motto was, "It pays to be shifty in a new country." And P. T. Barnum's favorite dictum is known to everybody: "There's a fool born every minute." Later came the creation of Peter Finlay Dunne, his Mr. Dooley, whose guiding principle was, "Trust everybody, but cut the cards!"

Are such caveats so different from those we use and need today, so many generations later? Ask any stockbroker, sales manager, credit bureau, lawyer, banker! "Keep your eyes peeled" is as good and useful a reflection of making it in contemporary life as it was in those long-gone generations. Remember that loveable thimblerigger and paragon of confidence men, Professor Harold Hill and his bandscam in the musical comedy, *The Music Man*? That was fiction. But the real thing is always with us in the form of an Al Capone, a Huey Long, a John Z. DeLorean, all of them stranger than fiction and twice as large. Every town and city in America has its real and comedic Professor Harold Hill. And we never tire of reading about them or of their fictional counterparts. This is not to say that our open-heartedness and our American decency, our legendary generosity to others, has diminished. It is just that our decent impulses and acts are always and everywhere tempered by a kind of redeeming, insuring cynicism that says, "Better keep your eyes peeled, sisters and brothers!" And we mean that to say precisely what Simon Suggs said one hundred and thirty-five years ago, and what Mr. Dooley meant at the turn of this century: "Here's my hand, friend, but the other one's cocked just in case . . ."

A final suggestion. Read the humor at random, skipping about in it, browsing among the chapters, trying some of this and some of that. Read the book as you might choose appealing food at a buffet or salad bar, tasting this and that, and blending things. When to move from one chapter into another? When your attention begins to wander at too many jokes, or too many fearsome critters, or tall tales, or bawdy stories. Just skip about, tasting two hundred years of our laughter and history, and you'll end your reading happy that you began it and much, much more understanding and proud of the laughing spirit that created the history of us all.

Chapter I
Tall Tales,
Whoppers and Windies

What is a tall tale? "An exuberant combination of fact with outrageous fiction," wrote Professor Walter Blair of the University of Chicago, himself no trivial teller of them. Frank Dobie, superb recorder of western folklore and humor, described the teller of tall tales as a "Poet who heightens fact and deals in illusions by creating a mood and an atmosphere favorable to the willing suspension of disbelief that constitutes poetic faith." Those are tall words in a tall description but not less than expected from a Texan.

Lowell Thomas, that superb radio personality and reconteur of a past generation, wrote: "The prevailing tone . . . is one of solemn factuality . . . with great pains to assert the scrupulous truth . . ." Of his Liars' Club, he wrote: "A grand air of sober veracity pervades the Tall Story Club as it might a pious brotherhood devoted to the eternal verities." You bet! Yes sir! For sure!

James Russell Lowell described the whopper as "an overplus of expression of wit." He illustrated his definition with the story of a man so tall that he got his hat wet a quarter-hour before the rain reached anyone else.

It has been said that the tellers of tall tales were artists in ascertaining the limits of their listeners' capacity for accepting deception. And if these limits were limitless . . . so much the better.

And yet another writer says: "A good tall story is a perfectly conceivable, imaginable, explicable, manageable and understandable happening. It is all of these "ables" except that it is impossible.

The tall tale is very much with us in talk and jokes. Recently one appeared that had a thimblerigger hauled up before the Judge for selling an elixir that would bring eternal youth to the buyer. Immortality by the drink! The Judge asked the sheriff to state the charges. "Judge," the sheriff began, "it sure is time to

*send this bum up the river. Why this con-artist is a repeat of-
fender. He's been selling this same danged pig-in-a-poke potion
for years, and been hauled into court for it at least four times . . .
in 1776, 1848, 1900, 1947.''*

*So here they are, a battery of windies, whoppers, tall tales or —
if you don't like poetry — just plain little old lies, told by
''altitudenous gentlemen'' ever since America was conceived.*

★   ★   ★   ★

In the early days, this old boy was hunting with a breech-
loading rifle when he saw six turkeys roosting on a forked limb.
But he only had one rifle ball left to shoot with! So he powdered,
primed, capped, and fired away in the most careful, exact manner, hoping to split that limb they roosted on. He did! And the
split limb snapped back together, pinning the claws of the
turkeys tight in the limb. All the old geezer had to do was to saw
off the limb, hoist it on his shoulder, and walk home with
enough turkey meat to last him for a fortnight.

★   ★   ★   ★

A few years later this same old boy was hunting for ducks.
This time he was not only short of balls, but had none at all, and
a skein of ducks was heading straight for him, strung out in a
single line! Making a quick decision, he powdered, used his
ramrod in place of a ball, put a cap on his gun, and fired! The
friction heated that rod so that when it skewered all twelve
ducks, the red-hot ramrod soon had them cooked. They fell at
the old boy's feet and, as soon as the ramrod, loaded with the
skewered ducks, had cooled, he put it on his shoulder and
walked home with enough cooked duck meat for a month!

★   ★   ★   ★

There's an old Massachusetts story about a huge flock of
geese caught in a terrible December ice storm. The ice was
followed by snow and then came a very hard, freezing rain. The
geese couldn't fly because their feathers were coated with ice. It
was the kind of ice storm when ice coats everything as thick as a

slice of mince pie. Well, those geese set up a fearsome racket, honking and all, so that this old boy goes out to see what the ruckus was all about. He sees these geese can't fly so he figures to have him a goose dinner and starts to drive them down the hill toward his house. But those geese were so weighted with ice that they could hardly waddle! When they hit the steepest part of the downhill walk, the ice on them caused them to tumble over and over and to roll on down through the wet, sticky snow, so that it stuck to them. By the time they hit the barnyard, they were rolled up tight as a big boy's snowball. They rolled on down until the barn stopped them cold and all that the old boy had to do was to gather them and pile them up outside, where they stayed frozen all winter. When this feller wanted a goose, he went to the pile, grabbed him a snowballed goose, and threw it against the barn wall to split it, then he shook the goose a bit and took it to the house, ready to thaw, then pluck, and then cook. Can't beat that!

★   ★   ★   ★

Another old geezer from up in Illinois tells about the time his wife ordered him out of a cold morning to get them a feed of ducks. So he goes out to his pond and comes up on the ducks to see them acting mighty queer. So he walks closer and discovers all those ducks' feet were frozen solid in the ice. Scared now, those ducks took off, and the entire surface ice, frozen to their feet lifted off the lake easy as pie. Well, those ducks — must have been a billion of 'em — lifted up just as easy as you please and took off with a mile-wide mirror of ice stuck to their feet. They headed south like they were migrating again. Of course the old boy was caught on the ice and was carried away with the ducks. And he'd never been aflying before! So he just enjoyed the experience . . . wasn't anything else he could do about it . . . only sit down and wait till the warmer weather down south slowly melted the ice and gradually lowered that flying cake of ice to the ground; and everybody just walked away — man and ducks — scot free. But there was sure some mighty tired ducks down in

Alabama that day. And one feller with a mighty cold bottom from sittin' on all that ice all that time.

★   ★   ★   ★

And there was a feller who told a story about his Grandpa. The old man told about the time, one winter, when there was wild game all around — deer, bear, and some panther (painter). But he hadn't a ball left to shoot with, only powder and cap! Thinking of the dear ones at home that he might never see again, a stream of tears fell down his ruddy cheeks and froze. He then loaded the frozen tear drops into his gun and fired. When the stream of tiny tear drops left the gun, the pressure had formed them into a single sliver of ice, a dagger of ice that could burst through even the toughest-hided bear or panther. That icy dagger of tears, on entering the head of the bear, or panther, or deer, by itself didn't actually kill the beast. Nope. It melted inside the critter and the cause of death was . . . water on the brain.

★   ★   ★   ★

Another old boy's Grandpa told of the time he ran out of balls but saw a cherry tree and quickly pitted enough fruit to load his gun with seeds and fire at a deer not too far from him. The deer was hit in the middle of his forehead but not killed. He ran away. But the next year, the hunter saw that very same deer with a cherry tree growing out of his forehead. It was in full bloom, the tree showing promise of yielding a bountiful supply of cherries, much earlier than normal, because that deer made for high-powered fertilizer and no doubt accelerated the growth of the tree, and the cherries. Nature is sure wonderful!

★   ★   ★   ★

They tell the story of the finest shot in Colorado. This old boy was hunting deer on his favorite mountain. He saw a deer, but it ran away, taking a well-worn path that led around that mountain. Since the hunter knew very well the course of all deer on that mountain, knew all of it about as well as he knew the back of his hand, he determined on an obvious course of action. He bent his rifle barrel precisely to fit the curve of that mountain, then aimed the rifle in the opposite direction from that in which the deer was running. Carefully calculating time, space, and friction, he fired. Halfway around the mountain, the bullet met the deer head-on and killed it. The old boy warned everybody not to try this shot except when shooting around a mountain, because if you try it on a flat prairie or plain, you are at the inside radius of the circle and cannot cross the circling trajectory of the bullet without being hit. You have to wait until the bullet is spent, which could take all day, and your girl friend might wonder what had happened to you and cast about for another feller. So be careful trying that circular shot!

★   ★   ★   ★

Another old boy told of his great English Pointer, the best bird dog he'd ever owned. One time he took this hunting dog to the city just for company. Suddenly, he realized that he was alone, that the dog was gone. Worried, he back-tracked only to find the dog on a tight, elegant point. It was the most humiliating thing that had ever happened! That such a fine bird dog could make so silly a mistake as to point non-existent quail or partridge or pigeons in the city was disgraceful. The old feller made up his mind to shoot the dog, right there and then. Luckily he looked up to see a sign just above him, toward which the dog pointed. It read:

A. Partridge
Attorney-at-Law

★   ★   ★   ★

There was this dog out in Indiana whose owner claimed it was the smartest dog in seven states. Every time the feller took up a rifle to go squirrel hunting, the dog would start out, *head up*, looking for squirrel. And if it was rabbits he wanted, the dog would go out, *head down*, sniffing the ground for rabbit scent. And if he took his shotgun along, that smart dog would go to pointing birds. One time a silly wag tried to fool that dog by showing up at the kennel with a fishing pole. The dog seemed confused and ran off into the woods. The owner was plumb embarrassed at this canine faux pas, and the feller with the pole nearly busted his gut haw-hawing. Disgusted, the owner of the dog finally set out to look for him only to find him a short piece into the woods busily pawing the ground. That smart dog was digging for worms!

★   ★   ★   ★

But perhaps the greatest hunter of all was a fellow who was out digging for clams. Another fellow came paddling up to him and they began to talk. "How's the duck shootin' down here?" asked the fellow. "First rate," he replied. "I got me about sixty ducks, five at a time, just as they come down the bay. Yes siree! I shot 'em and they just drifted up to my boat easy as pie, and like I say, that's how good duck huntin' is. "You don't say," said the other fellow. "You know who I am? No? Well, I'm the new game warden!" "You don't say so," said the clam digger. "That sure is a coincidence. You know who I am? I'm the biggest liar within forty miles!"

★   ★   ★   ★

In the adjoining county of Madison, there is a hill of considerable size called "Round Hill." The name is very appropriate, for the base of the hill forms a perfect circle. The preacher located one of his most remarkable experiences at that place. He was really a very successful hunter, but from his accounts it will be seen that he was a remarkable hunter as well. Talking to an admiring group of friends, he remarked:

"I once went to Round Hill a-hunting. In those days there was a forest around it. When I neared the hill a buck started up and took out around the hill. I followed for some time, but could not get a shot; so I bent my gun-barrel across my knee to correspond with the curve of the hill and fired, then the bullet followed the buck and killed him. I went on to where the buck had fallen and straightened the barrel. Near at hand, I saw some honey running out of a tree, where the ball had entered, and I drove a peg in the tree until I could return, which I did, in a few days, and me and my friends took home five pounds of splendid honey. But this, aside. I cut off the hind quarters from the buck, slung him across my shoulders, and started home. I had on a very large and loose pair of pants which turned out to my advantage, for when I reached the creek the water was up and I had to wade. When I got on the other side of the creek I took fifteen pounds of jumpin' perch out of my pants, and you may easily understand how we lived on the deer, honey, and fish for some time."

★   ★   ★   ★

"Many years ago," said he, "when I was a young man I had business in the State of Maine. It was during the winter and was exceedingly cold. I located an eagle's nest at the top of a crag and determined to capture one of the young eagles. To do this, I was compelled to climb an icicle for about fifty feet to reach the place. Just as I got the young bird the two old eagles appeared on the scene; and, to escape their beaks and claws, I slid down the icicle so fast that I set the seat of my pants on fire, and from that day to the present I have always been prejudiced against eagles."

★   ★   ★   ★

Of course, for every feller that tells a hunting story, there are at least a hundred that tell fishing tales.

Behold the fisherman!
He riseth early in the morning and disturbeth
The whole household.
Mighty are his prospects.
He goeth forth full of hope, and when the day
Is far spent he returneth — smelling of
Strong drink; and the truth is not in him.

★   ★   ★   ★

Dick Myers of Middletown, Illinois, tells of an intensive study conducted to determine how to successfully cook a bony, most resistant fish, the carp. Information was garnered world-wide, but the most useful recipe came from an old cowpuncher in Wyoming. This fellow-in-chaps always folded a flat of cowshit around the carp, just before cooking it. Then he baked the enfolded fish over a moderately hot fire of bullchips — or hardwood — until it was done. He advised that after cooking, the fish would taste not much better than if cooked in more traditional ways, but that the taste of cowshit was very much improved. After testing his method among several hundred Texas lovers of carp, the cowboy's solution to the international problem of cooking carp was proven not only true, but the best of all possible recipes submitted by world-wide cooks, professional and amateur.

Off the coast of Florida, this old boy was having trouble getting fish to bite. He used both minnows and worms but got not a nibble. Finally, he tried a new stunt. He dipped both the minnow and worm in good Kentucky moonshine, baited one hook with a minnow, the other with a worm. Almost at once he had a furious strike and, after a hard fight, managed to reel in a huge sea bass and there, around the neck of that bass, was that whiskeyed worm, strangling that bass to death! The minnow? Well, that minnow had hold of the bass's tail, and was shaking it so furiously that the poor fish couldn't swim a lick to get away!

Another good old boy and his buddy were fishing down in Mississippi when they noticed on the shore a blacksnake with a large frog in its mouth. Since frogs make excellent bait, they eased over to the shore and pinned that snake with a forked stick, then took the frog away from it. That big old snake looked so sad at such rough treatment that, knowing what a friend to mankind the blacksnake is, the men looked at each other, nodded, then gave the blacksnake a drink of good White Oak Mountain moonshine. The snake drank it, then wiggled away. The two friends cut up the frog and commenced to fish. In fifteen minutes there was a thump on that boat. One feller looked down to see that same snake looking up at him with another frog in its mouth. Not only that, but all day long, blacksnakes, watersnakes, all kinds of snakes kept acomin' and agoin' with frogs to trade for a slurp of good whiskey until it was all gone. Then the two fellers skeedaddled for fear of the snakes getting mad at them for disappointing them. They figured the snakes might upset the boat or take after them in some way. They said it was the dangdest experience they'd ever had. Now, they never go fishing with less than a case of good old White Mountain moonshine.

Then there was the time this same feller lost a five dollar gold piece over the side of his boat. Four years later he caught a fine, big fish, cut him open for dinner, and found that gold piece inside the fish! Not only that, but there were four half-dollars for four years' interest on his money!

Then there's the story of the pure-bred, blue-ribbon fish hound. The old boy who owned him threw a silver dollar into the river after first showing it to his fish hound. This feller thought the fish hound would dive in and retrieve it for him but he did something astonishing! That old hound dove in after the dollar — or so this old boy thought — but he came up with an eight-pound catfish and fifteen cents in change.

There is a feller out east who fishes off the coast of Maine. He goes out with a posthole digger, which is a kind of huge auger, only it is made of wood so it won't rust. With that posthole digger he dug a hole in the ocean. Almost at once, a marvelous fish, the shike, overcome with curiosity, rushed up the hole, shot to the top, and went aflyin' out of it. Then that shike took an enormous breath of air, becoming so inflated that he couldn't get back down that same hole. He was just too danged swollen to make it. So the eastern feller just grabbed the shike, put it in his bag, took it home and the family had shike chowder, fried shike, along with baked beans and whiskey that night for supper.

★   ★   ★   ★

But the queerest of all fish is the Tobacco Fish. To get him you cast a bait of tobacco. The fish comes to the surface to get him a chew, takes it, and submerges to enjoy a chaw. But there come a time when even a fish has got to spit, and that is the time of his undoing. When the fish comes to the surface to spit, the knowing, tobacco-wise fisherman is waiting to hit him on the head with his paddle. He does. Fish for dinner.

★   ★   ★   ★

Down in North Carolina, a man went fishing and caught a very special and quite darling bass that soon became adjusted to life out of water so that he could follow the man around. They became quite inseparable, until one day, on a long hike, they came to a creek with a bridge over it. By now, water disgusted that fish. But the man coaxed his friend the fish to cross the bridge, which had, unfortunately, a large crack in the path of the fish, through which it slipped and fell below into the water, where, in spite of the frantic efforts of his trainer, the poor fish drowned.

★   ★   ★   ★

Some bass in Florida lakes are so big that many fisherman, hooked to them, have been pulled overboard; and not a few have been lost that way! But now, to get a fishing license in that area, folks must pass a physical examination that includes indisputable proof that the applicant can bulldoze a steer, wrestle a man-eating Bengal tiger, and vanquish a 60 ft. boa constrictor . . . as well as swim for five minutes underwater. Those Florida bass sure are a caution, all right. Monstrous mean!

★   ★   ★   ★

Mr Frank L. DuMond, the 86-year-old doyen of the tall tale, is the American authority on the Sweatfish. Mr. DuMond

describes the critter in his book, "Tall Tales of the Catskills"
(New York: Atheneum, 1968). A shortened version of his ency-
clopedic description and analysis follows:

There used to be a lot of sweatfish around here in the Catskills. They were stranded when the arctic ice melted. To survive, these sweatfish had to gather in the sunlight so that they
could sweat up a storm until they had manufactured enough
sweat for a pond to swim in. You can see how versatile and self-
sufficient is the sweatfish! Another thing to remember about
them is that you can't catch them on a hook, because they must
swim backyard to keep the sweat out of their eyes, thus going
past the hook before they see it. So how do you catch them?
Easy: you take two augers, one big and one small. With the big
you bore a hole in the bottom at the middle of the boat. With the
small one you drill a small hole in the lower end of the boat so
that the water, coming in the big hole, can empty out of the
small one. Then you smear the rim of the big hole with peanut
butter (the chunky kind), so that the sweatfish, attracted by his
favorite bait, swims up through the big hole, backwards, of
course, with his tail first, whereupon you grab him by the tail.
Sometimes they come up so fast that the boat fills up with 'em,
and you got to row quickly to shore or the weight of all those
sweatfish'll swamp the boat. Many a man has been lost because
he didn't know that. But they sure do make fine eatin'. All that
reservoir of sweaty water gives them a great salty taste. That's
why they never spoil . . . too salty!

Out in Illinois they tell the story about a fisherman on the Illinois River who hooked a catfish so big and fast that it towed
the boat, lickety-split; towed that boat so fast, in fact, that it
burned the bottom right out of it!

Another feller in the same river, fishing from shore, hooked a
catfish that pulled him into the river and, gamely holding onto

his fishing rod, that feller was going so fast down the river that his shirt burned off, and he had to let go of his pole so's to fight the fire. Mighty big catfish, all right!

But life is not all about fish and wild game. Also does it deal with the work-a-day functions of living, the prosaic needs of all of us. Consider the following:

A stingy farmer mixed sawdust with laying mash for his hens. He normally got one or two eggs a day from his hens in laying season, but the eggs were good only for eating, not hatching. Why? Because of that sawdust feed, the hens hatched out chicks with one wooden leg! And not a few eggs hatched out woodpeckers!

That same farmer had a hog that ate several sticks of dynamite. Incautious, the hog got too close to a mule and got kicked so that the mule, barn, haystack and all the fences around the barnlot were blown to smithereens. And that farmer sure had him a mighty sick hog for nearly a week.

Grandpa told about the time things got so bad on the farm that they had hardly enough to eat. The chickens had even less. His laying hens got so thin they could drop through the cracks in the hen house floor to get the grain that had dropped through in bygone, better days. Of course there were very few eggs, and those they did lay were shaped like the hens, thin like silver dollars. Even when things got better, in the spring, those hens kept on laying silver-dollar-thin eggs. And the chicks that hatched out of those skinny eggs were shaped just like the hens and eggs — thin as pasteboard cutouts. They grew, all right, but every one of 'em was thin as a shingle and could walk right through a fair-sized crack in the barn wall. The farmer never could get enough meat to bother killing them for the table. Finally a trader came along and bought them all, then sold them for weather vanes and alarm clocks. Yep! He sure did.

★　　　★　　　★　　　★

"Let's see: they raise some wheat in Minnesota, don't they?" asked a Schoharie granger of a Michigander.

"Raise wheat! Who raises wheat? No, sir; decidedly no, sir. It raises itself. Why, if we undertook to cultivate wheat in that state it would run us out. There wouldn't be any place to put our house."

"But I've been told that grasshoppers take a good deal of it."

"Of course they do. If they didn't, I don't know what we would do. The cussed stuff would run all over the state and drive us out — choke us up. Those grasshoppers are a godsend, only there ain't half enough of 'em!"

"Is the wheat nice and plump?"

"Plump! Why, I don't know what you call plump wheat, but there are seventeen in our family, including ten servants, and when we want bread we just go out and fetch in a kernel of wheat and bake it."

"Do you ever soak it in water first?"

"Oh, no; that wouldn't do. It would swell a little, and then we couldn't get it in our range oven."

★　　　★　　　★　　　★

During the depression, a farmer was forced to feed his hens sawdust. As a result, one hen laid a knothole, and another laid eggs so like the feed that the family got splinters in their tongues from eating fried eggs. As you might expect, some of the eggs hatched out woodpeckers, and the only way the farmer's wife could cook them was to fry them for an hour and a half, then boil them in wood alcohol for another hour. But the good side of that sawdust feed was the flavor. Walnut sawdust gave walnut-flavored meat, and apple trees gave the eggs that flavor. Yet another bonus that sad year — when everybody really needed a break of some sort — was that the chickens grew so big and hearty on that sawdust feed that it took only nine of them to make a dozen. Yep!

★   ★   ★   ★

One hillman told of finding a tubful of turtle eggs. He raised the turtles, fattened them and set out to drive them to New Orleans, where turtle soup was bringing a good price. Since the Arkansas rocks injured their tender feet, he stopped and had them shod; but at the next ford the weight of the iron shoes drowned them all. He dammed the stream, threw in heated rocks, boiled the water, and made turtle soup. With the money from this enterprise he bought a farm in the hills. "But," he says, "I had me a lot o' bad luck. First off th' danged pumpkins jes' wore themselves to pieces draggin' over th' ground, on account th' vines growed so fast. But I shore had me a good stand o' corn. When shuckin' time come I sent th' least boy up a stalk. He had t' wear climbers I borrowed off'n a telephone lineman. Come dark afore he got up t' th' first ear and he was afraid t' climb down an' he had t' roost up thar all night. Thar was a powerful heavy frost that night an' all th' cornstalks weakened an' fell down. That crop was scattered all over Nebrasky an' Kansas, an' I had t' send money clear t' Montany so my least boy could come home on th' train."

★   ★   ★   ★

Stranger — I expect you are about the tallest kind of a coon there is in these diggings. Your little Buffalonian walks straight into things, like a squash vine into a potato patch.

I come down the other day in the steamboat Cleveland. She's pretty fixin'. Golly! Ain't she a smasher? Once coming down, a streak of lightning followed three miles and better. The Captain seeing it was gaining on us a little, so he told the man to starboard the helm and let it go by. It did go like a horse, and we were so near it that the passengers smelt brimstone. Then the Captain felt a little cheap, at first, about letting it beat him, and said the steam wasn't up; but I told him he did perfectly right to turn out, as there were so many women on board, and then there was so much iron, that it drew the lightning and helped it along, so it warn't fair play. You should have heard the thunder that came along just after it. Perhaps you don't know where I came from. Give us your fist now and I'll tell you all about it. When I'm at home I stops in Chuckahokee digging in the state of Indiana. We raised a mighty crop of wheat this year, I reckon upon nigh four thousand bushels, and a sprinklin' of corn, oats, potatoes and garden sass. You could hear the earth groan all round our settlement, the crops were so heavy, and that's what gives rise to the stories about the earthquakes. It was near enough to make a young earthquake to hear the corn grow as it did, and as to the potatoes, I'll be skinned alive, if ever I saw anything like it. Why, any one of them warm nights, you just go out into a little patch of fifty acres, close to the house, and hold your ear down, you could hear the young potatoes quarreling, and the old ones grumbling at them because they didn't lay along and stop crowding. I calculate you didn't raise such crops in these parts. Why one day one of our squash vines chased a drove of hogs better than half a mile, and they ran and squealed as if the old boy was after them. One little pig stubbed his toe and fell down and never was heard of afterwards. We got in pretty much all the crops, and I told the old man I would take a trip down east and see the old folks, grandfather and mother, aunts, and cousins, a pretty considerable heap of them I calculate down to old Vermont. So I packed up my plunder and started.

★   ★   ★   ★

"Yeah," said Old Zeke, "you sho' is tellin' de truth 'bout dat big old mosquito, 'cause my old man bought dat same piece of land and raised a crop of pumpkins on it and lemme tell y'all right now — mosquito dust is de finest fertilizer in de world. Dat land was so rich and we raised pumpkins so big dat we et five miles up in one of 'em and five miles down and ten miles acrost one and we ain't never found out how far it went. But my old man was buildin' a scaffold inside so we could cut de pumpkin meat without so much trouble, when he dropped his hammer. He tole me, he says, 'Son, Ah done dropped my hammer. Go git it for me.' Well, Ah went down in de pumpkin and begin to hunt dat hammer. Ah was foolin' 'round in there all day when I met a man and he ast me what Ah was lookin' for. Ah tole him my ole man had done dropped his hammer and sent me to find it for him. De man tole me Ah might as well give it up for a lost cause, he had been lookin' for a double mule-team and a wagon that had got lost in there for three weeks and he hadn't found no trace of 'em yet. So Ah stepped on a pin, de pin bent and dat's de way de story went.''

"Dat was rich land but my ole man had some rich land too," put in Toby Buckles. "My old man planted cucumbers and he went along droppin' de seeds and befo' he could git out de way he'd have ripe cucumbers in his pockets. What is the richest land you ever seen?''

"Well," replied E. Sommers, "my ole man had some land dat was so rich dat our mule died and we buried him down in our bottomland and de next mornin' he had done sprouted li'l jackasses.''

"Aw, dat land wasn't so rich," objected Gassy. "My old man had some land and it was so rich dat he drove a stob in de ground at de end of a corn-row for a landmark and next morning there was ten ears of corn on de corn stalk and four ears growin' on de stob.''

"Dat lan' y'all talkin' 'bout might do, if you give it plenty commercial-nal [commercial fertilizer] but my old man wouldn't farm no po' land like dat," said Ellis Tode. "Now, one year we was kinda late puttin' in our crops. Everybody else had corn a foot high when papa said, 'Well, chillun, Ah reckon we better plant some corn.' So I was droppin' and my brother was hillin' up behind me. We had done planted 'bout a dozen rows when Ah looked back and seen de corn comin' up. Ah didn't want it to grow too fast 'cause it would make all fodder and no roastin' ears so Ah hollered to my brother to sit down on some of it to stunt de growth. So he did, and de next day he dropped me back a note — says: 'Passed thru Heben yesterday at twelve o'clock sellin' roastin' ears to de angels.' ''

★   ★   ★   ★

"Yeah," says Estes Brown, "dat was some pretty rich ground, but whut is de poorest ground you ever seen?"

Bill Sampson spoke right up and said, "Ah seen some land so poor dat it took nine partridges to holler 'Bob White'."

"Dat was rich land, boy," declared Estes. "Ah seen land so poor dat de people come together and 'cided dat it was too poor to raise anything on, so they give it to de church, so de congregation built de church and called a pastor and held de meetin'. But de land was so poor they had to wire up to Jacksonville for ten sacks of commercial-nal before dey could raise a tune on dat land."

★   ★   ★   ★

Early in the forenoon Pete Rossiter came up and began inspecting the crops. "Oh, this is very well; very well, indeed, for Jersey," said Pete at last, as they sat on the fence by the cornfield, after their labors, smoking; "but nothing to what I have seen. In Tama County, Iowa, I once saw the corn growing to such an unprecedented height, and the stalks so exceptionally vigorous, that nearly every farmer stacked up, for winter firewood, great heaps of cornstalks, cut up into cordwood length by power saws run by the threshing engines. Oley Johnson, took advantage of the season to win a fortune by preparing cornstalks for use as telephone poles . . ."

★   ★   ★   ★

"A good illustration of nature's bounty happened some time ago in Cleger County, Nebraska," the tall tale began. "A seven-year-old daughter of Otis White was sent, in the middle of the forenoon, to carry a jug of switchel to the men, who were at work near the middle of one of those vast Nebraska cornfields. The corn was about up to little Betty's shoulders as she started, but as she went along it rose and rose before her eyes, shooting out of the soil under the magic influence of the sun and the abundant moisture. Almost crazed with fear, she hastened on; before she could reach the men, the stalks were waving above her head. The men were threatened in a like manner, but by mounting a little fellow on a big man's shoulders, to act as a lookout, they managed to get out, when they promptly borrowed a dog, to follow little Betty's trail. It was not until late in the afternoon that they reached her, where she lay, having cried herself to sleep, with the tear-stains streaking her plump cheeks.''

★   ★   ★   ★

"The soil of some of the Southern Missouri counties is so rich as to become an actual detriment to the farmer," observed Eckels. "In Clay County, a farmer, named Edwards, has been forced entirely to abandon the culture of corn, because the stalks, under the influence of the genial sun, mild air, and mellow soil, shoot up into the air so fast that they draw their roots after them; when of course, the plant dies as a rule. Cases have been known, however, where cornstalks thus uprooted and lifted into the air have survived for some time upon the climate alone.''

"Why," said Pete Rossiter, "we used to have the same trouble in Tennessee, but it was solved long ago by burying a heavy stone under each cornstalk and wiring the stalk down to it. I have known the price of stone to treble in one season in consequence of the purely agricultural demand.''

★   ★   ★   ★

In the Snake River Valley lives an old-timer who is known as Pegwell Pete. Old Pete comes to town now and then and boasts of the fertility of his land, but complains that he is unable to market the stuff. He grew pumpkins, but they were so large he could not get them on to a wagon, and then he ventured into potatoes. When, two years ago, a CCC camp was established nearby, Old Pete was approached by a man who wanted to buy a hundred pounds of spuds. "Only a hundred pounds?" he asked, scratching his pate. "No, I can't do it. I wouldn't cut a spud in two for no one.''

★   ★   ★   ★

Many years ago there lived a preacher in Menard County, whose name will not be given lest the feelings of his numerous descendants might be wounded. He was a man of great intellectual force and lived a blameless life, except for the wonderful stories he told, all of which he appeared to believe to be true.

He said that he once cleaned up a quarter of an acre of ground, fenced it in and sowed it in turnips. Some time after, he noticed that the turnips near the center were forced out of the ground, and thus continued outward until there was but one turnip top visible, and that was in the center of the patch. After careful investigation he found that this turnip had grown until it covered the entire field, forcing the others out. About this time he lost a valuable heifer, and after looking everywhere on the place, he found that she had eaten her way into the turnip. Said he: "I knew I would have to procure an enormous kettle in which to cook that turnip; so I went to the Peoria Works, in Kincaid county, and ordered it made. Three hundred men worked on it night and day for three weeks, and on Saturday night of last week, when it was completed, the head workman carelessly dropped his hammer, and just as we reached the spot on Monday morning early, we heard the hammer strike the bottom."

★   ★   ★   ★

Such timber, and such bottom land, why you can't preserve anything natural you plant in it unless you pick it young, things thar will grow out of shape so quick. I once planted in those diggins a few potatoes and beets: they took a fine start, and after that an ox team couldn't have kept them from growing. About that time I went off to Tennessee on bisiness, and did not hear from them things in three months, when I accidentally stumbled on a fellow who had stopped at my place, with an idea of buying me out. "How did you like things," said I. "Pretty well," said he; "The cabin is convenient, and the timber land is good; but that bottom land ain't worth the first red cent." "Why?" said I. " 'Cause it's full of cedar stumps and Indian mounds," said he, "and it can't be cleared." "Lord," said I, "them ar 'cedar stumps' is beets, and them ar 'Indian mounds' ar tater hills.''

As I expected, the crop was overgrown and useless: the sile is too rich, and planting in Arkansas is too dangerous. I had a good-sized sow killed in that same bottom land. The old thief stole an ear of corn, and took it down where she slept at night, to eat. Well, she left a grain or two on the ground, and lay down on them: before morning the corn shot up, and the percussion killed her dead. I don't plant any more: nature intended Arkansas for a hunting ground, and I go according to nature.

I took a handful of guano, that elixir of vegetation, and sowed a few cucumber seeds in it. Well, sir, I was considerable tired when I had done it, and so I just took a stretch for it under a great pine-tree, and took a nap. Stranger! As true as I am talking to you this here blessed minute, when I woke up, I was bound as tight as a sheep going to market on a butcher's cart, and tied fast to a tree. I thought I should never get out of that scrape, the cucumber vines had so grown and twisted round, and wound me and my legs while I was asleep! Fortunately, one arm was free, so I got out my jack knife, opened it with my teeth, and cut myself out, and off for Victoria again, hot foot. When I came into the town, says our captain to me, "Peabody, what in nature is that 'ere great yaller thing that's a sticking out of your pocket?" "Nothin'," says I, looking as 'mazed as a puppy nine days old, when he first opens his eyes, and takes his first stare. Well, I put in my hand to feel, and I pulled out a great big ripe cucumber, a foot long, that had ripened and gone to seed there.

★   ★   ★   ★

Sorry Country

Please goodness! but that's a poor country down yander; it makes the tears come into the kildeer's eyes when they fly over the old fields. Dod drot me, if you can even get a drink of cider!! They a'n't got no apples but little runts of things, about as big as your thumb, and so sour that when a pig sticks his tooth into 'em, he lays back his jaw, and hollers, you might hear him a mile; but it's "eat, pig, or die" — for it's all he's got. And then again, they're great for huntin' of foxes; and if you were to see their hounds! — lean, lank, labber-sized pups that are so poor they have to prop up agin a post-and-rail fence, 'fore they can raise a bark at my tincart. It's the poorest place was ever made.

The dogs, in a certain county in Maryland, are so poor that they have to lean against the fence to bark. The kildeers are so poor that they have to let down the draw-bars to enable them to go into a field; and the pigs are so poor that to prevent them from upsetting as they run down hill, they are compelled to suspend a lump of lead to their tails to balance them.

An eastern editor, in alluding to a rival town, says that it takes several of their pigs to pull up a blade of grass; that they are so poor, the foremost seizes the spear in his mouth, the balance having taken each other by the tail, when they give a pull, a strong pull, and a pull altogether, and if it breaks, the whole tumble to the ground for want of sufficient strength to support themselves. It must take three or four such pigs to make a shadow.

★   ★   ★   ★

West Virginia Hills

West Virginia is a hill-country state, and this has produced a type of farm surprising to newcomers within its borders. Planted fields seem to hang precariously on steep hillsides. The visitor is apt to be told by a native, quite earnestly, that the corn is sown by standing on one hillside with a gun and firing it into the opposite hillside. Pumpkins and squash, as soon as they begin to grow, have to be tethered to the cornstalks to hold them till harvest time. Cultivation on these slopes is so difficult that the native son at times will say with a perfectly straight face that he has to roughlock his harrow to get it down off the hill.

In the steep grazing country, it is told without even the suggestion of a smile that a breed of cattle has been developed with legs shorter on one side so they can graze around the hill without discomfort. The only herd of goats in the district had to be equipped with telephone linemen's climbers before they could get to pasture.

One man with an apple orchard on a steep hill just behind his house is said to have nothing to do when he harvests his crop except to open the gate to the orchard, shake the trees, and the apples roll right into his cellar.

A farmer with a cornfield on top of a high hill is reported to shuck out his corn and toss it down a natural chute of rock, so that when it gets to the bottom, all he has to do is to separate the corncobs from the shelled corn, put the corn in the bin for the winter, and stack up the corncobs in a little outhouse in case the mail-order catalogue should be used up.

There is also some extremely hardscapple country in West Virginia. A visitor in Webster Springs, having had supper at the hotel, went out for a smoke and a little walk. Zip! A cat ran past. He watched it in surprise. Zip! Zip! Two more cats ran by in the same direction. Within about fifteen minutes he saw twenty-seven cats, all running in the same direction. "Where are all those cats going" he asked a native. "Aw, don't pay no attention to that," the man replied. "They do it every day. It's seventeen miles down to the junction and that's the only place around here where they can find any dirt."

There is one place in the state where the country is so rough that the people have no teeth. The reason for this is said to be that level land is so scarce that cabin chimneys always open out close under the slope of the hills, and when beans are cooked in the fireplace, gravel from the hills runs down into the chimney and mixes with the beans, and the people wear out their teeth chewing on them. In this area folks always watch up the chimney to see the cows come home.

Some of the valleys are very narrow. The razorback hog is thought to have got his start in these narrow valleys: if he got too fat, he just naturally stuck between the walls of the valleys and had to get thin again before he could amble along. And there are valleys so narrow that the dogs wag their tails up and down. In fact, some valleys are so narrow that it is said you have to lie down and look up to see out; but one is so extremely narrow that the moonshine has to be wheeled out on a wheelbarrow early every morning, and the daylight wheeled in.

Windies are "windies," but the real wind makes windies true whoppers.

One time in a small town in Nebraska, about 1910, they had a terrible cyclone. There was a brush salesman out there, showing his wares at a farm house when that terrible cyclone struck and whirled that salesman through the air, destroying everything except the house and the farmer who was standing there talking. That cyclone ended up by depositing the salesman right back where he was, before the house, talking to the farmer. "Like I said just a few moments ago," the salesman resumed his pitch, "this here brush is jest like that cyclone and it'll sweep clean and thorough, jest like you just seen that cyclone do." Now, that's a real, live, never-lose salesman!

One of the early settlers out in Oklahoma was in big financial trouble, and he was down in the mouth. Well, about that time a twister hit his place, sucked up his rock-lined water well that he'd dug and lined with a rock casing. That twister dropped the casing over by the barn, upside down, but as good as new. He plastered that rock casing inside and out and ever since then he has used it as a silo! And from that old well that'd had the casing sucked up and out, he got him a gusher of an oil well that's still flowin'. Wait! There's more. Now that old boy has got him a summer home in Hyannis Port, and a winter home in Palm Beach. Twisters sure can be helpful.

There was this feller down in South Dakota who had just finished building a garage for a new Ford he'd ordered but hadn't had delivered. Well, about the time he finished that garage, a big cyclone hit, and that feller lit out for the storm cellar. When the storm was over and he came out and looked around, he found that in his new garage that cyclone had left him a brand-new Cadillac with a North Dakota license plate. No! No! Believe you me he was a church goin' feller, too, for sure.

But the wind sometimes dies in some places. There was such a lull, a dearth of wind in Maine one year, back in pioneer days, that they had to pass an ordinance forbidding the use of more than one windmill per township. There simply wasn't enough wind to go around in Maine, whose citizens are known to be taciturn. The Maine legislature sent an urgent request down to the Texas legislature, asking for the loan of a battalion of their tellers of windy tales. But there was such a drought down there, at that time, that those windy Texas fellers just didn't have enough spit so's to supply their own needs, much less to travel to Maine to increase the wind supply up there.

They say that out in Kansas the folks don't ever need to use hat hooks; they just lay their hats against the side of the barn that faces the wind, and the wind holds them there, good as a hat rack.

★   ★   ★   ★

Back in the "Dirty Thirties" a man and his wife got lost while driving in a dust storm. But they didn't realize they were lost, and driving in a circle, until they had filled their car with gas for the third time . . . at the same station.

★   ★   ★   ★

In Nebraska they rarely have wind vanes because all a feller has to do to know which way the wind is blowing is to look outside and see which way the barn tilts. And the wind vane they do use is normally a ten-foot log chain that the wind blows out to its full length, thus indicating the wind's direction. Still, they must be careful because sometimes the wind blows that chain mighty hard so that it whips around and the links begin to snap off the end of it. And when the wind blows that hard, a farmer must be sure that his hens don't put their hind ends into it because then, every time a hen lays an egg, the derned thing will be blown right back up her vent, and she has to set about laying that same derned egg all over again! One hen had to lay her egg eight times before she got smart and turned to face the wind. Only then could she lay her egg, once and for all.

★   ★   ★   ★

But Nebraska isn't the only state to suffer from severe winds. All the Plains States have them. For example, in Kansas, a farmer drilled a quarter of a mile of fence post holes. That night the wind blew so hard it blew the top soil away from the holes and left them standing above ground. The only thing he could do was to pile those post holes in his wagon, take them home, and cut them into 20" lengths to fit his wood stove.

★   ★   ★   ★

There was this Texas feller died and went to heaven where he talked with Ben Franklin, George Washington, Paul Bunyan, Franklin D. Roosevelt, Abraham Lincoln and lots of other nice folks from back east. Everybody sure like it up there. But this Texas feller didn't much seem to care for it. St. Peter asked him how come, and this Texas feller lifted up his halo, real courteous-like, and said, "Saint Pete, it sure is nice up here, all right, and I'm plumb satisfied for myself. But couldn't you make jest a little more room so's to let a few Americans up here, too?"

★   ★   ★   ★

One time there was a cowboy died, and he was from the Edwards Plateau in Texas. So he went to heaven and met up with St. Peter, who showed the cowpoke his new homestead. The cowboy saw a bunch of men tied to a stake, just like horses, and that puzzled him. So he asked how come? "Well," St. Peter said, "them fellers is all cowboys from the Edwards Plateau out in Texas. And sure as hell if we was to turn them old boys loose, they'd every one of 'em ride on back there."

★   ★   ★   ★

Carlos died and he also went to heaven. There he was greeted by St. Peter:
"Welcome. But where do you come from?"
"Dallas, Texas," Carlos said.
"And just where is that?"
"It's in . . . it's a city down there . . . well . . . hmmmm . . . St. Peter, you must know just where Dallas is!"
"Nope! Never heard of it. I think you're lyin', by gum!"
So Carlos asked for and got a map that proved there really was such a place down there. "Forgive me, my son," said the contrite St. Peter, "but, you see, we never had anybody from there before."

★   ★   ★   ★

Back in the days before steam, a four-masted sailing vessel was cruising twenty kilometers off the coast of Texas when the skipper noticed an odd kind of foggy cloud approaching from the west. It was most curious because the sea was calm. But the storm came on, and he discovered that it wasn't a storm at all, but an enormous cloud of mosquitoes, to escape which all the crew had to go below decks. When they emerged, the men discovered that every rope was gone and not a bit of canvas was left on the masts. Without sail, they drifted for days until finally washed ashore off Galveston. Going ashore, what was their surprise to see on the beach millions of mosquitoes, the same swarm that had attacked their ship. Only now each mosquito had on new canvas overalls, and each overall was cinched with a rope belt!

★   ★   ★   ★

Out in Texas there was this cowboy riding along herding his cattle when he noticed his horse had changed in color from roan to red. Touching the hide, he felt moisture and discovered that the horse was covered with blood, having been attacked by a swarm of baby mosquitoes. The horse grew so weak that they had to give him a blood transfusion! Luckily, there were several baby mosquitoes on hand to act as blood donors, and they saved the horse!

★   ★   ★   ★

One year, the government made an effort to get rid of mosquitoes. They tried to shoot them and then use them for food. The world has enough of the pests to feed itself if it only knew how to do it. The Department of Nutrition tried for several years to find a way to cook them but had to drop the project. At the last of several experiments, they had boiled a batch for four hours, and those mosquitoes were still so tough that it took a chain saw to carve them.

★   ★   ★   ★

Another cure to rid Americans of the critters was tried by the Agriculture Department. They approached a swarm to use DDT on it, but the mosquitoes grabbed the bottle and drank it. They did the same thing with Citronella. At last they discovered that the only way to kill them was with Missouri bootleg whiskey. Simple? Seems so. But the folks in the Show Me state were so outraged at the waste of good whiskey that the government had to abandon this promising scheme, or risk another Civil War.

★   ★   ★   ★

Mosquitoes are the curse of summer, while cold is the problem in winter. And it does get cold in some places. Take Minnesota, for example. It got so cold up there one winter that they had to use a blow torch to thaw the udders of their dairy cows. And for a month thereafter, all they could get out of those frosty udders and tits was ice cream — vanilla ice cream, the most ordinary flavor of all.

★   ★   ★   ★

That same hard winter, in the neighboring state of Wisconsin, it was so cold that the milk emerged in strings from the udders, and froze that way, like icicles. The milkers carried those milk-cicles like cordwood to the house, where they had to melt them on the stove before they could get a normal drink of milk.

★   ★   ★   ★

Up in Idaho, that winter, it got so cold that the flames froze in their kerosene lanterns. That was dangerous because it could cause disastrous fires when the flames melted. So the farmers out there had to stick around until the frozen flames thawed so they could blow out the wicks. Up in Montana, at that same time, the flames froze in the fireplaces. Of course, they chopped them out every morning, took the iced flame outside, and put it on the ground out of harm's way. But that was dumb! Because the hens came along and pecked and ate the icy fodder. Then, when the icy stuff melted inside them, they grew so hot that they laid nothing but hard-boiled eggs. For days! They say that to-day, eating in the best restaurants in that section of Montana, you can't get a native to order a hard-boiled egg, so bitter is the memory of that long, cold winter that froze fire.

★   ★   ★   ★

And in Michigan that winter, the sunbeams froze . . . it was that cold. But some good came of it; the farmers sawed the sunbeams into cordwood, then sliced 'em so that they had sunlight all night.

★   ★   ★   ★

But up in Canada, well, there it was really tough. The words that the Canucks spoke froze and fell to the ground and had to be collected in boxes, then taken to the stove to thaw out so's to know what was said. A feller was driving his car when he ran over some of those frozen words, hard words spoken in anger, and so sharp that they cut his tires something fierce. His tires mashed those words so badly that, when thawed, the conversation came out slurred. Fortunately, the tires didn't go flat, but stayed inflated because the air in them had frozen solid. But it did make for a pretty rough ride. His car had been painted a cheery, bright red, but it turned a dismal blue from all the cold. The man said he kind of liked it that color. You see, he was sort of a melancholy feller.

★   ★   ★   ★

Mark Twain told the story that in an earlier time, during just as cold a winter, the shadow of a ship's captain froze to the deck. They had to get six sailors each with ice picks to work on his shadow so as to get it loose and let the Captain get on with his work.

★   ★   ★   ★

A bunch of the fellers were sitting around Zeb Thompkins' store one day, and old Captain Billy Mansfield began to tell about his farm out in Arkansas. "Why, gentlemen, I've growed cornstalks thirty foot high, with seven or eight big ears on ever' stalk. 'Stead of a tassel thar was a round dingus like a gourd, an' when I busted one of 'em open thar was 'bout a quart o' shelled corn in it, for seed! Hit run two hundred and fifty bushel t' th' acre, an' maybe twenty bushel o' seed-corn in the gourds . . . I've raised alfalfy ten foot high an' twelve cuttin's a year, an' cowpeas so all-fired big th' cows cain't git 'em in their mouths! Thar's jest one thing you can't raise on my land, an' that's punkins. I planted a leetle patch o' punkins one year, an' th' vines growed up an' filled th' hull dang valley level full, plumb t' th' tops o' th' ridges. Th' hull country looked jest like a high prairie, an' so thick th' cattle couldn't find th' creek. But thar wasn't a single punkin fur's we could find out. Th' vines growed so dang fast they jest wore th' punkins plumb out, a-draggin' 'em over th' rocks!''

Once there was a simply splendid painter who was a marvel at realism. One time he painted a scene of a bitter snowstorm, so real that, because he didn't move away from it fast enough, that cold scene actually frosted his nose, toes, and fingers. After that he always wore winter clothing, including gloves, while painting winter scenes.

A cousin of that realistic painter also had problems, so excellent was his art. He painted flowers so enticing, so realistic, that one winter while he was painting a landscape, a bunch of bees was activated by the realism and swarmed all over his painting, seeking nectar from his painted flowers. Poor things grew so weak from lack of food and fruitless flying that they fell to the ground and froze to death. It's sure not easy to be an artist! *Sic semper ars.*

Summers, too, can be tough on folks. Especially when it is wet and muddy. There was this feller down in Alabama, who saw his friend coming down the middle of the road, and up to his knees in mud. "Sho seems kind of muddy out theah," the feller says. "Sho is!" the muddy traveller replied. "It's a danged good thang I'm asittin' atop this load of hay!" "An' how's yore boy Jonesy adoin'?" the other feller asks. "Jist fine. He's down below me driving the team.''

Then there was the tall Texan who was very rich. He went to Scotland and fell in love with Loch Lomond, so much so that he offered to buy it and put it in one tiny corner of his ranch where he had several thousand acres of idle land, just ideal for something like Loch Lomond. "I suppose ye have a pipeline on that gr-r-reat estate of yours?" the Scot asked.

"Shore do. I got me a pipeline runs from Texas to Chicago and on up to Montreal, over to New York, then down to Mexico and most ever' country down theah."

"Then it will be easy for ye to run a pipeline over her-r-re, to Loch Lomond. And if ye can *suck* as har-r-rd as ye can *blow*, why mon, ye'll have the whole Loch over to that Texas ranch before ye can say Loch Lomond!"

Of course, summer and the sun can be mighty salubrious. Take the Florida sun and its curative properties. They say that things were so tough in the undertaking business that they shot a gangster feller just to have a funeral so's the folks could see what a funeral was like. At graveside they opened the casket for a last look at the deceased. Well! When that Florida sun hit him, that gangster revived enough so's to reach for his gun. Those good folks had to shoot him again just so they could go on with the funeral. Now that's a healthy sun!

And the California sun has great power, too. There was this young feller out there who got word that his favorite aunt was dying in New York. He jumped on his bicycle and peddled back east as fast as he could go. He arrived just in time to rush with his bike to her bedside, where he let some of that good California air out of his bike tire so that she could take her last breath of it. The good woman inhaled twice only, but deeply, and she revived, and made an almost instant recovery.

And then there was the poor fellow with tuberculosis who was heading west for the air and sunshine of Colorado. When that special Colorado sun shone through the window of the train he was traveling on, bathing him in its healing properties, that sick feller leaped out the window and went running off toward

Denver just awhoopin' and ahollerin'. The last time they saw him he was with Barnum and Bailey circus as their head lion tamer. That's Colorado air for you!

They tell the story in Illinois, that during the terrible drought of 1933, a farm family of five persons had to eat an entire five acres of corn just to have one good, square meal. Think how bad it was in states with less fertile soil — like Iowa.

Talk about fog! There was this feller fishing from shore, and he was trying to bait his hook. But that danged fog was so thick that he stuck two fishhooks in his finger and didn't even know it till the fog lifted! But in spite of that fog, he caught a dozen walleye pike. Curiously, when the fog lifted he discovered that he'd been casting over dry land, but the fish had been swimming above the water and over dry land. You got to admit that sure was a danged thick fog!

You talk about fog! Well, there was this carpenter ashingling a house out in Vermont. That fog got so thick that he was nailing down shingles more by instinct than sight. But he was doing just fine until the fog lifted and he saw to his astonishment that he'd shingled one entire side of the roof and out onto the fog ten feet past the roof. He had shingled the fog!

In another hunting trip, Davy Crockett's companion showed him a squirrel eating sheep sorrel on a pine knot, and that feller claimed the squirrel was big as a barrel. Colonel Crockett poo-pooed the exaggeration, a fight began, and both were defeated. "Come to s'arch heads, both of ours was missin' as he'd bit off my head, and I'd swallered his'n."

You will be hearing more about Josh Billings in the chapter on

phunny phellows, where phonetic spelling and eye dialect rule the humor of that day. As the eye becomes adjusted to this odd way of spelling — a kind of screwed-up English — the reading becomes fun.

Josh Billings Corresponds with a "Hair Oil and Vegetable Bitters Man."

Dear Doktor Hirsute: — I reseaved a tin cup ov yure "Hair purswader," also a bottle ov yure "Salvashun Bitters," bi express, for which, I express my thanks.

The greenbak, which yu enklozed waz the kind ov purswader that we ov the press fully understand.

Yur hair grease, shall hav a reglar gimnastik puff, jist az soon az i kan find a spare time.

I tried a little ov it on an old counter brush in my offiss, this morning, and in 15 minnitts, the brussells grew long az a hosses tale, and i notis this afternoon, the hair begins tew cum up thru, on bak ov the brush, 'tis really wonderful! 'tis almoste Eureka! I rubbed a drop or two on the head ov mi cane, which haz bin bald for more than 5 years, and beggar me! if I don't hav to shave the cane handle, evry day, before I can walk out with it.

I hav a verry favrite cat, she iz one ov the Hambletonian breed ov cats, and altho she iz yung, and haint bin trained yet, she shows grate signs ov speed.

I thought I would just rub the corck ov the bottle on the floor, in the corner ov the room whare the cat generally repozes.

The consequents waz, sum ov the "purswader" got onto the hair ov the cat's tale.

When the cat aroze from her slumbers she caught sight ov her tale, which had growed tew an exalted size; taking one more look at the tale, she started, and bi the good olde Moses! sich running; across the yard! over the fence! up wun side ov an apple tree! and down the other! out into the fields, away! away! The laste i saw ov the cat, she waz pretty mutch awl tale.

I wouldn't hav took 10 dollars for the cat, with her old tale on her.

Slow trains have been a source of tall stories for generations. But over the years, Arkansas seems to have won the honors for the slowest, with Indiana following a close second.

I asked this conductor what time I could get the one o'clock train and he said: "Go home and hit the hay. You can get it whenever you want to." So I got the train and it sure was slow. When I told the conductor about the slowness of his train he told me that if I didn't like it I could get out and walk. I said: "I would, but my folks don't expect me until the train gets there."

Seated in front of me was a mother with her fat son — a big kid. She handed the conductor a half-fare ticket and he said: "That boy is too large to ride on a half-fare ticket. He's too danged old!" "Well," the mother said, "he sure as heck wasn't that way when he got on."

In the seat back of me sat an old geezer, 97 years old. He had a long grey beard; knit the thing himself — and of wire, too. But he had no hands. I said to him: "Where did you lose your hands?" and he replied, "Between the engine and the baggage car." Then I said, "Were you working on this road at the time?" He said, "Sure was. Newsboy on this very train, trip before last. But now I'm a shorthand writer for the railroad company."

About that time an elderly lady of 76 years passed by selling newspapers. She told me that she had the old man's job and then asked if I didn't want to read tomorrow's paper, but I told her that I'd read it yesterday!

And you talk about rough roads! Man, that road was up and down with curves and cut-backs and in-shoots. I noticed a sick lady on the train and I said to her, "Madame, you're too sick to be riding this train." But she told me: "It's doctor's orders. He told me to take a sea voyage!'' Well, that road got so danged rough that it jolted ten bucks out of my pocket that I never had. Then, suddenly, the jolting stopped while we seemed to be running real smooth-like. I asked the conductor: "How come we're moving so smoothly now?" and he said, "We're off the track now!"

Another time on this same train, the conductor noticed an old lady walking along the tracks in the same direction we were going. So he kind of slowed down and asked the old girl if she wouldn't like to hop aboard and ride the rest of the way to town. She thanked him and said, "No, sure nice of you, but it's just two or three miles farther, and I'm in a kind of hurry."

But you can talk about your slow trains through Arkansas and your snail specials over the Rockies, and then I'll tell you about a truly slow train in Indiana. I got on it to go up the state about seventy-five miles. The train ran so slow that I said to the conductor: "Look here, can't you ginger this thing up a little? If not, I'll get out and walk." He got sore at me. "Say, who's bossin' this train, anyhow!" "I know you are," I replied. "So go soak your head," he barked at me. That made me mad and I asked: "Who is the dead person on board this train?" "Why," he replied, "There ain't nobody dead on this train. How come you ask such a silly question?" "Well," I replied, "You're moving so danged slow I thought maybe you were heading up a funeral procession." Now that made him really mad and he jumped me. We had one whale of a fight, I can tell you, and I knocked the breath out of him and then felt so sorry that I ran down to the creek and got a hatfull of water, ran back, slopped it onto his face, brought him to, and we both caught the rear end of that train as it came by — and it wasn't a long train, either.

I was on that Indiana train so dern long that I wore out one of the cushions, and had train sores. You think I'm exaggerating? No siree! Why, a fellow took down with typhoid fever on that train, just after I got on, and when I got off at the end of my trip, that feller was sound and well, and he had a whale of a seige of it, too.

★   ★   ★   ★

But that feller with typhoid wasn't the worst of it. A rancher had on a carload of cattle headed for market, and a couple of cowboys to look after them. Now just before those cattle were loaded, one of the cowboys had got himself hitched, married, you know, and the next to last stop he got a telegram congratulating him on being the father of an eight pound boy!

Chapter II
Jokes From 1842-1912

If book-length humorous fiction is the novel, and shorter humorous fiction is the short story, and the condensed short story is a short-short story, then a good joke is simply a good short-short-short story. The triple-short story is one that Americans have always delighted to tell, listen to, exchange. Jokes are a part of our culture and reveal the concerns and doings of our past in brief ways sometimes more revealing than formal history. The joke is a kind of encapsulated cultural history.

Lately, collections of contemporary jokes have appeared increasingly in bookstores across the nation. This may indicate a shortage of interest in longer forms of humor, or it may tell us that there is increasing interest in not only telling good jokes, but in hearing and reading them . . . a rekindling of a consummate interest of an earlier time.

Here the jokes are arranged in a kind of rough subject-order so that the reader can get some notion of the matters of continuing concern to Americans, concerns with death, aging, law and lawyers, marriage and love, rustics, women's rights. And always the ethnic joke calling attention to the gauche, funny, and often clever doings of our then recent immigrants — the Irish, the Jews and, always, the Blacks. Today's ethnic humor considers and lampoons more recent immigrants . . . Poles and Chicanos, later ingredients added to our melting pot.

As expected, the largest group of jokes — always popular — is the pun, which never seems to go out of style. Puns may be the oldest form of humor in America.

★ ★ ★ ★

A census stopped at the house of an old farmer in the Arkansas hills.

"How many children have you got?"

"Nineteen."

"Big family!"

"Yes. The first thirteen of 'em was born before I found out the cause of 'em."

*   *   *   *

At the Texas border stands a signboard: "Beyond this sign lies Texas. All who can read come over."

*   *   *   *

Trucking, in an Arkansas dance means getting out on the floor and shaking all over. A fellow came to work one morning with his eyes blackened and bruises all over his face. "What happened?" he was asked. "Went to a dance last night. They said, 'Swing yo pahdner right an' left.' Ah did. Then they said, 'Grab yo pahdner.' Ah did. Then they called, 'Everybody staht truckin'.' Ah misunderstood."

*   *   *   *

"Where does Jess Skinker live?"
"Second hawg waller on the right after you pass Coon's Creek."

*   *   *   *

A visitor to a small Arkansas village noticed that every evening a native would pass with a drove of razorback hogs going north, and about sundown every evening he would return. One morning the visitor asked the native where he was going. He replied, "Over thar, tother side of the mountain."
"How far is it over there?"
"Three mile."
"Why do you take them over there?"
"To graze."
"Why don't you move over there?"
"What fur?"
"To save time!"
"Time! Hell, what's time to a hog?"

*   *   *   *

A backwoods girl asked another girl how old she was.

"I's six or seven, I ain't sho which."

"Well, is you still virtuous?"

"Yes."

"Well, you's jest six, then, 'cause I's seven."

★　　　★　　　★　　　★

A stranger traveling in the hills asked leave to pass the night at a farmer's house. The farmer replied that there was only one bed in the house, in which the guest was welcome, with him and his wife. At supper the guest ate very heartily of turnip greens and corn bread. He took repeated servings of the greens, but still his appetite was unsatisfied, and he went to bed hungry. During the night the farmer heard a disturbance among the horses and went to the barn to tie up a mare that had broken loose from her stall. The wife whispered, "Here's yore chanct! Hey! Mister. Here's yore chanct!" The stranger jumped out of bed, ran to the kitchen, and ate the rest of the turnip greens.

★　　　★　　　★　　　★

One task of an Arkansas farm boy is polin' the hawgs. He sticks the hawg on a pole an' holds him up to an oak tree to eat the acorns.

★　　　★　　　★　　　★

That man is so cheap! You know what he does to save haircut money? He freezes his hair and then just breaks them off!"

★　　　★　　　★　　　★

That same feller who froze his hair is so cheap he worked ten years trying to dry snow so he could sell it for salt.

★　　　★　　　★　　　★

A bumpkin sees a canebottom chair for the first time. "Now I cain't figure it," he said, "jist why in tarnation would a body go to the trouble to find all them holes jist to put straw around them?"

Then there was the feller who came home late and drunk, threw the candle in bed and blew himself out.

He's so dumb that when he saw an advertisement for a stove that would save half his fuel bill, he bought two so as to save 100%.

A traveler, returned from the wild west, was boasting of his exploits against the Indians. "By gum we made 505 of them wild critters jest run like hayll." "How come?" he was asked. "We ran and they ran after us!" he said.

A man was boasting of his ancient lineage, his distinguished ancestors who had come over on the Mayflower, and the farmer listening replied: "That's too bad, friend, because in my business we say: 'The older the seed, the worse the crop.' "

A man found a boy lying beside a steep hillside field. "How did you come here?"

"Fell outa the cawnfield."

Traveler before a hotel register in Leavenworth, Kansas, is about to sign when he sees a bed bug working his way across the page. "I've been bled by St. Joe fleas," he said, "and bit by Kansas City spiders, interviewed by Fort Scott greybacks, but I'll be damned if I was ever in a place before where the bedbugs looked over the hotel register to find out where your room was."

There is a man so cold-hearted that when a dog bit him, it froze teeth and gums.

★   ★   ★   ★

There's a man in Tennessee with such big feet that if he gets them wet in December, he doesn't catch cold until February.

★   ★   ★   ★

Game warden: "Ah hah! Caught you poaching. That'll cost ya."
Fisherman: "Now just a minute, officer. I wasn't fishing. I was only trying to drown this here worm."

★   ★   ★   ★

A retired dairyman has a compulsion that is a genuine complex. Every time he sees a container of water, he has an impulse to put some milk in it.

★   ★   ★   ★

There's some land in Nebraska so poor you can't raise a disturbance on it.

★   ★   ★   ★

Man in bed asleep falls out of bed. "I reckon," he says sleepily, "that I slept too near where I got in." "Nope," said his bed partner. "You was too near where you fell out."

★   ★   ★   ★

City slicker, gloating and preparing to fleece the country bumpkin: "If all flesh is grass, you're one whale of a load of hay."
Hay seed: "Mebbe so, mister, but judgin' from the way the asses on the street of thiseyer town is nibblin' at me, I shore ain't gonna last long."

★   ★   ★   ★

A hillbilly came to dine in a fine city restaurant. They started his dinner with shrimp and then served celery, whereupon he got up and started for the door. "My dear sir," asked the maitre d' hotel, "is something wrong?"

"I tried yore bugs and they's jist awful. An' I shore as hell don't want none of yore grass. Got plenty in my own pasture back home."

Prospective buyer: "Isn't three dollars a lot for a watermelon?"
Farmer: "You wouldn't think so, mister, if you'd set on a fence with a shotgun ever' night fer three weeks awatchin' thet watermelon patch."

Farmer being solicited to subscribe to the daily paper replies: "My paw died two years past and bedad, I ain't read yet the 'cumulation of newspapers he left behind."

Wouldn't the world be a richer place if the housefly, which lays 20,000 eggs a season, could be crossed with a hen?

Advice as to best way to raise strawberries. With a spoon.

To say that a man flies higher than he can roost is a lot more elevated language than to say he bites off more than he can chew.

It is said in Colorado, the spiders spin threads strong enough to sew on buttons . . . and the odd thing is, the spiders are tiny . . . not a bit bigger than blackbirds.

"A virgin for-r-rest iz a place," said the Irishman, "whur the hand o' man has niver yit set foot, be'dad."

My dear Murphy, why did you betray the confidence I placed in you when you promised never to reveal that secret?"
Murphy: "Betray? Nivir! I jist wasn't able to keep it to meself, so I give it away to a feller in whom I had more confidence than in me own self."

"Did you vote yesterday, Mike?"

"Shure an I did that . . . according to the instructions."

"And what were those?"

"Vote ayrly and often."

A black man signed his name with a D.D. after it. When asked what it meant, he replied: "I is a dog doctor."

Newly arrived Irish maid is sent to call a visitor to dinner. She sees him brushing his teeth before eating. "Bridget, is our guest ready?" the hostess asks. "Shur an' he is, mum, he's jist asharpenin' his teeth, he is."

"Why isn't Rory O'Keagan at Confession and Mass?" Father O'Toole asked Rory's wife.

"Begorra he's in a vurra bad way, Father, he is."

"Really? Is it Deism?"

"No, Father, worse yit."

"Soul o' me, an' is it . . . is it . . . atheism, I trust not?"

"Worse. Far worse."

"Thin phwat kin it be sister?"

"An' it's rheumatism, so tiz."

That Yankee trader is such a shrewd entrepeneur that if he was cast away on a desert island, he'd be up next mornin' selling maps to the inhabitants.

★   ★   ★   ★

Judge: "Now, Patrick, as to the charge. How do you plead, guilty or not?"

Patrick: "Faith an' I'll jist be about waitin' til I hears the ividence, y'r honor."

★   ★   ★   ★

A Scotch blacksmith was asked the meaning of metaphysics. He studied a bit, then replied, "When the par-r-ty listenin' dinna ken what the par-r-ty speakin' means, and when the par-r-ty speakin' dinna ken what he himself means, well, that is metaphysics."

★   ★   ★   ★

A drunken Irishman was leaning against a post watching a funeral procession. "Who's dead?" a passerby asked him. "Fellow in the coffin," he replied.

★   ★   ★   ★

"Murphy!" the boss hollered, "You're late again. The other men got here an hour before you!"

"Shure, and it's the tr-ruth, sur," Murphy replied. "But I'll even things this verra night, I will. I'll jist be lavin the job an hour early and that'll even things."

★   ★   ★   ★

It was the time for duels. A Frenchman and an Englishman quarreled, and a challenge to fight followed. Pistols were the weapons, and both, since they were cowards, agreed to fight in a dark room. The Englishman was to have the first shot. He groped his way to the chimney and fired up it, killing the Frenchman who had been hiding there.

★   ★   ★   ★

"Would ye mind takin' this coat fer me to Boston?" an Irishman asked a passenger in a coach going that way.

"I don't mind. But how will I ever find you to give it back?" asked the kind passenger.

"Twon't be no trouble atall," said Mike. "Fer I'll be in it all the way."

★   ★   ★   ★

A Negro woman lost patience when her lighter-colored son bullied her blacker son. "Rastus," she exclaimed, "you'd be jest as dahk as your brother if Ah hadn't got so fah behind in mah house rent!''

★   ★   ★   ★

"As I was goin' over the bridge," said Pete, "I met Pat Hewin. 'Hewin,' says I, 'How air ye?' 'Pretty well, thank ye, Donnelly,' says he. 'Donnelly,' says I, 'That ain't me name.' 'Faith, then no more is mine Hewin,' says he. So with that we looked at each other again an' sure enough, twarn't nayther of us.''

★   ★   ★   ★

They say that in the Civil War, an Irishman registered in the 75th Regiment so that he could be near his brother in the 74th Regiment.

★   ★   ★   ★

Friend commiserates with Irishman about missing the train. "Oh, Patty, you didn't run fast enough." "Shure an' I did, it's jist that I didna shtart soon enough."

★   ★   ★   ★

An Irishman wanted to learn French. "It'll cost you five dollars the first month," the instructor told him, "but only two dollars the second month." "Well," said Patrick, "ye can jist put me down as startin' the second month."

★   ★   ★   ★

A visitor from a distant land saw, for the first time, a black man standing on the corner. He rushed to him, tore his tie off and his collar open, screaming, "Mister! You're choking to death!"

★   ★   ★   ★

I get married and say to mine vife: "Every time I kiss you I giff you a dollar. Now I come home, open de box, und find two dolluh bills, and five dolluh bills, and ten dolluh bills, and fur coats and all tings I don't undershtand since I only giff you a dolluh ever' time I kiss you."

Wife: "Not eferbody so chipp like you."

★   ★   ★   ★

At a lodge they discussed the need to spend $100 for a new chandelier. Abe stands up and says, "Why for you vant to puy such a ting. Dere ain't one person in dis lodge vat know how to play it."

★   ★   ★   ★

"Mine brudder died."

"Too bad. What'd he die of?"

"He die of a pen on de seatus. They cut him from de front to de peck but dey couldn't find de pen on de seatus. Dey find absence. Den dey put him a box labeled 'Opened by mistake.' "

★   ★   ★   ★

Isaacs and Levy stop at a hotel and get ready for bed. Isaacs sniffs. "Levy! Iss dot you? Did you take a bath this week?" Levy turns. "Vy?" he asks. "Is von of tem missink?"

★   ★   ★   ★

Jake Cohen has found a winning formula at the race tracks. At first he found that if he won money one day, he lost it the next. Now he goes to the track only on alternate days.

★   ★   ★   ★

Husband and wife share a berth on a sleeping car. She needs to get a drink of water, but is afraid she can't find the right berth upon her return. "Dunt vurry. I'll stick my foot out in de aisle and you look for it ven you come back." She leaves. When she comes back, every berth has a man's foot stuck out in the aisle.

★   ★   ★   ★

That Sam is so cheap that he refused to buy his son a $25 bicycle, then promised a tricycle at $15, then finally told the boy to wait for winter and he'd get him an icycle.

★　　　★　　　★　　　★

"Vats a polar bear?" Isaac asks his wife. "A polar bear is from Alaska," she told him, "und walks around on de snow and sits down on a cake of ice." "Hah! Den I vont do it!" Isaac replies. "Vont do vat?" she asks. "Mrs. Cohen vants I should be a polar bear for her husband, his funeral. Some noive."

★　　　★　　　★　　　★

A planter orders his slave to climb a tree and thin the branches, but the slave procrastinates, and finally says: "Well, looky heah, massa, if I go up dar and fall down an' broke mah neck, dat'll be a thousan' dollars out'n yo pocket. Ain't it better you hire an Irishman to go up dah so dat when he fall down and kill hisself dat won't be no loss to nobody?"

★　　　★　　　★　　　★

Sad story of Abe, the son of Samuel. Abe was a fine musician. He played the piccolo and toured the country. When they got to Omaha, Senator Clark was so taken with the band that he invited them all to his home for a concert, after which he ordered all their instruments to be filled with gold. And there was poor Abe, son of Samuel, with that itty bitty piccolo.

★　　　★　　　★　　　★

Sammy says he never pays to get into a picture show. Says he walks in backwards and they figure he's walking out of it.

★　　　★　　　★　　　★

Ike and Greenie hated one another but found themselves where Ike was entertaining as a magician. As he's performing, he sees Greenie swipe a silver spoon and put it in his boot. In a while, Ike does an item disappearance stunt wherein he takes a spoon, places it carefully and obviously in his bosom, then tells the audience that he shall now make it reappear in Greenie's boot!

★　　　★　　　★　　　★

"Ike, this coat don't fit so good," the lady said, squirming about in the tight-fitting coat. "What'd you expect for five dollars," the salesman tells her, "an attack of epilepsy?"

Levy needs glasses and is in the office of the eye doctor who has him trying to read the letters on the card. "Can you read that first line now?" "No, I can't," says Levy. Moving it closer, the doctor asks, "Now?" "No," Levy replies. Closer and closer the sign is moved toward Levy until it can't go any closer. "I can't understand it," the doctor said. "Not even this close you can't read it?" "Nope. I never learned to read."

"So you're engaged to Becky? I heard she'd kissed every feller in Yonkers."

"So-o. Younkers ain't soch a big place."

Two Jews, best friends, agreed that the first one to die would be given five thousand dollars, to be placed in the coffin. Epstein dies first. Cohen puts a check for five thousand dollars in the coffin.

After much bargaining, the customer buys the fifteen dollar coat for three dollars. Next day he comes back, very angry. "That coat is chock full of moths," he yells. "Vat didya expect, Mister! For three dollars you vant mocking boids?"

When is a fishing boat like a pretty girl? When it's attached to a buoy.

Which travels faster, heat or cold? Heat! Why? Because you can always catch cold.

"This can't be beat," said the farmer as he pulled up a carrot.

★   ★   ★   ★

How to double and triple your money? You take the bill, fold it once, like this, then you fold it again, like this, and you see it's in-creases.

★   ★   ★   ★

There's no use expectin' a woman to see a joke unless it's marked down somethin'.

★   ★   ★   ★

When a cat entertains us at midnight from on top of the wall, it's not the cat we object to, but the *waul*.

★   ★   ★   ★

Title of the head nurse in a baby ward? Chief of the bawl room.

★   ★   ★   ★

Scientific question: If a little pebble had the guts to attack Goliath, what could it have done if it had only been boulder?

★   ★   ★   ★

Two of the worst puns of the year: The largest ant is the elephant. And the worst relation is a carb-uncle.

★   ★   ★   ★

Punster: "You blacksmiths all have at least one vise."
Blacksmith: "I suppose you mean we're good at forg-ery?"

★   ★   ★   ★

"Weight for the wagon," said the farmer as he helped his two-hundred-pound wife to her seat.

★   ★   ★   ★

How do you get rid of an extra T? Throw it in depot.

★   ★   ★   ★

What's the most dangerous breed of bat? The brickbat.

★   ★   ★   ★

It is said that the seers who made the wrong predictions at the greatest cost to humanity are the financiers.

★   ★   ★   ★

If brevity is the soul of wit, what's the heel? Why silence, fer shoe'r.

★   ★   ★   ★

The fellow who ate most of a half-picked goose said he felt down in the mouth over it.

★   ★   ★   ★

Although the rabbit is timid, no cook lives who can make it quail.

★   ★   ★   ★

Captain! I dropped my watch overboard. Is there any way to get it? Of course. Divers ways.

★   ★   ★   ★

Lawyer in carriage: "What's wrong, driver?"
Driver: "The horses are running away, Sir. Can't control them"
Lawyer: "Well, if you can't stop 'em, then run 'em into something cheap."

★   ★   ★   ★

"My work's dun," said the bill collector one evening.

★   ★   ★   ★

Sign in a bath house: "You can't make a silk purse out of a souse here."

★   ★   ★   ★

No part of a man can take so many blows as his nose.

★   ★   ★   ★

They say age improves all wines except the whine of a man.

★   ★   ★   ★

They say a pen may be driven, but a pencil does best when it's lead.

★　　　★　　　★　　　★

They say an actor's best friend is Benny Fits.

★　　　★　　　★　　　★

The owner of the local newspaper was faced with a bad business year, not enough customers. He was advised to walk five miles a day to increase circulation.

★　　　★　　　★　　　★

It's a truism that a young physician can make it only if he has patients.

★　　　★　　　★　　　★

A gun is not half so dangerous if the owner's not loaded.

★　　　★　　　★　　　★

How many sides to a tree? None: they're round. Wrong! Inside and outside.

★　　　★　　　★　　　★

What cheap hotel reminds you of a musical instrument? A vile-inn.

★　　　★　　　★　　　★

Why is a bowler like a divorced man? 'Cause he pays alley-money.

★　　　★　　　★　　　★

Couple has twins. When the first twin girl arrives, he names her Kate. When the second twin girl arrives, he names her Duplicate.

★　　　★　　　★　　　★

Epitaph on the stone of a collegian:

He loved his lager faithfully
　Who lieth buried here;
For even after he was dead
　He took another bier.

★   ★   ★   ★

What's the difference between a legal document and a cat? The document has pauses at the end of clauses while the other has clawses at the end of paw-ses.

★   ★   ★   ★

Although a Republic, two kings rule America. Jo-king and Smo-king.

★   ★   ★   ★

Do you know the kiss waltz? Is that the one played on a mouth organ?

★   ★   ★   ★

Fish should be selected on the basis of one's profession, as follows: Carpenter-sawfish. Shoemaker-sole. Jazz musician-drum fish. Policeman-starfish. Sea Captain-skipper. Lawyer-shark. Miser-goldfish. Schoolmaster-whale. Schoolboy-blubber. Cheese manufacturer-smelt.

★   ★   ★   ★

Two heads are better than one, they say, and it's especially true on a bass drum.

★   ★   ★   ★

An old sailor remarked that he supposed dancing girls wore their dresses at half-mast as a mark of respect for departed modesty.

★   ★   ★   ★

Dinner at a fashionable restaurant and the customer calls to his waiter. "Waiter," he asks, "what do you call this stuff?"
Waiter: "That's bean soup, sir."
Customer: "I don't care what it's been, what's it now!"

★   ★   ★   ★

John Jones doesn't object to the lick her law applied to Jane. Jane does believe in the liquor law applied to John, because when John does liquor, he does lick her. When John doesn't liquor, he doesn't lick her; therefore, if John can't liquor, he won't lick her — the conclusion she prefers.

How to say grace, with grace, when seated before the sole item of food on the table: a single beet. "Dear God . . . that beet's all. Amen."

A young man, a broker, married an obese, homely, but very wealthy widow. "It was not her face that attracted me, but her figure," he said.

★　　　★　　　★　　　★

Teacher: "Jupiter and Juno were husband and wife, yet Juno had Mars for a son but he wasn't Jupiter's. So why did they call him Mars?"
Pupil: "Because he was Mar's, but not Pa's."

★　　　★　　　★　　　★

A lady should always be excused for her bustle when she's a little behind.

★　　　★　　　★　　　★

Count on it, a lover of archery is an arrow-minded fellow.

★　　　★　　　★　　　★

A joint affair? Rheumatism.

★　　　★　　　★　　　★

Eggs come in layers.

★　　　★　　　★　　　★

And just how far can a widow with two kids go? One step-farther.

★　　　★　　　★　　　★

What is irony? The afternoon after the morning's washing.

★   ★   ★   ★

A western paper remarks that if the U.S. continues to ship feed grains to Europe, it'll soon be known as the fodderland.

★   ★   ★   ★

Want to see a religious uprising? Drop a handful of tacks in the family pew.

★   ★   ★   ★

"I may be stuck-up, but I'm not proud," said the butterfly that was pinned on the lady's bodice.

★   ★   ★   ★

What's the "Voice of the graves?" "Tomb's Tone."

★   ★   ★   ★

They say that the soil is so bad down in Texas that the only thing you can raise there is the dead.

★   ★   ★   ★

"Jack! I'm so glad to see you up and around," his friend said. "I heard you'd died."
"Nope. Rallied and pulled through."
"Great! How'd you do it?"
"Didn't do it. Doctor did. He fell sick and took to his bed at my critical time, so I made it."

★   ★   ★   ★

Young lady learns that her widowed mother is about to marry. She sits down and begins to cry. Why? Because she couldn't go a step-farther.

★   ★   ★   ★

A teacher's ruler is a wise board of education.

★   ★   ★   ★

Newlyweds, and the wife serves goulash to her husband. As he eats, she asks: "Do you love me as you use stew, dear?"

A shoe clerk's goodby: "Sole long."

As the Circuit Judge was trimming his grass in front of his house, a passerby remarked, "Yes. There must be lawn order."

"They didn't pick that stuff soon enough," said the little boy as he refused the limburger cheese.

Teacher: "Define excavate."
"It means to hollow out," answered 10-year-old pupil.
"Then please use it in a sentence."
"When hurt, the baby excavates," the boy replied.

First small boy: "Where are you in Sunday School?"
Second small boy: "We're in the middle of original sin."
Third small boy: "That ain't so much. We're already past redemption."

A boy enters a drug store on Kenzie Street. "Doctor, mother sent me to the sothicary pop, cos Bub's sick as the dickens with the phicken chox and she wants a thimble full of pollygollic in the din tipper cos we hadn't bot a gottle, and the kint pup's got the bine witters in it. Got any?"

A bill collector sent a boy to collect a $7.00 bill owed him. The kid comes back with the money and is given a quarter. "Mister," the kid asks, "Don't you think I ought to have something for my honesty?"

"It's so hot in here that the blood rushes to my head," said the sweet young thing.

"Plenty of room there, all right," whispered her rival to boy-friend.

★   ★   ★   ★

Sweet young thing walks up to her boyfriend just as another fellow walks away from him. "George," she asks, "Who was that nice looking young man who just left?"

"I don't know his name. I see him about. He's just a quon-dam acquaintance."

"George! If you can't speak without profanity in the presence of a lady, then you'd better follow your . . . your acquaintance."

★   ★   ★   ★

He: "Are you comfortable in that corner, dear?"
She: "Fine, honey."
He: "Quite sure you're not chilled?"
She: "Quite. Fine here."
He: "No draft?"
She: "Not at all."
He: "Well, then, would you mind changing places with me? I tend to catch cold in drafty, damp places."

★   ★   ★   ★

Why do ladies' teeth decay faster than men's? Because the friction of the tongue wears 'em out, and they have sugar lips.

★   ★   ★   ★

Told that her lawyer was lying at the point of death, client remarked: "Good heavens, won't even death make that man honest?"

★   ★   ★   ★

It is passing strange that women want to imitate men. A boa constrictor, one could understand. Or a rattlesnake, lion, or even an elephant. But a man? Damned poor judgment.

★   ★   ★   ★

City people coming out to the country always know a lot more about farming than the native, and they often provide good illustrative material for the country preacher. I know of one city woman who came out our way and sent for a native to help her make a flower garden. He dug out a bed, rounding it up nicely and smoothing it down with a rake. Then he asked, "What are you planning to plant here, ma'am?"

"I plan to put salivas in here," she replied proudly.

"Salivas? Salivas?" repeated the old farmer. "You don't mean salvias, do you?"

"I mean what I say. Do as you're told."

He did as he was told.

Then the city farmerette said, "Samuel, what would you suggest as a border around this bed?"

"Well, I'll tell you, ma'am," came the quick answer. "If you're going to have this great big bed of salivas here, I would suggest that you have a mighty wide border of spittoonias around the outside."

★   ★   ★   ★

Woman calls a Baptist minister to pray for her dying husband. "I'm pleased that you called me," the preacher said upon arrival, "But may I ask why you don't belong to a church?"

Wife: "But we do. The First M.E. at Downer's Prairie."

Preacher: "Forgive me for asking, but why didn't you call Brother Fink, the pastor at the First M.E.?"

Wife: "Well, Brother, it's like this. John may be dying of typhus, and you know how busy Brother Fink is? Well, we didn't want to expose him."

★   ★   ★   ★

A Quaker woman's sermon: "Three things I wonder at. That children throw sticks at fruit trees when, if they only waited, the fruit would fall of itself. Two, that men are so foolish and wicked as to go to war and kill each other when, if left alone, they'd die soon enough. Three, that young men woo women so unwisely as to go after them when, if they stayed at home, the young women would come after them."

The preacher saith that a hypocrite can no more get to heaven than a raccoon can climb up through a stovepipe with a teakettle tied to his tail.

In the community a clergyman was known for his interminable sermons. After services, one day, two parishioners were discussing this fault. "I don't understand how come Rev. Jones goes on and on and jest never quits sermonizing," one said. The other said: "He probably gets to writin' them sermons and is jest too lazy to quit."

*   *   *   *

At one time when Mr. Dow was traveling in the South, he asked permission to remain overnight. The woman of the house informed him that, her husband being away from home, he could not stay. He insisted that she should grant him permission, as there was no other house near to which he could go; but she positively refused, until he told her he was a preacher, and would sleep in the stable if he could do no better. This information, together with his long beard at once suggested to her who he was, and she accordingly inquired if he was Lorenzo Dow. Being answered in the affirmative, she waived her objections, and concluded that he might stay — probably more out of fear that evil might befall her if she turned him off than out of a wish to have him in the house.

Accordingly Mr. Dow put up, and about the usual hour retired to bed in a back room, where he had not lain long until he heard a man arrive, who he soon discovered was not the woman's husband. A series of jokes commenced between the woman and the man, which continued with a good deal of pleasantry till about midnight, when, all of a sudden, their pleasures were disturbed by a rap at the door, which announced that the husband had returned. Alarm and consternation followed. There was but one door, and at it stood the husband. To be caught there at that hour of the night would, to say the least of it, insure him a sound thrashing. To escape seemed impossible. At this critical juncture, when the ingenuity of man had failed, the quick perception of woman, as in most cases of emergency, found an expedient. At the foot of the bed stood a large gum full of raw cotton, in which she concealed the visitor. Then turning round very composedly, opened the door and received her husband.

But his lordship had been at the grogshop, and was in what the Irish schoolmaster called an "uproarious mood." "Hush, hush," said the wife, as the husband blundered in, and roared out, "Thunder and potatoes, Mag, and why didn't you open the door?" "Hush, my dear, hush! Lorenzo Dow is in the house." "O blood and tobacco! And is it Lorenzo Dow, the man who raises the Devil?" "Sure it is, and why don't you be still?" "Oh, by Saint Patrick, he shall come forth, and you shall see the Devil before you sleep." So blundering into the bedroom, Mr. Dow was compelled to come forth, and nothing would satisfy the husband but that Lorenzo must raise the Devil. Mr. Dow protested and urged his inability to perform such wonders; but no excuse would satisfy the uncompromising husband — he had heard that Dow could raise the Devil, and now that he had him in his house, he determined that he must. At length, said Mr. Dow, "If you will stand in the door and give him a few thumps as he passes, but not so hard as to break his bones, I will see if I can raise him." So saying, he took the candle in his hand, and walking up and down the room, Lorenzo touched the candle to the cotton, and said, "Come forth, old boy." Out jumped the hidden gentleman all in a blaze, and breaking for the door like a mass of living fire made good his escape, but not without first receiving a good rap over the shoulder from the husband's cudgel as he passed the threshold. The job was now done, Lorenzo had raised the Devil, and the husband thought it a real wonder performed by the Yankee preacher.

★   ★   ★   ★

Stories on the various denominations always go over well at any sort of gathering, but especially at a church one. The minister who can crack a joke on his own denomination gets off to a good start. I've done it many a time by telling about the Episcopal clergyman who was fatally ill. It seemed fitting for him to leave a message to his vestrymen. They brought him a pad and a pencil and with trembling fingers he wrote:

Go tell the vestry that I'm dead,
But they need shed no tears;
For though I'm dead I'm no more dead
Than they have been for years.

★   ★   ★   ★

An old lady in one of the parishes of Peter Cartwright, an early Methodist pioneer, often annoyed him by being more noisy than pious and by often going off on a high key. In a class meeting one day, when her soul was filled with ecstatic emotions, she rapturously cried out, "If I had one more feather in the wing of my faith, I would fly away and be with my Saviour!"

"Stick in the other feather, Lord," interjected Cartwright, "and let her go!"

★   ★   ★   ★

"You're looking well," said a friend to a ninety-five-year-old man.

"It's not my appearance that bothers me, these days, but my disappearance," the old boy replied.

★   ★   ★   ★

Mark Twain was criticized for not taking part in a dinner table conversation about "eternal life and future punishment." He replied: "Madame, excuse me my silence, but I do it out of respect since I have friends in both places."

★   ★   ★   ★

Chauncey M. Depew told this story. At a mountain funeral, a

busybody goes up to the bereaved wife to offer condolences. But she notices a grandfather clock in the corner and is surprised to see it. "When did y'all git that grandfather clock?" she asks. "Tain't no granfather clock," the widow tells her. "It's jes poor ol' Jake in his box. Had to stand him in the corner, thar, to make room fer the mourners."

Savoir faire, for sure. Mrs. Jones was called from the dinner table to the door to greet a stranger who told her: "Mrs. Jones, I have bad news to relate. Your husband just fell off his wagon and was killed. "Is it possible?" Mrs. Jones said softly, slowly. "So. I guess it is. Well, sir, you just wait until dinner's over, and you'll hear the biggest kind of weeping."

An honest, poor woman named Marie Plor residing near this city was 100 years old. When she lost her 80-year-old son, she said, weeping; "Ah, I always said I'd never be able to bring up that child."

When the condemned criminal was asked what style of death he wanted, he replied: "If it's all the same, I'll take old age."

Let us so live that when we pass away, our friends will not be immediately and uproariously reconciled to our death.

A Vermont editor has hit upon a great new way to collect from delinquent subscribers. He prints obituary notices of them.

Query: Is life worth living? Answer: Depends on the liver.

Lifestyle: The first thing in life that man takes is milk . . . the last is his bier.

★   ★   ★   ★

"Now that you've got glasses," his wife asked, "do you see better?"

"Sure, twice as good. A couple of glasses and I see double."

★   ★   ★   ★

"Could you tell me, shir, which is the other shide of the street?" a drunk stopped a passerby and asked.

"Over there. Other side."

"Thash what I told the feller over there on that shide, but he shaid it wush over here."

★   ★   ★   ★

Preacher to drunk: "If I was in your place I'd go out in the woods and hang myself."

Drunk: "If you wuz in my plaish, you'd never make it there."

★   ★   ★   ★

The doctor comes to the house where he's been treating the master of it. "How's Dad?" he asks the small son. "How's his appetite?" Small boy replies: "His appetite's still bad, but his drinkatite is good as ever."

★   ★   ★   ★

He's so bad about liquor that when he cuts himself, whiskey flows.

★   ★   ★   ★

A drunk comes staggering down the street, makes it to the liquor store, but collapses just in front of it. Little boy sees him, runs inside and announces to the owner: "Hey, Mister, your sign just fell down."

★   ★   ★   ★

A drunken lawyer appears in court to try a case at law. "I'm astonished to see you in this condition!" said the judge.

"Astonished? Wazzer maddur wi me, y'r honor?"

"To be plain, you're drunk!"

"Y'r honor, I been prac'sing here for fi'teen year, an' thass the firsht c'rect decishun I yever heard in dish court."

Jack, a murderer, is in court. He offers a friend on the jury five hundred dollars if he can get him off with a verdict of murder in the second degree. Friend succeeds: "Wasn't easy, Jack, I fought like hell; I was the only one, too. The rest of 'em wanted an acquittal, but I beat 'em."

Behind the locked doors of his office an Arkansas doctor administered to one female patient after another a kind of service not entirely therapeutic. During his absence his wife gratified a series of callers, beginning in the kitchen with the ice-man. At his return, the doctor found her lolling on the porch in a revealing posture.

"Why are you setting out here showing everything you got?"

"The landlord called to get the rent, and I'm drying the receipt."

A western congressman, wanting an allocation of funds for his state said that all the state needed was "water and good society." Congressman Thaddeus Stevens replied: "That's all that Hell needs!"

A visiting Englishman made fun of a hump-backed Yankee porter who was carrying his bags off the ship. "My dear fellow, what's that hump on your back?"

Porter: "Bunker Hill!"

The farmer raises the corn, the corn raises the whiskey, the whiskey raises the politicians, and the politicians raise all the hell and trouble we got in this country.

★   ★   ★   ★

"The politicians of my party have thrown me overboard," said a defeated candidate for public office. "But," he added, "I have enough strength to swim to the other side!"

★   ★   ★   ★

A lady once told how she could tell when she'd drunk too much: her husband's jokes began to seem funny.

★   ★   ★   ★

Early frontier bride looking at a menu in a big city restaurant: "What's patty de free grass, John?"
John, the new husband: "Must be French for celery, dear."

★   ★   ★   ★

Husband returns home to find his French servant girl smiling broadly. "Why so happy, Louise?" he asks her.
"Oh, Monsieur, eef you but knew! Zer was zis fran of yours, Monsieur Hector, an' he come an' he ask for you. But you was gone, alas. But eet make no matter. He vurry, vurry heppy to fine zat Madame was all alone in dis house, so dat he give me twenny dollair when he leave."

★   ★   ★   ★

"Tom!" said the girl to her sweetheart, "You've been paying your distentions to me long enough. Now I want to know your contentions! I just don't want to be kept in expense any longer and you'd better pop the answer or else. I can't stand this oleandering around!"

★   ★   ★   ★

Prescription for keeping a husband home nights. When he rings or knocks on the door to come in, after a long night on the town, whisper through the keyhole: "Is that you Willie?" When his name is John, well, you can bet he'll stay home and watch his pasture after that.

★   ★   ★   ★

A country bumpkin, half horse, half alligator, came to the

village and to the inn. To have fun with him, they do a mock marriage of him to a girl equally rustic. When the "preacher" learns that the two of them have taken it all seriously, he rushes to the room where they are staying and hollers: "Come on out. For heaven's sake, don't! I ain't a regular preacher, jes a make-fun one." The rustic sticks his head out the door, winks, and says, "Old hoss, y'all is too late."

Question: How long did Adam reign in Paradise before he sinned?
Answer: Till he got a wife.

Probabilities in the weather: When a man gets home at 2 A.M., it's likely to be stormy. When a husband gets an unexpected and enormous bill on his wife, it's likely to be thunder and lightning. When a man dies and leaves his widow lots of money and you see her walking with the executor, a change is imminent.

Woman returns to school from a picnic where she had chaperoned fourteen kids from the fourth grade. A stranger saw her and said, "Whew! Gee whiz Ma'am, are all those kids yours?"

"What d'ya take me for Mister," she replied, "an incubator?"

A condemned man, visited by his wife, was asked by her if he'd like his children present for the execution. He said "No."

"That's just like you, George," she said. "You never did let the kids have any fun."

Given a very tall girl and a very short fellow, how does he kiss her goodbye? He doesn't. He just looks up and says, "So long!"

★   ★   ★   ★

Somebody said that love was a tickling sensation of the heart that can't be scratched.

★   ★   ★   ★

A gentleman was speaking of the kindness of friends in visiting him; "Everybody has been so kind. Especially my mother-in-law who visited me twice this year and stayed six months each visit."

★   ★   ★   ★

A definition of love: a little sighing, a little crying, a little dying, and a great lot of lying.

★   ★   ★   ★

Talk about modesty! There's a young man of Cincinnati so modest he won't embrace an opportunity. He's engaged to a girl who fainted when she heard the naked truth.

★   ★   ★   ★

Many times, when I am introduced, the host will speak of my numerous occupations — farmer, minister, barber, and so forth. That always gives me a chance to tell of the barber who cut his customer all over the face, and then tried to patch up the cuts with pieces of brown paper. The man looked at himself in the when the torture was over, and he was so mad that the barber feared for his life.

"I'm sorry," said the barber. "I had bad luck with you." The customer pulled out a dollar bill and passed it over. The barber started to give back his change, but the customer roared, "Keep the change, man, keep the change. It's the first time I've ever met a man who was a barber, a paperhanger and a butcher at the same time."

★   ★   ★   ★

The last lines in a joke book:

If you pronounce this book not funny
And wish you hadn't spent the money
There soon will be a general rumor

That you're no judge of wit or humor

Philosopher: "The times are hard and getting harder. I fear very few will get out of it alive."

After a serious explosion, a bystander asked a policeman, "Did many die?"

"Yes, unfortunately. Twenty-six."

"Of the explosion?"

"Nope. Corroboration."

"Corroboration? What's that?"

"They tested to see if there was any risk in starting a wood fire with gasoline. The corroboration killed them."

A prisoner, just before his execution, is offered his choice of food for his last meal. "Peaches," he replied. "But they are not in season," the officer replied. "Never mind and don't worry about it," said the doomed prisoner, "I can wait!"

They tell the story of the Kentuckian who went west, as he said, "to get the hang of it." He did! Horse restored to rightful owner.

If you want to make a bald-headed man angry, accuse him of not cleaning the hair out of his comb.

A man requested a theatre ticket for half price on the grounds that he had only one eye. The theatre manager was shrewd and charged him double on the notion that with only one eye, it'd take him twice as long to see the show!

★   ★   ★   ★

One week,
The year had gloomily begun
For Willie Weeks, a poor man's
                SUN.
He was beset with bill and dun
And he had very little
                MON.
"This cash," said he, "won't pay me dues;
I've nothing here but ones and
                TUES."
A bright thought struck him, and he said,
"The rich Miss Goldirocks I will
                WED."
But when he paid his court to her,
She lisped, but firmly said, "No
                THUR!"
"Alas!" said he, "Then I must die!"
His soul went where they say souls
                FRI.
They found his gloves, and coat, and hat,
The Coroner upon them
                SAT.

★   ★   ★   ★

The Dollar volume in national sales of eggs is about $180,000,000. Hens, our prosperity.

★   ★   ★   ★

Isn't it odd that no matter how rich, important, dignified a man is, he can never resist the temptation to kick an empty tomato can.

★   ★   ★   ★

Schoolmaster: "What is life? It consists of money, a hoss, and a fashionable wife. And what is death? Death is a paymaster who settles everybody's debts, and gives a tombstone as a receipt for payment in full. And poverty? Poverty is the reward of merit that genius receives from a discriminating public. Religion? Doing unto others as you please without allowing them to return the compliment. Fame? Six lines of praise in a newspaper while living, and your fortune to your enemies when dead."

The adage "Don't count your chickens until they're hatched!" has been changed by a professor of etiquette to: "The producers of poultry should postpone census of their juvenile fowls until the period of incubation is fully accomplished."

A patron of a hotel sent a boy to fetch his clothes from the cleaners. The boy was very late, returning after the party had started. The man was furious. When the boy opened the door and handed him his clothes, the man said, "Are you the lad who took my clothes to the cleaners?"

"Yes sir! The same."

"I can't believe it!" said the irate man. "My, how you've grown!"

At a fourth-rate hotel, guests were annoyed by flies in their food. One wit stood and suggested to the manager that he put the butter on one plate and the flies on another and that he then let the guests mix them to suit their individual tastes.

One day there was a terrible windstorm in Kansas. Boulders the size of pumpkins were flying about, and the water pipes were sucked right out of the ground! But during it all, a Chinaman was sighted on top of a hill, flying a kite made of an iron shutter with a log chain for a tail, and no. 10 cable for string. That was some storm!

Isn't it surprising the number of people willing to draw a camel through the eye of a needle?

"Is he stingy?"

"Is he! Why that man is so stingy-mean that when he does spend a quarter, that danged thing turns over and over for days out of force of habit."

Some men get rich and fail. Some fail and get rich. But most fail to get rich.

Perhaps it is called "the upper crust" because you got to get through it before you come to the real meat and potatoes of our society.

Dying in poverty is not so bad. It's the living in it that's tough.

There's a whale of a lot of difference between a great man of wealth, and a man of great wealth. Them last is gettin' terrible common.

There may be some things I wouldn't do for a thousand dollars, but I don't just recall them at the present time.

Bill collector: "How often must I climb these three flights of stairs before I gets me money?"

Debtor: "Do you think I'm going to rent a first floor room just to accomodate my creditors?"

There's a woman in our town so badly cross-eyed that when she weeps tears out of her right eye, they fall on her left cheek.

A man was so absent-minded that he thought he had left his watch at home and then took it out of his pocket to see if he had time to go home to get it.

What can't be held for ten minutes although it's light as a feather? Answer: Your breath.

What's a bad sign in life? Your signature on another person's note.

★   ★   ★   ★

A clothing merchant put a coat and vest on a customer who then ran out the door with the merchandise on him. The merchant pursued along with a policeman who drew his gun and prepared to shoot the fleeing thief. "Shoot him in the pants, officer," the merchant yelled. "The coat and vest belong to me."

★   ★   ★   ★

In an auction room, a man lost his wallet with $300 in it. He rushed to the front and hollered an offer of a $75 reward. "I'll give $100" said one bidder. "$150" came from another. "$200" said a third. That wallet finally brought $1000!

★   ★   ★   ★

In a discussion about favorite fowl for dinner, the last speaker said he guessed he liked American eagles served on a gold dollar best of all.

★   ★   ★   ★

Two men discuss the theatre. One asks: "What did you think of the new play that opened last night?" The other replies: "Not much. What was good was not original, and what was original was not good."

★   ★   ★   ★

A Confederate officer in battle happened to bend over to bow down just as a cannonball went over his head and took off the head of the soldier behind him. "You see," the officer said, "A man never loses by politeness."

★   ★   ★   ★

An angry citizen stormed into the newspaper editor's office and pounded on the desk, saying: "Your paper is so damned bad, so poor in quality, that I don't intend ever again to take it."

"Good," said the editor. "Now your next-door-neighbor's morning paper will be safe!"

★   ★   ★   ★

City man to farmer: "How far is it to Butler, if I keep straight on?"

Reply: "Wall, if you're a goin' to keep straight on, it's about 25,000 miles, but if you turn round t'other way *it's about half a mile!*"

★   ★   ★   ★

Alexander H. Stephens, Vice President of the Confederacy, weighed only seventy-four pounds. One day he was arguing with a gigantic fellow from the far west. The big man loomed over Stephens and, in a great fury, overcome with anger, said: "You! You! Why I could swallow you whole, you quarter-pint, you!"

"If you did," Stephens replied, "You'd have more brains in your bowels than ever you had in your head."

★   ★   ★   ★

A flowery, long-winded orator, well into his speech began a sentence with: "I am speaking for the benefit of posterity when I say to you . . ."

Someone in the audience hollered out: "And if you don't quit and sit down soon, they'll all be here!"

★   ★   ★   ★

A Mississippi man gave his reason for seeking public office: "At the earnest solicitation from those whom I owe money, I have consented to become a candidate for County Treasurer."

Chapter III
Colonial and Frontier Humor:
A Rare Vintage

The ebullient, earthy and exaggerated humor that is typically American was retarded in time by two characteristics of our early settlements. First, the humor imitated that of the old country — England — and was decorous, witty, elevated and appropriate only for an established society. But it was hardly congenial to our frontier people, then in steady danger and flux. Second, life was harsh and frequently tragic. In Jamestown, in the winter of 1607, out of 104 men and boys, 51 died of disease and starvation. Such tragedy tends to shape a society's humor, and mute it.

But there was humor, as evidenced in the formal, erudite, haughty language of Nathaniel Ward, a colonist whose writing begins this chapter, and who lived 350 years ago. But much of that long-gone humor is too English for it to seem hilarious to contemporary ears.

During the next century, the colonies moved toward independence, and reached out in exploration of the frontier. These bold changes shaped our humor, and we began to develop our own style that reflected the unique person the American was becoming in the environment of this awesome land of wonder, surprise and excitement.

This development in the course of our humor is evidenced in the tall tales of the time. George Washington, for example, wrote of a mosquito so big and fierce that it pierced through shoe leather. Another man of the time wrote of a bear that bit a hole in a cow, then blew into that hole until the cow was big as a balloon, swelling until she burst! Another told of a spring in Mammoth Cave that gave forth a fountain of purest brandy!

Many of these whoppers were told to curious observers and writers sent from Europe to bring back news of how things were in the colonies, or what came to be the former colonies . . . that outrageous American experiment in self-government! Americans delighted in gulling these reporters, hornswoggling them with marvelously inventive and hilarious lies. One reporter was told that an earthquake had occurred that swallowed an entire river, just gulped it down and never so much as hiccuped! Such stories were believed because the land was so terrifying and mysterious, the teller so earnest and experienced, and the crowd listening was so grave — understanding the story and why it was told — that the reporter went back believing all that he had heard, and wrote about it as if the case of the disappearing river were gospel truth.

When Americans began to move west, American humor became original, unique, congenial, and perhaps immortal. A free-flowing language emerged that was innovative, often ungrammatical, wonderfully descriptive and congenial to our westering people. And the language told of an adventuresome people who could not be stopped in their effort to tame the land, a people who saw in much that they did a comical turn that caused them to laugh at it, and at themselves. And perhaps this ability to laugh, to be a laughing people, was a prime characteristic of their success.

Yet it is difficult for Americans — accustomed to the physically easy life of today — to understand and relate to the mentality of those pioneers who were moving west into the frightening and immense American wilderness west of the Alleghenies. There were real dangers — bear, panther, poisonous snakes, bad water, or no water, or too much water, cholera, malaria, typhoid fever, Indians, starvation and much more. Fully as fearful were the imagined dangers — the "fearsome critters" like the Hoopsnake, the Guyscutus and all those others. Then there were the frightening images left after listening to a plethora of tall tales about strangling ivy, caves that digested the unwary, whirlpools that drowned entire wagon trains, and the like.

But there is a way to get to the state of mind of those early Americans, those adventuring families who went west 165 years ago, and that is to learn of their humor, their fears and joys,

*triumphs and failures, all of which is to say . . . the way we
would have been in body and soul had we been there. In this
sense, their humor is their memorial and their history.*

★   ★   ★   ★

*Nathaniel Ward was a crotchety bachelor who lived in
America from 1634-1647. He is in the tradition of those who
still flail away at women's sometimes consummate interest in
fashion.*

"Should I not keep promise in speaking a little to women's
fashions, they would take it unkindly. I was loath to pester better matter with such stuff; I rather thought it meet to let them
stand by themselves, like the *Quae genus* [what gender] in the
grammar, being deficients or redundants, not to be brought
under any rule: I shall therefore make bold for this once, to borrow a little of their loose-tongued Liberty, and mispend a word
or two upon their long-waisted, but short-skirted Patience . . .

Gray Gravity itself can well beteem
That Language be adapted to the theme.
He that to Parrots speakes, must parrotise;
He that instructs a Fool, may act th' unwise.

It is known more than enough that I am neither Niggard, nor
Cynic, to the due bravery of the true gentry. I honor the woman
that can honor herself with her attire; a good text always
deserves a fair margin; I am not much offended if I see a trim fur
trimmer than she that wears it. In a word, whatever Christianity
or Civility will allow, I can afford with London measure; but
when I hear a nugiperous [inventing trifles] gentledame inquire
what dress the Queen is in this week: what the nudiustertian [of
the day before yesterday] fashion of the Court; with egg [desire]
to be in it in all haste, whatever it be; I look at her as the very
gizzard of a trifle, the product of a quarter of a cipher, the
epitome of Nothing, fitter to be kicked, if she were a kickable
substance, than either honored or humored."

★   ★   ★   ★

Dr. Alexander Hamilton, no relation to the American patriot, was born in Scotland of important parents. A physician, he came to the colonies, to Annapolis, in 1739. He suffered from a lung condition and prescribed a long trip for himself, from Annapolis to York, Maine, and back, in 1744. Fortunately, he was an excellent writer and kept a diary invaluable today in that it tells us much of those pre-Revolution people and their way of life. It tells us also something of Dr. Hamilton, a representative of the "better sort," and contemptuous of the common folks around him.

Annapolis, Wednesday, May 30th. [1744] I set out from Annapolis in Maryland . . . I put up att one Tradway's about 10 miles from Joppa . . . Just as I dismounted att Tradway's, I found a drunken club dismissing. Most of them had got upon their horses and were seated in an oblique situation, deviating much from a perpendicular to the horizontal plan(e), a posture quite necessary for keeping the center of gravity within its proper base for the support of the superstructure; hence we deduce the true physicall reason why our heads overloaded with liquor become too ponderous for our heels. Their discourse was as oblique as their position; the only thing intelligible in it was oaths and God dammes; the rest was an inarticulate sound like Rabelais' frozen words a thawing, interlaced with hickupings and belchings. I was uneasy till they were gone, and my landlord, seeing me stare, made that trite apology — that indeed he did not care to have such disorderly fellows come about his house; he was always noted far and near for keeping a quiet house and entertaining only gentlemen or such like, but these were country people, his neighbours, and it was not prudent to dissoblige them upon slight occasions. "Alas, sir!" added he, "we that entertain travellers must strive to oblige every body, for it is our dayly bread." While he spoke thus, our Bacchanalians, finding no more rum in play, rid off helter skelter as if the devil had possessed them, every man sitting his horse in a see-saw manner like a bunch of rags tyed upon the saddle.

I found nothing particular or worth notice in my landlord's character or conversation, only as to his bodily make. He was a fat pursy man and had large bubbies like a woman. I supped upon fry'd chickens and bacon, and after supper the conversation turned upon politicks, news, and the dreaded French war; but it was so very lumpish and heavy that it disposed me mightily to sleep. This learned company consisted of the landlord, his overseer and miller, and another greasy thumb'd fellow who, as I understood, professed physick and particular surgery. In the drawing of teeth, he practiced upon the house maid, a dirty piece of lumber, who made such screaming and squalling as made me imagine there was murder going forwards in the house. However, the artist got the tooth out att last with a great clumsy pair of blacksmith's forceps; and indeed it seemed to require such an instrument, for when he showed it to us, it resembled a horsenail more than a tooth.

★   ★   ★   ★

In 1728, William Byrd, II, led an expedition to survey the Virginia-North Carolina boundary. The following selections are from Byrd's journal written during that expedition.

Byrd was a landholder (179,000 acres!) political leader, slaveholder, lawyer, and a superb recorder of life in the early America of his day. His wit has been described as the medicine necessary to immunize himself against the "nervous apprehensions" of the wild and dangerous America of his day.

The Indians are generally tall and well proportioned, which may make full amends for the darkness of their complexions. Add to this that they are healthy and strong, with constitutions untainted by lewdness and not enfeebled by luxury. Besides, morals and all considered, I cannot think the Indians were much greater heathens than the first adventurers, who, had they been good Christians, would have had the charity to take this only method of converting the natives to Christianity. For, after all that can be said, a sprightly lover is the most prevailing missionary that can be sent amongst these or any other infidels.

★   ★   ★   ★

The only business here is raising of hogs, which is managed with the least trouble and affords the diet they are most fond of. The truth of it is, the inhabitants of North Carolina devour so much swine's flesh that it fills them full of gross humors. For want too, of a constant supply of salt, they are commonly obliged to eat it fresh, and that begets the highest taint of scurvy. Thus, whenever a severe cold happens to constitutions thus vitiated, 'tis apt to improve into the yaws, called there very justly the country distemper . . . First it seizes the throat, next the palate, and lastly shows its spite to the poor nose, of which 'tis apt in small time treacherously to undermine the foundation . . . the disputes that happen about the beauty the noses have in some companies much ado to carry it. Nay, 'tis said that once, after three good pork years, a motion had like to have been made in the House of Burgesses that a man with a nose should be incapable of holding any place of profit in the province; which extraordinary motion could never have been intended without some hopes of a majority . . . the distemper of laziness seizes the men oftener much than the women. These last spin, weave, and knit, all with their own hands, while their husbands, depending on the bounty of the climate, are slothful in everything but getting of children, and in that only instance make themselves useful members of an infant colony . . . One thing may be said for the inhabitants of that province, that they are not troubled with any religious fumes and have the least superstition of any people living. They do not know Sunday from any other day, any more than Robinson Crusoe did, which would give them a great advantage were they given to be industrious. But they keep so many Sabbaths every week that their disregard of the seventh day has no manner of cruelty in it, either to servants or cattle.

★   ★   ★   ★

It was now a great misfortune to the men to find their provisions grow less as their labor grew greater; they were all forced to come to short allowance and consequently to work hard without filling their bellies. Though this was very severe upon English stomachs, yet the people were so far from being discomfited at it that they still kept up their good humor and merrily told a young fellow in the company, who looked very plump and wholesome, that he must expect to go first to pot if matters should come to extremity. This was only said by way of jest, yet it made him thoughtful in earnest. However, for the present he returned them a very civil answer, letting them know that, dead or alive, he should be glad to be useful to such worthy good friends. But, after all, this humorous saying had one very good effect, for that younker [youngster] who before was a little inclined by his constitution to be lazy, grew on a sudden extremely industrious, that so there might be less occasion to carbonade [broil] him for the good of his fellow travelers.

★   ★   ★   ★

Surely there is no place in the world where the inhabitants live with less labor than in North Carolina. It approaches nearer to the description of Lubberland [a land of plenty and without work] than any other, by the great felicity of the climate, the easiness of raising provisions, and the slothfulness of the people . . . The men, for their parts, just like the Indians, impose all the work upon the poor women. They make their wives rise out of their beds early in the morning, at the same time that they lie and snore till the sun has risen one-third of his course and dispersed all the unwholesome damps. Then, after stretching and yawning for half an hour, they light their pipes, and, under the protection of a cloud of smoke, venture out into the open air; though if it happen to be never so little cold they quickly return shivering into the chimney corner. When the weather is mild, they stand leaning with both their arms upon the cornfield fence and gravely consider whether they had best go and take a small heat at the hoe but generally find reasons to put it off till another time . . . To speak the truth, 'tis a thorough aversion to labor that makes people file off to North Carolina, where plenty and a warm sun confirm them in their disposition to laziness for their whole lives.

★   ★   ★   ★

Edenton . . . is situate on the north side of Albemarle Sound . . . A dirty slash [marsh] runs all along the back of it, which in the summer is a foul annoyance and furnishes abundance of that Carolina plague, mosquitoes. There may be forty or fifty houses, most of them small and built without expense. A citizen here is counted extravagant if he has ambition enough to aspire to a brick chimney. Justice herself is but indifferently lodged, the courthouse having much the air of a common tobacco house. I believe this is the only metropolis in the Christian or Mahometan world where there is neither church, chapel, mosque, synagogue, or any other place of public worship of any sect of religion whatsoever. What little devotion there may happen to be is much more private than their vices. The people seem easy without a minister as long as they are exempted from paying him. Sometimes the Society for Propagating the Gospel has had the charity to send over missionaries to this country; but, unfortunately, the priest has been too lewd for the people, or, which oftener happens, they too lewd for the priest. For these reasons these reverend gentlemen have always left their flocks as arrant heathen as they found them. This much, however, may be said for the inhabitants of Edenton, that not a soul has the least taint of hypocrisy or superstition, acting very frankly and aboveboard in all their exercises.

★   ★   ★   ★

Mr. Kinchen had unadvisedly sold the men a little brandy of his own making, which produced much disorder, causing some to be too choleric and others too loving; insomuch that a damsel who assisted in the kitchen had certainly suffered what the nuns call martyrdom had she not capitulated a little too soon. This outrage would have called for some severe discipline, had she not bashfully withdrawn herself early in the morning and so carried off the evidence.

★   ★   ★   ★

As I sat in the tent, I overheard a learned conversation between one of our men and the Indian. He asked the Englishman what it was that made that rumbling noise when it thundered. The man told him merrily that the God of the English was firing his great guns upon the god of the Indians, which made all that roaring in the clouds, and that the lightening was only the flash of those guns. The Indian, carrying on the humor, replied very gravely he believed that might be the case indeed, and that the rain which followed upon the thunder must be occasioned by the Indian god's being so scared he could not hold his water.

★   ★   ★   ★

Our hunters killed a large doe and two bears, which made all other misfortunes easy. Certainly no Tartar ever loved horseflesh or Hottentot guts and garbage better than woodsmen do bear. The truth of it is, it may be proper food perhaps for such as work or ride it off, but, with our chaplain's leave, who loved it much, I think it not a very proper diet for saints, because 'tis apt to make them a little too rampant. And, now, for the good of mankind and for the better peopling an infant colony, which has no want but that of inhabitants, I will venture to publish a secret of importance which our Indian disclosed to me. I asked him the reason why few or none of his countrywomen were barren. To which curious question he answered, with a broad grin upon his face, they had an infallible secret for that. Upon my being importunate to know what the secret might be, he informed me that if any Indian woman did not prove with child at a decent time after marriage, the husband, to save his reputation with the women, forthwith entered into a bear diet for six weeks, which in that time makes him so vigorous that he grows exceedingly impertinent to his poor wife, and 'tis great odds but he makes her a mother in nine months. And thus much I am able to say besides for the reputation of the bear diet, that all the married men of our company were joyful fathers within forty weeks after they got home, and most of the single men had children sworn to them within the same time, our chaplain always excepted, who, with much ado, made a shift to cast out that importunate kind of devil by dint of fasting and prayer.

*   *   *   *

One of our people shot a large grey squirrel with a very bushy
tail, a singular use of which our merry Indian discovered to us.
He said whenever this little animal has occasion to cross a run of
water, he launches a chip or piece of bark into the water on
which he embarks and, holding up his tail to the wind, sails over
very safely. If this be true, 'tis probable men learnt at first the
use of sails from these ingenious animals, as the Hottentots
learnt the physical use of most of their plants from the baboons.

*   *   *   *

All the grandees of the Samponi nation did us the honor to
repair hither to meet us, and our worthy friend and fellow
traveler, Bearskin, appeared among the gravest of them in his
robes of ceremony. Four young ladies of the first quality came
with them, who had more the air of cleanliness than any copper-
coloured beauties I had ever seen, yet we resisted all their
charms, notwithstanding the long fast we had kept from the sex
and the bear diet we had been so long engaged in. Nor can I say
the price they set upon their charms was at all exorbitant. A
princess for a pair of red stockings can't, surely, be thought buying repentance much too dear.

*   *   *   *

All Indians have as great an aversion to hanging as the
Muscovites, though perhaps not for the same cleanly reason,
these last believing that the soul of one that dies in this manner,
being forced to sally out of the body at the postern, must needs
be defiled.

*   *   *   *

"UPON A FART"
William Byrd, II

Gentlest Blast of ill concoction,
Reverse of high-ascending Belch:

Th' only Stink abhorr'd by Scotsman,
Belovd and practic'd by the Welch.

Softest noat of Inward Gripeing
Sr Reverences finest part,
So fine it needs no pains of Wipeing,
Except it proves a Brewers fart.

Swiftest Ease of Cholique pain,
Vapor from a Secret Stench,
Is rattled out by th' unbred Swain,
But whispered by the Bashfull wench.

Shapeless Fart! we ne'er can show Thee
But in that merry Female Sport
In which by burning blew we know Thee
Th' Amuzement of the Maids at Court.

★   ★   ★   ★

During our Revolutionary War, the British started a rumor that a prophetic hen had laid an egg imprinted with the words: "Oh, America! Howe shall be thy conqueror," referring to British General William Howe. The poetic response indicates that Americans were not much persuaded.

"When eggs can speak what fools endite,
And hens can talk as well as write,
When crocodiles shed honest tears,
And truth with hypocrites appears;
When every man becomes a knave
And feels the spirit of the slave,
And when veracity again
Shall in a Tory's bosom reign;
When vice is virtue, darkness light,
And freemen are afraid to fight;
When they forget to play the men
And with the spirit of a hen
Desert the just and sacred cause,
And opening Heaven smiles applause

On such a bloody, barbarous foe,—
Then I'll be conquered by a Howe!"

★   ★   ★   ★

"In seventeen hundred and seventy-seven
General Burgoyne set out for Heaven;
But as the Yankees would rebel,
He missed his route, and went—to Hell!"

★   ★   ★   ★

Selections from early New England newspapers:

The New England Courant, January 29, 1722

Several Journeymen Gentlemen, (Some Foreigners and others of our own Growth) never sully'd with Business, and fit for Town or Country Diversion, are willing to dispose of themselves in Marriage as follows:

VIZ. Some to old Virgins, who by long Industry have laid up 500 pounds or prov'd themselves capable of maintaining a Husband in a genteel and commendable Idleness. Some to old or young Widows who have Estates of their first Husbands getting, to dispose of at their second Husbands Pleasure. And some to young Ladies under Age, who have their Fortunes in their own Hands, and are willing to maintain a pretty genteel Man, rather than be without him.

N. B. The above Gentlemen may be spoke with almost any Hour in the Day, at the Tick-Tavern in Prodigal Square, and will proceed to Courtship as soon as their Mistresses shall pay their Tavern Scores.

★   ★   ★   ★

New York Weekly Journal, December 31, 1733

We hear from Ridgefield, near the Country of Westchester, that one *William Drinkwater,* late an Inhabitant there proveing quarrelsom with his Neighbors and abusing to his Wife, the good Women of the Place, took the Matter into Consideration and laid hold of an Opportunity, to get him tied to a Cart, and there with Rods belaboured him on his Back, till, in striving to get away, he pulled one of his Arms out of Joint, and then they unti'd him. Mr. *Drinkwater* complained to sundrie Magistrates of this useage, but all he got by it was to be Laughed at; Whereupon he removed to *New-Milford* where we hear he proves a good Neighbour and a loveing Husband. *A remarkable Reformation ariseing from the Justice of the good Women.*

★　　　★　　　★　　　★

New York Weekly Journal, March 25, 1734

Philadelphia, March 12

We hear from Matfield in Bucks County, that on *Shrove Tuesday* last one *James Worthington,* after having eaten a hearty Meal of Beef and Pork, eat Forty one and a half boil'd Hens Eggs, and would have eaten more if some in Company had not taken them from him; he eat Bread and Salt plentifully with them, and said he could have eaten Ten more. He was not in the least Disordered with his Dinner, but eat a very hearty Supper about 5 or 6 Hours after.

★　　　★　　　★　　　★

Philadelphia, July 11.

On the 6th Instant at Bybery, one *James Worthington,* as he was reaping was so overcome with the excessive Heat of the Weather that he fell down, those about him removed him into the Shade, in Hopes that he would recover, but in vain, for he died immediately.

N.B. He was the Person mentioned in our Journal of the 25th of March last that eat 41 and a half hard boil'd Hens Eggs after a hearty Diner.

★　　　★　　　★　　　★

New York Weekly Journal, June 3, 1734

New York, June 3d.

Last week one *Thomas Copley,* was apprehended here, on Suspicion of Coining and uttering false Dollars, when he found himself discover'd he flung 18 in a Purse over the Fence into a Neighbouring Yard, some that he kept loose in his Pocket he dropt into the Privy, the Purse was immediately found but it is supposed that those which he dropt into the Privy are not all found.

★　　★　　★　　★

Boston *Weekly News-Letter,* March 20, 1735

A young Gentleman of Durham in Connecticut, had addressed a Lady in the Neighborhood with his solemn Protestations of Love, and asked for an approving Smile, and continued very Fervant in his Courtship, for about Two Years last past: But the young Woman, conscious of her superior Merit, always appeared with a forbidding Frown: This at last so discouraged the fond Courtier, that he gave over the pursuit; but being restless, he applys to his Father for Relief, by his kind Mediation; and he, being willing to help his favourite Son in this difficult Case, immediately mounts his Horse and away, to the Parents of the young Woman; and discoursing half an Hour with them, they agree and strike up a Match: The young Man being informed hereof, was so overcome with a sudden Joy, that he grew delirious, in which Frame he continued three Days, when it was termed Distraction: Hereon a Doctor was sent for, who coming, inquired the Cause, and finding it to be Love, he ordered the young Woman to be sent for, she came accordingly, and found her Captive raving: The sight of her revived him, and partly restored him, so much as enabled him to desire her to sit down; which done, he laid his Head on her Bosom, and slept for about an Hour and then awoke; but such sudden Raptures of Joy returning, proved strong for his Imagination, and losing the government of his Passions, in superextatick Joy made his Exit.

Contributed to the *William and Mary Quarterly,* XXIII, 2 (April 1966), 309-10 by Howard H. Peckham.

★　　★　　★　　★

Virginia Gazette, July 28, 1738

Last week a Team of five Horses and a Waggon with 2500 Weight of Tea, was seiz'd near Chichester in Sussex, by two Custom-house Officers, assisted by a Guard of Soldiers.

On Sunday last, Mr. Forster, Surveyor-General of the River, seiz'd a considerable Quantity of Tea at Woolwich, hid under some Hoop-Petticoats. The Owners of those Goods could be no experienced Smugglers, as is plain by their Choice of so improper a Place for Concealment, the Custom-House Officers being generally remarkable for having a natural Itch to rummage under Petticoats. ——— For, some time since, A Custom-House Officer being in the Pit at the Play-house, went to put his Hands up one of the Orange Wenches Petticoats, but the Girl knew him, and cry'd out, How, now, Mr. Tide-Waiter, there is nothing there *but what has been fairly Enter'd.*

★   ★   ★   ★

Ben Franklin was the exemplary wit of America's early times, the revolutionary and frontier days. He was one of the most remarkable and talented men we have produced. Carl Van Dorn describes him as "a harmonious human multitude," a man who mastered the natural, political, and social sciences of his time. He lived eighty-four years and did the work of a dozen accomplished men. His wit is as manifold as his talents, and his humor serves every generation.

But like Dr. Hamilton, Ben Franklin was not a man of the people. He loved comfort and witty companions, the sophisticated talk of the educated, and mingling with the high-born and wealthy. His humor is more English than of the American frontier he lived in, and he liked and wanted it that way.

In the following letter, Ben Franklin counsels a young friend on how best to control his libido.

June 25, 1745

My dear Friend,

I know of no Medicine fit to diminish the violent natural Inclinations you mention; and if I did, I think I should not communicate it to you. Marriage is the proper Remedy. It is the most natural State of Man, and therefore the State in which you are most likely to find solid Happiness. Your Reasons against entring into it at present, appear to me not well-founded. The circumstantial Advantages you have in View by postponing it, are not only uncertain, but they are small in comparison with that of the Thing itself, the being *married and settled*. It is the Man and Woman united that make the compleat human Being. Separate, she wants his Force of Body and Strength of Reason; he, her Softness, Sensibility and acute discernment. Together they are more likely to succeed in the World. A single Man has not nearly the Value he would have in that State of Union. He is an incomplete Animal. He resembles the odd Half of a Pair of Scissars. If you get a prudent healthy Wife, your Industry in your Profession, with her good Economy, will make a Fortune sufficient.

But if you will not take this Counsel, and persist in thinking a Commerce with the Sex inevitable, then I repeat my former Advice, that in all your Amours you should *prefer old Women to young ones*. You call this a Paradox, and demand my Reasons. They are these:

1. Because as they have more Knowledge of the World and their Minds are better stor'd with Observations, their Conversation is more improving and more lastingly agreeable.

2. Because when Women cease to be handsome, they study to be good. To maintain their Influence over Men, they supply the Diminution of Beauty by an Augmentation of Utility. They learn to do a 1000 Services small and great, and are the most tender and useful of all Friends when you are sick. Thus they continue amiable. And hence there is hardly such a thing to be found as an old Woman who is not a good Woman.

3. Because there is no hazard of Children, which irregularly produced may be attended with much Inconvenience.

4. Because thro' more Experience, they are more prudent and discreet in conducting an Intrigue to prevent Suspicion. The Commerce with them is therefore safer with regard to your Reputation. And with regard to theirs, if the Affair should happen to be known, considerate People might be rather inclin'd to excuse an old Woman who would kindly take care of a young

Man, form his Manners by her good Counsels, and prevent his ruining his Health and Fortune among mercenary Prostitutes.

5. Because in every Animal that walks upright, the Deficiency of the Fluids that fill the Muscles appears first in the highest Part: The Face first grows lank and wrinkled; then the Neck; then the Breast and Arms; the lower Parts continuing to the last as plump as ever: So that covering all above with a Basket, and regarding only what is below the Girdle, it is impossible of two Women to know an old from a young one. And as in the dark all Cats are grey, the Pleasure of corporal Enjoyment with an old Woman is at least equal, and frequently superior, every Knack being by Practice capable of Improvement.

6. Because the Sin is less. The debauching of a Virgin may be her Ruin, and make her for Life unhappy.

7. Because the Compunction is less. The having made a young Girl miserable may give you frequent bitter Reflections; none of which can attend the making an old Woman *happy*.

8. (thly and Lastly) They are *so grateful!!* Thus much for my Paradox. But still I advise you to marry directly; being sincerely

Your affectionate Friend.

★   ★   ★   ★

Rules for Making Oneself a Disagreeable Companion.
Ben Franklin. 1750

RULES, by the Observation of which, a Man of Wit and Learning may nevertheless make himself a *disagreeable* Companion.

Your Business is to *shine;* therefore you must by all means prevent the shining of others, for their Brightness may make yours the less distinguish'd. To this End,

1. If possible engross the whole Discourse; and when other Matter fails, talk much of your-self, your Education, your Knowledge, your Circumstances, your Successes in Business, your Victories in Disputes, your own wise Sayings and Observations on particular Occasions, &c. &c. &c.

2. If when you are out of Breath, one of the Company should

seize the Opportunity of saying something: watch his Words, and, if possible, find somewhat either in his Sentiment of Expression, immediately to contradict and raise a Dispute upon. Rather than fail, criticise even his Grammar.

3. If another should be saying an indisputably good Thing; either give no Attention to it; or interrupt him; or draw away the Attention of others; or, if you can guess what he would be at, be quick and say it before him; or, if he gets it said, and you perceive the Company pleas'd with it, own it to be a good Thing, and withal remark that it had been said by Bacon, Locke, Bayle, or some other eminent Writer: thus you deprive him of the Reputation he might have gain'd by it, and gain some yourself, as you hereby show your great Reading and Memory.

4. When modest Men have been thus treated by you a few times, they will chuse ever after to be silent in your Company; then you may shine on without Fear of a Rival; rallying them at the same time for their Dullness, which will be to you a new Fund of Wit.

Thus you will be sure to please *yourself.* The polite Man aims at pleasing *others,* but you shall go beyond him even in that. A Man can be present only in one Company, but may at the same time be absent in twenty. He can please only where he *is,* you wherever you are *not.*

★   ★   ★   ★

Proud, "macho" men of an earlier day settled serious insult with a duel that was surrounded with all the punctillo, the rigamarole of that classic action. Sometimes they fought to the death, but most often not. Here Benjamin Franklin handles himself wittily when challenged to fight.

" 'SIR:

" 'I have two objections to this duel matter. The one is, lest I should hurt you; and the other is, lest you should hurt me. I do not see any good it would do me to put a bullet thro' any part of your body. I could make no use of you when dead for any culinary purpose, as I would a rabbit or turkey. I am no cannibal to feed on the flesh of men. Why then shoot down a human creature, of which I could make no use? A buffalo would be better meat. For though your flesh may be delicate and tender; yet it wants that firmness and consistency which takes and retains salt. At any rate, it would not be fit for long sea voyages. You might make a good barbecue, it is true, being of the nature of a raccoon or an opossum; but people are not in the habit of barbecuing anything human now. As to your hide, it is not worth taking off, being little better than that of a year old colt.

" 'It would seem to me a strange thing to shoot a man that would stand still to be shot at; inasmuch as I have been heretofore used to shoot at things flying or running or jumping. Were you on a tree now, like a squirrel, endeavoring to hide yourself in the branches, or, like a raccoon, that after much eyeing and spying, I observe at length in the crotch of a tall oak, with bough and leaves intervening, so that I could just get sight of his hinder parts, I should think it pleasurable enough to take a shot at you. But as it is there is no skill or judgment requisite either to discover or take you down.

" 'As to myself, I do not much like to stand in the way of anything harmful. I am under apprehensions you might hit me. That being the case, I think it most advisable to stay at a distance. If you want to try your pistols, take some object, a tree or a barn door about my dimensions. If you hit that, send me word, and I shall acknowledge that if I had been in the same place, you might also have hit me.' "

Ben Franklin here tells of another duel he knew about.

A Gentleman in a Coffee-house desired another to sit farther from him. "Why so?" "Because, Sir, you stink," "That is an affront, and you must fight me." "I will fight you, if you insist upon it; but I do not see how that will mend the Matter. For if you kill me, I shall stink too; and if I kill you [you] will stink, if possible, worse than you do at present."

★   ★   ★   ★

Extracts from Poor Richard's Almanac by Benjamin Franklin

Kind Reader,

Encouraged by thy former Generosity, I once more present thee with an Almanack, which is the 7th of my Publication. — While thou are putting Pence in my Pocket, and furnishing my Cottage with Necessaries, *Poor Dick* is not unmindful to do something for thy Benefit. The Stars are watch'd as narrowly as old *Bess* watch'd her Daughter, and told a Tale of their Influences and Effects, which may do thee more good than a Dream of last Year's Snow.

Ignorant Men wonder how we Astrologers foretell the Weather so exactly, unless we deal with the old black Devil. Alas! 'tis as easy as pissing abed. For Instance; The Stargazer peeps at the Heavens thro' a long Glass: He sees perhaps TAURUS, or the great Bull, in a mighty Chase, stamping on the Floor of his House, swinging his Tail about, stretching out his Neck, and opening wide his Mouth. 'Tis natural from these Appearances to judge that this furious Bull is puffing, blowing, and roaring. Distance being consider'd, and Time allow'd for all this to come down, there you have Wind and Thunder. He spies perhaps VIRGO (or the Virgin) she turns her Head round as it were to see if any body observ'd her; then crouching down gently, with her Hands on her Knees, she looks wistfully for a while right forward. He judges rightly what she'd about: And having calculated the Distance and allow'd Time for its Falling, finds that next Spring we shall have fine *April* shower.

★   ★   ★   ★

But what signifies our Wishing? Things happen, after all, as they will happen. I have sung that *wishing Song* a thousand times, when I was young, and now find, at Fourscore, that the three Contraries have befallen me, being subject to the Gout and the Stone, and not being yet Master of all my Passions. Like the proud Girl in my Country, who wish'd and resolv'd not to marry a Parson, nor a Presbyterian, nor an Irishman; and at length found herself married to an Irish Presbyterian Parson.

★   ★   ★   ★

A Surgeon I met with here excused the Women of Paris, by saying, seriously, that they *could not* give suck; *"Car,"* dit il, *"elles n'ont point de tetons."* He assur'd me it was a Fact, and bade me look at them, and observe how flat they were on the Breast; "they have nothing more there, " said he, "than I have upon the Back of my hand." I have since thought that there might be some Truth in his Observation, and that, possibly, Nature, finding they made no use of Bubbies, has left off giving them any.

★   ★   ★   ★

Davy Crockett was born in eastern Tennessee in 1786, and died in defense of the Alamo, in Texas in 1836. He is our most typical frontiersman of that period. In their monumental work: THE RISE OF AMERICAN CIVILIZATION, Charles and Mary Beard tell of Davy Crockett: "The politics of the frontier was the politics of backwoodsmen, and if a type of the age is needed . . . it may well be David Crockett, whose autobiography is one of the prime human documents for the American epic yet to be written."

But for a judgment of his reputation, here is the report of Captain R. G. A. Levinge, a British traveler who visited Louisville in 1839. "Everything here is Davy Crockett. He was a member of Congress. His voice was so rough it could not be described — it was obliged to be drawn as a picture. He took hailstones for 'Life Pills' when he was unwell — he picked his teeth with a pitchfork — combed his hair with a rake — fanned himself with a hurricane, wore a cast-iron shirt, and drank nothing but creosote and aquafortis. Almanacs bear his name, and he snored so loud that he was obliged to sleep at a house in the next street for fear of waking himself. He had a farm, which was so rocky, that, when they planted the corn, they were obliged to shoot the grains into the crevices of the rocks with muskets; and, on another part of his property, the stones were so thick that the ducks couldn't get their bills between them to pick up the grasshoppers; in short, he was a devil of a fellow. He could whip his weight in wild cats — drink the Mississippi dry — shoot six cord of bear in one day — and, as his countrymen say of themselves, he could jump higher, dive deeper, and come up dryer than any one else. Then he could slide down the slippery end of a rainbow, and was half-horse, half-alligator, and a bit of snapping turtle. Even his domestic animals were the most cunning in the world, and he possessed a cat which, having lost her kittens, was so 'cute' that she was observed moaning for several days at the door of a sausage-maker."

The mystique surrounding Davy Crockett has continued to our own day when, in 1955, Walt Disney introduced him to a generation of American kids. Davy Crockett coonskin caps were everywhere, as were fringed shirts, Davy Crockett toy weapons, songs, and the entire paraphernalia needed to bring alive that larger-than-life figure.

Davy Crockett went to Texas to fight in our Texican War. There, in the battle of the Alamo, February 23 to March 6 of 1836, he met his death. It was that tragic ending that fittingly completes the awesome legend of his life.

The first selection, CROCKETT'S SONG, is a prose poem so lyrical that one is touched, and yet wants to grin, to laugh upon reading it. It is one of the most exuberant, joyous, "don't-it-feel-good" prose poems ever written. Doubtless, Walt Whitman knew it, and Abraham Lincoln. Doubtless they grinned and chuckled and, perhaps, laughed out loud at it. Certainly they passed it around among their contemporaries. And one can imagine Carl Sandberg chuckling with it, making notes from it for his great poem, THE PEOPLE, YES.

Anyone who has ever walked into a brilliant, cold, bracing winter morning, taken a deep breath that brought on an exhilaration to quicken the step, square the shoulders, light-up a cocky grin as the spirit soared — anyone who has experienced that will understand Davy Crockett's song and consider it a personal testimonial.

Crockett's Song

One January morning it was so all-screwen-up cold that the forest trees war so stiff that they couldn't shake, and the very day-break froze fast as it war tryin' to dawn. The tinder-box in my cabin would no more ketch fire than a sunk raft at the bottom o' the sea. Seein' that daylight war so far behind time, I thought creation war in a fair way for freezin' fast.

"So," thinks I, "I must strike a leetle fire from my fingers, light my pipe, travel out a few leagues, and see about it."

Then I brought my knuckles together like two thunder clouds, but the sparks froze up afore I could begin to collect 'em — so out I walked, and endeavored to keep myself unfriz by goin' at a hop, step, and jump gait, and whistlin' the tune of "fire on the mountains!" as I went along in three double quick time. Well, arter I had walked about twenty-five miles up the peak o' Daybreak Hill, I soon discovered what war the matter. The airth had actually friz fast in her axis, and couldn't turn round; the sun had got jammed between two cakes o' ice under the wheels, an' thar he had bin shinin' and workin' to get loose, till he friz fast in his cold sweat.

"C-r-e-a-t-i-o-n!" thought I, "this are the toughest sort o' suspension, and it mustn't be endured — somethin' must be done, or human creation is done for."

It war then so antedeluvian and premature cold that my upper and lower teeth an' tongue war all collapsed together as tight as a friz oyster. I took a fresh twenty pound bear off o' my back that I'd picked up on the road, an' beat the animal agin the ice till the hot ile began to walk out on him at all sides. I then took an' held him over the airth's axes, an' squeezed him till I thaw'd 'em loose, poured about a ton on it over the sun's face, give the airth's cog-wheel one kick backward, till I got the sun loose — whistled "Push along, keep movin'!" an' in about fifteen seconds the airth gin a grunt, and begun movin' — the sun walked up beautiful, salutin' me with sich a wind o' gratitude that it made me sneeze. I lit my pipe by the blaze o' his top-knot, shouldered my bear, an' walked home, introducin' the people to fresh daylight with a piece of sunrise in my pocket, with which I cooked my bear steaks, an' enjoyed one o' the best breakfasts I had tasted for some time. If I didn't jist wake some mornin' and go with me to the office o' sunrise!

★   ★   ★   ★

A Brief Autobiography of Davy Crockett

I was born in a cane brake, cradled in a sap trough, and clouted with coon skins; without being choked by the weeds of education, which do not grow *spontinaciously* — for all the time that I was troubled with *youngness,* my cornstealers were *na'*trally used for other purposes than holding a pen; and *rayly* when I try to write my elbow keeps coming round like a swingletree, and it is easier for me to tree a varmint, or swallow a bear than to write. Some persons tickle up their fancies to the scribbling point, and then their pen goes like a fiddler's elbow. Of books the divil a one have I read, except Tom Toe and The Axes of the Apostles. And although my I *dears* run through me like an hour glass that never wants turning, if I only know'd how to scrawl the alphabet, I'd soon row some of the larned ones up *Salt River* — for

Honor and fame from no condition rise;
Axe well your part and down the tree soon lies.

For it's the grit of a fellow that makes the man; and I'm half chicken hawk and steel trap. So I will just let you know, reader, what I think about gineral matters and things in particular.

★   ★   ★   ★

Davy Crockett Meets His Equal

One day as I was sitting in the starn of my broad horn, the old Free and Easy, on the Mississippi, taking a horn of midshipman's grog, with a tin pot in each hand, first a draught of whiskey, and then one of river water, who should float down past me but Jo Snag; he was in a snooze, as fast as a church, with his mouth wide open; he had been ramsquaddled with whiskey for a fortnight, and as it evaporated from his body, it looked like the steam from a vent pipe. Knowing the feller would be darned hard to wake, with all this steam on, as he floated past me I hit him a crack over his knob with my big steering oar. He waked in a thundering rage. Says he, halloe stranger, who axed you to crack my lice? Said I, shut up your mouth, or your teeth will get sunburnt. Upon this he crooked up his neck and neighed like a stallion. I clapped my arms and crowed like a cock. Says he, if you are a game chicken, I'll pick all the pin feathers off of you. For some time back I had been so wolfy about the head and shoulders, that I was obliged to keep kivered up in a salt crib to keep from spiling; for I had not had a fight for as much as ten days. Says I, give us none of your chin music, but set your kickers on land, and I'll give you a severe licking. The fellow now jumped ashore, and he was so tall he could not tell when his feet were cold. He jumped up a rod. Says he, take care how I lite on you, and he gave me a real sockdologer that made my very liver and lites turn to jelly. But he found me a real scrouger. I brake three of his ribs, and he knocked out five of my teeth and one eye. He was the severest colt that ever I tried to break. I finally got a bite hold of his posterious, that he could not shake off. We were now parted by some boatmen, and we were so exorsted that it was more than a month before either could have a fight. It seemed to me like a little eternity. And although I didn't come out second best, I took care not to wake up a ring tailed roarer with an oar again.

★   ★   ★   ★

An Early Fight on the Frontier

At last the war broke out, and then I marched under General Jackson against the English at New Orleans. When we was about starting for New Orleans, I composed the celebrated song, well known to every backwoodsman, and which was wonderfully admired at the time, beginning with,

> "Come all you bold Kentuckians, I'd have you all to know
> That for to fight the enemy, we're going for to go."

I believe it was this song that did more than any thing else, towards getting me to Congress, for when it was seen that I had talents, I grew very popular all at once. Before I went home from the wars, I met a big fellow on the Levee at New Orleans, who thought to take advantage of my youth, and begun black-guarding me about my countrymen, for he did'nt belong to Kentucky himself, Says he, 'You call yourselves half horse and half alligator, but I'll let you know that I'm whole alligator with a cross of the wild-cat.' I jumped up and snapped my fingers in his face, and told him that I did'nt care the fag end of a johnny cake for him, and I spit right in his mouth. With that he came at me with his mouth wide open; he just missed my ear, and I snapped at his nose and seized it between my teeth. He roared and struggled but I held on like a pair of pinchers, until at last off came his nose. 'That's into you,' says I, 'for an alligator — you see I'm crossed with the snapping turtle!'

Well, I went home once more, and found every thing pretty much as I left it, and fell to hunting bears right away. In one season I killed twenty-five bears, besides two wild cats and a possum. I was out one day and got benighted, when I laid down to sleep by the side of a river. I laid my head on a great log, and closed my eyes. I had'nt been long asleep before the log began to move, and I jumped on my feet, when what should the log be but a great crocodile. He raised his head and opened his pesky great mouth to bite me in two. I jumped right down his throat. He whisked about and thrashed up the ground like an earth-quake for a few minutes, but presently he give over completely choked to death, and I found hard work to get out again.

★   ★   ★   ★

Crockett's Coon Story

That Colonel Crockett could avail himself, in electioneering, of the advantages which well-applied satire ensures, the following anecdote will sufficiently prove:

In the canvass of the congressional election of 18—, Mr. ✱✱✱✱ was the Colonel's opponent — a gentleman of the most pleasing and conciliating manners — who seldom addressed a person or a company without wearing upon his countenance a peculiar good humored smile. The Colonel, to counteract the influence of this winning attribute, thus alluded to it, in a stump speech:

"Yes gentlemen, he may get some votes by *grinning*, for he can *out grin* me, and you know I ain't slow — and to prove to you that I am not, I will tell you an anecdote. I was concerned myself — and I was fooled a little of the damn'dest. You all know I love hunting. Well, I discovered, a long time ago, that a 'coon couldn't stand my grin. I could bring one tumbling down from the highest tree. I never wasted powder and lead, when I wanted one of the creturs. Well, as I was walking out one night, a few hundred yards from my house, looking carelessly about me, I saw a 'coon planted upon one of the highest limbs of an old tree. The night was very *moony* and clear, and old Ratler was with me; but Ratler won't bark at a 'coon — he's a queer dog in that way. So, I thought I'd bring the lark down, in the usual way, *by a grin*. I set myself — and, after grinning at the 'coon a reasonable time, found that he didn't come down. I wondered what was the reason — and I took another steady grin at him. Still he was *there*. It made me a little mad; so I felt round and got an old limb about five feet long — and, planting one end upon the ground, I placed my chin upon the other, and took *a rest*. I then grinned my best for about five minutes — but the damn'd 'coon hung on. So, finding I could not bring him down by grinning, I determined to have him — for I thought he must be a droll chap. I went over to the house, got my axe, returned to the tree, saw the 'coon still there, and began to cut away. Down it came, and I run forward; but damn the 'coon was there to be seen. I found that what I had taken for one, was a large knot upon a branch of the tree — and, upon looking at it closely, I saw that *I had grinned all the bark off, and left the knot perfectly smooth.*

"Now fellow-citizens," continued the Colonel, "you must be convinced that, in the *grinning line*, I myself am not slow — yet, when I look upon my opponent's countenance, I must admit that he is my superior. You must all admit it. Therefore, be wide awake — look sharp — and do not let him grin you out of your votes."

★   ★   ★   ★

Davy Crockett Steals a Little Lovin'

In the spring of '34 when I was going home from Congress I came the nearest being chawed up, that ever I did. After staying all night at Memphis, where I slept so *sound* (i.e. made such a noise a snoring) that the neighbors could'nt sleep for some distance from the hotel. From fatigue I was so drowsy they were obliged to open my eyes with a pickaxe. Well arter breakfast I started in the stage alone with the driver. At the distance of two or three miles from the house, at a point where the road was covered with stumps of trees, he drew up, and tying the reins up at the front window, he said to me, 'look to the reins till I come back.' He was obliged to go a little way to give out some sowing he said. Before I could say a word he was out of sight behind the trees. He kept me holding on to the reins for nearly half an hour, when I began to smell a rat, and was just on the point of getting out to go arter him, when he made his appearance from behind the trees. After he got on his box, I began to blow him up for staying so long. Says he 'the fact is I have a girl a little ways off; I always stop when I pass and make some of the passengers hold the horses. I have built a house and got a negro wench to wait on her.' Thinks I what would the Post Master General say if he knowed that the great Southern Mail was stopped half an hour every day or two to let a stage driver see his doxy. But says I to myself, Crockett keep dark and squat low. So on our arrival at the next hotel, instead of going on with him, I pretended I should stop till arternoon and take the stage to Natches and go down the Mississippi. But no sooner had the driver started than I cut out for the gal's house in the woods. I quickly got into her good graces, as she was 'nothing loth,' as the poets say. I kept her company for two days, when as we were up in the loft of the house which had a ladder and trap door to get to it, all at once, whose voice should I hear but the stage driver's below, inquiring for his doxy. Zounds! here was a pretty predikyment. I must either play possum by jumping out of the window and running off, or jump down and fight. I found I must do the latter, as the

window was so small I could'nt get out of it. As quick as the
critter saw me, he flew into such a rage that he crooked up his
neck and neighed like a stud horse, and dared me down. Says I,
stranger! I'm the boy that can double up a dozen of you. I'm a
whole team just from the roaring river. — I've rode through a
crab apple orchard on a streak of lightning. I've squatted lower
than a toad; and jumped higher than a maple tree; I'm all brimstone but my head, and that's aquafortis. At this he fell a cursing
and stamping, and vowed he'd make a gridiron of my ribs to
roast my heart on. I kicked the trap door aside, and got sight at
the varmint; he was madder than a buffalo, and swore he'd set
the house on fire. Says I take care how I lite on you; upon that I
jumped right down upon the driver, and he tore my trowsers
right off of me. I got hold of his whiskers and gave them such a
twitch that his eyes stuck out like a lobster's. He fetched me a
kick in the bowels that knocked all compassion out of them. I
was driv almost distracted, and should have been used up, but
luckily there was a poker in the fire which I thrust down his
throat, and by that means mastered him. Says he, stranger you
are the yellow flower of the forest. If ever you are up for Congress again, I'll come all the way to Duck river to vote for you.
Upon this I bade them good morning, and proceeded on my
journey. This adventure I never told to Mrs. Crockett.

★   ★   ★   ★

Davy's Last Fight

At the last canvass for a Member of Congress, in our district, I
told my constituents, if they did not re-elect me, they might go to
hell, and I'd got to Texas. I was beaten, for they made choice of
a man with "a timber toe" [wooden leg]. And I am now about
to cut out to that country, to help give the Mexicans a licking. I
have got my Almanac ready for the printer, so as to be ahead of
all others, and if he don't git it printed early, when I come back
I'll lite on him like a Martin. As prehaps I shall be absent some
time, I have left reading and pictures enough to make several
Almanacs, and a *lit*-arary friend has promised to git the

"*Gastronomical* calculations" made for me. I want nothing more to do with Gastronomy, and the "see-less-tial bodies," for I was appointed by the President to stand on the Alleghany Mountains and wring the Comet's tail off. I did so, but got my hands most shockingly burnt, and the hair singed off my head, so that I was as bald as a trencher. I div right into the Waybosh river, and thus saved my best stone blue coat and grass green small clothes. With the help of Bear's grease, I have brought out a new crop, but the hair grows in bights and tufts, like hussuck grass in a meadow, and it keeps in such a snarl, that all the teeth will instantly snap out of an ivory comb when brought within ten feet of it. Talking of crops, they say Texas is the place; and the land is so rich, if you plant a crowbar at night it will sprout tenpenny nails before morning. And the soil is so deep one can't raise any long sarce — it all gits pulled through the other side. Our land in West Tennessee is merely frog pasture to it. Reader, "good bye," I'll "go where glory waits me," and I'll go through the Mexicans like a dose of salts.

★   ★   ★   ★

Davy the Judge of Men

The creturs of the forest is of different kinds, like humans. Some is stupid and some is easy to larn. The most knowing cretur that ever I seed war a barr that my darter Pinetta picked up in the woods. It used to follow her to church, and at last it got so tame, it would cum into the house, and set down in one corner of the fire-place to warm itself. I larned it to smoke a pipe and while it sot in one corner smoking, I sot in the other with my pipe. We couldn't talk to one another; but we would look, and I knowed by the shine of his eye what he wanted to say, though he didn't speak a word. The cretur would set up o'nights when I war out late, and open the door for me. But it war the greatest in churning butter. It did all that business for the family. At last it got so civilised that it caught the hooping cough and died. My wife went to the minister and tried to get him to give the barr a christian burial: but the skunk war so bigotted that he wouldn't

do it, and I told him the barr war a better christian than he
ever war.

★   ★   ★   ★

Davy "Explunctificates" His Passion

Thar ar a grate menny kinds of larning. I found it out when I
went to Kongress. Thar ar your mattymatticks, your jommy-
trees, your sighentifficks, and your axletrissity. I nose nothin
about the other wons, but the axletressity is a screamer. Thar
war a feller in Washington that put the thunder and litening into
glass bottles, and when a feller had the roomatiz, or the Saint
Vitals dance, he would put the axletressity into his corpse jist
like pouring whiskey into a powder horn, and it cured him as
clean as a barked tree. So I seed how 'twas done; and intarmined
whenever ennything aled me to try it, only I didn't keer about
the bottles, for I thort I could jist as well take the litening in the
raw state as it cum from the clouds. I had been used to drink out
of the Massissippy without a cup, and so I could take the litening without the bottles and whirligigs that belongs to an axle-
tressityfying masheen. It fell out that sum two yeers arter I had
ben to see this axletrissity, I got a leetle in love with a pesky
smart gal in our cleering, and I knowed it war not rite, seeing I
war a married man. So I combobbolated on the subject and at
last I resisted that I would explunctificate my passions by axletressity, so it must be done by bringing it rite on the hart and
driving the love out of it. So I went out into the forrest one arternoon when thar war a pestiferous thunder gust, I opened my
mouth, so that the axletressity might run down and hit my hart,
to cure it of love. I stood so for an hour, and then I seed a
thunderbolt a cummin, and I dodged my mouth rite under it,
and plump it went into my throte. My eyes! it war as if seven
buffaloes war kicking in my bowels. My hart spun round
amongst my insides like a grindstone going by steem, but the
litening went clean through me, and tore the trowsers cleen off
as it cum out. I had a sore gizzard for two weeks arterward, and
my inwards war so hot that I use to eat raw vittals for a month

arterward, and it would be cooked befour it got farely down my throte. I have never felt love since.

$$\star \qquad \star \qquad \star \qquad \star$$

Davy the Humane

One day I war out in the forest with kill-devil, and thar war a deep snow on the ground, and I seed a Fox crossing my track, and jumping up in the snow, but couldn't get ahead, tho' he tried hard to get out of my way. So I telled growler to be still and I walked along as if I didn't see him: for Davy Crockett war never the man to take advantage of a feller cretur in distress.

$$\star \qquad \star \qquad \star \qquad \star$$

Davy Piles It On Thick

"Mr. Speaker.

Who—Who—Whoop—Bow—Wow—Wow—Yough. I say, Mr. Speaker; I've had a speech in soak this six months, and it has swelled me like a drowned horse; if I don't deliver it I shall burst and smash the windows. The gentleman from Massachusetts [Mr. Everett] talks of summing up the merits of the question, but I'll sum up my own. In one word I'm a screamer, and have got the roughest racking horse, the prettiest sister, the surest rifle and the ugliest dog in the district. I'm a leetle the savagest crittur you ever *did see*. My father can whip any man in Kentucky, and I can lick my father. I can outspeak any man on this floor, and give him two hours start. I can run faster, dive deeper, stay longer under, and come out drier, than any *chap* this side the big *Swamp*. I can outlook a panther and outstare a flash of lightning, tote a steamboat on my back and play at rough and tumble with a lion, and an occasional kick from a *zebra*. To sum up all in one word *I'm a horse*. Goliah was a pretty hard colt but I could choke him. I can take the rag off — frighten the old folks — astonish the natives — and beat the Dutch all to smash — make nothing of sleeping under a blanket of snow — and don't mind being frozen more than a rotten apple.

"Congress allows *lemonade* to the members and has it

charged under the head of stationery — I move also that *whiskey* be allowed under the item of *fuel*. For *bitters I can suck away at* a noggin of aquafortis, sweetened with brimstone, stirred with a lightning rod, and skimmed with a hurricane. I've soaked my head and shoulders in Salt River, so much that I'm always corned. I can walk like an ox, run like a fox, swim like an eel, yell like an Indian, fight like a devil, spout like an earthquake, make love like a mad bull, and swallow a bear whole without choking if you butter his head and pin his ears back.''

★　　　★　　　★　　　★

. . . and Thicker and Thicker . . .

Friends, fellow-citizens, brothers and sisters: On the first Tuesday previous to next Saturday you will be called on to perform one of the most important duties that belong to free white folks — that are a fact. On that day you will be called upon to elect your members to the Senate and House of Representatives in the Congress of the United States, and feeling that in times of great political commotion like these, it becomes you to be well represented, I feel no hesitation in offering myself as a candidate to represent such a high-minded and magnanimous white set.

Friends, fellow-citizens, brothers and sisters: Carroll is a statesman, Jackson is a hero, and Crockett is a *horse!!*

Friends, fellow-citizens, brothers and sisters: They accuse me of adultery; it's a lie — I never ran away with any man's wife, that was not willing, in my life. They accuse me of gambling, it's a lie — for I always plank down the cash.

Friends, fellow-citizens, brothers and sisters: They accuse me of being a drunkard, it's a d—d eternal lie, — for whisky can't make me drunk.

★　　　★　　　★　　　★

. . . and Yet Thicker!

I'm that same David Crockett, fresh from the backwoods, half-horse, half-alligator, a little touched with the snapping-turtle; can wade the Mississippi, leap the Ohio, ride upon a streak of lightning, and slip without a scratch down a honey locust; can whip my weight in wild cats, — and if any gentleman pleases, for a ten dollar bill, he may throw in a panther, — hug a bear too close for comfort, and eat any man opposed to Jackson.

★   ★   ★   ★

Davy Wins an Election

One day, when I was getting ready to go down into Green Swamp for a mess of rattlesnakes, Luke Wing, Grizzle Newcome, and Batt Wiggle, cum to my house to try to coax me to set up for Congress. I told them I didn't understand them kind of splunctifications; but they told me it was sartain the country would be ruined if I didn't go to Congress. So I seed thar war no other way, and so I got ready to go round among the 'lectors, and argufy upon it. I went down to Hay Hollow and ketched a pesky great alligator, and made a bridle for him of painter's hides, and then I got on his back, and rid up to Bear Cleering, whar thar war a whole heap of fellows talking politicks. I driv rite in among 'em, and my crockodile opened his mouth as wide as Black Cave, and they war all astonished. It did wonders for my election. When he opened his mouth every tooth in his head counted for a voter, and when I driv through 'em, I yelled seven times as loud as a hull drove of injins, and then I crowed till my eyes stuck out two inches. 'Tother candidate begun to think he had a smart chance of losing his 'lections; so he got on the stump to speechify. But I driv my alligator right up to the spot, and he opened his mouth wider than ever, as if he was goin to swallow the feller, and he jumpt off that stump, and run and hollered murder, and was never seen arterward, and so I won the 'lection.

★   ★   ★   ★

Davy's Kind of Music!

Folks may talk and crow as much as they can about the roar of Niagara, the growlin o' the sea, and the barkin o' them big iron bull dogs called cannons, but give me a hull team of storm-brewed thunder, an your other natral music is no more than a penny trumpet to the hand organ of a hurrycane. By the great bein above, a reglar round roarin savage peal o' thunder is the greatest treat in all creation! it sets everything but a coward an a darned culprit shouting in the very heart and soul till both on 'em swell so etarnal big with nat'ral glorification that one feels as if he could swoller the entire creation at a gap, hug the hull universe at once, then go to sleep with his entire nater, so full of thunder glory, that he'll wake up with his head an entire electrical machine, and his arms a teetotal thunderbolt. Jist give me a touch o' this sort o' natral music afore I go to sleep, another night; arter I wake up, I feel my bump of veneration for old mammy nater so all mountain big, that I can kneel down an hug old Mississippi, bust a big rock, an feel strong enough to do the duty of an entire saw mill.

★　　★　　★　　★

Colonel Davy Crockett was not alone among the ring-tailed roarers on our frontier. Among others there were Mike Fink, Ralph Stackpole, Billy Earthquake and some mighty powerful women, although the society was male-oriented, with women more notable for their contribution to the homes in the wilderness, rather than the more dramatic physical conquest of it.

These ring-tailed roarers did not fight to kill but to overcome, to "put down" in order to vanquish, then establish and maintain the "pecking order" in the hierarchy of feisty roarers. Muscle, not the gun, was their tool to establish order. Macho? Of course. However, since physical strength and courage were essential to its conquest, Macho would not have been an opprobrious term on the frontier but, rather, one of honor.

"The Wall-eyed Harbinger of Desolation"

" ' "Let all the sons of men b'ar witness!" sings this gent, as he goes skatin' stiff-laig about in a ring like I relates, arms bent, an' back arched; "let all the sons of men b'ar witness; an' speshully let a cowerin' varmint, named Sam Enright, size me up an' shudder. I'm the maker of deserts an' the wall-eyed harb-binger of desolation! I'm kin to rattlesnakes on my mother's side; I'm king of all the eagles an' full brother to the b'ars! I'm the bloo-eyed lynx of Whisky Crossin', an' I weighs four thousand pounds. I'm a he-steamboat; I've put a crimp in a cat-a-mount with nothin' but my livin' hands! I broke a full-grown allagator across my knee, tore him asunder an' showered his shrinkin' fragments over a full section of land! I hugged a cinnamon b'ar to death, an' made a grizzly plead for mercy! Who'll come gouge with me? Who'll come bite with me? Who'll come put his knuckles in my back? I'm Weasle-eye, the dead shot; I'm the blood-drinkin', skelp-t'arin', knife-plyin' demon of Sunflower Creek! The flash of my glance will deaden a whiteoak, an' my screech in anger will back the panther plumb off his natif heath! I'm a slayer an' a slaughterer, an' I cooks an' eats my dead! I can wade the Cumberland without wettin' myse'f, an' I drinks outen the spring without touchin' the ground! I'm a swinge-cat; but I warns you not to be misled by my looks! I'm a flyin' bison, an' deevastation rides upon my breath! Whoop! whoop! whoopee! I'm the Purple Blossom of Gingham Mountain, an' where is that son of thunder who'll try an' nip me in the bud! Whoop! whoopee! I'm yere to fight or drink with any sport; ary one or both! Whoopee! Where is the stately stag to stamp his hoff or rap his antlers to my proclamations! Where is the boundin' buck! Whoopee! whoop! whoop!" ' "

★   ★   ★   ★

Nimrod Wildfire Explains Himself

(From a review of an early play: *Lion of the West*, in 1831)

The *Lion of the West* was played on Friday evening, and drew a crowded house, notwithstanding the inclemency of the weather. The principal character in this production is, to use his own elegant language, a *screamer*. Some idea of his peculiarities may be formed from the following slight sketch which he gives of an affair between himself and a raftsman.

"I was ridin' along the Mississippi in my wagon, when I come acrost a feller floatin' down stream, settin' in the starn of his boat fast asleep! Well, I hadn't had a fight for ten days — *felt as tho' I should have to kiver myself up in a salt barrel to keep* — so wolfy about the head and shoulders. So, says I, 'Hulloa, strannger! if you don't take keer your boat will run away with you!' So he looked up at me slantindicler, and I looked down on him slantindicler — he took out a chor o' tobaccer, and says he, 'I don't value you tantamount to *that!*' and then the varmint flapped his wings and crowed like a cock. I ris up, shook my mane, crooked my neck, and neighed like a horse. He run his boat plump, head-foremost ashore. I stopped my wagon and sot my triggers. 'Mister,' says he, 'I can whip my weight in wildcats, and ride straight through a crab-apple orchard on a flash of lightning. Clear meat-ax disposition; the best man, if I a'nt, I wish I may be tetotaciously exfluncted!' "

The two belligerents join issue, and the Colonel goes on to say —

"He was a pretty severe colt, but no part of a priming to such a feller as me. *I put it to him mighty droll* — in ten minutes he yelled Enough! and swore I was a rip-staver! Says I, *'A'nt I the yaller flower of the forest!* and I'm all brimstone but the head, and that's aquafortis!' Says he, *'Stranger, you're a beauty!* and if I only know'd your name, I'd vote for you next election.' Says I, 'My name is Nimrod Wildfire — half horse, half alligator and a touch of the airthquake — that's got the prettiest sister, fastest horse and ugliest dog in the District, and can outrun, outjump, throw down, drag out and whip any man in all Kaintuck.' "

★   ★   ★   ★

A "Screamer" of the 1840s

Once thar war a deep snow on the ground, and I sot out to make a call on my friend Luke Twig, as it war a leisure day, and I war goin' to be idle. Luke lived next door to me, only about fifteen mile off, and so I war goin' to foot it. Jest as I got up by Brush Hollow, the snow war as deep as my middle, the wind blowed so hard that I went into a hollow tree to warm myself. I hung kill-devil up and begun to thrash my hands, when a wolf cum along, and looked in. He stared right up in my face, as much as to ax leave to pick a breakfast off of any part of me he wanted. I war so astonished at his imperdence that I stood right still a minit. Then the wolf turned about, and war going off, when the end of his tail stuck through a big knot hole in the tree. I ketched hold and pulled his tail through. He jumped and twitched and tried to get away, and screeched like a dying hawk. I tied his tail into a big knot and fastened it with a strap, so that he couldn't haul it out, and left him thar to amuse himself. I could hear him holler all the way till I got to Luke Twig's house.

★   ★   ★   ★

Roaring Ralph Stackpole

"Cunnel," said he, "you're a man in authority, and my superior officer; wharfo' thar' can be no scalping between us. But my name's Tom Dowdle, the rag-man!" he screamed, suddenly skipping into the thickest of the throng, and sounding a note of defiance; "my name's Tom Dowdle, the rag-man, and I'm for any man that insults me! log-leg or leather-breeches, green-shirt or blanket-coat, land-trotter or river-roller, — I'm the man for a massacree!" Then giving himself a twirl upon his foot that would have done credit to a dancing-master, he proceeded to other antic demonstrations of hostility, which when performed in after years on the banks of the Lower Mississippi, by himself and his worthy imitators, were, we suspect, the cause of their receiving the name of the mighty alligator. It is said, by naturalists, of this monstrous reptile, that he delights, when the returning warmth of spring has brought his fellows from their holes, and placed them basking along the banks of a swampy lagoon, to dart into the centre of the expanse, and challenge the whole field to combat. He roars, he blows the water from his nostrils, he lashes it with his tail, he whirls round and round, churning the water into foam; until, having worked himself into a proper fury, he darts back again to the shore, to seek an antagonist. Had the gallant captain of horse-thieves boasted the blood, as he afterwards did the name, of an "alligator half-breed," he could scarce have conducted himself in a way more worthy of his parentage. He leaped into the centre of the throng, where, having found elbow-room for his purpose, he performed the gyration mentioned before, following it up by other feats expressive of his hostile humor. He flapped his wings and crowed, until every chanticleer in the settlement replied to the note of battle; he snorted and neighed like a horse; he bellowed like a bull; he barked like a dog; he yelled like an Indian; he whined like a panther; he howled like a wolf; until one would have thought he was a living menagerie, comprising within his single body the spirit of every animal noted for its love of conflict. Then, not content with such a display of readiness to fight the field, he darted from the centre of the area allowed him for his exercise, and invited the lookers-on individually to battle. "Whar's your buffalo-bull," he cried, "to cross horns with the roarer of Salt River? Whar's your full-blood colt that can shake a saddle off? H'yar's an old nag can kick off the top of a buckeye! Whar's your cat of the Knobs? your wolf of the Rolling Prairies? H'yar's the old brown b'ar can claw the bark off a gum-tree! H'yar's a man for you, Tom Bruce! Same to you, Sim Roberts! to you, Jimmy Big-nose! to you, and to you, and to you! Ar'n't I a ring-tailed squealer? Can go down Salt on my back, and swim up the Ohio! Whar's the man to fight Roaring Ralph Stackpole?"

★   ★   ★   ★

Ain't Nobody Puts Mike Fink Down

I'm a Salt River roarer! I'm a ring-tailed squealer! I'm a reg'lar screamer from the ol' Massassip'! WHOOP! I'm the very infant that refused his milk before its eyes were open, and called for a bottle of old Rye! I love the women an' I'm chockful o' fight! I'm half wild horse and half cock-eyed alligator and the rest o' me is crooked snags an' red-hot snappin' turkle. I can hit like fourth-proof lightnin' an' every lick I make in the woods lets in an acre o' sunshine. I can out-run, out-jump, out-shoot, out-brag, out-drink, an' out-fight, rough-an'-tumble, no holts barred, ary man on both sides the river from Pittsburgh to New

Orleans an' back ag'in to St. Louiee. Come on, you flatters, you bargers, you milk-white mechanics, an' see how tough I am to chaw! I ain't had a fight for two days an' I'm spilein' for exercise. Cock-a-doodle-do!

★   ★   ★   ★

The "Big Snag of the Desert"

The bully of Salt River war named Skippoweth Branch. He slept in his hat, chawed his vittles with his foreteeth, and could scream through his nose. He sunned himself in a thunder storm, went to meeting on two horses, never turned out for man or beast; and was sworn to lick every thing he saw, escept his own father and mother. He would walk ten miles, at any time of day or night, for a fight. He called himself the great oak that grows half its length underground, and turns up its roots unexpected. He sometimes took the name of floating iron and melted pewter, red hot cannon balls, and Big Snag of the Desert. He said he lived on the mountains and eat thunder, that he had a neckcloth at home made of double chain lightning, and that he could never come to his full height till the clouds were lifted a peace. He called himself a west wind full of prickles, a dose for old Kaintuck and a drawing plaster for the Allegheny mountains. The fact is he war too smart to live long, and screamed himself to death, one night, to show his spirrit. I knowed him when he war a boy, and seed him when he war a man, and went to his funeral when he war ded. He war the pride of the country, and could outscream seven catamounts tied together.

★   ★   ★   ★

Little Billy from the No'th Fo'k of Muddy Run

As we were passing by the court-house, a real "screamer from the Nob," about six feet four in height, commenced the following tirade: — "This is *me*, and no mistake! Billy Earthquake, Esq., commonly called Little Billy, all the way from No'th Fork of Muddy Run! I'm a small specimen, as you see, a remote circumstance, a mere yearling; but cuss me if I ain't of the true imported breed, and I can whip any man in this section of the country. Whoop! won't *nobody* come out and fight me? Come out, some of you, and die decently, for I'm spileing for a fight, I hain't had one for more than a week, and if you don't come out I'm flyblowed before sundown, to a certingty. So come up to taw!

"Maybe you don't know who Little Billy is? I'll tell you. I'm a poor man, it's a fact, and smell like a wet dog; but I can't be run over. I'm the identical individual that grinned a whole menagerie out of countenance, and made the ribbed nose baboon hang down his head and blush. W-h-o-o-p! I'm the chap that towed the Broad-horn up Salt River, where the snags were so thick that the fish couldn't swim without rubbing their scales off! — fact, and if any one denies it, just let 'em make their will! Cock-a-doodle-doo!

"Maybe you never heard of the time the horse kicked me, and put both his hips out of joint — if it ain't true, cut me up for catfish bait! W-h-o-o-p! I'm the very infant that refused its milk before its eyes were open, and called out for a bottle of old Rye! W-h-o-o-p! I'm that little Cupid! Talk about grinning the bark off a tree! — 'tain't nothing; one squint of mine at a bull's heel would blister it. O, I'm one of your toughest sort, — live for ever, and then turn to a white oak post. I'm the ginewine article, a real double acting engine, and I can out-run, out-jump, out-swim, chaw more tobacco and spit less, and drink more whiskey and keep soberer than any man in these localities. If that don't make 'em fight (walking off in disgust) nothing will. I wish I may be kiln-dried and split up into wooden shoe-pegs, if I believe there's a chap among 'em that's got courage enough to collar a hen!"

★   ★   ★   ★

Mike Fink and Davy Crockett

I expect, stranger, you think old Davy Crockett war never beat at the long rifle; but he war tho. I expect there's no man so strong, but what he will find some one stronger. If you havent heerd tell of one Mike Fink, I'll tell you something about him, for he war a helliferocious fellow, and made an almighty fine shot. Mike was a boatman on the Mississip, but he had a little cabbin on the head of the Cumberland, and a horrid handsome wife, that loved him the wickedest that ever you see. Mike only worked enough to find his wife in rags, and himself in powder, and lead, and whiskey, and the rest of the time he spent in nocking over bar and turkeys, and bouncing deer, and sometimes drawing a lead on an injun. So one night I fell in with him in the woods, where him and his wife shook down a blanket for me in his wigwam. In the morning sez Mike to me, 'I've got the handsomest wife, and the fastest horse, and the sharpest shooting iron in all Kentuck, and if any man dare doubt it, I'll be in his hair quicker than hell could scorch a feather.' This put my dander up, and sez I, 'I've nothing to say agin your wife, Mike, for it cant be denied she's a shocking handsome woman, and Mrs. Crockett's in Tennessee, and I've got no horses. Mike, I dont exactly like to tell you you lie about what you say about your rifle, but I'm d——d if you speak the truth, and I'll prove it. Do you see that are cat sitting on the top rail of your potato patch, about a hundred and fifty yards off? If she ever hears agin, I'll be shot if it shant be without ears.' So I plazed away, and I'll bet you a horse, the ball cut off both the old tom cat's ears close to his head, and shaved the hair off clean across the skull, as slick as if I'd done it with a razor, and the critter never stirred, nor knew he'd lost his ears till he tried to scratch 'em. 'Talk about your rifle after that, Mike!' sez I. 'Do you see that are sow away off furder than the eend of the world,' sez Mike, 'with a litter of pigs round her,' and he lets fly. The old sow give a grunt, but never stirred in her tracks, and Mike falls to loading and firing for dear life, till he hadn't left one of them are pigs enough tail to make a tooth-pick on. 'Now,' sez he, 'Col. Crockett, I'll be pretticularly ableedged to you if you'll put them are pig's tails on again,' sez he. 'That's onpossible, Mike,' sez I, 'but you've left one of 'em about an inch to steer by, and if it had a-been my work, I wouldn't have done it so wasteful. I'll mend your host,'

and so I lets fly, and cuts off the apology he'd left the poor
cretur for decency. I wish I may drink the whole of Old
Mississip, without a drop of the rale stuff in it, if you wouldn't
have thort the tail had been drove in with a hammer. That made
Mike a kinder sorter wrothy, and he sends a ball after his wife as
she was going to the spring after a gourd full of water, and
nocked half her koom out of her head, without stirring a hair,
and calls out to her to stop for me to take a plizzard at what was
left on it. The angliferous critter stood still as a scarecrow in a
cornfield, for she'd got used to Mike's tricks by long practiss.
'No, no, Mike,' sez I, 'Davy Crockett's hand would be sure to
shake, if his iron war pointed within a hundred mile of a
shemale, and I give up beat, Mike, and as we've had our eye-
openers a-ready, we'll now take a flem-cutter, by way of an anti-
formatic, and then we'll disperse.'

★   ★   ★   ★

Mike Fink's Brag

. . . "Hurray for me, you scapegoats! I'm a land-screamer —
I'm a water-dog — I'm a snapping-turkle — I can lick five times
my own weight in wildcats. I can use up Injens by the cord. I
can swallow bears whole, raw or cooked. I can out-run, out-
dance, out-jump, out-dive, out-drink, out-holler, and out-lick,
any white thing in the shape o' human that's ever put foot
within two thousand miles o' the big Massassip. Whoop! holler,
you varmints! — holler fur the Snapping Turkle! or I'll jump
straight down yer throats, quicker nor a streak o' greased
lightening can down a bear's! . . . I'm in fur a fight, I'll go my
death on a fight, and a fight I must have, one that'll tar up the
arth all round and look kankarifferous, or else I'll have to be
salted down to save me from spiling, as sure nor Massassip
alligators make fly traps o' thar infernal ugly jawrs."

★   ★   ★   ★

"Wimmin Was Wimmin in them Days"

My first sweetheart gave me this description of herself:

"You just ought to see me rigged out in my best. My bonnet is a hornet's nest, garnished with wolves' tails and eagles' feathers. My gown's made of a whole bear's hide, with the tail for a train. I can drink from the branch without a cup, shoot a wild goose flying, wade the Mississippi without getting wet, out scream a catamount, and jump over my own shadow. I've good, strong horse sense, and I know a woodchuck from a skunk. I can dance down any fellow in Arkansas, and cut through the bushes like a pint of whisky among forty men. Your Sal."

☆   ★   ★   ★

Oak Wing's Sister: The Dressmaker

One day when Oak Wing's sister war going to a baptizing, and had her feed in a bag under her arm, she seed a big bear that had come out from a holler tree, and he looked first at her, then at the feed, as if he didn't know which to eat fust. He kinder poked out his nose, and smelt of the dinner which war sassengers maid of bear's meat and crocodile's liver. She stood a minute an looked at him, in hopes he would feel ashamed of himself an go off; but he then cum up and smelt of her, and then she thort twar time to be stirring. So she threw the dinner down before him, an when he put his nose to it, to take a bite, she threw herself on him, an caught the scuff of his neck in her teeth; an the bear shot ahead, for it felt beautiful, as her teeth war as long an as sharp as nales. He tried to run, an she held on with her teeth, an it stript the skin clear off of him, an left him as naked as he was born, she held on with her teeth till it cum clear off the tale. The bear was seen a week arterwards up in Muskrat Hollow, running without his skin. She made herself a good warm petticoat out of the pesky varmint's hide.

★   ★   ★   ★

Colonel Coon's Wife Judy

It's most likely my readers has all heered of Colonel Coon's wife Judy. She wore a bearskin petticoat, an alligator's hide for an overcoat, an eagle's nest for a hat, with a wild-cat's tail for a feather. When she was fourteen years old, she wrung off a snapping turtle's neck and made a comb of its shell, which she wears to this day. When she was sixteen years old she run down a four year old colt, and chased a bear three mile through the snow, because she wanted his hair to make a tooth brush. She outscreamed a catamount, on a wager, when she was just come of age; and sucked forty rattlesnake's eggs to give her a sweet breath, the night she was married. It was not at all likely that Judy would throw herself away on any young feller that was a mind to set up a claim to her, and so many of 'em found they were barking up the wrong tree and getting their fingers pricked with a chestnut burr. At last, one Tennessee roarer, that never backed out for any thing short of a mammouth, heard of Judy's accomplishments, and 'tarmined to try his flint agin her steel. So he got into a jumper on a cold winter night, and drove through the woods towards her father's house. He begun to scream before he got within sight of the log hut where Judy lived, and his voice was heard five mile off. Judy's heart begun to beat when she heard him, for she knew whoever he was, he was a whole steamboat. When he got to the house, he give one leap from his jumper, dashed down the door, and bounced into the middle of the room. "Tom Coon, by Jingo!" cried every one in the house — for he was no stranger by fame, though they had never seen him before. Judy right away set down in a corner of the room to try his spunk, and said not a word, good or bad. He pulled half a dozen eyes out of his pocket, and flinging 'em down on the floor, swore with a round oath he'd place any man's eyes by the side of them that dared to say a word agin Judy! Judy then jumped up like a frog and said, "Tom Coon, I'm yours for life — I know what you've come for, and I'll be your wedded wife without any more fustification about it." So Tom got Judy and all her plunder. Tom took her into Tennessee with him right away, and begun to make a little clearing in the midst of the wood, when Judy soon gave him a specimen of her talents. For, being out one evening to a tea-squall, about ten mile off, in coming home through the wood, she found a nest of young wild-cats in the stump of a tree. She said nothing about it when she went home, but let her toenails grow till they were an inch long, when she started all alone, one morning, and went to the nest, and, jumping in upon the young wild-cats, stamped them to death with her feet. It was quite a tough job, and they bit her legs most ridiculously; but she stood up to the scratch, though they scratched her backsides so tarnaciously they've never itched since.

★   ★   ★   ★

Sal Fink, the Mississippi Screamer

I dar say you've all on you, if not more, frequently heerd this great she human crittur boasted of, an' pointed out as *"one o' the gals"* — but I tell you what, stranger, you have never really set your eyes on *"one of the gals,"* till you have seen Sal Fink, the Mississippi screamer, whose miniature pictur I have here give, about as nat'ral as life, but not half as handsome — an' if thar ever was a gal that desarved to be christen — *"one o' the gals,"* then this gal was that gal — and no mistake.

She fought a duel once with a thunderbolt, an' came off without a single scratch, while at the fust fire she split the thunderbolt all to flinders, an' gave the pieces to Uncle Sam's artillerymen, to touch off their canon with. When a gal about six years old, she used to play see-saw on the Mississippi snags, and arter she war done she would snap 'em off, an' so cleared a large district of the river. She used to ride down the river on an alligator's back, standen upright, an' dancing *Yankee Doodle,* and could leave all the steamers behind. But the greatest feat she ever did, positively outdid anything that ever was did.

One day when she war out in the forest, making a collection o' wild cat skins for her family's winter beddin, she war captered in the most all-sneaken manner by about fifty Injuns, an' carried by 'em to Roast Flesh Hollow, whar the blood drinkin' wild varmints detarmined to skin her alive, sprinkle a leetle salt over her, an' devour her before her own eyes; so they took an' tied her to a tree, to keep till mornin' should bring the rest o' thar ring-nosed sarpints to enjoy the fun. Arter that, they lit a large fire in the Holler, turned the bottom o' thar feet towards the blaze, Injun fashion, and went to sleep to dream o' thar mornin's feast; well, after the critturs got into a somniferous snore, Sal got into an all-lightnin' of a temper, and burst all the ropes about her like an apron-string! She then found a pile o' ropes, too, and tied all the Injun's heels together all round the fire, — then fixin' a cord to the shins of every two couple, she, with a suddenachous jerk, that made the intire woods tremble, pulled the intire lot o' sleepin' red-skins into that ar great fire, fast together, an' then sloped like a panther out of her pen, in the midst o' the tallest yellin', howlin', scramblin' and singin', that war ever seen or heerd on, since the great burnin' o' Buffalo prairie!

★   ★   ★   ★

Friendship and Adultery on the Frontier

Jedediah was very fond of his neighbor's wife, and went with his friend Elnathan to see her one afternoon. Jedediah went up stairs and left Elnathan below to watch. Presently the husband came home, and greeted Elnathan cordially. He told him that he had long suspected Jedediah of improper tenderness towards his wife, and said, 'As you are his intimate friend, you may tell me whether you think he is guilty.'

'I have known my friend Crawfish for twenty years,' replied Elnathan, 'and would not be afraid to stake my head that he is above doing a bad action.'

★   ★   ★   ★

A revealing source of early humor is found in the South-western press, some samples of which are presented below.

He who steals a million is only a financier. He who steals a half million is only a defaulter. He who steals a quarter of a million is a swindler. He who steals a hundred thousand is a rogue. He who steals fifty thousand is a knave. But he who steals a pair of boots or a loaf of bread is a scoundrel, and deserves hanging.

March 1863

★   ★   ★   ★

A shrewd little fellow, who had just begun to read Latin, astonished his maiden instructress, who was fast approaching a "Certain Age," by the following translation: 'VIR, a man; GIN, a trap; VIRGIN, a man trap.'

April 1863

★   ★   ★   ★

B. P., who went from here to Fort Wingate a few days ago, passed the night at the Rito, unable to sleep for several hours on account of the chinchas which amused themselves racing over his body. After midnight he sent one of the house for a leg of mutton, paying him a dollar for his services. Putting the meat in the middle of the floor, the chinchas went to the banquet and B. P. slept very well until morning. We publish this remedy for the public good.

June 1863

★   ★   ★   ★

A judge trying a case out West had proceeded about two hours, when he observed: "Here are only eleven jurymen present; where is the twelfth?" "Please, your honor," said one of the eleven, "he has gone away about some business, but he has left his verdict with me."

December 1865

★   ★   ★   ★

"I say boy, is there anything to shoot about here?" inquired a sportsman of a boy he met.

"Well," was the reply, "nothing just about here but the schoolmaster is down the hill yonder — you can pop him over."

January 1866

★   ★   ★   ★

A student at one of our colleges had a barrel of ale deposited in his room — contrary, of course, to rules and usage; he received a summons to appear before the President who said:

"Sir, I am informed you have a barrel of Ale in your room."

"Yes, sir."

"Well, what explanation can you make?"

"Why, the fact is, sir, my physician advised me to try a little every day as a tonic, and, not wishing to stop at the various places where the beverage is retailed, I concluded to have a barrel taken to my room."

"Indeed. And have you derived any benefit from the use of it?"

"Ah, yes, sir. When the barrel was first taken to my room, ten days since, I could scarcely lift it. Now I carry it with the greatest ease."

We believe the student was discharged without a special reprimand.

December 1867

★   ★   ★   ★

A couple of fellows who were pretty thoroughly soaked with bad whiskey got into the gutter. After floundering about for a few minutes one of them said: "Jim, let's go to another house; this hotel leaks."

December 1867

★   ★   ★   ★

The fellow who got up the following, understood *himself* adzactly. Hear him!

> If I was a lokle editor,
>   Wouldn't I have a time?
> I wouldn't print a cussed word
>   For less than a $ a line.
>
> I'd get my grub and licker free,
>   & tickets for the shows,
> I wouldn't pay for buggy hier
>   & wouldn't I war good close!

December 1869

★   ★   ★   ★

One Pablo Padilla who has been for a long time engaged in stealing stock, etc. was overtaken on Saturday last by a fit of remorse, (or something else) and hung himself on a tree near Peralta.

January 1872

★   ★   ★   ★

A baby girl knelt down to pray one morn.
The mother said, "My love,
Why do we ever say, give us our daily bread?
Why not ask for a week or more?"
The baby bent her head in thoughtful mood
Towards the floor: "We want it fresh!" she said.

May 1872

★   ★   ★   ★

Within the past three weeks the town of Loma Parda in Mora County, New Mexico has lost four of its citizens by violence. They became too intimately associated with their neighbor's stock, and were strung up by the sufferers, who had more faith in a stout lariat than in stone walls.

June 1872

★   ★   ★   ★

Yesterday we were informed of a "muss" that took place in one of our fashionable saloons. A man called for a drink and swallowed it before going down in his pockets to see whether he had the wherewith to pay for it. He didn't find it, after a careful search, and told the man behind the bar to "mark down on the slate." This the bar keeper refused to do on the ground that he "didn't do credit business," where upon the honest customer "skinned off" his clothes and passed them over the counter to be held as security for the drink until morning, when he promised to call and redeem them. The tumbler wrestler became very angry at this, swore he didn't keep a pawnshop, and finally jumped the counter and kicked the poor fellow out following him to the sidewalk and part of the way home, laying on vigorously all the time. The abused man took it all without a word or an attempt at resistance, until he thought he had received about a drink's worth, when he turned round and gave the enraged saloon keeper, one of the most exhaustive threashings that ever human frame was subjected to!

September 1872

★   ★   ★   ★

A fellow leaning over the wagon bridge a few nights ago, getting rid of a load, finally threw himself up from his boots. He followed the rest of himself to the bed of the river and when he came to, expressed himself as feeling much better but that the water was mighty cold and the stones all fired hard.

October 1873

★   ★   ★   ★

The Mesilla *News* continues to smack its chops over the "Pie Biters" of that place, and well it may, for a more voracious set of pie-ous cusses cannot be found than those who roam around the sand hills of that aborial town. (Aborial is a dictionary word.) But Mesilla was not the only town that fostered pie biters. Las Cruces also had its lover of delicate pastery, and the aperture in his face was such — no matter about the opening — that his friends were willing to back him to the extent of their last evidence of Uncle Sam's indebtedness. So a challenge was sent and accepted, a match made, and the champions of the two towns met, hungry and cadaverous, but eager for the contest. We now give the remainder of the account in the words of our special correspondent: "The pies were to be mince and one inch thick, Mesilla to bite first, and no bite to count unless it reached to the center of the pie. Mesilla piled up nine and shut down on them without an effort. Las Cruces elevated his head and closed his jaw over eleven. (Great enthusiasm among his friends.) Mesilla came up to the scratch, or bite, manfully, and flopped his lip over a dozen successfully. (Odds offered on Mesilla.) Las Cruces at this point said, "Well, it's time to stop this nonsense, hand me fifteen." They were given him; he smiled, laid the back of his head on his shoulders and came down on the bundle of pies like an alligator on a mouthful of flies. But his teeth did not come together. He struggled and jerked, but it was no use. Three of his teeth broke and his hold gave away. On examining, a dog collar was found in the center pie, and Las Cruces had got his teeth tangled in the bundle. Jack Martin, the referee, decided in favor of Mesilla on the ground that everything was fair in a mince pie."

Our special gained a few stamps on the result, as he followed Barela and Davis in betting. The dog collar was recognized as belonging to Davis' missing purp.

January 1874

★   ★   ★   ★

"Signor Don Jose," said his Honor. "You stand charged with having filled your ugly corpus with tanglefoot whiskey, willfully, deliberately, and from a premeditated design to disturb the peace and quiet of a day that is held sacred by every patriotic American." "Los Americanos son carajoes," interrupted the prisoner. "Shut up your ugly mug," said the Judge, "or you will be committing for contempt. You got drunk, and kicked up a row on the Fourth of July, and then finished by spreading yourself out in the street to broil, and started a barbeque for bluetailed flies, do you consider that a proper way to celebrate the glorious Fourth?" "El Cuatro de Julio no vale nada, que viven Guadalupe Hidalgo." "Five dollars and costs," said his Honor. "Broke es de Banke," replied Jose, as he sorrowfully took up his line of march towards the jail.

July 1877

★   ★   ★   ★

The *New Mexican* man seems to be the victim of a troublesome infirmity; from the symptoms recently manifested we conclude that he is afflicted with the "bots." In sympathy we recommend a mild course of "aloes and turpentine." This remedy is highly recommended in case of other beasts of burden thus afflicted, and we see no reason why it should not prove equally effective in the case of an *ass*. Suffering of any kind, even of a brute arouses our sympathies.

September 1877

★   ★   ★   ★

The *NEWS & PRESS* barbarously designates the young gentlemen of that locality as "young bucks." Wonder what name it would give the young ladies.

January 1878

★   ★   ★   ★

The following hints, intended for young men for the first time entering fashionable society, will, if closely followed, be productive of beneficial results:

Don't joke about the food on the table. Don't whistle and beckon to the sausage. Never call the hash mystery, and, above all things never ask your host where the butter had its hair cut last.

Don't eat your soup with your fork, this is an unpardonable breach of good manners. Remember that your knife is the proper utensil.

Always eat all you wish while at the table, for it is very unmannerly to fill your pockets with pie or pudding. Remember the twelfth commandment — eat all you want but pocket none.

When you have finished eating don't shove your chair back against the wall and put your feet upon the table. Place them carefully in the lap of the gentleman or lady sitting next to you.

If you see anything you don't want don't ask for it.

Never put the napkin rings or spoons in your pocket as this is not an act of refinement, and may leave your conduct open to criticism.

Some persons use their bread to dry their plate with, this is intolerable. The pocket handkerchief is the proper article in this emergency.

After the meal, wine is generally brought in. In assisting your nearest friend you should not use the vulgar phrase, "Well, Cully, will you have a ball?" This is ungentlemanly in the extreme. Use the elegant expression, "Sir, will you have a Santa Fe straight, a Southwestern smile, or a Chicago stunner?"

November 1878

★   ★   ★   ★

Richard Coeur de Lion was the most stylish man in England of his time. When he put on his tin helmet and cast iron ulster, and a pair of laminated steel boots, and picked up a club with an iron knob and a steel spike in the end, and set forth on a crusade, the fashionable society of that day considered him just "dressed to kill." And so he was. And one time when he was dressed up that way a fellow killed him.

April 1878

★   ★   ★   ★

WANTED FOR A SOBER FAMILY — a man of light weight, who fears the Lord and can drive a team of horses. He must occasionally wait tables, join in household prayer, look after some burros and read a chapter in the Bible. He must, God willing, rise at 7 in the morning, and obey his master and mistress in lawful commands; if he can dress hair, sing psalms and play cribbage, the more agreeable. Note: he must not be familiar with the maid servants, lest the flesh should rebel against the spirit and he should be induced to walk in the thorny paths of the wicked. Wages $7.00 a month and a place to rest his weary head and body.

January 1880

★   ★   ★   ★

The following joke on one of the professional "mashers" in Santa Fe is first-rate, but at the same time is naughty; so naughty that no lady who doesn't blush ought to read it.

And yet there will not be a person in Santa Fe who reads the first part of this paragraph, of either sex, who will not turn the paper upside down to see what is the joke referred to, in spite of the warning given above.

March 1880

★　　　★　　　★　　　★

Mr. A. J. Fountain, through the Silver City *Southwest,* complains of the *NEW MEXICAN'S* recent mention of him taking exception of the manner in which the paragraph was worded. The *NEW MEXICAN* simply stated that "Mr. A. J. Fountain hadn't lied for a long time" and is perfectly willing to acknowledge it was mistaken.

August 1880

★　　　★　　　★　　　★

Saloon keepers are indirectly a great aid to the cause of temperance. Were it not for the fact that they are always careful to fill the beer glass half of foam few of their customers would go home sober.

August 1880

★　　　★　　　★　　　★

A North Carolina woman stabbed a man who attempted to hug her. This proves that all women are not enthusiastically in favor of a free press.

September 1880

★　　　★　　　★　　　★

Women resemble flowers. They shut up when they sleep.

October 1880

★　　　★　　　★　　　★

A woman was testifying in behalf of her son, and swore he had worked on a farm ever since he was born. The lawyer who cross-examined her said: "You assert that your son has worked upon a farm ever since he was born?" "I do." "What did he do the first year?" "He milked." The lawyer evaporated.

October 1880

★　　　★　　　★　　　★

Wanted, at this office, an able-bodied, hard-featured, bad-tempered, not-to-be-put-off and not-to-be-backed-down, freckle faced young man, to collect for this paper; must furnish his own horse, saddle-baggs, pistols, whiskey, bowie-knife and cowhide.

We will furnish the accounts. To such we promise constant and laborious employment.

June 1874

★   ★   ★   ★

Timkins aroused his wife from a sound sleep the other night, saying that he had seen a ghost in the shape of an ass. "Oh let me sleep," was the reply from the irate dame, "and don't be frightened at your shadow."

August 1874

★   ★   ★   ★

"Mother bring me my little kitten," is the latest popular ballad. The mew-sick is fair so far as we are able to judge, but words seem to have been scratched off rather hurriedly, and strung out to such a length there is a feeling of relief when the singer comes to a paws.

August 1874

★   ★   ★   ★

Somebody says Mr. Gladstone is engaged in writing a work on hell. A long and active political life should make him as familiar with that subject as is possible for a mere inhabitant of earth to be. But would it not be well for him to wait for a little more light on the subject when he might treat it with more warmth than he can at present?

August 1874

★   ★   ★   ★

An Indiana jury recently returned a written verdict of "Blode to pieces by a biler bursting."

April 1875

★   ★   ★   ★

"Self made men are very apt to worship their maker."

April 1875

★   ★   ★   ★

The Albuquerque *Review* is crying for the wholesale clearing out of the thieves of that town, and the Socorro *Sun* calls it a movement to depopulate the town.

August 1874

★   ★   ★   ★

Loaded to the muzzle: "What is this man charged with?" asked the judge. "With whiskey, yer honor," replied the sententious policeman.

May 1882

★   ★   ★   ★

General Phil Sheridan and staff passed through the city yesterday in an elegant private coach bound for Washington.

The party is in excellent spirits as the following will show.

Reporter — hat in hand and smiling blandly — "General, I am a member of the great daily press. I have been deputized by the owners of the *Las Vegas Gazette* to propound to you a few interrogations.

"Where are you going, General? Where have you been traveling to, and what is your program in the future?"

General Sheridan replied thusly: "It is none of your G— D—— business, sir."

March 1883

★   ★   ★   ★

Fred Bean, an Iowa stripling, has married the daughter of a Sioux Chief. The tribe will now enjoy Bean's-Whoop, or Bean's-Soup — or perhaps it be spelled Bean's-Siouxp?

June 1883

★   ★   ★   ★

Unworthy namesake of the gentle Nazarene exchanging bellicose chin music — Naughty Jesus Gonzales jawed Jesus Candelaria in an ungodly way, whereupon the latter skipped to the nearest dispenser with justice who mulcted this timid Jesus for costs for not jawing back and knocking the holy excrement out of 'tother Jesus.

October 1883

★   ★   ★   ★

The cowboys are not all college graduates as some sentimental people suppose. A cowboy near Hell Canon recently posted up the following notice: "If any man's or woman's kows or Oxes gets in these oats, his or her's tail will be cut off, as the case may be."

December 1884

★   ★   ★   ★

Some lousy, fistulous, carrion-scented, worm-eaten and otherwise deformed human miscarriage, walking on its hind legs and having a remote resemblance to the animal man, has added another to the horrid list of his infamous acts by cutting off the nose of a colt, the property of Nicolas Candelaria! Such a wretch ought to be mashed to a jelly between two limberger cheeses without benefit of clergy, and the remains of his hideous cadaver chopped into sausage and fed to the dogs.

January 1884

★   ★   ★   ★

Baked beans is the national dish of Boston, New Mexico and Egypt. The bean is an unpretending little vegetable, but we hear good reports from it wherever it is used for food.

February 1884

★   ★   ★   ★

This frontier story of 1849, was sent to THE SPIRIT OF THE TIMES by an Iowa correspondent with the nom de plume of "Skyscraper." He was traveling in the forests of Arkansas and stayed the night in a log cabin where an old man lived alone. After a hearty supper of bear meat he asked his host how long since he had settled there.

"Stranger," says he, "I ain't the first settler; I bought this clearing from a fellow they called Tussle Jim, sometimes Long Jim; they called him 'Tussle Jim' cause he was sich a rantankerous fighter. Jim said he settled here when the Ingens and Bar war thick as simmons, and a mity hard time he had on it, trying to keep things straight. His stock wasn't very large, only an old cow and a sow, but the sow littered every month or so, and the old cow had a calf every year — she never failed but once. One winter it was so cold that she concluded to hold over, and not have a calf in the spring, but she made it up afterwards, for the next spring she had a calf and a yearling! She was a great cow, Jim said, and considerate. The old sow didn't do so well, the bar got the persuasion of her, and, whenever her back war turned, they wisited her family and enticed some of them off. Jim didn't like sich carryings on, but he couldn't help himself, the varmints never left a track, so Jim had to grin and bear it. Well, one cold winter, (the same one the old cow held over) Jim was hunting three or four miles from here, and going round the root of a big hollow tree that had fallen down, he seed some bones that looked mity like his pigs's, so he fired his rifle in the hole three or four time, and when he listened he heered a noise like as if somethin' war smothering in blood. Jim thought he'd killed a wolf, and as he wanted a skin for the baby to sleep on, he concluded to crawl in and get the varmint out. So he crept in feet foremost, pulling his rifle arter him, and when he got to the 'tuther end, a matter of fifty feet, he felt back, and found he hadn't killed a wolf, but a young cub bar. Jim war mity glad, and commenced pulling it out, but before he got half way he seed the hole darkened, and he knowed it war the old she. Jim was so skeered, he didn't know what to do till she war rite over him, but he fired down her throat, and she fell dead. Jim's feelins war mity relieved at first, 'till he tried to push her back (cause she filled the hole chock full, and he couldn't get over,) and he found she wouldn't budge an inch. He thought to cut her to pieces, and felt for his knife — but it warn't there! Scissors! wasn't that a fix! Jim said he war rite down worried, if he could only get the tarnal thing behind him, he wouldn't care a cuss, he'd crawl rite straight out and go home; but she wasn't behind him — so he fell to studying, and studied a long spell, and then, as there was no other way, he took hold on her nose with his teeth and commenced eating, and before dark the old she was behind him!

"Jim says it are a fact, and he thrashed Jo Larkins nearly to death cause he said he didn't much more than half believe it, so I suppose it are."

★   ★   ★   ★

The following exerpt from THE ARKANSAS TRAVELER was printed in 1876 and is the best of many versions printed since 1858, having the most authentic dialect and the best lines.

Arkansas was considered "the pits" among all American frontier states, back then, and continued to be so regarded until recent years. It had the most undeveloped, brazen, funny and illiterate people in the Union, or so the canard went, and that reputation (untrue and undeserved, of course) continued until quite recently. The last comedian to make Arkansas his "shtik" was Bob Burns.

A lost and hungry traveler approaches the cabin of an Arkansas squatter. He needs to "bed down" and loses no time asking the squatter if he might do so.

Traveler.—Halloo, stranger.

Squatter.—Hello yourself.

T.—Can I get to stay all night with you?

S.—No, sir, you can't git to —

T.—Have you any spirits here?

S.—Lots uv 'em; Sal seen one last night by that ar ole hollar gum, and it nearly skeered her to death.

T.—You mistake my meaning; have you any liquor?

S.—Had some yesterday, but Ole Bose he got in and lapped all uv it out'n the pot.

T.—You don't understand; I don't mean pot liquor. I'm wet and cold and want some whiskey. Have you got any?

S.—Oh, yes — I drunk the last this morning.

T.—I'm hungary; havn't had a thing since morning; can't you give me something to eat?

S.—Hain't a durned thing in the house. Not a mouffull uv meat, nor a dust uv meal here.

T.—Well, can't you give my horse something?

S.—Got nothin' to feed him on.

T.—How far is it to the next house?

S.—Stranger! I don't know, I've never been thar.

T.—Well, do you know who lives here?

S.—Yes zir!

T.—As I'm so bold, then, what might your name be?

S.—It might be Dick, and it might be Tom; but it lacks right smart uv it.

T.—Sir! will you tell me where this road goes to?

S.—It's never gone any whar since I've lived here; It's always thar when I git up in the mornin'.

T.—Well, how far is it to where it forks?

S.—It don't fork at all; but it splits up like the devil.

T.—As I'm not likely to get to any other house to night, can't you let me sleep in yours; and I'll tie my horse to a tree, and do without anything to eat or drink?

S.—My house leaks. Thar's only one dry spot in it, and me and Sal sleeps on it. And that thar tree is the old woman's persimon; you can't tie to it, 'caze she don't want 'em shuk off. She 'lows to make beer out'n um.

T.—Why don't you finish covering your house and stop the leaks?

S.—It's been rainin' all day.

T.—Well, why don't you do it in dry weather?

S.—It don't leak then.

T.—As there seem to be nothing alive about your place but children, how do you do here anyhow?

S.—Putty well, I thank you, how do you do yourself?

T.—I mean what do you do for a living here?

S.—Keep tavern and sell whisky.

T.—Well, I told you I wanted some whisky.

S.—Stranger, I bought a bar'l more'n a week ago. You see, me and Sal went shars. After we got it here, we only had a bit betweenst us, and Sal she dind't want to use hern fust, nor me mine. You see I had a spiggin in one eend, and she in tother. So she takes a drink out'n my eend, and pays me the bit for it; then I'd take one out'n hern, and give her the bit. Well, we's getting long fust-rate, till Dick, durned skulking skunk, he born a bole on the bottom to suck at, and the next time I went to buy a drink, they wont none thar.

T.—I'm sorry your whisky's all gone; but, my friend, why don't you play the balance of that tune?

S.—It's got no balance to it.

T.—I mean you don't play the whole of it.

S.—Stranger, can you play the *fiddul?*

T.—Yes, a little, sometimes.

S.—You don't look like a fiddlur, but ef you think you can play any more onto that thar tune, you kin just try it.

(The traveler takes the fiddle and plays the whole of it.)

S.—Stranger, tuck a half a duzen cheers and sot down. Sal, stir yourself round like a six-horse team in a mud hold. Go round in the hollar whar I killed that buck this mornin', cut off some of the best pieces, and fotch it and cook it for me and this gentleman, d'rectly. Raise up the board under the head of the bed, and got the ole black jug I hid from Dick, and gin us some whisky; I know thar's some left yit. Til, drive ole Bose out'n the bread-tray, then climb up in the loft and git the rag that's got the sugar tied in it. Dick, carry the gentleman's hoss round under the shead, give him so fodder and corn; much as he kin eat.

Til.—Dad, they ain't knives enuff for to sot the table.

S.—Whar's big butch, little butch, ole case, cob-handle, granny's knife, and the one I handled yesterday! That's nuff to sot any gentleman's table, outer you've lost um. Durn me, stranger, ef you can't stay as long as you please, and I'll give you plenty to eat and to drink. Will you have coffey for supper?

T.—Yes, sir.

S.—I'll be hanged if you do, tho', we don't have nothin' that way here, but Grub Hyson, and I reckon it's mighty good with sweetnin'. Play away, stranger, you kin sleep on the dry spot to-night.

T.—(After about two hours fiddling.) My friend, can't you tell me about the road I'm to travel to-morrow?

S.—To-morrow! Stranger, you won't git out'n these diggins for six weeks. But when it gits so you kin start, you see that big sloo over thar? Well, you have to git crost that, then you take the road up the bank, and in about a mile you'll come to a two-acre-and-a-half corn-patch. The corn's mitely in the weeds, but you needn't mind that: jist ride on. About a mile and a half or two miles from thar, you'll cum to the damdest swamp you ever struck in all your travels; it's boggy enouff to mire a saddle-blanket. Thar's a fust rate road about six feet under thar.

T.—How am I to get at it?

S.—You can't git at it nary time, till the weather stiffens down sum. Well, about a mile beyant, you come to a place whar thar's no roads. You kin take the right hand ef you want to; you'll foller it a mile or so, and you'll find it's run out; you'll then have to come back and try the left; when you git about two miles on that, you may know you're wrong, fur they ain't any road thar. You'll then think you're mity lucky ef you kin find the way back to my house, whar you kin cum and play on thara'r tune as long as you please.

Chapter IV
A Gallery of Fearsome Critters

It is hard to know what to call the beasts of American mythology: lies, whoppers, windies, or all three! But because they are so innocent and comically imaginative, let us call these beasties part of a comical bestiary of poetical critters.

Almost every western society has had a bestiary of such critters, and all have taken them seriously; all, that is, except American society, which invented them for the sheer hell of it and the joy to be had in telling about them.

Julius Caesar told in all seriousness of a four-legged creature he had seen that could not lie down because it had no joints in its legs (it slept leaning against a tree!). Egypt has its jinns, Japan its kappas, Ireland its fairies, and so on, all believed in and passed down through the generations. Even the Bible has its fearsome critters, such as in the Book of Job, 41:11-12. Here the Lord tells Job of the wonders of behemoth, a critter of frightening proportions:

> *His sneezings flash forth light,*
> *And his eyes are like the eyelids of the morning.*
> *Out of his mouth go burning torches,*
> *And sparks of fire leap forth.*

And Isaiah, too, has something to say about this critter Leviathan: In Chapter 27:1, we read:

> *In that day the Lord with his sore and great and strong sword*
> *will punish leviathan the slant serpent, and leviathan the*
> *   tortuous serpent,*
> *and He will slay the dragon that is in the sea.*

Psalms, too, talks about these critters in 74-14:

> *Thou didst shatter the heads of the sea-monsters in the waters.*
> *Thou didst crush the heads of Leviathan.*

Thus, we see that fearsome critters have a long and illustrious serious history, one that goes back "till the memory of man knoweth not to the contrary."

But Americans do not play second fiddle to any nation devising these critters. We invent, devise, create them better than anyone else: naturally! But only for the fun of it. And our television and cinema reflect our penchant for fearsome critters. One has only to recall recent imagined beasties that we have made a part of our comical bestiary of poetical critters: Mickey Mouse and Donald Duck, E.T., and Yoda, to see that we are still at it.

The telling of a tall tale about a fearsome critter takes a talented tale-teller or, rather, two of them. In his book on these critters, Henry Tryon has described his own experience with two masterful tale-tellers describing a fearsome critter.

"My first personal introduction to a specific 'critter' was while fighting fire on Attean Lake in 1908. Dick Fisher had landed me a summer job in the woods, but the cruising work had been suddenly interrupted by the bad fires which broke out that year. I was utterly new and green; but it just happened that the principal introducers, Sam Clarke and Walter Laurison (I wonder where they are now?) selected another youngster as a victim. This lad opened the way by remarking that on the trail back to camp that afternoon he had heard an extraordinary, screech-like cry which he could not identify. Given this opening, the teamplay developed between the two older men was simply marvelous. 'How did it go?' inquired Sam, full of seeming fatherly interest. 'Oh, I don't think I could imitate it,' replied the lad. A moment's pause. 'Reckon it was one o' them tree-squeaks,' put in Walter at the precise psychological moment; 'they're common hereabouts in July.' 'What's a tree-squeak like?' asked the victim, deliberately putting his foot in the trap. 'Wa-al—' drawled Sam, and the game was on. It was like watching two highly skilled bridge players. Sam would lead with a colorful bit of description, and Walter would follow suit with an arresting spot of personal experience, every detail being set forth with the utmost solemnity, and with exactly the correct degree of emphasis. At the end, so deftly had the cards been played that the listener was completely convinced of the animal's existence. This method of presentation is widely used. For the best results, two narrators who can "keep the ball in the air" are necessary, and perhaps an occasional general question is tossed to someone in the audience, such inquiries being invariably accorded a grave, corroborative nod."

★   ★   ★   ★

The Guyuscutus

Our literary zoo of poetical critters offers first a fearsome beast the record of which is almost as old as that of America. Every generation has heard of the Guyuscutus. Abraham Lincoln was reminded of the account you are about to read when Confederate warships failed to be seen at an expected naval battle the President had gone to witness.

The SPIRIT OF THE TIMES — a great early newspaper devoted to sports and humor — in 1845 printed this account of the Guyscutus. It tells about two "flat-broke" Yankees who used a Guyscutus to fill their empty pockets with hard cash extracted from the pockets of a gullible and too curious audience of "southroners."

A good story is told by somebody — we don't recollect who — of a couple Yankees who chanced to be traveling at the South, and had run short of funds. Out of "tin," and out at the toes, they hit upon the following expedient to raise the rhino.

By dint of address they contrived to come it over the printer, and procured a quantity of hand-bills, giving notice to the denizens of the town where they were stopping, that "a *monster* Guyuscutus," of the genus "*humm,*" would be exhibited on the following day, at a certain place — admittance 25 cents, children half price. A curtain was obtained, which was drawn across one end of the apartment where the show was to come off, and the time having arrived, one of the worthy pair performed the part of doorkeeper and receiver-general, while his companion in sin was busy behind the screen (which was so arranged as to prevent discoveries) where he kept up an incessant and most unearthly moaning, while the company were entering and being seated. The hour having at last arrived for the show to commence, the doorkeeper left his post, and marching across the hall, which was crowded with men, women and children, he disappeared behind the curtain. Immediately after his exit a terrific howling, and chaffering commenced, in the midst of which the clattering of chains and a heavy fall or two, were distinctly heard. A terrific struggle appeared to be going on behind the green baize, and an occasional "Oh! ah-hold hard, Jim" — "hit him on the head" — "that's it" — "no it isn't," etc., were heard for some minutes by the audience in front, who by this time had become greatly excited, and not a little alarmed. Amidst the call for the "manager" the exclamations were heard — "he'll break his chains" — "*there he goes!*" — and the doorkeeper rushes from behind the scenes, hatless and breathless, his hair on end, while he shouts at the top of his lungs — "Save yourselves, gentlemen! Save your children! *The Guyuscutus is loose!*" Everyone stampeded! Nobody saw again either Yankees or entrance money.

★   ★   ★   ★

The Guyuscutus has spawned varieties of related critters, cousins of a sort, one could call them, and such is the Gowrow, a critter that, like the Guyuscutus, lends itself to those in need of cash, and just in the nick of time in every case.

The Gowrow

The Gowrow is a critter that looks like a giant lizard twenty feet long, with enormous tusks. The critter is hatched from an egg that's as big as a beer keg. King-size. The Gowrow operates somewhat like the Guyuscutus, as described by a fellow who captured one, and described the circumstances surrounding the event: "Presently the earth swayed as if another earthquake were taking place. The waters of the lake began to splash and roar like the movement of the ocean waves . . ." And so on, until the Gowrow emerges as a kind of cross between an elephant and a dinosaur. Another fellow claims to have caught one of them by

HYLTON

GOWROW

feeding it a wagon load of dried apples, which so swelled the critter that it could not squeeze back into its burrow. After muzzling and binding it, the fellow hauled it to town to a huge tent and thereafter sold tickets at two bits each to see the beast. There was a capacity audience. Then came: "A roar, followed by the sound of shots and chains clanking was heard from backstage and the showman, bloodied and tattered, rushed out shouting, "Run for your lives, the Gowrow has broke loose." The report has it that the tent collapsed, women screamed, and the crowd lit out for safer places.

★   ★   ★   ★

The Sidehill Dodger

But the most storied of all fearsome critters is the Sidehill Dodger which is also called the Sidehill Hoofer, Sidehill Wowser, Gwinter, Prock, Yamhill Lunkus, Packabore, and lots more! This odd beast has legs on one side considerably shorter than those on the other side.

This odd condition came about over millenia, and was caused by constant grazing on steep hillsides, in a single direction, circling the steep mountains in search of grass. As is plainly seen, this present condition makes it quite impossible for the Dodger to walk on level ground; only a hillside allows the Dodger to graze with its short legs uphill as it walks, its longer set of legs holding it erect and level and balancing things from its downhill side.

The eggs of the Dodger are huge, one of them making breakfast for twenty-five men! At the end of its tail there are two tough hooks to attach itself to the top of a cliff and, by hanging therefrom, to rest itself.

There are two varieties of Sidehill Dodger: one that feeds clockwise with short legs on the uphill *right* side, and one that feeds counter-clockwise with short legs on the uphill *left* side. If the twain should meet, look out! The only way they can pass is to fight one another to the death. The loser rolls over and down the mountain, unable to rise because of its unbalanced legs, and thus frees the way for the other. A man caught in the middle between the two fighting Dodgers has only to take a step uphill, or down, to escape, since the Dodger cannot veer to one side or the other without falling down to its death. But should it forget, and pursue the man, uphill or down, it loses its balance, falls over and cannot raise itself erect again. It lies there screaming until it starves to death.

In trying to capture one of these beasts for Ringling Brothers circus, a posse of Sidehill Dodger hunters chased one completely around a mountain and into a blind canyon where they congratulated themselves that finally they had it trapped. But at the last minute, the critter turned itself inside out and ran around the other way, its legs reversed so that it could escape. And that's why you never see a Sidehill Dodger in a Ringling Brothers circus.

It is said that in the early days, the Sidehill Dodger migrated to California from New England. The flat prairies of the Middle West caused them no end of trouble until they discovered that if a Dodger with short legs on the right could team up with a counter-clockwise Dodger whose legs were short on the left side, both sets of short legs in the middle and out of the way, each Dodger leaning against the other, they then could navigate the endless miles of level prairie on the level. Thus it is seen that cooperation is not confined to the human species. In fact, some of the Sidehill Dodgers who paired up in this way became so attached that they decided to go through life side-by-side, as a team. In this way the Dodgers discovered that they could not only inhabit the steep slopes of the mountain states, as singles, but could team up with each other, with each set of long legs outside, short legs paired inside, achieving a perfect, paired balance on the level, and living a double life on the prairie, thus proving the marvelous symbiosis that nature employs to perpetuate a species otherwise doomed.

SIDE HILL DODGER

★   ★   ★   ★

The Hoopsnake

When they begin to learn about nature, and snakes, most kids hear about the Hoopsnake, a critter that takes its tail in its mouth to form a wheel of itself, and in this form can roll toward or away from battle. Marvelous tales of the Hoopsnake are told in every American generation, and each adult expands on the story.

There are two qualities that run through all the stories about this fabulous snake: that it attacks when threatened, and that its venom is deadly and can do queer things to not only humans that it strikes but inanimate objects as well. Here is an example: A Hoopsnake felt threatened by a wagon back around the turn of the century. It whipped itself into a hoop, rolled downhill at terrific speed, striking at the horse-drawn wagon, hitting the wagon's wood tongue. The tongue began to swell until the venom spread beyond it and welled over into the axle, which then swelled, causing the wheels to lock so that the wagon was immobilized for ten days. But this wagoneer was considered lucky because in another, similar case, the tongue swelled mightily until it put so much pressure on the ring binding it to the ox-yoke that the tongue exploded under the pressure, killing both oxen, and causing the driver to be mighty fidgity for a week.

In yet another illustrative example, a feller was hoeing weeds in his garden when a Hoopsnake decided to attack. It did, hitting the hoe handle, which then swelled so much that the feller sawed ten fence posts out of that old hoe handle. And they weren't piddly line-posts, either, they were big, heavy end and brace posts of the kind that cost a lot of dollars in the auction ring.

★   ★   ★   ★

The legends go far back, and the Hoopsnake often goes by other names. John Lawson describes one as the Horn Snake, back in 1709, in his "A New Voyage to Carolina."

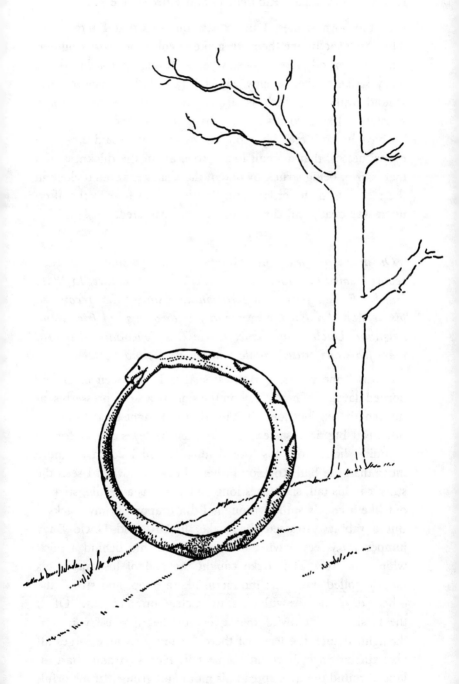

HOOP SNAKE

HYLTON

Of the horn snakes, I never saw but two that I remember. They are exactly like the rattlesnake in color, but rather lighter. They hiss exactly like a goose when anything approaches them. They strike at their enemy with tail (and kill whatsoever they wound with it), which is armed at the end with a horny substance, like a cock's spur. This is their weapon.

I have heard it credibly reported, by those who said they were eye-witnesses, that a small locust tree, about the thickness of a man's arm, being struck by one of these snakes at ten o'clock in the morning, then verdant and flourishing, at four in the afternoon was dead, and the leaves red and withered.

★   ★   ★   ★

On down the years, others reported on the snake and each report seemed to embellish the critter's horrific nature. In 1859, Harden E. Taliaferro, a superb southern story teller, recounted his version through the eyes and mouth of his old friend and neighbor, Uncle Davy Lane. Uncle Davy encountered one of these fearsome critters while hunting on Round Peak.

It was "one uv the curiousest snakes I uver seen in all my borned days . . . There it lay on the side uv a steep presserpis, at full length, ten foot long, its tail strait out, right up the presserpis, head big as a sasser, right toards me, eyes red as forked lightnin', lickin' out his forked tongue, and I could no more move than the Ball Rock on Fisher's Peak. But when I seen the stinger in his tail, six inches long and sharp as a needle, stickin' out like a cock's spur, I thought I'd a drapped in my tracks." But a rabbit distracted the snake, luckily, and Uncle Davy jumped forty feet down the mountain and hid behind a thick white oak tree. The snake caught the end of his tail in his mouth, rolled down the mountain like a hoop, and struck the other side of the tree with his stinger, clean up to his tail. "Of all the hissin' and blowin' that uver you hearn sense you seen daylight, it tuck the lead. Ef there'd a bin forty-nine forges all ablowin' at once, it could't a beat it. He rared and charged, lapped round the tree, spread his mouf and grinned at me orful, puked and spit quarts and quarts of green pisen at me, an' made the air stink with his nasty breath." Uncle Davy seized his gun, Bucksmasher, and finally shot the snake between the eyes. "Soon as he were dead as a herrin'; all the leaves was wilted like a fire had gone through its branches." When Uncle Davy passed by three weeks later, the "Whole tree was dead as a door-nail."

In Mississippi, Ike Smith was out in his garden with his favorite hoe, weeding away to beat sixty! Suddenly he sees this Hoopsnake coming at him. He throws up that hoe for a guard and the snake hit it a lick, then rolled on. That hoe had a fine, mahogony handle and Ike was some fearful that he might lose it. Sure enough, the handle starts to swell. And it swelled and it swelled until Ike called his boys to bring the wagon. They did and Ike and his ten kids hauled that huge mahogany log to town to the sawmill where they cut 7000 board feet of lumber out of it. And that's how the Smith Lumber Yard got its start down there, got to material to open up with, and the seed money to finance the business. Yes sir!

There was another feller down in Texas had about as good luck as Ike Smith. The Hoopsnake struck his axe handle of good white ash wood, and when it swelled, he, too, hauled it in his wagon to town and got it sawed into enough wood to build him a house. But this feller didn't come out ahead, as did Ike Smith, because when he painted that house, the kerosene thinner took all the poison out of the wood, and it began to shrink on him. It shrank and shrank until it was hardly bigger than a bird house, and a small one at that. Ike had to build himself another house, all right, but that bird house of his was known as the most elaborate and refined in all of Texas. It was a beauty. How many birds can boast a 12-room house? And with three bathrooms?

★   ★   ★   ★

A similar story occured to a feller out in Illinois. He was standing alongside a slender sapling when he saw a Hoopsnake rolling hell-bent-for-election toward him. He stepped aside in the nick of time and that snake buried its stinger in the sapling. That little tree swelled up to the size of a mighty oak and the feller cut it down, took it to town, and had it sawed into boards. Then he built an enormous cow barn out of that wood, but he made the same mistake as the feller from Texas. He had kerosene in his paint (for paint thinner) and it took the poison out. His barn shrunk down to a tiny facsimile of itself but it sure made a fine dog house. The cows were desolate at losing their home, just stood around looking resentfully at the hound dog lying around so comfortably in his new dog house. But there was nothing to be done about it. That lucky dog had the only dog house in Illinois with automatic waterers, and a hay mow to sleep in.

★   ★   ★   ★

In all that time, only one fatal accident happened as the result of Hoopsnake venom. The snake struck at a man, missed him but hit the tree alongside him. That tree died, of course, and the man forgot all about it. Too bad, because he should have remembered. Well, that feller was out hunting one day, some five years later, and after his lunch under that same very dead tree, he took his knife and cut a toothpick out of it and foolishly picked his teeth, pricked his gums and was dead of the poison before nightfall.

★   ★   ★   ★

Down in Arkansas they tell the story of two Ozark boys standing in front of the village store watching the town character peddle down the street on his early American bicycle, the one that had the enormous front wheel and the tiny one behind. "Here comes the Devil," one boy said, "And he's a-ridin' a hoop snake!" The other little boy says, "Sho is. An' they's a young hoop snake a-follerin' like a colt."

★   ★   ★   ★

In the past, when traveling, the Hoop Snake rolled toward its destination in an east-west direction, or clockwise. But about one hundred years ago, the female of the species became infected with an odd disease, the Latin name of which is *Traces Overthrowum,* a disorienting illness that reverses certain previous life-patterns. Thus, the female Hoop Snake reversed its ancient pattern of movement and became a west-to-east mover, or one that moved counter-clockwise. Since the males were immune to this disease, it is obvious why the species has all but disappeared. Only at six o'clock and twelve o'clock were the reptiles close enough for breeding, and then only the most outrageously speedy and lightning-quick males could get the job done. Thus it is that so few Hoop Snakes are sighted today.

★   ★   ★   ★

The Rubber Snake

There have been only three reports of sighting a Rubber Snake, but all of them are in essential agreement. One reporter calls the Rubber Snake the most obliging reptile critter in the world. He saw one obliging critter hook his *tail* in the ring at the top of a family's laundry pole in their backyard, then snake his way down that pole and wriggle forty feet to another pole across the yard, then climb that second pole and tie his *front* end into the ring at the top of the pole. The good wife in that family was able to hang a week's washing on that line! To expedite drying, the family trotted out a roll of good old-time jazz and played it on their pianola so that the obliging Rubber Snake could have entertainment while he served as the laundry line. The Rubber Snakes have, it seems, an advanced sense of rythm as evidenced by the wonderful hootchy-kootchy dances that snake performed while the waving and bouyant clothes dried faster and faster. The shirts did a minuet, the pants did a jig, blouses did a hula-hula, sox did the old soft shoe, while wash dresses did a splendid fox trot until ever bit of that clothing was dry three hours before the neighbors'.

CACTUS CAT

★   ★   ★   ★

The Cactus Cat

This critter is known only in the State of Arizona, and mainly in the area around Phoenix, Prescott, and Tucson. Often seen in pioneer days, modern civilization has caused its near extinction. Few there are today who have seen the Cactus Cat, but once seen, that cat is never forgotten. Its hair is barbed like a porcupine's quills so that its "fur" must be stroked as the barbs lay. Or else. It's tail is forked in two places so that as it walks, dragging it tail behind it (just like little Bo Peep's sheep) it leaves a very well-swept path for others to follow. This causes it to be named, in some high-toned quarters, the Neat-Tail Cat. But its most noteworthy feature is the bony protuberances that line the front and back of its front legs. These extrusions are very sharp so that when the cat travels its rounds, it slashes the base of every cactus it passes, moving always in a circuitous route. Thus it manages to return toward the end of the week to the cactus first slashed to find it exuding an aromatic juice in a high state of fermentation. The Cactus Cat greedily consumes the heady beverage and soon becomes infected with a variety of feline intoxication, making up words to popular tunes like "Yes sir! That's My Baby," and "There Ain't Nothin Like My Cactus Cat—My Pussy." When the Cactus Cat becomes too giddy to continue on, it climbs into a comfortable notch of one of the cactus plants, fastens itself securely with recycled catgut, and falls asleep, giving the wounded cactus plants time to heal. When the Cactus Cat awakens, it begins its rounds all over again, giving credence to the popular belief that the Cactus Cat has eighty-one lives; seventy-two of them due to the pickling effect of the cactus effluent, nine of them due to the nature of a cat-type critter.

★   ★   ★   ★

The Squonk

Another rare critter is the Squonk. It is a cuddly, cute beast that few have seen, and those few have glimpsed it only along the eastern seaboard. It is a shy animal, traveling mostly at

HYLTON

SQUONK

night. The reason for its shyness is that it is covered with a kind of eczema, or pimples, from head to tail and is unhappy over this most of the time. It is a truly melancholy beast subject to deep fits of depression, whereupon it sheds tears, the liquid falling profusely enough to allow hunters to follow its trail of salty, moist liquid. If a hunter corners the beast, it may even dissolve itself in tears. There is one case on record where one was actually captured, put in the hunter's game bag, and forgotten until the hunter heard sounds that went "blurb," "gurgle," "blurp," whereupon he put down the bag, looked into it, and discovered that the poor critter had dissolved itself in tears and all that was left was a pool of salty water through which air arose going "blurb," "gurgle," "blurp." Since that day, only four have been sighted, and those on frosty, moonless nights when the Squonk becomes nearly moribund, sighs repeatedly and can be heard weeping intermittently over its pimply condition. Usually, the sorrowful sound of the Squonk emenates from neighborhood cemeteries.

Addendum: There is a long-standing story in upstate New York to the effect that a departed Squonk had its tombstone engraved with these simple if heart-rending words: "Pimples is Hell."

★   ★   ★   ★

The Bildad

In upper Maine they tell of an odd critter that gives off a noise like a canoe paddle struck flat against the water, a sound that comes out as a resounding "SPLAT!" If you were ever in those parts, and chanced to hear a "SPLAT" like that, you probably heard the oh-so-elsusive critter, the Bildad, out fishing for his dinner. This critter has kangaroo-like hind legs, and short, nondescript front ones. Its feet are webbed, like a duck's, and it has a hooked bill of enormous weight, so heavy in fact that the head is forced down, giving it a prayerful, penitent look. It fishes for its dinner in this manner: immobile and in a crouch on some grassy point jutting into a lake, it awaits the surfacing of a trout

BILDAD

or bass seeking an insect for its own dinner. When the fish surfaces, the Bildad leaps from its crouch, soars out over the water, and just a shade beyond where the fish surfaced, whereupon it drops like a shot and strikes the finny *pisces* a tremendous blow with its tail, stunning it so that it is easily mouthed by the Bildad which then swims calmly to shore with its dinner. The ability of the Bildad to do such lightning-like broadjumps is simply not to be believed! Some jumps carry the Bildad forty-fifty feet out into the lake! The United States Olympic team has long sought a Bildad in order to study just what quality or chemical make-up allows it to jump so much farther than our Olympic champions. It is believed that possession of this knowledge, kept secret would enable the United States to win all places at the Olympic games broadjump on into the forseeable future. Thus, there may be something of international importance about this critter.

Lumberjacks tell of the delicious taste of the Bildad. But such tales are altogether hearsay since nobody has ever come forward to say that they have actually tasted one of these critters. We do know that one day they actually caught and prepared a Bildad for dinner as a savory stew. In the process of cooking it, one man tasted the stew, as good cooks must do, whereupon his body stiffened, his eyes bugged, he jumped five feet straight up in the air, and then took off for the lake. From the shore he leaped out over the water in a *fifty-foot broadjump,* landing in a squatting position, both arms striking the water in an ear-splitting "SPLAT!" Unfortunately, the poor fellow sank like a brick, and his body was never recovered. And since that fatal jump, no lumberjack has ever dared to touch Bildad meat — assuming they could get it — not even with a ten-foot pole. No sir!

Addendum: But the search goes on spurred by the possibility that the Russians, too, know about the Bildad and may be scouting upper Maine even at this very time in an effort to get a Bildad before we do, so that they can defeat US at the next Olympics.

The National Olympic Committee has requested that we ask all readers to keep an eye and ear peeled, in their native habitat,

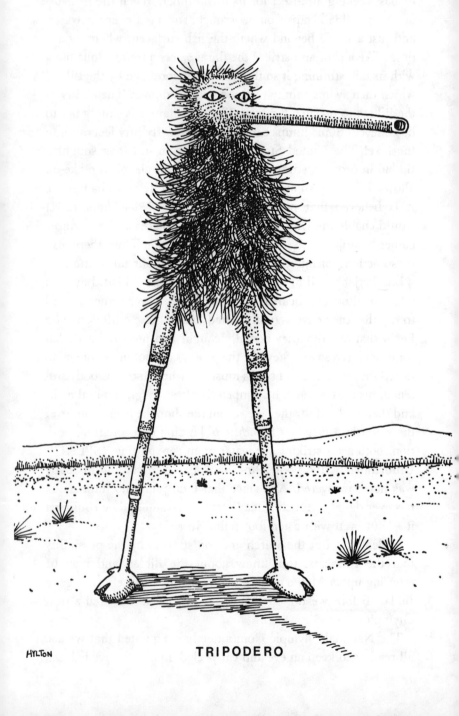

HYLTON

TRIPODERO

in the hope that someone, somewhere, will sight a Bildad that can then be captured and analyzed with a view to sustaining our national honor at the next Olympic games.

★   ★   ★   ★

The Tripodero

This odd critter has telescoping legs, a trait that allows it, when in thick brush, to extend its legs so that its head is above the brush, and it can look unobstructedly for its victim for lunch. The body of the Tripodero is thick and squat and ideal for thrusting through heavy brush. Its head is long and thin, something like the nozzle on a fire hose. Now . . . when the Tripodero has elevated its head above the brush, and has sighted game, its quarry, suitable for lunch, the critter aims its head at the victim, regurgitates a golf-ball-size pebble that it keeps stored in its stomach in a special pouch nature has provided it for just this purpose. Holding the pebble at the ready in its nozzle-like mouth, the Tripodero takes careful aim, breathes deeply once to steady itself, then fires the pebble at the quarry in a whooshing action precisely like that of the biblical David with his slingshot against Goliath.

Once the shot is fired, the Tripodero retracts its legs, thus lowering itself so that it can burrow through the thick brush to claim its lunch, be it a rabbit, a raccoon, or a rat. Wonderfully, the fat of its victims provides the grease needed to keep its telescoping legs working smoothly, thus providing another example of symbiosis in nature.

★   ★   ★   ★

The Whirling Whimpus

This curious critter lives among the hardwood forests of Southern Illinois and can be found throughout the Ozarks. Without doubt it has been responsible for the disappearance of more Ozark hunters and trappers than any other cause.

A block-buster beast, it can grow tall as eight feet, is shaped like a fifty-gallon barrel, and is covered with rough fur. The

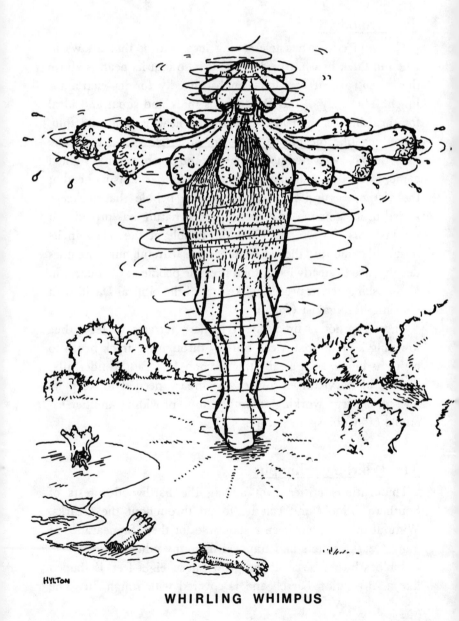

WHIRLING WHIMPUS

horse-like rear legs join at the fetlock to create a single, broad and dangerous hoof. The front legs are long, sinewy and powerful; each leg ending in a paddle-like form, something like a steak-thick ping-pong paddle.

The Whirling Whimpus is carnivorous, with deer, bear, rabbit, sheep, cattle, *humans* all part of its diet. It is a versatile eater and a superb hunter. It pursues its prey as follows: about sunset it stations itself near a bend in the trail, and then begins to whirl around and around, spinning on that huge and single rear hoof. One observor claims that he has clocked a Whirling Whimpus whirling at 2500 m.p.h. This same observor warns that it is dangerous to get too close to the Whimpus when it first begins to rev up and whirl since, at that early state of whirl, the air is terribly churned, roiled so that it can blow a man right into the next county if he's too close to it. However, that is all that can happen up to 1500 r.p.m. After that, look out! Approaching 2500 r.p.m., the Whirling Whimpus spins so fast that it becomes quite invisible and the only evidence of its presence is a terribly high-pitched, murderous moaning sound that is blessedly inaudible to most ears. But for ears tuned to its high-decibel moan, it is terribly dangerous, because the moan is so extraordinarily seductive, enticing the hearer with a kind of sexy, syncopated sound, that it draws the listener as surely as catnip draws cats. The titillated listener walks with increasing speed toward the moan-music until he enters the area flailed by the Whirling Whimpus, whereupon he is at once macerated — as if too long in a wine-press — into a viscous, sweet liquid that sticks to the front paddles of the Whimpus. The critter then slows down and prepares to eat its sweet and liquid and, sadly, sometimes human dinner.

Addendum: One current observer claims to have sighted a Whirling Whimpus coming out of a tavern in the town of Toonerville, Mo., in mid-afternoon of a mid-week in mid-July of mid-1983. The critter seemed pleased, satisfied and wore the typical grin of a satiated Whirling Whimpus. In view of this rare sighting, tavern frequenters are urged to keep their eyes open for

WAMPUS CAT

HYLTON

other tavern-happy Whirling Whimpuses, and to report them to their nearest Department of Vital Statistics, because it is possible that we are witnessing an evolutionary change of the dietary habits of this critter. It may be changing from a carnivorarian to an alcoholicarian, and this portends immeasurably safer paths through Ozark trails frequented by Ozark hunters and trappers . . . as well as creating a new category of customer for our liquor industries.

★   ★   ★   ★

The Wampus Cat

This feline critter is distinguished by a right foreleg shaped like a very long surgeon's forceps. It is said that a northwoods veterinarian operated on the shoulder of a Wampus Cat and forgot to remove the forceps when he sewed up the wound. That forgotten forceps took root and a genetic change occured that gave all ensuing Wampus Cats a forceps for a right front leg. A rare specimen, the only known Wampus Cat ever to be on display, is in the city museum at Lake Nebagamon, Wisconsin. The right leg of that stuffed critter, when extended to its full, forceps-like length, measures sixteen feet!

But the Wampus Cat can be very useful. During an epidemic of eagles in Montana, a flock of Wampus Cats was imported, placed on several mountain tops, and set to catching the pestiferous eagles. They were successful. They would crouch on a mountain top, hunker down unobstrusively, create in a soaring eagle an uncontrollable desire to see just what in heck such an oddly misplaced cat was doing on that particular mountain top. The eagle would fly lower and lower, looking and looking, and when close enough, the Wampus Cat would snake out its forceps-like leg, and snag the eagle. If hungry, the Wampus would eat the eagle; feathers, beak, nails and all. If not, it would pluck the more beautiful, useful feathers and give them to the neighboring Indians for their headdress. The Indians, out of gratitude, would never trap or shoot a Wampus Cat, and that is one reason why there are so few to be seen in museums. But the

Wampus Cat is not much to look at. The hide is mostly quills, and the color is "akin to that of a Christmas tie."

But a problem developed. The Wampus Cat grew so happy in its new habitat that it refused to leave, proliferated, and became a menace, in that the loud clanking of its metallic front leg, working at garnering eagles and other birds, was so loud and so constant that the inhabitants in valleys below could not sleep. It was like a steady anvil song atop those mountains! To get rid of the Wampus Cats, and get some sleep, the valley inhabitants invented imitation eagles made of light metal, power-operated. When these eagles were flown close to a Wampus Cat, the latter would reach out, clamp down on them and yowl like heck at the pain from those metal bones. It was like trying to chew a ceramic cherry. The region was soon clear of the critters!

★   ★   ★   ★

But the reputation of the Wampus Cat lingered on and proliferated with time, bringing the most outlandish stories about them. Here is how an early observer, Henry H. Tryon, described those stories.

Since the first specimen was discovered scratching false blazes on mountain trails, the Wampus Cat has been blamed for a variety of forest tribulations. If a Wampus wades a stream, the fish won't bite for seven days. When the Wampus is on the prowl the only game abroad is the fool hen. The howl of the Wampus on a lonely night will curdle a crock of sourdough. Females of the species may be killed only with a crosscut saw. The males, practically indestructible, carry in their fur the germ of blister rust. Under the influence of a full moon, the glare from their eyes starts forest fires. Their footprints are visible only in solid rock. They steal prospectors' picks to brush their teeth.

Now those are canards of the worst sort. But that is what happens when we make judgments about people or animals or things about which, or whom, we are unfamiliar.

★   ★   ★   ★

The Swamp Auger

The following three fearsome critters were vouched for by Henry Tryon in his 1939 book entitled (what else?) FEARSOME CRITTERS. The first critter is a deceptively harmless and charming fish that resembles a common lake or river snag and is, therefore, named the Swamp Augur. This fish-like reptile lays in wait for fisherman in rowboats, and can await them for a week, a month, sometimes for years. But when his great day comes, and the rowboat approaches what appears to be a snag but is really a Swamp Auger, the critter at once snuggles under the boat and, with its auger-like proboscis, drills a three-inch hole in the bottom before you can say Jack Robinson. The boat sinks at once unless you know what to do. The trick is to carry a jar of McDonald's special hamburger seasoning, and to sprinkle it on the augur-nose, causing it to sneeze with delight and to hold its proboscis tight in the hole, plugging it securely while it actually pleads, by snorting, for more of the marvelous seasoning. The savvy fisherman will, with one hand, row toward shore while with the other he sprinkles seasoning (between sneezings) in the nostrils of the Swamp Augur. Once ashore, the fisherman can thank his lucky stars that the Swamp Augur is addicted to McDonald's special hamburger seasoning.

Caveat: never go back to that same lake because the Swamp Augur never forgets the delicious sneezes you gave him and will wait all its remaining life for a return engagement. Should you be so foolish as to fish that lake again, you can be sure the Swamp Augur, wiser from his experience with you the last time, will not let you leave him ever again. To be forewarned is to be foreseasoned.

★   ★   ★   ★

The Whiffenpoof
(Sometimes called the Gilli-Galoo Fish)

This fish has the imposing Latin name: *Pisces absurdus tumescens*, but for us to use the high-falutin Latin seemed, for an

AGROPELTER

outdoors writer, merely an affectation. So we chose not to use it. We hope the reader will understand. But here is The Gilli-Galoo.

This tasty fish is found in "perfectly round lakes," assuring its rarity and its perpetuation. To take a Gilli-Galoo, the fisherman/hunter (both skills are needed as will be seen) boats around the lake, following the circumference exactly. When he has made three complete rounds, thus dizzying the following Gilli-Galoo, the hunter/fisherman bores a rectangular hole in the water at the exact point where he commenced his round-trip, then baits the hole on all four sides with chunky peanut butter (the smooth kind won't do). When the Gilli-Galoo sees or scents the luscious bait, he comes to the surface of the square hole and commences to lap-up the tasty bait. Allow the Gilli-Galoo to become totally engrossed in his banquet, then spit tobacco or snuff juice in his eye. The critter at once becomes so enraged that he swells with anger until wedged tight and can then be easily caught by excising the water around him and removing the square package — water, fish, and all — to your creel.

A caveat. One young feller tried to use marijuana smoke instead of tobacco or snuff juice, but the results were disastrous. The fish elongated, then shot up through the hole into the air where it flew around and around the lake getting higher and higher until lost from view. Obviously, that is no way to catch a Gilli-Galoo. All are advised to stay with traditional methods, either tobacco or snuff — or both.

★   ★   ★   ★

The Agropelter

This critter has been sighted in American forests from Maine to northern California. It is a recognized menace that every person vacationing or working in dense, coniferous forests should be aware of. Its menace arises in the fact that when disturbed, its method of strike is to tear a limb from the tree of its choice, and then to hurl it with deadly accuracy, striking and burying the person that disturbed it. Responsible authorities believe that the plethora of persons who have disappeared while in northern forests is due in no small measure to the lethal aim of the Agropelter.

An important aspect to its menace arises because only one person has ever seen and identified the critter. He is David Matthews of San Clemente, California. Luckily, Mr. Matthews is an indefatigable naturalist who is aware of the Agropelter so that, one day while wandering the Mt. Shasta region of Northern California, observing the Stripe-Rumped Caleyeopea — his special interest — he heard the sharp cra-a-ack of a snapped-off limb. He had time only to turn, and a moment only to see an Agropelter in process of snapping off a huge limb, then elevating and hurling it at him with indescribable velocity. He had only time to begin a dodge when the limb hit him on his east side and permanently bent him in the shape of what orthopedists call "the Right-Angle Syndrome, east phase." The patient is left in a half-square shape so that he/she can walk only in square configurations. Mr. Matthews is something of a wit and grins wryly when he says he doesn't mind his present shape since before it he had always "gone around in circles."

Matthews had only a brief glimpse of the Agropelter, but his is the only responsible view of it that we have. "That critter," said Mr. Matthews, "had a face like a gorilla, and a body heavily haired and spotted just like a leopard so that it was superbly camouflaged. The arms were very long — thirty feet at least, it seemed to me — and they were shaped like tree limbs, but were flexible as bull whips, whipping about to find the exact kind of limb. Before it got me, I managed to see the critter wrap its arms around the limb of its choice and snap it off (that was the 'cra-a-ack' I heard) then hurl it at me so speedily that I could not dodge. It hit me on the left, east side leaving me in the square condition in which you see me."

So much for the most credible witness we have. Nevertheless . . . all forest workers and wanderers are advised to be on the lookout for the Agropelter as described by Mr. Matthews, for better or worse, since his is as they say, "the only game in town.''

Anyone who truly views an Agropelter is requested to get in touch with this publisher, who will then make the information available to all states wherein the Agropelter is known to so-journ.

★　　★　　★　　★

The Central American Whintosser

William T. Cox, forester and author of FEARSOME CREATURES OF THE LUMBERWOODS wrote in 1909 about critters that compete with man for *lebensraum* in these United States. One of these critters is the Central American Whintosser, a curious beast that immigrated here in 1906. At first it was content to stay along the "coastal ranges of California," Mr. Cox states, but by 1983 the critter had migrated to almost every state west of the Mississippi. It is known everywhere for its furious irascibility. The critter is just plain mean! It's not that it bites or claws but that the commotion it stirs is worse than any bite or clawing. The Whintosser's head and tail are fastened to its body by almost frictionless swivels that, when angry, are whirled at unbelievable speeds, and create such a turbulence that nothing is safe. Some folks, caught by the whirling winds of the Whintosser say the power of the air is of extreme hurricane force taking everything not nailed or tied down before it. It is especially hard on male wigs, female false eyelashes and nails, formal dinner settings, and automobiles in used-car lots.

The body of the Whintosser is long and rectangular with a set of four legs on each of its four sides, a condition that renders it immune to windstorms, including its own, since whichever way the critter is blown, it lands on its feet, on one side or the other. For some reason the Whintosser resists killing in the usual way, probably because the whirling tail and head deflect arrows, bullets, clubs, etc. But Irving Dilliard, a seasoned hunter from Collinsville, Illinois, discovered that if the beast is enticed by its favorite food — hot tamales — into a culvert of the exact size, its

HYLTON

CENTRAL AMERICAN WHINTOSSER

feet are all on the surface at the same time, forcing it to walk in four directions at once, thus tearing itself apart.

The toenails of the Central American Whintosser offer us their only useful addition to our American culture. These one hundred and sixty toenails, gathered from the ten toes on sixteen feet, on four sets of four legs, are much coveted by the fashion-conscious American female. In the November 31, 1983, issue of *Women's Wear Daily*, bible to the women's fashion industry, an entire section was devoted to the stunning jewelry being made from the chameleon-like toenails of the Whintosser. These toenails have the uncanny quality of changing color to harmonize with any outfit a woman wears. Thus, as may be seen by even the most fashion-ignorant, this toenail item is invaluable in necklaces, earrings, brooches and pins, rings, bellybuckles, and the like.

Women's Wear Daily strongly recommends these gems of toenails be worn by the plainer sort of woman whose ordinary looks are not normally noticed by suitors beguiled by the scintillating and evanescent — if unpredictable — beauty of the Whintossers' ultimate appendage or, to phrase it otherwise, its soignee toenails.

★   ★   ★   ★

The Slidedown Bolter
(Macrostoma saxiperrumptus)

In the mountains of Colorado, where in summer the woods are becoming infested with tourists, much uneasiness has been caused by the presence of the Slide-Rock Bolter. This frightful animal lives only in the steepest mountain country where the slopes are greater than 45 degrees. It has an immense head, with small eyes, and a mouth somewhat on the order of a sculpin, running back beyond its ears. The tail consists of a divided flipper, with enormous grab-hooks, which it fastens over the crest of the mountain or ridge, often remaining there motionless for days at a time, watching the gulch for tourists or any other hapless creature that may enter it. At the right moment, after sighting a

SLIDE DOWN BOLTER

HYLTON

tourist, it will lift its tail, thus loosening its hold on the mountain, and with its small eyes riveted on the poor unfortunate, and drooling this skid grease from the corners of its mouth, which greatly accelerates its speed, the Bolter comes down like a toboggan, scooping in its victim as it goes, its own impetus carrying it up the next slope, where it again slaps its tail over the ridge and waits. Whole parties of tourists are reported to have been gulped at one swoop by the Slide-Rock Bolter, and guides are becoming cautious about taking parties far back into the hills. The animal is a menace not only to tourists but to the woods as well. Many a draw through spruce-covered slopes has been laid low, the trees being knocked out by the roots or mowed off as by a scythe where the Bolter has crashed through from the peaks above.

A forest ranger, whose district includes the rough country between Ophir Peaks and the Lizard Head, conceived the bold idea of decoying a Slide-Rock Bolter to its own destruction. A dummy tourist was rigged up with plaid Norfolk jacket, knee breeches, and a guide book to Colorado. It was then filled full of giant powder and fulminate caps and posted in a conspicuous place, where, sure enough, the next day it attracted the attention of a Bolter which had been hanging for days on the slope of Lizard Head. The resulting explosion flattened half the buildings in Rico, which were never rebuilt, and the surrounding hills fattened flocks of buzzards the rest of the summer.

Addendum: back in January of 1982, just before dark, a skier named Bernard Skiwax was schussing slowly homeward when he noticed what appeared to be a small avalanche moving downhill off the slope below him. He watched it with some trepidation soon turned into stunned interest that finally stopped him in his tracks. The snowslide appeared to undulate rather than slide! And it seemed to have an animal, rather than an avalanche contour! He squinted hard through the dusk and made out a beast that very much resembled the elusive Slide-Rock Bolter (the skier was an avid collector of American folktales, and so knew all about such critters) only the critter seen on the slope was all-white, and had several enormous hooks

STAND UPRITE

on its tail. What really drew his attention was the fact that each hook was loaded with mittens, gloves, ski caps, dark glasses, odd skis, poles, in short, the entire apparatus that skiers use. Frightened at what he saw, Mr. Skiwax hurtled homeward to his lodge where he breathlessly told his story to a goggle-eyed, incredulous set of rosy-cheeked, if exhausted, skiers sitting around the fire. Complete silence met his story. Was it horror? Medieval terror at the unknown? Disbelief? Too much alcohol?

Finally the savant of the group, 80-year-old Stamford Conn, broke the silence. "So that's where my mittens went," he ejaculated. Another joined in with, "So that's what happened to my ski cap!" "And my skis!" shouted another. On and on it went until all could account for every stitch and piece of lost equipment.

At last they lapsed into silence, overcome by the enormity of their discovery, the scientific wonder of it, the austerity of Max's revelation.

But! That was the last sighting of a Snow-White Bolter, the presumed mutation and present embodiment of the infamous Slide-Rock Bolter. Was Bernard Skiwax's late-night sighting an apparition? Hallucination? Wishful thought? Too many Martinis while en route to the lodge? No one knows. But all skiers are urged to be alert when on ski slopes at dusk when, it is believed, the movement of the Snow-White Bolter against the dark background of night, makes it then, and only then, visible to the human eye. Think of the significance of the finding! Millions of dollars in clothing and equipment — now the presumed diet of the Snow-White Bolter — will be saved. And perhaps, just maybe, the explanation for a number of missing skiers, and others, in the vicinity of Aspen will have been found.

★   ★   ★   ★

The Standuprite

The first recorded sighting and description of this type of critter was that of Julius Caesar in his Commentaries, on his expedition to Gaul (6th Book, Chapter 27). He described the typically jointless legs of this huge critter, a fact that disallows it to lie down to sleep. To sleep, it must recline against a tree or, in rare instances when in treeless terrain, against a building such as an outhouse. The physical fact is that if the Standuprite falls flat on the ground, it cannot ever arise because it cannot bend its jointless legs so as to get up — and is doomed.

One of the few American sightings and descriptions was done by Henry Tryon in this century. He gave us a graphic view of the Northwoods variety of this critter, describing it as thirteen feet tall and weighing nearly two tons when mature. Its totally bald head is covered with lumps and bumps and sumps that would cause "the best phrenologist in the world to throw in his hand if asked to make a reconnaissance of this party's dome." Tryon went on to describe the hair of the critter as resembling pine needles. Its diet consists of pine knots and pine cones and, as might be expected, it leaks pine pitch from every pore of its enormous body. The sticky pitch exudate traps and destroys the mosquitos coming from the northern swamp and lake areas, rendering the otherwise unbearably mosquito-ridden region habitable by man. Hence, the Standuprite is a benign critter.

The most recent sighting was done by a farmer in Arkansas who wrote a Ph.D. thesis on a variant of the critter, describing its hair as, curiously, resembly cotton thread and not pine needles. Too, its diet had changed from pine knots to cotton seeds so that instead of leaking pitch, it leaked cottonseed oil that the children of the farmer gathered to use to pop their popcorn.

The Arkansas farmer recognized the terrific strength of the Standuprite and trained it to pull his plow over his very steep hillside fields. The long, unbending, spear-like legs of the critter were ideal for holding to the row on these terribly steep fields. And the production was wonderful, the critter plowing more acres in one day than an eight-horse team could plow in a week. But there was a serious problem; the power behind those straight, sharp legs that pulled the plow so well, also punched myriad eight-to-ten inch holes in the rocky soil so that the plow wheels, in passing over the deep holes or pits, made the ride for the farmer so rough and bumpy that he developed unbearably severe hemorrhoids, jarred loose the fillings in his teeth, and suffered addled brains for several days each Spring. Clearly, the Standuprite was then no substitute for the horse in Arkansas agriculture.

Bird watchers and other outdoors folks are requested to keep their eyes peeled for slanted trees, or buildings, a sure indication that the Standuprite has leaned against them to sleep, employing the only way it can to get some rest. Usually there is a favorite sleeping or bedding grounds, so that an entire row or clump of trees; or slanted outbuildings, can be observed bending in odd directions thereby indicating the area is used by the Standuprite.

The other clue is the adherence of the hair of the critter to the bark of the tree leaned against. In the South, of course, the hair will be easily seen as the white, cotton-like thread it is. In the Northwoods, the clue is the smeared exudate, the black pitch of the critter that adheres to the tree slept against. Check the exudate for mosquitoes — it should be matted with them.

When the observer sights the habitat described above, he should report it to the nearest office of the Department of Agriculture. It is believed that the Standuprite may yet solve our most serious agriculture problem: the high cost of farm fuels. Now that shock-absorbing springs and cushions are on all farm implements, the Arkansas rider of the plow should no longer be subjected to the teeth-jarring, soul-shaking ride behind the Standuprite while plowing, but should have as cushiony a ride as if things were on the level. If the theory proves correct, millions of gallons of fossil fuels will be saved. Further, the much cheaper, home-grown cottonseed is fuel enough for the Standuprite, thus reducing the cottonseed surplus plaguing Southern agriculture, while saving billions of bucks in unneeded gas and oil.

As of date of publication, the capture of a Standuprite and its successful adapatation to American agriculture offers the greatest hope for a successful solution to the nation's fuel conservation problem.

SUKHALUCK

En passant, it is worth mentioning that other industries are awaiting with intense interest further developments in adapting the Standuprite to their needs — the trucking industry, for example!

★   ★   ★   ★

The Sukhaluck

This critter, known in the Northwoods as the Rumtifusel, but in the Midwest as the Sukhaluk, is deadly although unbelieveably slow of movement. The Sukhaluk plays upon the biblical caveat advising us not to covet our neighbor's possessions. In short, it uses everyman's greed to feed itself.

The Sukhaluk is large, strong, and has a voracious appetite. The body is wide and long with a thick coating of mink-like hair resembling nothing so much as a luxurious mink coat. This coat-like appearance is flattened to further its appeal to its prey. To use an earlier description of it, the body is flattened "the way old Hank McGinnis looked after he'd rolled off the porch roof following the annual firemen's dinner, and sort of spread himself so flat we just slid him edgewise between a couple of shed doors for a coffin." A graphic description of the dissimulating Sukhaluk, for sure, and one to remember.

The shape of the critter lends itself to its food-gathering method. It drapes itself over a roadside fence, or a barn lot gate, or a fallen log near the highway so that the curious (and covetous) viewer goes up to its innocence hoping it truly is an abandoned mink coat, his for the taking. That is fatal curiousity! Because the Sukhaluk envelopes the greedy one and its many sucking pores that line the inside of its pelt, begin to suck all the juices and solids out of that feller's body. In less time than it takes to say Sukhaluk, a pile of bones is all that remains of that greedy feller.

Only one has been captured, and that one in Illinois. David Kenney, Director of the Department of Conservation, had sought for years to find one of these critters and at last he did come upon one. He threw a large fishnet over the critter, im-

m. HYLTON

BOADF
or
fill-a-maloo

mobilizing it, then gathered it in his arms and put it in the truck compartment of his car, then drove off toward the Department's laboratory. He had proceeded only a mile or so when a huge explosion blew out the entire rear of his car . . . and only then did Kenney recall his mistake. He had two spare tires in that compartment, and the Sukhaluk had sucked all the air out of them, more air than it could hold, and it exploded! Luckily, Director Kenney was not hurt, but his vehicle was a wreck. And that was the closest science has come to capturing a Sukhaluk.

All observors are advised not to attempt a personal capture of one of these critters. When one is sighted, call the nearest Forestry Service office for help in securing the critter.

★   ★   ★   ★

The BOADF

(Bird-of-a-different-feather)

The Boadf is a most unusual bird, although it is well-known in history, sightings going back to Pharaonic times in pyramidal Egypt. Its principal distinction lies in its flying habits, since it never faces forward in flight, but to the rear, caring not a whit for where it is going, but only for where it has been.

This bird has held several names throughout history, from Aves Reverso, in Roman times, to Goofus Bird in early teutonic days, to Flu-fly Bird in Medieval England, to Assbakburd during the bawdy Rennaissance. But all these birds were nothing other than our native Boadf in that they always flew backwards, built their nests upside down, and issued their same odd cry that sounds like the squeal of a Boeing 707 when its wheels hit the runway.

The Boadf flies well with geese or ducks, joining them in their flights at vernal and autumnal equinox. The Boadf takes a position in the skein of ducks or geese exactly like a tail gunner protecting the rear against diving Stukas. Its position is at the rear flange of the inverted V, in the center, for good visibility, so that it can protect the skein against marauding eagles or hawks. When attacked, the Boadf disgorges grit, sand, gravel and blackberry thorns melded in a kind of sharp, hard cud, or quid, shooting the lethal wad with unerring accuracy at the attacker, destroying it and saving the entire skein of ducks and geese so that it can proceed to the hunters awaiting it further south. This protection of the skein by a bird that flies backward is a classic example of a symbiotic relationship in nature.

★   ★   ★   ★

The Doodang

Joel Chandler Harris

"I wish," said the little boy, sitting in the doorway of Uncle Remus's cabin and watching a vulture poised on motionless wing, "I wish I could fly."

The old man regarded him curiously, and then a frown crept up and sat down on his forehead. "I'll tell you dis much, honey," he said, "ef eve'ybody wuz ter git all der wishes, de wide worl' 'ud be turned upside down, and be rollin over de wrong way. It sho would!" He continued to regard the little boy with such a solemn aspect that the child moved uneasily in his seat on the doorstep. "You sho does put me in min' er de ol' Doodang dat useter live in de mudflats down on de river. I ain't never see 'im myse'f, but I done seed dem what say dey hear tell er dem what is see 'im.

"None un um can't tell what kinder creetur de Doodang wuz. He had a long tail, like a yallergater, a great big body, four short legs, two short years, and a head mo' funny lookin dan de rhynossyhoss. His mouf retched fum de cen'er his nose ter his shoulder blades, and his tushes wuz big 'nough, long 'nough, and sharp 'nough fer ter bite off de behime leg uv a elephant. He could live in de water, er he could live on dry lan', but he mos'ly wallered in de mud-flats, whar he could retch down in de water and ketch a fish, er retch up in de bushes and ketch a bird. But all dis ain't suit 'im a 'tall; he got restless; he tuck ter wantin things he ain't got; and he worried and worried, and groaned and growled. He kep' all de creeturs, fur and feather, wide awake fer miles aroun'.

"Bimeby, one day, Brer Rabbit come a-sa'nterin by, and he ax de Doodang what de name er goodness is de matter, and de Doodang say dat he wanter swim ez good ez de fishes does.

"Brer Rabbit say, 'Ouch! you make de col' chills run up and down my back when you talk 'bout swimmin in de water. Swim on dry lan' ol' frien' — swim on dry lan'!'

"But some er de fishes done hear what de Doodang say, and dey helt a big 'sembly. Dey vow dey can't stan' de racket dat he been makin. De upshot uv de 'sembly wuz dat all de fishes 'gree fer ter loan de Doodang one fin apiece. So said, so done, and when dey tol' de Doodang 'bout it, he fetched one loud howl, and rolled inter shaller water. Once dar, de fishes loan't 'im eve'y one a fin, some big and some little, and atter dey done dat, de Doodang 'skivver dat he kin swim des ez nimble ez de rest.

"He skeeted about in de water, wavin his tail fum side ter side, and swimmin fur and wide. Brer Rabbit wuz settin off in de bushes watchin. Atter while de Doodang git tired, and start ter go on dry lan', but de fishes kick up sech a big fuss, and make sech a cry, dat he say he better gi' um back der fins, and den he crawled out on de mudflats fer ter take his nap.

"He ain't been dozin so mighty long 'fo' he hear a mighty big fuss, and he look up and see dat de blue sky wuz fa'rly black wid burds, big and little. De trees on de islan' wuz der roostin place, but dey wuz comin home soon so dey kin git some sleep 'fo' de Doodang set up his howlin and growlin, and moanin and groanin. Well, de birds ain't mo'n got settle' 'fo' de Doodang start up his howlin and bellerin. Den de King-bird flew'd down and ax de Doodang what de name er goodness is de matter. Den de Doodang turn over in de mud, and howl and beller. De King-bird flew'd aroun', and den he come back and ax what der trouble is. Atter so long a time, de Doodang say dat de trouble wid him wuz dat he wanted to fly. He say all he want wuz some feathers, and den he kin fly ez good ez anybody. Den de birds hol' a 'sembly, and dey all 'gree fer ter loan de Doodang a feather apiece. So said, so done, and in a minnit er mo' he had de feathers aplenty. He shuck his wings, and ax whar'bouts he mus' fly fer de fust try.

"Brer Buzzard say de best place wuz ter de islan' what ain't got nothin but dead trees on it, and wid dat, de Doodang tuck a runnin start, and headed fer de place. He wuz kinder clumsy, but he got dar all right. De birds went 'long fer ter see how de Doodang 'ud come out. He landed wid a turrible splash and splutter, and he ain't hardly hit de groun' 'fo' Brer Buzzard say he don't want his feather fer ter git wet, and he grabbed it. Den all de birds grabbed der'n, and dar he wuz. Days and days come and went, and bimeby Brer Rabbit wanter know what done gone wid de Doodang. Brer Buzzard say, 'You see my fambly settin in de dead trees? Well, dar's whar de Doodang is, and ef you'll git me a bag, I'll fetch you his bones!' And den Brer Rabbit sot back and laugh twel his sides ache!"

"Anyhow," said the little boy, "I should like to fly." "Fly, den," replied Uncle Remus; "Fly right in de house dis minnit, ter yo' mammy!"

Chapter V
Oh, Those Phunny Phellows!

*T*he group of literary comedians, known as Phunny Phellows, titillated Americans between 1855-1895. These comics used busted English and fractured grammar to increase the punch of their funny writings and lectures, and they used this cacographic technique not only because it was funny, but because its use punctured the inflated, sentimental, and purple prose, poetry, and the affected mannerisms so much in vogue by the then fashionable writers.

The use of the technique of mispelled words and odd grammar was old, going back to ancient Greek times, and continuing with Shakespeare, Rabelais, Ben Franklin, and on up to our own day, in backwoods, isolated areas.

The reader is cautioned not to be discouraged too soon over the tortured grammar and awful spelling. Very quickly the swing of the language will come, and the reading will seem quite natural, even fun. For as Ben Franklin's advice to a friend expressed it:

> You need not be concern'd in writing to me about your bad Spelling: for in my opinion as our Alphabet now Stands, the bad Spelling, or what is call'd so, is generally the best, as conforming to the Sound of the Letters and of the Words. To give you and Instance, a Gentleman receiving a Letter in which were these Words, Not fining Brown at hom, I delivered you Meseg to his yf. The Gentleman finding it bad Spelling, and therefore not very intelligible, call'd his Lady to help him read it. Between them they pick'd out the meaning of all but the yf, which they could not understand. The lady propos'd calling her Chambermaid; for Betty, says she, has the best Knack at reading bad Spelling of any one I know. Betty came, and was surpriz'd

that neither Sir nor Madam could tell what yf was; why, says she, y,f spells Wife, what else can it spell? And indeed it is a much better as well as shorter method of Spelling Wife, than Doubleyou, i, ef, e, which in reality spells Doubleyifey.

In 1866, James Russell Lowell, had his character, Hosea Bigelow, evaluate phonetic spelling: "I allus do, it kind of puts a noo soot of close onto a word, thisere funatick spellin' does, an' takes 'em out of the prison dress they wair in the dixonary."

But Josh Billings has the last word: "There is just az mutch joke in bad spelling, as thar iz in looking Kross-eyed, and no more."

★　　　★　　　★　　　★

ARTEMUS WARD *(Charles Farrar Browne, 1834-1867)*

Artemus Ward was one of the most popular literary characters ever created in the United States and the most popular during his short life. His early life was not signally noteworthy, with slight schooling and early years spent as a wandering journeyman printer. But he hit on a writing style that suited his time. By the use of fractured grammar and ruptured spelling, he made fun of the literary poseurs of his day. He took great delight in satirizing the philsophers, ministers, generals, professors—all the eggheads of his time...and Americans loved him for it. They made him rich by buying his books and attending his lectures. His first book sold 40,000 copies, a tremendous number for that day, and the equivalent, in today's figure, of 265,000.

Brown was a prodigious drinker and that helped to end his life shortly before his thirty-third birthday. In reply to a telegram asking what he would take to lecture in California, he wired back: "Brandy and water!" But tuberculosis destroyed him.

His writing is full of word-play: "moral bares," highly manured prose," "women's rites," and of very "malignant grammar."

In 1864, he went to England and was a tremendous success. The English loved his puns, his anti-climactic punch lines, peculiar appearance, and his odd delivery. They mourned for him after he died there in 1867. Oddly, the English remembered the hundredth anniversary of his death, but Americans had already forgotten him.

Browne was most helpful to other Phunny Phellows. He got Josh Billings his start, as well as Petroleum V. Nasby and Bill Arp. He seemed to be a man without envy, ever anxious to help his fellow man. Perhaps this generous quality was obvious in his personality, his speaking manner so that he won audiences not only because of his wit and manner but because of his obvious kindness.

★ ★ ★ ★

ONE OF MR. WARD'S BUSINESS LETTERS

To the Editor of the——

Sir—I'm movin' along—slowly along—down tords your place. I want you should rite me a letter, sayin how is the show bizniss in your place. My show at present consists of three moral Bares, a Kangaroo (a amoozin little Raskal—t'would make you larf yerself to deth to see the little cuss jump up and squeal) wax figgers of G. Washington Gen. Tayler John Bunyan Capt. Kidd and Dr. Webster in the act of killin Dr. Parkman, besides several miscellanyus moral wax statoots of celebrated piruts & murderers, &c. ekalled by few & exceld by none. Now Mr. Editor, scratch orf a few lines sayn how is the show bizniss down to your place. I shall have my hanbills dun at your offiss. Depend upon it. I want you should git my hanbills up in flamin stile. Also git up a tremenjus excitemunt in yr. paper 'bowt my onparaleld Show. We must fetch the public sumhow. We must wurk on their feelins. Cum the moral on 'em strong. if it's a temperance community tell 'em I sined the pledge fifteen minits arter Ise born, but on the contery ef your peple take their tods, say Mister Ward is as Jenial a feller as we ever met, full of conwiviality, & the life an sole of the Soshul Bored. Take, don't you? If you say anythin abowt my show say my snaiks is as harmliss as the new-born Babe. What a interestin study it is to see a zewological animal like a snaik under perfeck subjecshun! My Kangaroo is the most larfable little cuss I ever saw. All for 15 cents. I am anxyus skewer your infloounce. I repeet in regard to them hanbills that I shall git 'em struck orf up to your printin office. My perlitercal sentiments agree with yourn exackly. I know thay do, becawz I never saw a man whoos didn't.

Repectively yures,

A. WARD

P. S.—You scratch my back & Ile scratch your back.

★   ★   ★   ★

Note: In 1862, President Lincoln surprised his cabinet, assembled for a reading of a draft of The Emancipation Proclamation, by first reading Artemus Ward's "High-Handed Outrage at Utica." Mr. Lincoln was friendly with Ward who visited him in the White House.

★   ★   ★   ★

HIGH-HANDED OUTRAGE AT UTICA

In the Fall of 1856, I showed my show in Utiky, a trooly great city in the State of New York.

The people gave me a cordyal recepshun. The press was loud in her prases.

l day as I was givin a descripshun of my Beests and Snakes in my usual flowry stile what was my scorn disgust to see a big burly feller walk up to the cage containin my wax figgers of the Lord's Last Supper, and seize Judas Iscarrot by the feet and drag him out on the ground. He then commenced fur to pound him as hard as he could.

"What under the son are you about?" cried I.

Sez he, "What did you bring the pusillanimous cuss here fur?"

and he hit the wax figger another tremendous blow on the hed.

Sez I, "You egregious ass, that air's a wax figger—a represen-tashun of the false 'Postle."

Sez he, "That's all very well for you to say, but I tell you, old man, that Judas Iscarrot can't show hisself in Utiky with im-punity by a darn site!" with which observashun he caved in Judassis hed. The young man belonged to 1 of the first famerlies in Utiky. I sued him, and the Jury brought in a verdick of Arson in the 3d degree.

★　　★　　★　　★

ON FORTS

Every man has got a Fort. It's sum men's fort to do one thing, and some other men's fort to do another, while there is numeris shiftliss critters goin round loose whose fort is not to do nothin.

Shakspeer wrote good plays, but he wouldn't have succeded as a Washington correspondent of a New York daily paper. He lackt the requisite fancy and imagginashun.

That's so!

Old George Washington's Fort was not to have any public man of the present day resemble him to any alarmin extent. Whare bowts can George's equal be found? I ask, & boldly anser no wheres, or eny where else.

Old man Townsin's Fort was to make Sasparilla.

"Joy to the world! anuther life saved!" (Quotation from Townsin's advertisemunt.)

Cyrus Field's Fort is to lay a sub-machine tellegraf under the boundin biller of the Ocean, and then have it Bust.

Spauldin's Fort is to make Prepared Gloo, which mends everything. Wonder ef it will mend a sinner's wicked ways. (Im-promptoo joke.)

Zoary's Fort is to be a female circus feller.

My Fort is the great moral show bizniss & writin choice famer-ly literatoor for the newspapers. That's what's the matter with *me*.

&c., &c., &c. So I mite go on to a indefnit extent.

Twict I've endeavored to do things which thay wasn't my Fort. The fust time was when I undertuk to lick a audacious cuss who cut a hole in my tent & crawled thru. Sez I, "my gentle Sir go out or I shall fall onto you putty heavy." Sez he, "Wade in, Old wax figgers," whareupon I went for him, but he caught me powerful on the head & knockt me through the tent into a cow pastur. He pursued the attack & flung me into a mud puddle. As I aroze & rung out my drencht garments I koncluded fightin wasn't my Fort. Ile now raise the curtain upon Seen 2nd: It is rarely seldom that I seek consolation in the Flowin Bole. But in a certain town in Injianny in the Fall of 18—, my orgin grinder got sick with the fever & died. I never felt so ashamed in my life & I thought I'd heist in a few swallows of something strengthin. Konsequents was I heisted in so much I dident zactly know where bouts I was. I turnd my livin wild beests of Pray loose into the streets and spoilt all my wax wurks. I then Bet I could play hoss. So I hitched myself to a Canal boat, there bein two other hosses hitcht on also, one behind and anuther ahead of me. The driver hollerd for us to git up, and we did. But the hosses bein unused to such a arrangemunt begun to kick & squeal and rear up. Konsequents was I was kickt vilently in the stummuck & back, and presuntly I found myself in the Canal with the other hosses kickin & yellin like a tribe of Cusscaroorus savages. I was rescued, & as I was bein carried to the tavern on a hemlock board I sed in a feeble voice, "Boys, playin hoss isn't my Fort."

MORAL—Never don't do nothin which isn't your Fort, for if you do you'll find yourself splashin round in the Canal, figgeratively speakin.

★   ★   ★   ★

INTERVIEW WITH PRESIDENT LINCOLN.

I have no politics. Not a one. I'm not in the bisness. If I was I spose I should holler vociferously in the streets at nite and go home to Betsy Jane smellin of coal oil and gin, in the mornin. I should go to the Poles early. I should stay there all day. I should see to it that my neighbors was thar. I should git carriges to take the cripples, the infirm and the indignant thar. I should be on guard agin frauds and sich. I should be on the look out for the infamus lies of the enemy, got up jest before election for perlitical effect. When all was over and my candydate was elected, I should move heaven & earth—so to speak—until I got office, which if I didn't git a office I should turn round and abuse the Administration with all my mite and maine. But I'm not in the bizniss. I'm in a far more respectful bizness nor what politics is. I wouldn't give two cents to be a Congresser. The worst insult I ever received was when sertain citizens of Baldinsville asked me to run fur the Legislater. Sez I, "My friends, dostest think I'd stoop to that there?" They turned as white as a sheet. I spoke in my most awfulest tones & they knowed I wasn't to be trifled with. They slunked out of sight to oncet.

Therefore, havin no politics, I made bold to visit Old Abe at his homestead in Springfield. I found the old feller in his parler, surrounded by a perfect swarm of office seekers. Knowin he had been captain of a flat boat on the roarin Mississippy I thought I'd address him in sailor lingo, so sez I, "Old Abe, ahoy! Let out yer mailsails, reef home the forecastle & throw yer jib-poop overboard! Shiver my timbers, my harty!" (N. B. This is ginuine mariner langwidge. I know because I've seen sailor plays acted out by them New York theater fellers.) Old Abe lookt up quite cross & sez, "Send in yer petition by & by. I can't possibly look at it now. Indeed, I can't. It's onpossible, sir!"

"Mr. Linkin, who do you expect I are?" sed I.

"A office-seeker, to be sure," sed he.

"Well, sir," sed I, "You's never more mistaken in your life. You hain't gut a office I'd take under no circumstances. I'm A. Ward. Wax figgers is my perfeshun. I'm the father of Twins, and they look like me—both of them. I cum to pay a friendly visit to the President elect of the United States. If so be you wants to see me, say so, if not, say so & I'm off like a jug handle."

"Mr. Ward, sit down. I'm glad to see you, Sir."

"Repose in Abraham's Buzzum!" sed one of the office-seekers, his idee bein to get off a joke at my expense.

"Well," sez I, "if all you fellers repose in that there Buzzum thar'll be mighty poor nursing for some of you!" whereupon Old Abe buttoned his weskit clear up and blusht like a maiden of sweet 16. Jest at this point of the conversation another swarm of office-seekers arrove & come pilin into the parler. Sum wanted post offices, sum wanted collectorships, sum wanted foreign missions, and all wanted sumthin. I thought Old Abe would go crazy. He hadn't more than had time to shake hands with 'em, before another tremendous crowd cum poring onto his premises. His house and dooryard was now perfeckly overflow-ed with office-seekers, all clamerin for a immejit interview with Old Abe. One man from Ohio, who had about seven inches of corn whiskey into him, mistook me for Old Abe and addrest me as "The Pra-hayrie Flower of the West." Thinks I you want a office pretty bad. Another man with a gold-heded cane and a red nose told Old Abe he was "a second Washington & the Pride of the Boundliss West."

Sez I, "Squire, you wouldn't take a small post offiss if you could git it, would you?"

Sez he, "A patriot is above them things, sir!"

"There's a putty big crop of patriots this season, ain't there Squire?" sez I, when *another* crowd of office seekers pored in. The house, dooryard, barns, woodshed was now all full, and when *another* crowd cum I told 'em not to go away for want of room as the hog-pen was still empty. One patriot from a small town in Michygan went up on top the house, got into the chimney and slid into the parlor where Old Abe was endeverin to keep the hungry pack of office seekers from chawin him up alive without benefit of clergy. The minute he reached the fireplace he jump up, brusht the soot out of his eyes, and yelled:

"Don't make eny appointments at the Spunkville postoffiss till you've read my papers. All the respectful men in our town is signers to that there dockument!"

"Good God!" cried Old Abe, "they cum upon me from the skies—down the chimneys, and from the bowels of the earth!" He hadn't more'n got them words out of his delicate mouth before two fat office seekers from Wisconsin, in endeverin to crawl between his legs for the purpose of applyin for the tollgateship at Milwaukee, upset the President elect, & he would have gone sprawlin into the fireplace if I hadn't caught him in these arms. But I hadn't more'n stood him up straight before another man cum crashing down the chimney, his head strikin me violently again the inards and prostratin my voluptuous form onto the floor. "Mr. Linkin," shouted the infatuated being, "my papers is signed by every clergyman in our town, and likewise the skoolmaster!"

Sez I, "You egregious ass," gettin up & brushin the dust from my eyes, "I'll sign your papers with this bunch of bones, if you don't be a little more careful how you make my bread basket a depot in the future. How do you like that air perfumery?" sez I, shoving my fist under his nose. "Them's the kind of papers I'll give you! Them's the papers *you* want!"

"But I workt hard for the ticket; I toiled night and day! The patriot should be rewarded!"

"Virtoo," sed I, holdin' the infatuated man by the coat-collar, "virtoo, sir, is its own reward. Look at me!" He did look at me, and quailed before my gase. "The fact is," I continued, lookin' round on the hungry crowd, "there is scarcly a office for every ole lamp carrid round during this campaign. I wish thare was. I wish thare was foreign missions to be filled on various lonely Islands where epydemics rage incessantly, and if I was in Old Abe's place I'd send every mother's son of you to them. What air you here for?" I continued, warmin up considerable, "can't you giv Abe a minute's peace? Don't you see he's worried most to death? Go home, you miserable men, go home & till the soil! Go to peddlin tinware—go to choppin wood—go to bilin' soap—stuff saugages—black boots—git a clerkship on sum respectable manure cart—go round as original Swiss Bell Ringers—becum 'original and only' Campbell Minstrels—go to lecturin at 50 dollars a nite—imbark in the peanut bizniss—*write for the Ledger*—saw off your legs and go round givin concerts, with touchin appeals to a charitable public, printed on your handbills—anything for an honest living, but don't come round here drivin Old Abe crazy by your outrageous cuttings up! Go home! Stand not upon the order of your goin', but go to onct! If in five minits from this time," sez I, pullin' out my new sixteen dollar huntin cased watch and brandishin' it before their eyes, "Ef in five minits from this time a single sole of you remains on these here premises, I'll go out to my cage near by, and let my Boy Constrictor loose! & ef he gits amung you, you'll think old Solferino has cum again and no mistake!" You ought to have seen them scamper, Mr. Fair. They run of as tho Satun hisself was arter them with a red hot pronged pitchfork. In five minits the premises was clear.

"How kin I ever repay you, Mr. Ward, for your kindness?" sed Old Abe, advancin and shakin me warmly by the hand. "How kin I ever repay you, sir?"

"By givin the whole country a good, sound adminstration. By porein oil upon the troubled waturs, North and South. By pursuein' a patriotic, firm, and just course, and then if any State wants to secede, let 'em Sesesh!"

"How 'bout my Cabinet, Mister Ward?" sed Abe.

"Fill it up with Showmen, sir! Showmen, is devoid of politics. They hain't got any principles. They know what the public wants, North & South. Showmen, sir, is honest men. Ef you doubt their literary ability, look at their posters, and see small bills! Ef you want a Cabinit as is a Cabinit fill it up with showmen, but don't call on me. The moral wax figger profession mustn't be permitted to go down while there's a drop of blood in these veins! A. Linkin, I wish you well! Ef Powers or Walcutt wus to pick out a model for a beautiful man, I scarcely think they'd sculpt you; but ef you do the fair thing by your country you'll make as pretty a angel as any of us! A. Linkin, use the talents which Nature has put into you judiciously and firmly, and all will be well! A. Linkin, adoo!"

He shook me cordially by the hand—we exchanged picters, so we could gaze upon each others' liniments, when far away from one another—he at the hellum of the ship of State, and I at the hellum of the show bizniss—admittance only 15 cents.

★　　★　　★　　★

THE WIFE

"Home they brought her warrior dead:
　　She nor swooned, nor uttered cry.
　All her maidens, watching, said,
　　'She must weep, or she will die.' "

The propriety of introducing a sad story like the following, in a book intended to be rather cheerful in its character, may be questioned; but it so beautifully illustrates the firmness of a woman when grief and despair have taken possession of "the chambers of her heart," that we cannot refrain from relating it.

Lucy M—— loved with all the ardor of a fond and faithful wife, and when he upon whom she had so confidingly leaned was stolen from her by death, her friends and companions said Lucy would go mad. Ah, how little they knew her!

Gazing for the last time upon the clay-cold features of her departed husband, this young widow—beautiful even in her grief; so etheral to look upon, and yet so firm!—looking for the last time upon the dear familiar face, now cold and still in death—oh, looking for the last, last time—she rapidly put on her bonnet, and thus addressed the sobbing gentlemen who were to act as pall-bearers:—"You pall-bearers, just go into the buttery and get some rum, and we'll start this man right along!"

★   ★   ★   ★

A ROMANCE—WILLIAM BARKER,
THE YOUNG PATRIOT

I

"No, William Barker, you cannot have my daughter's hand in marriage until you are her equal in wealth and social position."

The speaker was a haughty old man of some sixty years, and the person whom he addressed was a fine-looking man of twenty-five.

With a sad respect the young man withdrew from the stately mansion.

II

Six months later the young man stood in the presence of the haughty old man.

"What! *you* here again?" angrily cried the old man.

"Ay, old man," proudly exclaimed William Barker. "I am here, your daughter's equal and yours."

The old man's lips curled with scorn. A derisive smile lit up his cold features; when, casting violently upon the marble centre table an enormous roll of greenbacks, William Barker cried—

"See! Look on this wealth. And I've tenfold more! Listen, old man! You spurned me from your door. But I did not despair. I secured a contract for furnishing the Army of the —— with beef—"

"Yes, yes!" eagerly exclaimed the old man.

"—and I bought up all the disabled cavalry horses I could find—"

"I see, I see!" cried the old man. "And good beef they make, too."

"They do! they do! and the profits are immense."

"I should say so!"

"And now, sir, I claim you daughter's fair hand!"

"Boy, she is yours. But hold! Look me in the eye. Throughout all this have you been loyal?"

"To the core!" cried William Barker.

"And," continued the old man, in a voice husky with emotion, "are you in favor of a vigorous prosecution of the war?"

"I am, I am!"

"Then, boy, take her! Maria, child, come hither. Your William claims thee. Be happy, my children! and whatever our lot in life may be, *let us all support the Government!*"

★   ★   ★   ★

JOSH BILLINGS (Henry Wheeler Shaw, 1818-1895)

Josh Billings is quite the most charming and contempory of all the phunny phellows, those literary hatchet men dedicated to the execution of the stilted and over-refined language and manners of their day. He came from an illustrious family, both his father and grandfather serving as United States Congressmen. But Josh seemed a more modest sort, failing to get through college (he was booted out early in his sophomore year), a fact that must have influenced his estimate of himself in terms of politics. He made his home in Poughkeepsie, New York, where he worked as an auctioneer and real estate agent, writing for the local paper but without much acclaim. Then he wrote a short piece titled ESSA ON THE MULE, and it was an instant success, appearing in newspapers across the land. He was paid $1.50 for the piece! But its widespread reprinting caused him to exclaim "I think I've struck oil!" And he had.

In New York, Artemus Ward and Josh Billings swigged a liquid lunch together, entertaining one another uproariously. After that, Ward helped Josh find an editor who published his first book: JOSH BILLINGS FARMERS' ALMANAX. This book was one of ten he published. He sold a million copies within ten years, a sales record that gives some notion of how popular were the phunny phellows, Josh Billings in particular.

A critic remarked: "There is always a higher purpose peeping out from the quaint fancies and odd expressions of Josh Billings." Then he went on to say that one of those purposes was to prick and puncture the literary pretensions of the time.

Prof. Walter Blair, University of Chicago, describes the category of phunny phellows and their purposes in this way: "Dressed in their brilliant bumpkin overalls, comic writers spoke up in aphorisms for old American beliefs." Josh Billings was the outstanding writer and lecturer of that genre of comedians: funny but principled. President Abraham Lincoln thought so much of him that he remarked: "Next to William Shakespeare, Josh Billings is the greatest judge of human nature the world has ever seen." Mighty high praise, indeed, and enough to introduce that kind, endearing, and very American humorist: Josh Billings.

The piece that brought Josh Billings national publicity—and success:

THE MULE

The mule is half hoss and half Jackass, and then comes tu a full stop, natur diskovering her mistake.

They weigh more, accordin tu their heft, than any other creature, except a crowbar.

They kant hear any quicker, nor further than the hoss, yet their ears are big enuff for snow shoes.

You can trust them with any one whose life ain't worth any more than the mules. The only way tu keep the mules in a pasture, is tu turn them into a meadow joining, and let them jump out.

They are reddy for use, just as soon as they will do tu abuse.

They hain't got any friends, and will live on huckle berry brush, with an occasional chance at Kanada thistels.

They are a modern invention, i don't think the Bible deludes tu them at tall.

They sell for more money than any other domestik animal. Yu cant tell their age by looking into their mouth, any more than you could a Mexican cannons. They never have no dissease that a good club wont heal.

If they ever die they must kum rite tu life agin, for i never herd noboddy sa "dead mule."

They are like some men, verry corrupt at harte; ive known them tu be good mules for 6 months, just tu git a good chanse to kick sumbody.

I never owned one, nor never mean to, unless thare is a United Staits law passed, requiring it.

The only reason why they are patient, is because they are ashamed ov themselfs.

I have seen eddikated mules in a circus.

They could kick, and bite, tremendous. I would not say what I am forced tu say against the mule, if his birth wasn't an outrage, and man wasn't tu blame for it.

Any man who is willing tu drive a mule, ought to be exempt by law from running for the legislatur.

They are the strongest creeturs on earth, and heaviest according to their sise; I herd tell ov one who fell off from the tow path, on the Erie Kanal, and sunk as soon as he touched bottom, but he kept rite on towing the boat tu the next station, breathing thru his ears, which stuck out ov the water about 2 feet 6 inches; i didn't see this did, but an auctioneer told me ov it, and i never knew an auctioneer tu lie unless it was absolutely convenient.

★   ★   ★   ★

LAFFING

Anatomically considered, laffing iz the sensashun ov feeling good all over, and showing it principally in one spot.

Morally considered, it iz the next best thing tew the 10 commandments.

Philosophikally considered, it beats Herrick's pills 3 pills in the game.

Theoretically considered, it can out-argue all the logik in existence.

Analitically considered, any part ov it iz equal tew the whole.

Constitushionally considered, it iz vittles and sumthing tew drink.

Multifariously considered, it iz just az different from ennything else az it is from itself.

Phumatically considered, it haz a good deal ov essence and some boddy.

Pyroteknically considered, it iz the fire-works of the soul.

Syllogestically considered, the conklushuns allwus follows the premises.

Spontaneously considered, it iz az natural and refreshing az a spring bi the road-side.

Phosphorescently considered, it lights up like a globe lantern.

Exudatiously considered, it haz all the dissolving propertys ov a hot whiskey puntch.

But this iz too big talk for me; these flatulent words wuz put into the dicshionary for those giants in knolledge tew use who hav tew load a cannon clean up tew the muzzell with powder and ball when they go out tew hunt pissmires.

But i don't intend this essay for laffing in the lump, but for laffing on the half-shell.

Laffing iz just az natral tew come tew the surface as a rat iz tu cum out ov hiz hole when he wants tew.

Yu kant keep it back by swallowing enny more than yu can the hiccups.

If a man *can't* laff there iz sum mistake made in putting him together, and if he *won't* laff he wants az mutch keeping away from az a bear-trap when it iz set.

I have seen people who laffed altogether too mutch for their own good or for ennyboddy else's; they laffed like a barrell ov new cider with the tap pulled out, a perfekt stream.

This is a grate waste ov natural juice.

I have seen other people who didn't laff enuff tew giv themselfs vent; they wuz like a barrell ov nu sider too, that wuz bunged up tite, apt tew start a hoop and leak all away on the sly.

There ain't neither ov theze 2 ways right, and they never ought tew be patented.

Sum folks hav got what iz called a hoss-laff, about haffway between a growl and a bellow, just az a hoss duz when he feels hiz oats, and don't exackly know what ails him.

Theze pholks don't enjoy a laff enny more than the man duz hiz vittles who swallows hiz pertatoes whole.

A laff tew be nourishsome wants tew be well chewed.

Thare iz another kind ov a laff which i never did enjoy, one loud busst, and then everything iz az still az a lager beer barrell after it haz blowed up and slung 2 or 3 gallons ov beer around loose.

There iz another laff which I hav annalized; it cums out ov the mouth with a noize like a pig makes when he iz in a tite spot, one sharp squeal and two snickers, and then dies in a simper.

This kind ov a laff iz learned at femail boarding-skools, and dont mean anything; it iz nothing more than the skin ov a laff.

Genuine laffing iz the vent ov the soul, the nostrils ov the heart, and iz jist az necessary for health and happiness as spring water iz for a trout.

Thare iz one kind ov a laff that i always did recommend; it looks out ov the eye fust with a merry twinkle, then it creeps down on its hands and knees and plays around the mouth like a pretty moth around the blaze ov a candle, then it steals over into the dimples ov the cheeks and rides around in thoze little whirlpools for a while, then it lites up the whole face like the mello bloom on a damask rose, then it swims off on the air, with a peal az clear and az happy az a dinner-bell, then it goes back agin on golden tiptoze like an angel out for an airing, and laze down on its little bed ov violets in the heart where it cum from.

Thare iz another laff that noboddy can withstand; it iz just az honest and noizy as a district school let out tew play, it shakes a man up from hiz toes tew hiz temples, it doubles and twists him like a whiskee fit, it lifts him up off from hiz chair, like feathers, and lets him bak agin like melted lead, it goes all thru him like a pickpocket, and finally leaves him az weak and az crazy az tho he had bin soaking all day in a Rushing bath and forgot tew be took out.

This kind ov a laff belongs tew jolly good phellows who are az healthy az quakers, and who are az easy tew please as a gall who iz going tew be married to-morrow.

In conclusion i say laff every good chance yu kan git, but don't laff unless yu feal like it, for there ain't nothing in this world more harty than a good honest laff, nor nothing more hollow than a hartless one.

When yu do laff open yure mouth wide enuff for the noize tew git out without squealing, throw your hed back az tho yu was going tew be shaved, hold on tew your false hair with both hands and then laff till your soul gets thoroly rested.

But i shall tell yu more about theze things at sum future time.

★   ★   ★   ★

KISSING

I hav written essays on kissing before this one, and they didn't satisfy me, nor do I think this one will, for the more a man undertakes to tell about a kiss, the more he will reduce his ignorance to a science.

Yu cant analize a kiss any more than yu can the breath of a flower. Yu cant tell what makes a kiss taste so good any more than yu can a peach.

Enny man who can set down, whare it is cool, and tell how a kiss tastes, haint got any more real flavor to his mouth than a knot hole haz. Such a phellow wouldn't hesitate to describe Paridise as a fust rate place for garden sass.

The only way to deskribe a kiss is to take one, and then set down, awl alone, out ov the draft, and smack your lips.

If yu cant satisfy yureself how a kiss tastes without taking another one, how on arth can you define it to the next man.

I have heard writers talk about the egstatic bliss thare waz in a kiss, and they really seemed to think they knew all about it, but these are the same kind ov folks who perspire and cry when they read poetry, and they fall to writing sum ov their own, and think they hav found out how.

I want it understood that I am talking about pure emotional kissing, that is born in the heart, and flies to the lips, like a humming bird to her roost.

I am not talking about your lazy, milk and molasses kissing, that daubs the face ov any body, nor yure savage bite, that goes around, like a roaring lion, in search ov sumthing to eat.

Kissing an unwilling pair ov lips, iz az mean a victory, az robbin a bird's nest, and kissing too willing ones iz about az unfragant a recreation, az making bouquets out ov dandelions.

The kind ov kissing that I am talking about iz the kind that must do it, or spoil.

If yu search the records ever so lively, yu cant find the author ov the first kiss; kissing, like mutch other good things, iz anonymous.

But there iz such natur in it, such a world ov language without words, such a heap ov pathos without fuss, so much honey, and so little water, so cheap, so sudden, and so neat a mode of striking up an acquaintance, that i consider it a good purchase, that Adam giv, and got, the fust kiss.

Who can imagine a greater lump ov earthly bliss, reduced to a finer thing, than kissing the only woman on earth, in the garden of Eden.

Adam wasn't the man, i don't beleave, to pass sich a hand.

I may be wrong in my conclusions, but if any boddy can date kissing further back, i would like tew see them do it.

I don't know whether the old stoic philosophers ever kist any boddy or not, if they did, they probably did it, like drawing a theorem on a black board, more for the purpose of proving sumthing else.

I do hate to see this delightful and invigorating beverage adulturated, it iz nectar for the god, i am often obliged tew stand still, and see kissing did, and not say a word, that haint got enny more novelty, nor meaning in it, than throwing stones tew a mark.

I saw two maiden ladys kiss yesterday on the north side ov

Union square, 5 times in less than 10 minutes; they kist every time they bid each other farewell, and then immediately thought ov sumthing elwse they hadn't sed. I couldn't tell for the life ov me whether the kissing was the effect ov what they said, or what they said waz the effekt ov the kissing. It waz a which, and tother, scene.

Cross-matched kissing iz undoubtedly the strength ov the game. It is true there iz no statute regulashun aginst two females kissing each other; but i don't think thare iz much pardon for it, unless it iz done to keep tools in order; and two men kissing each other iz prima face evidence ov deadbeatery.

Kissing that passes from parent to child, and back agin seems to be az necessary az shinplasters[1], to do bizness with; and kissing that hussbands give and take iz simply gathering ripe fruit from ones own plum tree, that would otherwise drop off, or be stolen.

Therefore i am driven tew konklude, tew git out ov the corner that mi remarks have chased me into, that the oil ov a kiss iz only tew be had once in a phellow's life, in the original package, and that iz when...

Not tew waste the time ov the reder, i hav thought best not tew finish the above sentence, hoping that their aint no person ov a good educashun, and decent memory, but what can recolekt the time which i refer to, without enny ov mi help.

★   ★   ★   ★

MARRIAGE

Marriage iz a fair transaction on the face ov it.

But thare iz quite too often put up jobs in it.

It iz an old institushun, older than the pyramids, and az full ov hyrogliphicks that noboddy can parse.

History holds its tongue who the pair waz who fust put on the silken harness, and promised tew work kind in it, thru thick and

1. Paper money

thin, up hill and down, and on the level, rain or shine, survive or perish, sink or swim, drown or flote.

But whoever they waz they must hav made a good thing out ov it, or so menny ov their posterity would not hav harnessed up since and drove out.

Thare iz a great moral grip in marriage; it iz the mortar that holds the social bricks together.

But there ain't but darn few pholks who put their money in matrimony who could set down and giv a good written opinyun why on earth they cum to did it.

This iz a great proof that it iz one ov them natral kind ov accsidents that must happen, jist az birds fly out ov the nest, when they hav feathers enuff, without being able tew tell why.

Sum marry for beauty, and never discover their mistake; this iz lucky.

Sum marry for money, and—don't see it.

Sum marry for pedigree, and feel big for six months, and then very sensibly cum tew the conclusion that pedigree ain't no better than skimmilk.

Sum marry tew please their relashuns, and are surprized tew learn that their relashuns don't care a cuss for them afterwards.

Sum marry for love without a cent in their pocket, nor a friend in the world, nor a drop ov pedigree. This looks desperate, *but it iz the strength ov the game.*

If marrying for love ain't a success, then matrimony iz a dead beet.

Sum marry becauze they think wimmin will be scarse next year, and liv tew wonder how the crop holds out.

Sum marry tew git rid ov themselfs, and discover that the game waz one that two could play at, and neither win.

Sum marry the second time to git even, and find it a gambling game, the more they put down, the less they take up.

Summ marry tew be happy, and not finding it, wonder where all the hapiness on earth goes to when it dies.

Sum marry, they can't tell whi, and liv, they can't tell how.

Almost every boddy gits married, and it iz a good joke.

Sum marry in haste, and then set down and think it careful over.

Sum think it over careful fust, and then set down and marry.

Both ways are right, if they hit the mark.

Sum marry rakes tew convert them. This iz a little risky, and takes a smart missionary to do it.

Sum marry coquetts. This iz like buying a poor farm, heavily mortgaged, and working the balance ov yure days tew clear off the mortgages.

Married life haz its chances, and this iz just what gives it its flavour. Every body loves tew phool with the chances, becauze every boddy expects tew win. But i am authorized tew state that every boddy don't win.

But, after all, married life iz full az certain az the dry goods biziness.

Sum never marry, but this iz jist az risky, the diseaze iz the same, with no other name to it.

The man who stands on the bank shivering, and dassent, iz more apt tew cetch cold, than him who pitches hiz head first into the river.

Thare iz but phew who never marry becauze they *won't* they all hanker, and most ov them starve with slices ov bred before them (spread on both sides), jist for the lack ov grit.

Marry young! iz mi motto.

I hav tried it, and kno what i am talkin about.

If enny boddy asks yu why yu got married, (if it needs be), tell him, *yu don't recollekt.*

Marriage is a safe way to gamble—if yu win, yu win a pile, and if yu loze, yu don't loze enny thing, only the privilege ov living dismally alone, and soaking yure own feet.

I repeat it, in italicks, *marry young!*

Thare iz but one good excuse for a marriage late in life and that iz—*a second marriage.*

★   ★   ★   ★

TIGHT BOOTS.

I would jist like to kno who the man waz who fust invented *tite boots*.

He must hav bin a narrow and contrakted kuss.

If he still lives, i hope he haz repented ov hiz sin, or iz enjoying great agony ov sum kind.

I hav bin in a great many tite spots in mi life, but generally could manage to make them average; but there iz no sich thing az making a pair of tite boots average.

Any man who can wear a pair ov tite boots, and be humble, and penitent, and not indulge profane literature, will make a good husband.

Oh! for the pen ov departed Wm. Shakspear, to write an anethema aginst tite boots, that would make ancient Rome wake up, and howl agin az she did once before on a previous oc-cashun.

Oh! for the strength ov Herkules, to tear into shu strings all the tite boots ov creation, and scatter them tew the 8 winds ov heaven.

Oh! for the beauty ov Venus, tew make a big foot look hand-some without a tite boot on it.

Oh! for the patience ov Job, the Apostle, to nurse a tite boot and bless it, and even pray for one a size smaller and more pinchfull.

Oh! for a pair of boots big enough for the foot ov a mountain.

I have been led into the above assortment ov *Oh's!* from hav-ing in my posseshun, at this moment, a pair ov number nine boots, with a pair ov number eleven feet in them.

Mi feet are az uneasy az a dog's nose the fust time he wears a muzzle.

I think mi feet will eventually choke the boots to death.

I live in hopes they will.

I suppozed i had lived long enuff not to be phooled agin in this way, but i hav found that an ounce ov vanity weighs more than a pound ov reason, especially when a man mistakes a big foot for a small one.

Avoid tite boots, mi friend, az you would the grip of the devil; for many a man haz caught for life a fust rate habit for swareing by encouraging hiz feet to hurt hiz boots.

I hav promised mi two feet, at least a dozen ov times during my checkered life, that they never should be strangled agin, but i find them to-day az full ov pain az the stummuk ache from a suddin attak ov tite boots.

But this iz solemly the last pair ov tite boots i will ever wear; i will hearafter wear boots az big az mi feet, if i have to go barefoot to do it.

I am too old and too respectable to be a phool enny more.

Easy boots iz *one* of the luxurys ov life, but i forgit what the other luxury iz, but i don't know az i care, provided i can git rid ov this pair ov tite boots.

Any man can have them for seven dollars, just half what they cost, and if they don't make his feet ake wuss than an angle worm in hot ashes, he needn't pay for them.

Methuseles iz the only man, that i can call to mind now who could hav afforded to hav wore tite boots, and enjoyed them, he had a great deal ov waste time tew be miserable in, but life now days, iz too short, and too full ov actual bizzness to phool away enny of it on tite boots.

Tite boots are an insult to any man's understanding.

He who wears tite boots will have too acknowledge the corn.

Tite boots hav no bowells or mercy, their insides are wrath, and promiskous cussing.

Beware ov tite boots.

★   ★   ★   ★

FASHION—FURY—FELLOW—FUN—FUSS—
FLUNKY—FRETS—FITS—FINIS

FASHION

Fashion is a goddess.

She iz ov the masculine, feminine and nuter gender.

Men worship her in her masculine form—wimmin in her feminine form, and the excentrics in her nuter gender.

She rules the world with a straw, and makes all her suppliants.

She enslaves the poor az well az the ritch, she kneels in sanctuarys, pomps in cabins, and leers at the street corners.

She fits man's foot with a pinching boot, throttles him with a stubborn collar, and dies his mustash with darkness.

She trails the ritch silks ov wimmin along the filthy sidewalks, leads sore-eyed lap dogs with a string, and banishes helpless children to murky nurserys, in the care ov faithless hirelings.

She cheats the excentric with the clap-trap of freedom, and makes him serve her in the habiliments ov the harlequin.

Yea, verily.

FUN

Fun is the soul's vent.

Fun iz whare the crudaitys eskape, where she kiks up her heels, and runs snorting around the lot, unhaltered, and az eager az an eskaped convikt.

Fun iz a safety-valve that lets the steam pressure off from the boiler, and keeps things from bussting.

Fun iz the dansing particles, which fli off from the surface ov unbottled cider, it iz the senseless frolic ov the spring lamb in the clover, it iz the merry twinkle that creeps down tew the korner ov the parson's eye, to stand in the sunlite, and see what's going on.

Fun iz az carliss az a colt, az happy az a bridegroom, and az silly az a luv-sick skool-girl.

Fun iz the holy day wisdum ov the sage, the phools pholly, and everybody's puppet.

Next tew the virtew in this world, the *fun* in it iz what we can least spare.

Truly! O! truly!

FRET

Fret iz a canker, a gangreene, a blister, a boil, salt on a sore place, and a sliver everywhare.

Fret iz frickshun, a dull lancet, a gimblet.

Fret makes a yung man act like an old one, and an old man act like a yung one.

Fret iz a grind stone, whare he holds hiz noze on, haz tew do hiz own turning.

Fret haz burnt more holes thru a man's koppers that all the other hot things, it haz killed az often az the doktors hav, and iz az lawless, and senseless, az a goose.

Fret makes the husband a tyrant, the wife a plague, the child a nuisance, an old maid terrible, and a bachelor disgusting.

Fret makes home a prizon, and puts teeth into the gums ov all life's misfortunes.

I bet! thou bet! he, she, or it, bets!

FURY

Fury iz the tornado ov the inner man, a thunder shower, a black kloud phull ov litening, a tiger out ov hiz cage, a maniac armed, a bull in fli time.

Fury knows no law only its strength, like a rocket, it whizzes till it busts, and when it haz bust, like a rocket, it iz but a senseless and burnt reed.

Fury iz the argument ov tyrants, and the revenge ov the imbecile, the courage ov the kat, and the glowing embers ov dispair.

Fury makes the hornet respektabel, and the pissmire a laffing stock, it makes the eagle allmost human, and clothes the little wren, battling for her brood, with a halo sublime.

Indeed! Indeed!

FITS

Fits are the moral tumblings ov man's natur, the back summersets ov hiz disposishun, the flying trapez ov the critter himself.

Fits prompt him tew climb a greast pole, tew fite a wind mill at short range, to go too near a mule's heels, and to make a cussed phool ov himself generally.

Fits taketh a man bi the end ov hiz noze, and leadeth him into back lots.

Fits hav no conshience, and no judgment.

Fits jerk a man from the path ov duty, they knock him crazy at noontime, they seize him at twilite, and twist him early in the morning.

Sum men, and sum wimmen, are good only in fits, and bad only in fits, when they haint got a fit they are unfit for ennything.

Yes, i think so.

FUSS

Fuss iz like an old setting hen when she cums off from her nest.

Fuss iz like cold water dropt in hot grease—it sputters, and sputters, and then sputters agin.

Fuss iz haff-sister to Hurry, and neither ov them cant do enny thing without gitting in their own way and stepping on themselfs.

There iz more fuss in this world than there iz hurry, and there iz a thousand times more ov either ov them than there iz ov dispatch.

Fuss works hard all day, and don't do enny thing, goes to bed tired at night, then gits up next morning, and begins agin whare she left off.

Oh, dear! Why iz this such?

FLUNKEY

Flunkeys are just abuv loafers, and just belo fellows.

They ain't masculine, feminine, nor nuter—they are just human dough.

They hav the courage ov a spring chicken, the ferocity ov a cricket, the combativness ov a grasshopper, and the bakbone ov an angleworm.

They are human dough made to order, and baked az yu choose.

Ain't it orful?

FINIS

Finis iz the end ov all things—the happiest place in the whole job.

All things on earth hav an end to them, and i kant think ov but phew things now that hain't got two.

A ladder haz two ends to it, and the surest way tew git to the top ov it iz to begin at the bottom.

Finis iz the best and only friend that menny a man in this world ever haz, and sum day Finis will be the autocrat ov the universe.

Bully for yu, Finis.

★   ★   ★   ★

BILL ARP (Charles Henry Smith, 1826-1903)

Bill Arp was a typical Georgia backwoodsman, and a friend of Charles Henry Smith, who "took him off"—Arp's language and morality—to perfection, and used his name for a nom de plume. Smith himself had a university education, was a lawyer, judge, state senator, soldier, farmer, and an altogether refined and cultivated southerner. His character, Bill Arp, unlike Locke's Petroleum V. Nasby, represented the thoughts and values of the citizens of the Confederacy—their glory as well as their racism and bigotry.

Smith was one of the best-loved men in all the Southland. In the words of the Savannah Press: "In the dark days he kept Southern hearts from breaking." Further: "His handling of the negro and southern dialect is trustworthy and accurate. His war-time sketches are valuable...for the insight they give into

Southern attitudes and sentiments." A biographical note says of him: "Perhaps no author has ever more thoroughly represented the people he wrote for, or has had a more sympathetic audience."

Whereas Locke's Petroleum V. Nasby represents a deliberate attempt to portray southern values in such a way that the Union soldiers could joyfully go to war to destroy them, Smith's Bill Arp offers a just and true portrayal of the South and its people at that time.

To understand Bill Arp, today's reader must place himself back in the desperate, depressed times of that vicious and deadly American Civil War that claimed half-a-million American casualties! Once placed back then, the reader can imagine the brave, resourceful, but out-gunned and out-manned Confederate troops desperately short of the materials needed to fight their revolutionary war. Smith/Arp was a soldier in that sorry situation and his defiant, satirical letters to President Lincoln reflect the "up yours" attitude of the ill-starred Confederate G.I.

★   ★   ★   ★

BILL ARP TO ABE LINKHORN

ROME, GA., Aprile 1861.

MR. LINKHORN–SUR: These are to inform you that we are all well, and hope these lines may find you in *statue ko.* We received your proklamation[1]; and as you have put us on very short notis, a few of us boys have conkluded to write you, and ax for a little more time. The fact is, we are most obleeged to have a few more days, for the way things are happening, it is utterly unpossible for us to disperse in twenty days. Old Virginy, and Tennessee, and North Callina, are continually aggravatin us into tumults and carousements, and a body can't disperse until you put a stop to sich unruly condukt on their part. I tried my darndest yisterday to disperse and retire, but it was no go; and besides, your marshal here ain't doing a darned thing—he don't

1. President Lincoln's Proclamation to the rebels to disperse their militia within twenty days.

read the riot act, nor remonstrate, nor nothing, and ought to be turned out.

The fact is, the boys round here want watchin, or they'll take sumthin. A few days ago I heard they surrounded two of our best citizens, because they was named Fort and Sumter. Most of em are so hot that they fairly siz when you pour water on em, and thats the way they make up their military companies here now—when a man applies to jine the volunteers, they sprinkle him, and if he sizzes they take him, and if he don't they don't.

Mr. Linkhorn, sur, privately speakin, I'm afeerd I'll git in a tite place here among these bloods, and have to slope out of it, and I would like to have your Skotch cap and kloak that you travelled in to Washington[1]. I suppose you wouldn't be likely to use the same disgize agin, when you left, and therefore I would propose to swap. I am five feet five, and could git my plow breeches and coat to you in eight or ten days if you can wait that long. I want you to write to me immeditly about things general-ly, and let us know wherebouts you intend to do your fightin. Your proklamation says somethin about takin possession of all the private property at "All Hazards." We can't find no such place on the map. I thought it must be about Charleston, or Savannah, or Harper's Ferry, but they say it aint anywhere down South. One man said it was a little Faktory on an island in Lake Champlain, where they make sand bags. My opinion is, that sand bag bisness won't pay, and it is a great waste of money. Our boys here carry there sand in there gizzards, where it keeps better, and is always handy. I'm afeered your Govern-ment is givin you and your kangaroo a great deal of onnecessary trouble, and my humble advice is, if things don't work better soon, you'd better grease it, or trade the darned old thing off. I'd show you a slite-of-hand trick that would change the whole con-cern into buttons quick. If you don't trade or do sumthin else with it soon, it will spile or die on your hands, sertain.

1. On his way to his inauguration as President, Mr. Lincoln got word of an assassination attempt. The Pinkerton detective agency spirited him from the railroad car and secretly on to Washington. Mr. Lincoln later regretted his move, feeling that it was cowardly and that the people would resent it. The "skotch cap and kloak" were his disguise.

Give my respekts to Bill Seward[1] and the other members of the kangaroo. What's Hannibal[2] doin? I don't hear anything from him nowadays.

Yours, with care,

BILL ARP.

P.S.—If you can possibly xtend that order to thirty days, do so. We have sent you a CHECK at Harper's Ferry (who keeps that darnd old ferry now? its giving us a heap of trubble), but if you positively won't xtend, we'll send you a chek drawn by Jeff Davis, Borygard[3] endorser, payable on sight anywhere.

Yours,

B.A.

★   ★   ★   ★

When Locke, the creator of Petroleum V. Nasby was asked by a reporter to describe his creation, he replied: "Why he's a nickel-plated son-of-a-bitch . . ." And he was! Locke created Nasby as a kind of strawman to be despised and laughed at by the Union forces of the North. He managed this by creating Nasby as a sterotypical citizen of the Confederacy, thus building a character easy to hate, to fight, and to kill. Every war needs hatreds to justify the hard times and the fighting, and Locke created in Petroleum V. Nasby a character passing easy to despise since Nasby stood for slavery and bigotry.

Nasby's view of his imagined confederates in the South was stated in a way to vilify the southern secessionists: "It takes a moderately smart man to be vicious enuff to come tu me; he hez to hev sense enuff to distinguish between good and evil, cussedness enuff to deliberately choose the latter, and brains enuff to do suthing startlin in that line."

Abraham Lincoln kept a pamphlet of Nasby letters in his office, and jokingly offered to "swap places" with Locke if he would teach him to do his kind of writing. And Mr. Lincoln's secretary of the Treasury, George S. Boutwell said—and only half-jokingly—that the crushing of the rebellion was due to three

1. William Seward, Secretary of War.
2. Hannibal Hamlin, Vice President of the United States.
3. Jefferson Davis, Confederate President; P.T.G. Beauregard, Confederate General.

forces; the Army, the Navy and the Nasby Letters! Most important politicians of the North quoted from them. In their time, these letters did yeoman service for the anti-slavery cause, and gave to the tormented nation the heart's balm and ease that only laughter could bring.

David Ross Locke came from an old and always staunchly anti-slavery family from New York state. He was a journeyman printer and newspaper editor of wide experience, and was a superb judge of the needs of the American people of the North during their time of war troubles. He wrote to meet those needs.

★　　　★　　　★　　　★

PROPOSES TO CELEBRATE THE FOURTH OF JULY.

WASHINGTON, Joon the 12th, 1862.

I am in Washington, and wont be home for some time, on account uv biznis pertainin to the re-organization uv the Dimekratik party. I will give sufficient notice uv my comin, so that my frends may surprise me by gittin up a procession to escort me from the cars to my hotel.

The object uv this letter is to suggest a plan for the appropriate celebrashun uv the fourth uv July — the birthday of our Liberties — the day on which Freedom wus proclaimed to all men, exceptin niggers, and them havin a visible admixter uv African blud, et settery. I want to see a pure Dimekratik celebration fer wunst. Let me suggest the following order fer a procession:—

1st. Marshel in uniform uv Home Guard, decorated with a winder sash over the left shoulder.

2d. Banner with inscription, "The Union ez it wuz — under Buchanan![1] the constitooshn ez it is, with some variations."

3d. Barrel containing native corn juice, inscribed, "Our platform."

4th. Carriage containin speaker, reader, and chaplin — ef wun of our perswashin kin be procured.

5th. Wagon with a nigger a lyin down, and my esteemd friend

1. President of the U.S., preceding Pres. Lincoln

a standin onto him — a paregorical illustrashun uv the superiority uv the Anglo-Saxon over the Afrikin races.

6th. Soljers uv the present war. (A few may be procured frum the military prison at Chicago, where they are at present unconstitutionally confined, fer this occasion).

7th. The courthouse officials, with banner and inscription, "Our saleries — we will defend em to the last."

8th. Citizens on hossback with bottles.

9th. Citizens in carriages with bottles.

10th. Citizens on foot with bottles.

(Space on each side reserved for citizens a lyin down with empty bottles.)

11th. Candidates for office, all walkin on their knees.

Procession to form so that the head will rest on the distillery, and the tail on the court-house, representin the beginnin and end uv our glorious party.

On arrivin at the grove, the follerin exercises may be had:

Singin — National ode, "We've Cuffee by de wool."

Readin Vallandigum's[1] address.

Oration — "Nigger: his Past, Present, and Futur" — by myself.

Singin — Patriotic song —

> "Sambo, ketch dat hoe,
>   And resign dat vain idee:
> We've got de power, you know,
>   And you never kin be free."

Benediction, by myself.

In the evenin it would be appropriate to hev fireworks, and perhaps I might be induced to deliver an oration on "Nigger: his Past, Present, and Futur."

Sich a celebrashun would elevate the spirits uv the faithful, and help materially towards makin a triumph this autumn.

PETROLEUM V. NASBY

1. Clement Vallandigham was an Ohio Congressman and Copperhead exiled to the Confederacy for disloyalty.

★   ★   ★   ★

SHOWS WHY HE SHOULD NOT BE DRAFTED[1]

August the 6th, 1862.

I see in the papers last nite that the Government hez instituted a draft, and that in a few weeks sum hundreds uv thousands uv peaceable citizens will be dragged to the tented field. I know not wat others may do, but ez for me, I cant go. Upon a rigid examination uv my fizzleckle man, I find it wood be wus nor madness for me to undertake a campane, to-wit:—

1. I'm bald-headid, and hev bin obliged to wear a wig these 22 years.

2. I hev dandruff in wat scanty hair still hangs around my venerable temples.

3. I hev a catarrah.

4. I hev lost, since Stanton's order to draft, the use uv one eye entirely, and hev chronic inflammashen in the other.

5. My teeth is all unsound, my palette aint exactly rite, and I hev hed bronchitis 31 years last June. At present I hev a cough, the paroxisms uv which is friteful to behold.

6. I'm holler-chestid, am short-winded, and hev always had pains in my back and side.

7. I am afflicted with chronic diarrear and kostivniss [constipation]. The money I hev paid (or promise to pay), for Jayneses karminnytiv balsam and pills[2] wood astonish almost anybody.

8. I am ruptured in nine places, and am entirely enveloped with trusses.

9. I hev varicose veins, hev a white-swellin on one leg and a fever sore on the uther; also one leg is shorter than tother, though I handle it so expert that nobody never noticed it.

10. I hev corns and bunyons on both feet, wich wood prevent me from marchin.

1. One of the most surprising results of the conscription was the amount of disease disclosed among men between "eighteen and forty-five," in districts where quotas could not be raised by volunteering.
2. A patent medicine to relieve colic, grippe, and flatulence!

I dont suppose that my political opinions, wich are aginst the prosecution uv this unconstitutional war, wood hev any weight, with a draftin officer; but the above reasons why I cant go, will, I make no doubt, be suffishent.

PETROLEUM V. NASBY

★　　★　　★　　★

IS FINALLY DRAFTED.

CAMP UV THE 778TH OHIO KIDNAPT MELISHY, TOLEDO, October the 17th, 1862.

I am here, clad in the garb of slavery! Nasby, clothed in a bob-tailed blue coat, a woolin shirt, and blue pants, with a Austrian musket in his hands, a going thro the exercise! Good hevings! wat a spectacle!

The draft was over, and I thought that once more I'd visit my native land. Gaily I stepped abord the boat that was to carry me from British shores — gaily I say, for my money hed given out some weeks before, and I hed earned a precarious subsistence a sawin wood in partnership with a disgustin mulatto, and I looked forward with joyful anticipation to the time when I should again embrace Louiser Jane (the pardner uv my buzzum), and keep my skin perpetually full uv the elixir uv life, out uv her washin money. Joyfully I sprang off the boat onto the wharf at Toledo, when a heavy hand was laid onto my shoulder. Twas a soljer! The follerin conversation ensued:

"Wat wantest thou, my gentle friend?"

"I want yoo, my gay Canadian."

"On wat grounds?" retorted I.

"On the ground uv eludin uv the draft," sez he.

"You're mistaken," sez I; "I'm a Ablishnist — a emissary. I hev bin a spreadin the bread uv life among the poor colored brethrin in Canada, and am jest returnin to run thru another lot. Let me pass, I entreat thee, nor stay me in my good work."

"Not much," sez he. "I know better. You're a butternut."

"How knowst thou?" sez I.

"Yoor nose," sez he. "That Bacchus beacon light wuz never got out uv spring water."

"Yoor knowledge uv men and things is too much for me. I confess, and surrender at discretion — do with me ez thou wilt."

And he did. I wuz led out to camp, and wuz allowed to volunteer to fite against my convictions — against my brethren, who hev taken up arms in a rightous cause. So be it. Hentzforth the name uv Nasby will shine in the list uv martyrs.

Amid the dark, deep gloom that envelopes me, one ray uv light strikes me. I hev seen the election returns, and when I seed em, I yelled Hallelogy! Me and another victim uv Linkin's tyranny, who is a Dimekrat (he wuz a postmaster under Pres. Buchanan, and when removed by Linkin, dident give up the balance uv money he had on hand, fearin twood be used to subvert our free institutions), had a jubilee. We smuggled a bottle uv condensed ecstacy, and celebratid muchly.

"The North's redeemed!" shoutid I.

"Let the eagle scream!" yelled he.

"The Quakers hev voted!" shoutid I.

"Abolitionism dead!" screamed he.

"Dimokrasy's triumphed!" laft I; and so on, until after midnite, when, completely exhausted, we sank into slumber, with a empty bottle atween us.

PETROLEUM V. NASBY.

P.S. — Tell Louiser Jane that I may never see her again — that should it be my fate to perish on the battle-field, amid the roar uv battle and the horrors uv miscellaneous carnage, my last thought, ez life ebbs slowly away, shall be uv her; and ask her if she can't send me half or three quarters uv the money she gits fer washin, ez whisky costs fritefully here.

P.V.N.

★   ★   ★   ★

One of the famous Nasby satires, of southern attitudes, that were so influential in the North during the Civil War and, for that reason, so much admired by President Lincoln, General

Grant, and others.

PREACHES ON "THE PRODIGAL SUN"

CHURCH UV THE NEW DISPENSASHUN,
January 31, 1864.

My brethren and sistern: I shall make some remarks this mornin based upon the bootiful parable of the prodigal son. I would read 2 you the passage but the Bible I hev is the only wun in the township, and I lent it yisterday 2 Squire Gavitt, who sed swearin witnesses on almanacs wouldn't do in hoss cases, and he hasn't brung it back. The skripter sez, in substance:

There was a certain man who hed 2 suns. The youngest hed a taste fer that branch uv agricultural pursuits known ez sowin wild oats, so he asked the old man fer his share uv the estate. He got it, turned it into greenbacks, and went off. He commenced livin high—boardin at big hotels, and keepin trottin hosses, and playin billiards, and sich. In about a year he run thru his pile, and wuz dead broke. Then his credit playd out, and he wuz in a tite place for his daily bread. The idea struck him that he hed better put for home, which he did. The old man saw him a comin, and he run out and met him, and give him a new coat, and a order for a pair of shoes, and killed a fat calf, and hed flour doins. The oldest boy objected 2 these, sayin, "Lo I hav servd thee these menny years, and thou never madest no splurge over me, but when this thy son, who hez fooled away his pile, returns, you kill calves and sich." Then the old man retorts sayin, "My sun who wuz lost is found, the sheep who went astray is cum back, let us be merry."

My brethern, this parable applies ez well to the present time ez though it wuz made fer it. Uncle Samuel is the old man, the suthern wing uv the Dimocratic party is the prodigal, and the Abolitionist is the oldest son. The south got tired and went off on its own hook. It has, I make no doubt, spent the heft uv its substance, and will shortly conclude to come home. Now the grate question uv the hour is how shall he be received. My friends, the Dimocratic rule is to foller the scripter wen you can make a point by so doin. In this pertickeler case Godliness is gain, halleloogy, therefore, let us be Godly. Let Uncle Samuel see the repentant prodigal afar off — let him go out to seek him, or send Fernand Wood[4], and when he hez found him let him fall, not upon his neck, but at his feet — let him put onto him the purple robe which is royalty and upon his hand a ring, which is dominion, which is a improvement upon scripter.

But the Abolishnist, who is the elder son, steps up and sez, "Nary. He wuz a doin well, and he wented out from us, takin all that wuz his own, and such az he could steel, all uv which he hez spent upon such harlots as African slavery, State rights, and Suthren independence, which last two mentioned is whited sepulchres. I sent my sons Grant, and Rosencranz[5], and Ben Butler[6] after him, but lo! when he wuz strong and vigorous he did despitefully use them. Now that he is weak from hunger, let him brindle. Ef we take him to our bossoms, let him cum on his knees, let him cast off the harlots that hav seduced him, that ther may be no more trubble in all the land."

My brethren, we must take him back ez the old man did in the bible. Why, do you ask? Because he wuz always the old man's pet, and had things his own way. We wuz his frends and shared with him the stealins, but sence he went out the Abolishun brother and his friends hav controlled things and where air we? Echo answers nowhere! We occupy low places in the sinagogue, and the doggery keepers [saloons] go mornin about the streets and refuse to be comforted because their cash is not plenty, and ef we take back the prodigal shorn of his strength, of what avail is he to us? He must cum back as strong as ever, he must bring his harlots with him — he must RULE! Then shall we hev the Post Orfises, and then shel we again live on the fat uv the land, dodgin the curse of labor. Brethrin, let us be diligent in this great work, instant in seeson and out of seeson.

A collecshun wuz takin' up fer the purpose uv sending a mis-

4. Fernando Wood, Mayor of New York City.
5. General Rosenkranz of the Union Army.
6. General Ben Butler of the Union Army.

sionary to Massachusits, which yielded 7 dollars. Ez the amount wouldn't pay the ralroad fare, it wuz voted to apply it to havin my boots half-sold and buyin a new handkurcheef.

PETROLEUM V. NASBY
Paster uv sed Church in charge.

★　　　★　　　★　　　★

ORPHEUS C. KERR (Robert Henry Newell, 1836-1901)

Newell was the son of a wealthy, famous inventor who gave him a superior education in New York private schools. He began his career as a writer-editor for New York City newspapers, developing his nom de plume — Orpheus C. Kerr (Orpheus Seeker). So popular was Orpheus C. Kerr that four volumes of his writing were published during the years 1861-1864 — Civil War years.

A biography of Newell stated that he deserved "a permanent place in the history of American burlesque writing", referring to his parodies of many of the best-known writers of his day. And Abraham Lincoln told General Meigs — who had not read the Orpheus Kerr papers: "Anyone who has not read them is a heathen!"

Newell made a delightful distinction between wit and humor: "Humor is the sunshine of the language, wit its lightning."

As one critic said of him: "His humor demands an uproarious reader."

Washington, D.C., October 26th 1862

It pains me to say, my boy, that Captain Villiam Brown so far forgot himself on Wednesday, upon discovering the non-arrival of the spectacles, that he used language of an incedeniary description against the beloved General of the Mackerel Brigade, thereby proving himself to be one of those crazy fanatics who are trying to ruin our distracted country. He said, my boy, that the adored General of the Mackerel Brigade was a dead-beat, and furthermore observed that he would be very sorry to take his word.

Such language could not pass unnoticed, and a Court of Inquiry, composed of Captains Bob Shortly, Samyule Sa-mith, and Colonel Wobert Wobinson, was instantly called. The Court had a decanter and tumbler only, to aid its deliberations, it being determined by the War Department that no fact which could be detected even by the aid of a glass, should go uninspected.

Villiam having been summoned to the presence, Samyule declared the Court in session, and says he:

"The sad duty has become ours, to investigate certing charges against a brother in arms which has heretofore been the mirror of chivalry. It is specified against him:

" 'First—That said Captain Villiam Brown, Eskevire, did affirm, declare, avow, testify, and articulate, with his tongue, licker, and organ of speech, that the General of the Mackerel Brigade was a dead-beat.

" 'Second—That aforesaid Captain Villiam Brown, Eskevire, did proclaim, utter, enunciate, fulminate and swear, that he would not take the word of the General of the Mackerel Brigade.'

"What has the culprit to say to these charges? Did he say that our idolized Commander was a dead-beat?"

Villiam smiled calmly, and says he: "The chaste remark exactly fits the orifice of my lips."

"Confine yourself to English," says Colonel Wobinson, majestically. "What do you mean by the observation?"

"Why," says Villiam, pleasantly, "I meant, that before he was beaten he must be dead. And after death, you know," says Villiam, reaching one hand abstractedly toward the decanter, "after death, you know, we must all b'eaten by worms."

This explanation, my boy, was satisfactory, and conveyed a grave moral lesson; but the court felt convinced that the second charge could not be thus simply answered.

Captain Samyule Sa-mith set down the tumbler for a moment, and says he:

"You're not guilty on the first count, Villiam; but didn't you say that you wouldn't take the word of the General of the Mackerel Brigade?"

"Which I did," says Villiam.

"And what excuse have you to offer, my trooper?" says Captain Bob Shorty, pointing the question with his spoon.

"Is the general a gentleman?" says Villiam, searchingly.

The court believed him to be such.

"Ah!" says Villiam, "then if he's a gentleman, he always *keeps* his word, and of course it is impossible to *take* it."

Verdict of "not guilty, with a recommendation to mercy."

Courts of Inquiry, my boy, are calculated to draw out the rich humor of military character, and are equally useful and appropriate with all other jokes, in times of devastating war.

Yours, smilingly,
ORPHEUS C. KERR

★   ★   ★   ★

Washington, D.C. August 30, 1862

The uniform of the Southern Confederacy is much respected by many of our officers, my boy, and is the only guise in which a fellow-being may scrutinize the national strategic works with entire safety.

Thus attired, I joined the Mackeral Brigade in its cheerful work of pushing Richmond away from its martial front, and having penetrated to the rear where horrible carnage was being wrought in the frantic ranks of the Confederacy, I beheld the idolized General of the Mackerel Brigade anxiously searching for something upon the ground. In a moment, he looked up, and says he to the warriors in his neighborhood:

"My children, have you seen anything of a small black bottle that I placed upon the grass, just now, when I turned to speak to my aid?"

A Mackerel chap coughed respectfully, and says he: "I guess it was taken by some equestrian Confederacies, which has just made another raid."

"Thunder!" says the General, "that's the third bottle I've lost in the same way within an hour." And he proceeded slowly and thoughtfully to mount his horse, which stood eyeing him with funereal solemnity and many inequalities of surface.

Turning to another part of the line, my boy, I beheld Captain Villiam Brown and Captain Bob Shorty in the act of performing a great strategic movement with the indomitable Conic Section, many of whom were employing the moment to take a last look at the canteens presented to them before leaving home by their devoted mothers. A number of reckless Confederacies had just crossed a bridge spanning a small stream near by, and the object of this daring movement was to suddenly destroy the bridge before they could retreat and then make prisoners of the whole.

It was a sublime conception, my boy — it was a sublime conception, and rich with strategy.

Like panthers surrounding their unsuspecting prey, the wily Mackerels swept noiselessly across the bridge, applied their axes with the quickness of thought, and in a moment the doomed structure fell splashing into the water. It was beautiful to see Villiam's honest exultation at this moment; his eyes brightened like small bottles of brandy with the light shining through them, and says he:

"We have circumvented the Confederacy. Ah!" says Villiam, proudly; "the United States of America is now prepared to continue in the exchange business, and —"

He paused. He paused, my boy, because he suddenly observed that Captain Bob Shorty had commenced to scratch his head in a dismal manner.

"I'm blessed," says Captain Bob Shorty, in a cholerical manner — "I'm blessed if I don't think there's some mistake here, my military infant!'

"Ha!" says Villiam, with dignity; "do you discover a flaw in the great chain woven by the United States of America around the doomed Confederacy?"

Captain Bob Shorty again scratched his head, and says he:

"I don't wish to make unpleasant insinuations; but it seems to me that this here body of infantry has left itself on the wrong side of the stream!"

And so it had, my boy. By one of those little mistakes which will sometimes occur in the most victorious armies, the Conic Section had thoughtlessly *crossed the bridge* before destroying it, thus leaving themselves on one side of the river, while the riotous Confederacies were on the other.

How they got across again, at a fordable place higher up, just in time to see the Confederacies cross again, at a fordable place lower down, I will not pause to tell you, as such information might retard enlistments.

★   ★   ★   ★

Washington, D.C., November 7th, 1862

The late election in New York, my boy, has electrified everybody except our Honest Abe, who still goes about smiling, like a long and amiable sexton, and continues to save our distracted country after the manner of an honest man. On Tuesday night, a high moral Democratic chap, of much watch-seal, who had just received a dispatch all about the election, went to see the Honest Abe, for the express purpose of telling him that the Democratic party had been born again, and was on the point of protesting against everything whatsoever, except the Constitution of our forefathers. He found the Honest Abe cracking some walnuts before the fire, my boy, and says he:

"The celebrated Democratic organization, of which I am Assistant Engineer, has carried the State of New York in a manner impossible to express, and will now proceed to demand of you a vigorous prosecution of that unnatural strife in which are involved our lives, our liberties, and the pursuit of happiness. We admire to see your harmless honesty," says the chap, blandly, "and we believe you to be a fresh egg; but we protest against the arbitrary arrest of men which is patriots, only conservatively Democratic; and we insist upon a vigorous prosecution of Constitutional hostilities against our misguided brothers who are now offering irregular opposition to the Government."

The Honest Abe cracked a walnut, and says he: "You say, neighbor, that the organization still insists upon a vigorous prosecution of the war?"

The Democratic chap sliced a toothpick from the arm of the chair with his knife, and says he: "That is the present platform on which we are *E pluribus unum*."

"Well," says the Honest Abe, "I believe that you mean well; but am reminded of a little story.

"When I was practicing law out in Illinois," says the Honest Abe, twisting the bow of his black necktie around from under his left ear, "there was an old cock, with two sons, living near me in a tumble-down old shanty. He lived there until half his roof blew off one windy night, and then he concluded to move to a new house, where the chimney didn't take up all the upper story. On the day when he moved, he'd got most all his traps changed to the other residence, and had sent one of his sons to see that they were all got safely indoors, when suddenly a shower commenced to come up. The old man and his other off-spring, who had stayed to hurry him, were taking up a carpet from the floor at the time the first dose of thunder cracked, and the offspring says he, 'Hurry up, old crazy-bones, or we'll be ketched in the freshet before you get up this here rich fabric.' The stern parent heeded the admonition, and went ripping away the carpet around the edges of the room, until he came near where the offspring was standing, and there it stuck. He pulled, but it wouldn't come, and he says, says he: "Pears to me that dod-rotted tack must be a tenpenny nail — it holds on so.' You see, the old screw was very blind without his specs," says the Honest Abe, buttoning his vest askew, "and he couldn't see just where the tack was. Another peal of thunder at this moment made the irascible offspring still madder, and he says, says he: 'You misabul old cripple, if you don't hurry up we'll be ketched, I tell you!' As he made this dutiful remark he went stamping to the window, and at the same moment the cantankerous tack came out, and the aged parent went over on his back with the carpet up to his chin. He got up and dusted, and says he: 'Well, now, that *is* cur'ous — how suddent it went. Then he proceeded to rip away again, until it came near the window, and there it stuck once more. The wild offspring saw him tugging again, and it made him so wrathy that he says, says he: 'Why in thunder didn't you take the nails out first, you crooked old sinner, you? It's enough to make me weep afresh for the old woman, to see how you —' But he didn't finish his observation; for, as he walked toward where the hammer lay, the tack came out, and the old 'un went to bed again under the carpet. Up sprang the sad parent, spitting rags, and he says, says he: 'Well now, how cur'ous — to think it should come so suddent!' Still on he went, until the carpet was all up from around the edges; but when he tried to draw it away on his shoulder, it was fast somewheres yet. R-r-rum-bum-boom! went the thunder; and says the infuriated offspring, says he: 'Well, I never did see such a blundering old dad as you be. We'll be ketched in the rain as sure as grasshoppers; and all because you didn't take my advice about the hammer in the first place.' The poor old 'un tugged, and pulled, and panted, and says he: 'Well, now, it *is* cur'ous, I swun to massey. There can't be no tacks way out in the middle of the floor here, can they?' To make sure, the old blind-pate was going down on his knees to take a mouse-eye view, when all of a sudden he gave a start, and he says, says he: 'Why, 'pears to me, Sammy, *you're standin' on the carpet yourself!*' And so he was — so he was," says the Honest Abe, smiling into the fire, "and that was the why the carpet had stuck fast in so many places."

"Now," says the Honest Abe, poking the Democratic chap in the ribs with his knuckles; "if your organization wants me to move vigorously in this war, tell them not to be standing on my carpet all the time. Otherwise, I must still keep tacking about."

The Democratic chap had been slowly rising from his chair as this small moral tale drew toward its exciting conclusion, and at the last word he fled the apartment with quivering watch-seal.

Our President, my boy, has a tale for every emergency, as a rat-trap has an emergency for every tail.

★ ★ ★ ★

Dr. George W. Bagby (1828-1883) was a staunch Virginian and one of the most popular southern writers of a kind of humor

*that helped sustain the morale and the mores of the Con-
federacy. Curiously, he was thoroughly trained as a physician
and practiced for a brief time with his physician father. But
Bagby's interests were literary, not medical. Further, in his day
the physical demands of a medical practice were terribly heavy,
wearing, and for the "dyspeptic" and fragile young physician,
too punishing. He therefore turned to writing, as more suitable
to his talent and uncertain health.*

*As did Artemus Ward and Josh Billings, Bagby traveled the
lecture circuit, giving humorous lectures at which he was
wonderfully successful in the South, but far less so in the North
where his southern views on the righteousness of the Confederate cause satirized the Union and, of course, dampened the
enthusiasm of northerners for his wit. This becomes understandable when we read his "History Uv the Waw," where he writes
these imperishable lines: "The world iz full uv corns maid to be
trod on, especially by histoarians uv thar own times; and be
durn ef I don't inten to tred on as many of 'em as I possibly kin.
But Confedrit corns, I shall tred litely on um." He goes on to
irony, excoriating the news coming from the War Department at
Washington: "Far frum imitating the exampul of the Waw
Department at Washintun, and tellin uv the truth recklssly and
regardllss of consequences, I shall not hesitate, whenever it suits
my puppus, to tell the most infernel lies that ever issued from
mortal man . . ." Of course, his southern readers relished the
sarcasm, the delicious mockery in that kind of humor.*

*Some notion of the veneration for him that was felt by his
southern readers can be sensed from the eulogy his fellow
Virginian, and then famous novelist, John Esten Cooke,
delivered at the time of his death: "Never in Virginia letters
shall we see his like again."*

*Mozis Addums and Jud Brownin were two pen names that Dr.
Bagby used. In the second selection, with Jud Brownin, the
humor will seem particularly apt by anyone who has ever been
transported — by great music played superbly — to faraway
lands and places.*

FLIZE
By Mozis Addums

I hate a fli.

A fli is got no manners. He ain't no gentlemun. He's an in-trooder, don't send in no card, nor ask a introduction, nor don't knok at the front door, and never, never thinks uv takin off his hat.

Fust thing you know he is in bed with you and up your nose — tho what he wants up there iz a mystery — and he invites hisself to breakfast, and sets down in yore butter, without brushin his pants.

He helps hisself to sugar, and meat, and molasses, and bread, and preserves, and vinnegar, and everything — don't wait for no invitashum. He's got a good appetite, and jist as soon eat one thing as anuther.

'Taint no use to challenge him for taking liberties; he keeps up a hostile correspondence with you, wether or not, and shoots hisself at you like a bullet, and he never misses, never.

He'll kiss yore wife 20 times a day, and zizz and zoo, and ridikule you if you say a word, and he'd rather you'd slap at him than not, cause he's a dodger uv the dodginest kind. Every time you slap, you don't slap him, but slap yo'self, and he zizzes and points the hind leg uv skorn at you till he aggravates you to distraction.

He glories in lightin every pop on the exact spot whar you drove him from, wich proves the intention to tease you. Don't tell me he ain't got no mind; he knows what he is after. He's got sense, and too much ov it, though he never went to school a day in his life except in the sugar dish. He's a mean, malignant, audacious, premedditated cuss.

His mother never paddled him with a slipper in her life. His morals was neglecktid, and he lacks a good deal of humility mightily. He ain't bashful a bit, and I doubts if he blushes often. In fact, he was never fetched up at all.

He was born full grown; he don't get old, neither. Things gits old, but he never gits old — and he's impudent and mischevus to the day uv his death.

He droops in cold wether, and you kin mash him on a winder-pane, but you've jest put your finger in it. He cums agin next year, and a heap mo with him. 'Taint no use.

One fli to a family might do for amusement, but the good uv so many flize I bedog if I kin see. Kin you?

I have thought much abut flize, and I has noticed how oftin they stops in thar deviltry to comb thar heads and scratch thar nose with thar forelegs, and gouge thar arm-pits under thar wings, and the tops of thar wings with thar hind legs, and my candid opinion ar that flize is lousy; they itches all the time, is miserable, and that makes em bad-tempered, and they want to make other people miserable, too.

Ef that ain't the philosophy of flize, I give it up.

Altho a fli don't send in his card, he always leaves one, and I don't like it. 'Taint pretty if 'tis round. He can't make a cross-mark — only a dot — and he is always a dottin whar there ain't no i's. There is no end to his periods, but he never comes to a full stop.

Sich handwritin is disagreeable.

He's a artist, but his fresco and his wall-paperin I don't ad-mire. Thars too much sameness in his patterns. His specs is the only specs that don't help the eyes. You can't see through um, and you don't want too.

I hate a fli.

Durn a fli.

★   ★   ★   ★

Anton Rubenstein (1829-1894) was a Russian child prodigy who came to be the world's foremost pianist and one of the great composers of all time. From 1868 on, for twenty years, he toured American cities on an annual schedule, and was enor-mously popular in his piano concerts. In the following story, a country rustic (early hillbilly) hears a piano, and a piano concert, for the first time. The pianist is Rubenstein, and Dr. Bagby records the country bumpkin's impressions.

JUD. BROWNIN'S ACCOUNT OF
RUBENSTEIN'S PLAYING

"Jud, they say you heard Rubenstein play, when you were in New York."

"I did, in the cool."

"Well, tell us about it."

"What! me? I might's well tell you about the creation of the world."

"Come, now; no mock modesty. Go ahead."

"Well, sir, he had the blamedest biggest, catty-cornedest pianner you ever laid eyes on; somethin' like a distracted billiard table on three legs. The lid was heisted, and mighty well it was. If it hadn't been he'd a-tore the entire insides clean out, and scattered 'em to the four winds of heaven."

"Played well, did he?"

"You bet he did; but don't interrup' me. When he first set down he appeard to keer mighty little 'bout playin', and wished he hadn't come. He tweedle-leedled a little on the treble, and twoodle-oodle-oodled some on the base — just foolin' and boxin' the thing's jaws for bein' in his way. And I says to a man settin' next to me, says I, 'what sort of fool playin' is that?' And he says, 'Heish!' But presently his hands commenced chasin' one another up and down the keys, like a passel of rats scamperin' through a garret very swift. Parts of it was sweet, though, and reminded me of a sugar squirrel turnin' the wheel of a candy cage.

" 'Now,' I says to my neighbor, 'he's showin' off. He thinks he's a doing of it; but he ain't got no idee, no plan of nothin'. If he'd play me up a tune of somekind or other, I'd —'

"But my neighbor says 'Heish!' very impatient.

"I was just about to git up and go home, bein' tired of that foolishness, when I heard a little bird waking up away off in the woods, and calling sleepy-like to his mate, and I looked up and I see that Ruben was beginnin' to take some interest in his

business, and I set down agin. It was the peep 'o day. The light
come faint from the east, the breeze blowed gentle and fresh,
some more birds waked up in the orchard, then some more in
the trees near the house, and all begun singin' together. People
begun to stir, and the gal opened the shutters. Just then the first
beam of the sun fell upon the blossoms; a leetle more and it
tetched the roses on the bushes, and the next thing it was broad
day; the sun fairly blazed; the birds sang like they'd split their
little throats; all the leaves was movin', and flashin' diamonds of
dew, and the whole wide world was bright and happy as a king.
Seemed to me like there was a good breakfast in every house in
the land, and not a sick child or woman anywhere. It was a fine
mornin'.

"And I says to my neighbor, 'that's music, that is.'

"Then, all of a sudden, old Ruben changed his tune. He
ripped and he rar'd, he tipped and tear'd, he pranced and he
charged like the grand entry at a circus. 'Peared to me that all
the gas in the house was turned on at once, things got so bright,
and I helt up my head, ready to look any man in the face, and
not afeard of nothin'. It was a circus, and a brass band, and a
big ball, all goin' on at the same time. He lit into them keys like
a thousand of brick, he give 'em no rest, day nor night; he set
every livin' joint in me a-goin', and not bein' able to stand it no
longer, I jumpt spang onto my seat, and jest hollered:

" 'Go it, my Rube!'

"Every blamed man, woman and child in the house rose on
me, and shouted, 'Put him out! put him out!'

"Put your great-grandmother's grizzly grey greenish cat into
the middle of next month!' I says. 'Tech me if you dare! I paid
my money, and you jest come a-nigh me.'

"With that, some several policemen run up, and I had to sim-
mer down. But I would a fit any fool that laid hands on me, for I
was bound to hear Ruby out or die.

"He had changed his tune again. He hopped like light ladies
and tip-toed fine from end to end of the keyboard. He played
soft, and low, and solemn. I heard the church bells over the

hills. The candles in heaven was lit, one by one. I saw the stars rise. The great organ of eternity began to play from the world's end to the world's end, and all the angels went to prayers. Then the music changed to water, full of feeling that couldn't be thought, and began to drop — drip, drop, drip, drop — clear and sweet, like tears of joy fallin' into a lake of glory. It was sweeter than that. It was as sweet as a sweetheart sweetenin' sweetness with white sugar, mixt with powdered silver and seed diamonds. It was too sweet. I tell you the audience cheered. Ruben he kinder bowed, like he wanted to say, 'Much obleeged, but I'd rather you wouldn't interrup' me.'

"He stopt a minute or two, to fetch breath. Then he got mad. He run his fingers through his hair, he shoved up his sleeves, he opened his coat tails a leetle further, he drug up his stool, he leaned over, and, sir, he just went for that old pianner. He slapt her face, he boxed her jaws, he pulled her nose, he pinched her ears and he scratched her cheeks, till she farly yelled. He knockt her down and he stomped on her shameful. She bellowed like a bull, she bleated like a calf, she howled like a hound, she squeeled like a pig, she shrieked like a rat, and then he wouldn't let her up. He run a quarter-stretch down the low grounds of the base, till he got clean into the bowels of the earth, and you heard thunder galloping after thunder, through the hollows and caves of perdition. The house trembled, the lights danced, the walls shook, the floor come up, the ceilin' come down, the sky split, the ground rockt — heavens and earth, creation, sweet potatoes, Moses, nine-pences, glory, ten-penny nails, my Mary Ann, hallelujah, Samson in a persimmon tree, Jeroosalem, Tump Tompson in a tumbler-cart, roodle-oodle-oodle-oodle — BANG!

With that *bang!* he lifted hisself bodily into the air, and he come down with his knees, his ten fingers, his ten toes, his elbows and his nose, striking every single solitary key on that pianner at the same time. The thing busted and went off into seventeen hundred and fifty-seven thousand five hundred and forty-two hemi-demi-semi-quivers, and I know'd no mo'.

Chapter VI
Abraham Lincoln's Stories

We Americans view our greatest citizens in dignified, solemn, usually grave images, especially our deceased presidents. It is difficult for us to imagine raucous laughter and a knee-slapping response to jokes from George Washington, Thomas Jefferson, Ulysses S. Grant, Calvin Coolidge, or John F. Kennedy. Such great men, saddled with world-shaking responsibility, evoke in us veneration and sobriety — but hardly a grin. The single exception is Abraham Lincoln, our most honored and noblest citizen about whom more has been written than any other, except Jesus. And yet the voluminous writings about him rarely have much to say about the humor in the man. His wit and humor seem to most biographers something reductive, almost out of place in so important a man. Too, the quasi-sanctity that has come to surround him is strengthened by the unique respect in which the rest of the world holds him, so that, as the generations pass, we tend to forget the plebian side of him, his engagingly human parts so wonderfully revealed through his sense of humor. His wise and funny stories represent a welcome extension to the legacy that this great man gave and gives to generations of Americans. His stories, jokes, sayings represent a kind of cement that binds up our often-exacerbated, yet shared, American humanity.

The President was frequently criticized for his levity during our bloody Civil War. But the unrelieved anguish of that awful conflict required the therapy humor could provide to maintain his mental equilibrium, to grant him proper perspective with problems, and to keep in mind the meaning of that pertinent passage from Proverbs: "For surely there is a future."

But how could he refrain from laughter and those funny stories and jokes when to consider his own background and the circumstances that had led him to the highest post in the nation were the vital stuff of humor? For one thing, the sheer oddity, the fantastic incongruity that had brought him from a raw fron-

tier life with only a year of schooling — in a "blab" school at that — to President of the United States where he must direct his Cabinet filled with distinguished men of far more formal education and "refined" living than he had, was a "study in contrasts" that at times must have overwhelmed him with its fantasy and tickled his funnybone to the core.

Again, to simply recall those early years in log cabins — when in the winter of 1816, in Indiana, the Lincolns lived in a three-sided hutch, a "half-faced camp" open on the fourth side with only a roaring fire to keep out the cold — just to contrast those spartan years with his present prestigious home with servants, superb furnishings, comforts, conveniences must have seemed to him a wryly funny switch of fate.

More! Certainly he saw the humorous anomaly of his job when he thought of his disorderly office in Springfield, where grain had sprouted on the unswept office floor, and his filing system was so bad that he wrote in his hat: "When you can't find it anywhere else, look in here!" And yet it was required of him that he bring method and order and cohesiveness to an entire nation even if he had to lead a Civil War to do it.

As if all this were not humorously skewed enough, the President had all of his adult life suffered depression — "hypochonria," as he called it, or "Hypo," a sadness his friends remarked about. And yet, despite his periodic melancholy, this superior man was expected to lift up and sustain the depressed morale, the sad soul of the Union lest it be overwhelmed by "the blues" and quit to allow the South to secede and destroy the Union.

Clearly, there were incongruity, incommensurateness, hilarious irony and paradox in this great man's public life so that, commonsensical and clear-eyed as he was, he must have grinned at all those wildly unpredictable switches and divagations his life had taken. Of course it is true, as he said in his Farewell Address to his Springfield friends — in a kind of prayer — that just as divine help had been needed by President George Washington, so would it be needed by himself because: "With-

out the assistance of that Divine Being, who ever attended him, I cannot succeed. With that assistance I cannot fail." Obviously, the President had that assistance. And yet when one recalls the story of the two Quakers discussing Mr. Lincoln's entry into heaven, one wonders if Deity might all along have been sharing the joke and the humor of Mr. Lincoln's life as President. The Quaker story had one of them asking why the other doubted that Mr. Lincoln would get into heaven, especially after the President had recited his many virtues, and contributions to mankind, while on earth. "How could thee doubt that St. Peter will let him enter?" asked the one Quaker. "Because," replied the other, "The Lord will think that Abraham is only joking."

As to his own jokes and stories, most were not original with him but were adaptations of those heard on the 8th Judicial Circuit in Illinois, or ones that he found in weekly newspapers and magazines — like Harper's Weekly — or in collections of jokes such as Joe Miller's Joke Book. His neighbor and friend in Springfield, Issac R. Diller, said: "I do not think Mr. Lincoln ever brought forth from his imagination a single story, but that they were based on what he had seen or heard. Many of them were so changed that the man who invented them would not have recognized his work." He himself told one observer that he reckoned about half the stories attributed to him were, in fact, told by him. But there are so many stories from so many honorable people over so many years that we cannot foreclose the notion that he did tell them. And the truth of the matter is only relative since, if honorable people said he told them a story, and if it sounds right, fits what we know about him, his style, cleverness, taste, wit, etc., then it is not only gratifying to assume he told it, but it is also a reasonable judgement.

His talent at story telling was recognized everywhere. It helped that he was a fine actor, using his 6' 4" height, his very long arms and legs, that unforgettable and mobile face to drive home the "nib," the point of his stories. Too, he had a keen ear for dialect, telling stories in German accent, or with an Irish lilt, or with the drawl and elisions of Black speech. Night after night

*while on the Judicial Circuit, for six months of the year, story
telling was his recreation, and that of gatherings of the towns-
people, visitors, judges, lawyers — even the jurymen — all having fun together, sometimes until early morning.*

*But the jokes and stories were not told simply for the entertain-
ment of the groups that heard them. These stories helped to
make his name known throughout the areas that could bring
him legal clients and votes in political contests. For Mr. Lincoln
had learned the secret of the Yankee peddlers before him, a
secret still holding true, that a well-told, funny story is an easy,
sure, and amusing way to build customers and clients, to influence juries and judges, to convince voters, or, as we say today,
to "win friends and influence people."*

*Not all of the stories were "nice," fit for the "parlor." Sadly,
most of the bawdy ones were suppressed by his early biographers, and so lost to us. In a revealing letter, Leonard Swett, an
old friend of Mr. Lincoln, advised Billy Herndon not to include
the many off-color stories in the Lincoln biography he was
preparing. Swett told Billy to "excise" the raunchy stories since
to include them would hurt the sale of his book and, more, that
people did not want to read about such things, and would not
believe that Mr. Lincoln had told them.*

*These dirty stories must have been something special because
an unfriendly writer said of him: "the foulest in his jests and
stories of any man in the country." That was ridiculous, of
course, but Mr. Lincoln was a product of our American frontier,
along with Daniel Boone, Davy Crockett, Andrew Jackson and
a host of others who mixed the animal with the human to build
this nation. Their ways were of physical strength, of the body,
with the sexual muscle as important a part of work and leisure
as any other. A reading of Davy Crockett, or his frontier contemporaries, reveals how direct and uninhibited these frontier
souls were. And their qualities were Mr. Lincoln's, refined and
subdued in him, of course, by his contact with "the better sort"
in Illinois and Washington — but always there.*

Curiously, this witty, laughing, joking genius was at heart a melancholy man. In 1840-41, Mr. Lincoln suffered a terrible depression that ended — for a time — his engagement to Mary Todd, and led him to retreat from society. "If what I feel were to be equally distributed to the whole human family," he wrote to his law partner, John Stuart, "there would not be one cheerful face on earth." This recurrent sadness, or melancholy, was integral to his life. His friend, U.S. Supreme Court Justice David Davis, said that Mr. Lincoln joked to "whistle down sadness." And this facet of his nature offers us yet another insight to Abraham Lincoln for, as Mark Twain said: "The secret source of humor itself is not joy but sorrow. There is no humor in heaven." Certainly, one "secret source of humor" in Mr. Lincoln was exactly that, a kind of immedicable woe.

The following stories serve to remind us of both the deep sadness and the elevated joy that were part of Abraham Lincoln's wisdom and personality. They show humor as an important facet of the persona who was our greatest American, and who was also our finest example and symbol — both in reality and hope — of the unceasing American effort to create a nation of "Lincoln-hearted" men and women.

The Early Years

When a boy in Kentucky, Mr. Lincoln wrote these lines in a school book.

> Abraham Lincoln
> his hand and pen
> he will be good but
> god knows when

> Abraham Lincoln is my nam(e)
> and with my pen I wrote the same
> I wrote in both haste and speed
> and left it here for fools to read

In 1841, the primary officers of the State of Illinois, including James Shields the State Auditor, signed an unpopular proclamation refusing the State's *own paper money in payment of taxes and debts to the State, accepting only gold or silver. Shields and the other principle officers were Democrats, but only Auditor Shields, a feisty, belligerent, mannered but talented Irish immigrant, was made the scapegoat for the proclamation. Abraham Lincoln, prominent Whig (the opposition that would evolve into the Republican Party), his future wife Mary Todd, and her friend Julia Jayne, wrote four insulting letters to the Springfield newspaper, the* Sangamo Journal, *excoriating Auditor James Shields. Mr. Lincoln wrote the second of these letters and when Shields discovered this, he challenged him to a duel. Mr. Lincoln accepted! As the challenged party, he chose sabers for weapons and all went to Bloody Island, in the Mississippi River near St. Louis, to fight. Luckily, the duel was averted at the last minute. Of the one letter that Mr. Lincoln wrote, the great Lincoln scholar, Roy Basler, had this to say: "It displays an ability to portray character, a skill in handling dialogue, a realistic humor, and a biting satire, which mark him at this time the potential equal of his Southern contemporaries . . . if not of the later Mark Twain." Lincoln's letter begins with "Jeff" accusing Democrat Shields of being a Whig. Jeff is talking to "Aunt Beca," the sage of "Lost Township."*

'Why, Jeff, you're crazy — you don't mean to say Shields is a whig.'

'Yes I do.'

'Why, look here, the proclamation is in your own democratic paper as you call it.'

'I know it, and what of that? They only printed it to let us democrats see the deviltry the whigs are at.'

'Well, but Shields is the Auditor of this loco — I mean this democratic State.'

'So he is, and Tyler appointed him to office.'

'Tyler appointed him?'

'Yes (if you must chaw it over) Tyler[1] appointed him, or if it wasn't him it was old granny Harrison[2], and that's all one. I tell you, aunt Becca, there's no mistake about his being a whig — why his very looks shows it — every thing about him shows it — if I was deaf and blind I could tell him by the smell. I seed him when I was down in Springfield last winter. They had a sort of a gatherin there one night, among the grandees, they called a fair. All the galls about town was there, and all the handsome widows, and married women, finickin about, trying to look like galls, tied as tight in the middle, and puffed out at both ends like bundles of fodder that hadn't been stacked yet, but wanted stackin pretty bad. And then they had tables all round the house kivered over with baby caps, and pin-cushions, and ten thousand such little nick-nacks, trying to sell 'em to the fellows that were bowin and scrapin, and kungeerin about 'em. They wouldn't let no democrats in, for fear they'd disgust the ladies, or scare the little galls, or dirty the floor. I looked in at the window, and there was this same fellow Shields floatin about on the air, without heft or earthly substance, just like a lock of cat-fur where cats had been fightin.

'He was paying his money to this one and that one, and tother one, and sufferin great loss because it wasn't silver instead of State paper; and the sweet distress he seemed to be in, — his very features, in the exstatic agony of his soul, spoke audibly and distinctly — "Dear girls, it is *distressing,* but I cannot marry you all. Too well I know how much you suffer; but do, *do* remember, it is not my fault that I am *so* handsome and *so* interesting."

'As this last was expressed by a most exquisite contortion of his face, he seized hold of one of their hands and squeezed, and held on to it about a quarter of an hour. O, my good fellow, says I to myself, if that was one of our democratic galls in the Lost Township, the way you'd get a brass pin let into you, would be about up to the head. He a democrat! Fiddle-sticks! I tell you,

1. John Tyler, 10th U.S. President.
2. William Henry Harrison, 9th U.S. President.

aunt Becca, he's a whig, and no mistake; nobody but a whig could make such a conceity dunce of himself.'

'Well,' says I, 'may be he is, but if he is, I'm mistaken the worst sort. if it turns out that Shields is a whig; considerin you shall be a whig if he turns out a democrat.'

'A bargain, by jingoes,' says he, 'but how will we find out.'

'Why,' says I, 'we'll just write and ax the printer.' 'Agreed again,' says he, 'and by thunder if it does turn out that Shields is a democrat, I never will——'

'Jefferson—Jefferson—'

'What do you want, Peggy.'

'Do get through your everlasting chatter some time, and bring me a gourd of water; the child's been crying for a drink this live-long hour.'

'Let it die then, it may as well die for water as to be taxed to death to fatten *officers of State*.'

Jeff run off to get the water though, just like he hadn't been sayin any thing spiteful; for he's a rail good hearted fellow, after all, once you get at the foundation of him.

I walked into the house, and 'why Peggy,' says I, 'I declare, we like to forgot you altogether.' 'O yes,' says she, 'when a body can't help themselves, every body soon forgets 'em; but thank God by day after to-morrow I shall be well enough to milk the cows and pen the calves, and wring the contrary one's tails for 'em, and no thanks to nobody.' 'Geod evening, Peggy,' says I, and so I sloped, for I seed she was mad at me, for making Jeff neglect her so long.

And now Mr. Printer, will you be sure to let us know in your next paper whether this Shields is a whig or a democrat? I don't care about it for myself, for I know well enough how it is already, but I want to convince Jeff. It may do some good to let him, and others like him, know *who* and *what* these *officers of State* are. It may help to send the present hypocritical set to where they belong, and to fill the places they now disgrace with men who will do more work, for less pay, and take a fewer airs while they are doing it. It ain't sensible to think that the same men who get us into trouble will change their course; and yet its pretty plain, if some change for the better is not made, its not long that neither Peggy, or I, or any of us, will have a cow left to milk, or a calf's tail to wring.

Yours, truly,   Rebecca------.

★   ★   ★   ★

During an address before the Young Men's Lyceum, in Spring-field, Illinois, Mr. Lincoln read a poem on women's chastity, the subject of his speech that night.

> Whatever spiteful fools may say—
> Each jealous ranting yelper—
> No woman ever played the whore
> Unless she had a man to help her.

★   ★   ★   ★

"The fact is," said Lincoln, "that I don't much like a cut-and-dried sermon. When I hear a man preach, well, I want to see him act like he was fighting bees!"

★   ★   ★   ★

The following story is Billy Herndon's version of an Abraham Lincoln favorite, a story he often told: "Parson John Bullin's Lizards," by George Washington Harris, a wonderful tale set in East Tennessee.

LIZARD

An old-line Baptist preacher rose up in the pulpit of his country meeting house, and in a loud voice announced his text thus: "I am the Christ whom I shall represent today."

He was dressed in coarse linen pantaloons and a shirt of the same material. The pants, manufactured after the old fashion, with baggy legs, were made to attach to his frame without the aid of suspenders. A single button held his shirt in position, and that was at the collar.

About this time a little blue lizard ran up his roomy pantaloons. The old preacher, not wishing to interrupt the steady flow of his sermon, slapped away on his leg, expecting to arrest the intruder, but his efforts were unavailing, and the little fellow kept on ascending higher and higher.

Continuing the sermon, the preacher loosened the central button which graced the waistband of his pantaloons, and with a kick off came that easy-fitting garment.

But, meanwhile, Mr. Lizard had passed the equatorial line of the waistband and was calmly exploring that part of the preacher's anatomy which lay underneath the back of his shirt.

Things were now growing interesting, but the sermon was still grinding on. The next movement on the preacher's part was for the collar button, and with one sweep of his arm off came the tow linen shirt. The congregation sat for an instant as if dazed; at length one old lady in the rear part of the room rose up, and, glancing at the excited object in the pulpit, shouted at the top of her voice: "If you represent Christ, then I'm done with the Bible."

—Lincoln to Herndon, in *The Hidden Lincoln.*

★   ★   ★   ★

Dennis Hanks, half-brother of Lincoln, told the story about the hard times of those early days when there was rarely enough to eat. Once, only a single potato graced the table at dinner, but Thomas Lincoln bowed his head and asked the blessing over it. Mr. Lincoln remarked: "I call them mighty poor blessings, Pa."

★   ★   ★   ★

At a ball in Springfield, Lincoln asked Mary Todd, his future wife, if she'd dance with him, saying: "I want to dance with you in the worst way." Mary accepted. After the dance, she said, "well, you weren't joking. You did want to dance with me in the worst way. And you did! The very worst . . ."

★   ★   ★   ★

"I never knew his equal," said T. G. Onstot, son of the New Salem cooper, "in the role of storyteller. His power of mimicry was very great. He could perfectly mimic a Dutchman, Irishman, or Negro."

★   ★   ★   ★

During the Blackhawk War, Captain Lincoln, quite inexperienced and only recently elected Captain, was marching a squadron across a field when he came to a gate. "I could not for the life of me remember the proper word of command for getting my company 'endwise,' so that it could get through the gate; so, as we came near it, I shouted: "This company is dismissed for two minutes, when it will fall in again on the other side of the gate'." Lincoln often told that story, using it to illustrate politics: "And I sometimes think that the gentlemen in yonder (Congress) who get into a tight place in debate would like to dismiss the House until the next day, then take a fair start."

★   ★   ★   ★

Mr. Lincoln made a speech in Springfield on 26 December 1839, and he referred to Democrats who took public funds and absconded.

They are most distressingly affected in their heels with a species of "running itch." It seems that this malady of their heels, operates on these sound-headed and honest-hearted creatures, very much like the cork-leg, in the comic song, did on its owner: which, when he had once got started on it, the more he tried to stop it, the more it would run away. At the hazard of wearing this point thread bare, I will relate an anecdote, which seems too strikingly in point to be omitted. A witty Irish soldier, who was always boasting of his bravery, when no danger was near, but who invariably retreated without orders at the first charge of an engagement, being asked by his Captain why he did so, replied: "Captain, I have as brave a heart as Julius Caesar ever had, but some how or other, whenever danger approaches, my cowardly legs will run away with it."

★   ★   ★   ★

Mr. Lincoln addressed the Temperance Society in Springfield in 1842 saying: "There is something so ludicrous in *promises* of good, or *threats* of evil, a great way off, as to render the whole subject with which they are connected, easily turned into ridicule. 'better lay down that spade you're stealing, Paddy, — if you don't you'll pay for it at the day of judgment.' 'By the powers' replied Paddy, 'if ye'll credit me that long, begorra, I'll jist be about takin' another.' "

★   ★   ★   ★

In 1846, G. W. Harris, a young law student studying in the Lincoln-Herndon law office in Springfield, Illinois, wrote a letter to a friend. The friend was ailing and Harris offered some advice:

I wish you co[uld] be in the office about two hours, to hear Lincoln tell his tales and anecdotes, of which he has any amount. I think you would laugh yourself well in that length of time. I sometimes have to hold my sides at times, so convulsed with laughter as to be almost unable to keep my seat. I have seen a dozen or more, with their hands on their sides, their heads thrown back, their mouths open, and the tears coursing down their cheeks, laughing as if they would die, at some of Lincoln's jokes . . .

★   ★   ★   ★

President Van Buren stopped for the night at Rochester, Ill., a little town east of Springfield, and a delegation including Mr. Lincoln rode out to be with him there. That night Lincoln entertained with his stories until the President insisted that "his sides were sore with laughing."

★   ★   ★   ★

When James Quarles was trying a case in Tennessee, Lincoln said, Quarles produced all the evidence he could, then rested his case secure and certain that he had won. But the defense brought a witness who swore so tellingly that Quarles was made to seem a fool . . . and so lost the case.
"How come you didn't get that feller to swar on yore side," a friend asked him?
"I didn't know him," Quarles replied.
"I shoulda told you about that feller," his friend replied,

"because he'd swar fer you jest as easy as he'd swar for t'other side. That's his business, Jedge, that feller takes in swarin' fer a livin."

★   ★   ★   ★

Herndon recorded that Lincoln was most adroit in outwitting people who came to him to get information which he did not wish to divulge. In such cases Lincoln did most of the talking, "swinging around what he suspected was the vital point, but never nearing it, interlarding his answers with a seemingly endless supply of stories and jokes." Later, of course, the visitor, "Blowing away the froth of Lincoln's narratives, would find nothing left."

★   ★   ★   ★

Mr. Lincoln was appointed by the court to defend a man accused of stealing hogs. Asked for the facts, the defendant advised his attorney (Lincoln) not to worry about facts, but to "jump in and fight 'em on general principles." These, he was certain, would clear him. "But there are half-a-dozen witnesses . . . who will swear against you and state that they saw you steal the hogs!" Mr. Lincoln warned him. "Never you mind that," the defendant told Mr. Lincoln, "you just do like I told you . . . use general principles and I can't lose."

Puzzled and yet intrigued by his client, Mr. Lincoln reluctantly took the job of defending the man. And no one was more surprised to hear the jury announce an acquittal of his client, than Mr. Lincoln.

Taking the man outside to a bench on the courthouse lawn, Mr. Lincoln insisted on knowing the facts, the truth, and the man did not hesitate to tell them. "I did steal them hogs and a whale of a lot more'n they accused me of doin'. And I sold ever' last one of 'em to this one on that jury, or that one. They was all buyers of them hogs, ever' last one of 'em. How else you figger I knew I'd be let off, Mr. Lincoln?"

★   ★   ★   ★

"His stories may be literally retold," said Henry C. Whitney in yet another comment on Mr. Lincoln's humor, "every word, period, and comma, but the real humor perished with Lincoln. . . . He provoked as much laughter by the grotesque expression of his homely face as by the abstract fun of his stories."

★   ★   ★   ★

Mr. Lincoln often told the story of his stagecoach ride with a friendly, generous Kentuckian who, during the long trip, offered him a chew of tobacco, then later a cigar, then later a drink of brandy, all of which Mr. Lincoln refused. At the end of the trip, the Kentuckian turned to Mr. Lincoln and said: "I may never see you again, and I don't want to offend you but . . . my experience has taught me that a man who has no vices has damned few virtues!"

★   ★   ★   ★

In Danville, Illinois, at a jury trial, Lincoln's friend and associate in the law, Ward H. Lamon, tried a case before a jury, altogether unaware that he had a huge rip in the seat of his pants. As a joke, the attorneys in the courtroom passed a note around requesting funds to be given to Lamon to repair his britches. But Mr. Lincoln refused, writing: "I do not like the end in view."

★   ★   ★   ★

Billy Herndon, Mr. Lincoln's law partner, once asked if Lincoln believed in heredity. Mr. Lincoln thought for awhile, then allowed as how he did. "You know that feller Jack_____, out at New Salem, Billy?" he asked.

"Sure I do. Had four boys. Mean as all get out. But what's that got to do with the question of heredity?"

"Plenty, Billy. Now old Jack suffered from some kind of incurable diarrhea that was almost uncontrollable. Messy situation! And it so happens that every danged one of his four sons is a shitass just like his daddy!"

★   ★   ★   ★

And Lincoln's friend, Leonard Swett, declared that while the humor was sometimes "broad", it was not told for that reason. "When hunting for wit he had no ability to discriminate between the vulgar and refined substances from which he extracted it," Swett pontificated, "it was the wit he was after, the pure jewel, and he would pick it up; out of the mud or dirt just as readily as he would from the parlor table."

★   ★   ★   ★

A friend of Mr. Lincoln's, Moses Hampton, wrote to him in 1848. In the letter, Hampton made a curious remark that makes one wish he had elaborated on this tantalizing question:

"Do you remember the story of the old Virginian stropping his razor on a certain *member* of a young Negro's body which you told . . . ?"

And in the same letter:

"I want this application to be like your story of the old woman's *fish* — gets *larger* the more it is handled —"

★   ★   ★   ★

"If a man broached a subject which he did not wish to discuss, he told a story which changed the direction of the conversation. If he was called upon to answer a question, he answered it by telling a story."

★   ★   ★   ★

The Middle Years

One evening, after court on the 8th Judicial Circuit, the lawyers were having a heated discussion with so much loud talk and rude behavior that nobody could make sense out of the arguments. Mr. Lincoln managed to quiet things long enough to tell this story:

"A friend of mine, a preacher, was traveling from Beardstown to Quincy where he was due to preach. He rode his horse through the pitch-black night that was made even darker by heavy storm clouds. The thunderclaps were like a continuous, heavy cannonade, and the preacher had all he could do to control his horse. And it was so dark he could hardly see, finding his way by intermittent flashes of lightning that came too infrequently. At last, he was lost. He stopped his horse, got to the ground, and went to his knees to pray. 'Dear God,' the preacher fervently prayed. 'I'm lost. Don't know where I am. But it would sure help if you could give me a little less noise and a lot more light.' "

The lawyers got the point and, after the laughter had died down, the discussion proceeded in good order.

★   ★   ★   ★

Lincoln was discussing the mistakes sometimes made at the bar. The discussion put him in mind of a joke about a lawyer and a minister riding through the country together. Asked what he did about mistakes, the lawyer said he mended the large ones and tended to forget about the small ones. "But tell me, Reverend Jones, what do you do about mistakes?"

"Pretty much as you do," the minister replied. "Just the other Sunday, I stated in a sermon that the devil was the father of all liars, but I had a slip of the tongue. I said; 'of all lawyers'. But it was a small mistake so I forgot about it."

★   ★   ★   ★

Billy Herndon described social life on the 8th Judicial Circuit, in Illinois.

"In the evening, after the court business of the day was over and book and pen had been laid [down] by the lawyers, judges, jurymen, witnesses, etc., the people generally would meet at some barroom, 'gentlemen's parlor,' and have a good time in story-telling, joking, jesting, etc., etc. The barroom, windows, halls and all passageways would be filled to suffocation by the people, eager to see the 'big ones' and to hear their stories told by them . . . Lincoln would tell his story and then followed Engle and then came Murray and thus this story-telling, joking, jesting, would be kept up till one or two o'clock in the night, and thus night after night till court adjourned for that term. In the morning we would all be sore all through from excessive laughing — the judges, the lawyers, jurymen, witnesses, and all. Our sides and back would ache. This was a gay time and I'll never see it again.''

★   ★   ★   ★

The following story is a good example of a story attributed to Mr. Lincoln despite the lack of evidence that he had told it. But the story is so witty, sly, buoyant, and so much resembles the kind of stories that we know he told, that the editor is certain it belongs in the collection. It simply sounds like a Lincoln story!

In a famous railroad case that Mr. Lincoln won against all odds, nobody was more surprised than the opposing attorney who asked Mr. Lincoln how on earth he had managed to win what had seemed such a cut-and-dried win for him. Mr. Lincoln explained: "Last night at the tavern, I was present and so were the members of the jury. Too bad you weren't there but good for me that you were absent. Well, I told them a number of stories and the one that seemed to tickle them most was the one about the little farm boy who came running into the house, yelling to his father: 'Pa! Hey Pa! The hired man has got sis up in the hayloft. She's raising her skirts and he's dropping his britches and they's fixin' to pee all over our new hay up thar in the mow!''

"Well, the father thought about that for a bit, then looked down at his small son and said: 'Son, you got your facts jest right, but you got your conclusion dead wrong!' "And that," said Mr. Lincoln, "was my concluding statement to the jury. I said: 'worthy counsel for the defense has got his facts right but his conclusions wrong.' And the jury laughed for five minutes! You remember?" The other attorney grinned in sudden understanding.

★   ★   ★   ★

In 1839, when Mr. Lincoln was thirty years old, the opposing

Springfield newspaper counseled him about falling into the bad habit of telling stories. They advised him "to correct this clownish fault before it grows upon him."

★   ★   ★   ★

Lincoln once told the story of a citizen's remark at Decatur, Illinois, where Lincoln won the Republican nomination for the Presidency. The fellow came from the southern part of Illinois, a part dominated by Democrats. He walked up to Lincoln and said:

"So you're Abe Lincoln?"

"Yes, that is my name."

"They say you're a self-made man."

"Well, yes; what there is of me is self-made."

"Well, all I've got to say," said the man after a careful once-over of the Republican candidate, "is that it was a damned bad job!"

★   ★   ★   ★

Lincoln had a peculiar gait, rather more indirect than straight ahead. When asked why he walked that way he replied, "Oh, my nose is crooked and so, you see, I have to follow it."

★   ★   ★   ★

One night Lincoln walked inside a crossroads tavern. He was cold and wet and wished to sit by the fire to dry off. But there were more people sitting around the fire than he had reckoned on, so that he could not get close. He ordered the innkeeper to take a peck of catfish to his horse.

"He can't eat catfish," said the innkeeper. "No horse can."

"You just try it and see," said Lincoln. "Go ahead."

The crowd all rushed after the landlord to see the marvelous sight of Lincoln's horse eating catfish.

Returning, the innkeeper said "He won't eat them, just as I told you."

"Then you can bring them to me and I'll eat them" said Lincoln from his comfortable seat near the fire, a seat he had taken when it was vacated by the curious who had gone to see a horse eat catfish!

In New York, Lincoln discovered that a thief had picked his pocket and taken his watch. He put an advertisement in the New York *Herald* that read, "stolen, a watch worth a hundred dollars. If the thief will return it, he shall be informed, gratis, where he may steal one worth two of it, and no questions asked."

A favorite story of Lincoln's was about Springfield. It seems that a traveling evangelist applied to the Secretary of State, in Springfield, to use the hall of the House of Representatives for his lecture. The Secretary of State, Thomas Campbell, asked: "May I know what is to be the subject of your lectures?"

"Certainly," was the reply. "I plan to discuss the second coming of our Lord."

"It'll just waste your time trying it," Campbell told him, "for if the Lord has been in Springfield once, He's got more sense than to come a second time."

His friend, Judge David Davis described him in the act of telling a story: "His little grey eyes sparkled; a smile seemed to gather up, curtain-like, the corners of his mouth; his frame quivered with suppressed excitement; and when the point — or 'nub' as he called it — came, no one's laughter was heartier than his."

This artfully confused story was written by Abraham Lincoln for a clerk in the court at Springfield.

"He said he was riding bass-ackwards on a jass-ack, through a pattoncotch, on a pair of baddle-sags, stuffed full of binger-gred, when the animal steered at a scump, and the lirrup-steather broke, and throwed him in the forner of the kense, and broke his pishing-fole. He said he would not have minded it much, but he fell right into a great tow-curd . . . He said about bray-dake he came to himself, ran home, seized up a stick of wood and split the axe to make a light, rushed into the house, and found the door sick abed, and his wife standing open. But thank goodness, she is getting right hat and farty again.''

*   *   *   *

Professor Charles Strozier, in his superb, revealing and epic psycho-history of Abraham Lincoln: "Lincoln's Quest for Union," described some of the humor as "distinctly anal."

*   *   *   *

One time Lincoln's friend, Judge David Davis, was going through the docket to dispose of such cases as could be dealt with summarily, when he came to a long bill in chancery, drawn by a good but very lazy lawyer named Snap. "How come," he asked the lawyer "you found enough energy to get up this long bill in chancery?"

"I dunno, Judge," the lawyer said, rutching about in his seat, very ill-at-ease.

"Why, it's astonishing, ain't it, Lincoln?" the judge asked turning to him, quite sure he'd get a response.

He did! Lincoln replied: "I knew a lazy preacher, just like Snap, over there. He used to write endless sermons and somebody asked him why he made them so durned long. 'It's jest that I gits to writin' the thangs, and I suppose I'm jest too durned lazy to stop,' the preacher replied."

*   *   *   *

Judge David Davis said, "if the day was long and he was oppressed, the feeling was soon relieved by the narration of a story. The tavern loungers enjoyed it, and his melancholy, taking to itself wings, seemed to fly away."

*   *   *   *

When in Congress, Mr. Lincoln made speeches in support of

General Zachary Taylor, and against General Lewis Cass. Cass had been in the Blackhawk War and bragged about his many brave exploits there. To put him down, Mr. Lincoln made the following speech.

"By the way, Mr. Speaker, did you know that I am a military hero? Yes sir; in the days of the Blackhawk War I fought, bled, and came away. Speaking of General Cass's career reminds me of my own. I was not at Stillman's defeat, but I was about as near as Cass was to Hull's surrender; and, like him, I saw the place very soon afterwards. It is quite certain I did not 'break my sword,' for I had none to break; but I bent my musket pretty badly on one occasion. If Cass broke his sword, the idea is he broke it in desperation. I bent my musket by accident. If General Cass went in advance of me in picking whortleberries, I guess I surpassed him in charges upon the wild onions. If he saw any live, fighting Indians, it was more than I did; but I had a good many bloody struggles with mosquitoes, and, although I never fainted from loss of blood, I can truly say I was often very hungry. Mr. Speaker, if I should ever conclude to doff whatever our Democratic friends may suppose there is of black-cockade federalism about me, and thereupon they shall take me up as their candidate for the Presidency, I protest they shall not make fun of me, as they have of General Cass, by attempting to write me into a military hero."

★   ★   ★   ★

When Lincoln was a Congressman from Illinois, the only federal office he was ever to hold until elected President, he took a firm stand against the Mexican War. He thought it an unwarranted act of agression. He said that our going into Mexico reminded him of a farmer back in Illinois, who when accused of being greedy about land, declared, "Me? Hell, I ain't greedy. I only want the lands that jine my own."

★   ★   ★   ★

"O Lord, wasn't he funny," exclaimed Usher F. Linder,

himself a noted humorist. "Any remark, any incident brought from him an appropriate tale."

In discussing a foppish dandy who strutted about boasting of his sexual exploits, Mr. Lincoln remarked that the only time the fop had his "flesh" in anything was the time he slipped, fell on his hand and jammed his finger up his ass!

And Lincoln biographer David Donald mentions "an extensive cycle of ribald and Rabelaisian stories . . . for the most part unprintable and unfortunately gradually becoming lost."

During the famous Lincoln-Douglas debates in Illinois, both men were traveling on the same train, Senator Douglas in his private car, Abraham Lincoln in the coach! Mrs. Douglas wanted to chat with Mr. Lincoln, left her private car, and walked to his seat. She did not notice the stove pipe hat resting on the seat beside Mr. Lincoln, and sat down on it! Shocked, embarrassed, unsure of what to do or say, she simply squirmed, wiggled, rutched about, tongue-tied with embarrassment. Mr. Lincoln let her suffer just a bit, then said: "Mrs. Douglas, let me advise you. No matter how hard you try, or how long you may work at the thing, I have to counsel you that the derned thing'll never fit."

Stephen Douglas's arguments at the Freeport, Illinois, debates were blasted by Lincoln's description of them. They were, he said, "as thin as the homeopathic soup that was made by boiling the shadow of a pigeon that had starved to death."

Stephen A. Douglas remarked during the famous debates: "Every one of his stories seems like a whack upon my back . . . Nothing else — not any of his arguments or any of his replies to

my questions — disturb me. But when he begins to tell a story, I feel that I am to be overmatched."

During one of the debates, Lincoln entered the building where the contest was to take place. A fellow named Joe, rooting for Douglas, said to Lincoln as he entered: "Abe, keep your eye on 'Doug' or the first thing you know will be that you don't know nothing." Lincoln replied: "Joe, I'm sorry to see you violating the law as you do." Joe was startled and replied. "How am I violating the law, Lincoln?"

"Why, don't you know it is against the law to open up a rum hole without a license?"

"When did I ever open up a rum hole?" Joe asked. Lincoln pointed to Joe's mouth. "You got one right there," he said, and walked on into the building.

Lincoln had failed at everything he ever tried, Douglas charged, at farming, teaching, liquor selling, and the law; and he was trying to fail at politics. Lincoln stood and said that Douglas had presented the facts.

"It's true, every word of it. I've tried a lot of things, but there's one thing that Douglas forgot. He told you that I sold liquor, but he didn't mention that while I had quit my side of the counter the judge still remains on his."

Mr. Lincoln advised the family preacher on how to tell a story: "If you have an auditor who has the time, and is inclined to listen, lengthen it out slowly as if from a jug. If you have a poor listener, hasten it, shorten it, shoot it out of a pop-gun."

At one of the debates against Douglas, Lincoln remarked that Douglas had said that his father was a cooper, by trade, and had taught him the craft. Speaking of the father's excellent craftsmanship, Lincoln remarked: "I have no doubt, however, that he was a good one for . . ." and here he bowed gently toward Stephen Douglas, "his father has made one of the best whiskey casks I have ever seen!"

Losing the nomination by his party for United States Senator, Mr. Lincoln was asked how the defeat had left him feeling. He said: "Somewhat like the boy in Kentucky who stubbed his toe while running. He said he was too big to cry, and it hurt too much to laugh."

When he was guest speaker at a banquet hosting editors of various newspapers, in 1856, Mr. Lincoln remarked that he felt out of place in such a gathering. To explain he told about an extremely ugly man who met a witch of a woman on the road he was traveling. She looked him over and told him that he was the ugliest man she had ever seen. "What you say may be true, Madam Witch," said the shamed fellow "But I was born that way and cannot help it."

"No, I suppose not," the Witch replied, "but you might stay at home."

"In our walks about the little towns where courts were held," said Henry C. Whitney, a fellow lawyer on the Circuit, "he saw ludicrous elements in everything, and could either narrate some story from his storehouse of jokes, else he could improvise one."

Once Mr. Lincoln stayed with a pompous Judge who was also a legislator. The judge was given to using big words. Mr. Lincoln heard him tell his hired man that their ox, "Big Brindle" had lately been breaking out of the barn lot and generally tearing things up, his own and his neighbors. He ordered the servant "to impound Big Brindle in order that I may hear no animadversion on his eternal depredations."

The hired man walked away completely puzzled as to what

the Judge wanted him to do. But his wife explained that all that was needed was to put the ox securely in his pen. This he did. The next day, during a dinner party with many guests, the Judge asked the hired hand if he had impounded Big Brindle.

"Yes, I did, sire; but Old Brindle transcended the impanel of the impound, and scatterlophisticated all over the equanimity of the forest." The company burst out laughing, and the Judge was embarrassed. "What do you mean by that, sir?" he asked.

"Why, Colonel, I simply said that Old Brindle, being prognosticated with an idea of the cholera, ripped and teared, snorted and pawed dirt, jumped the fence, tuck to the woods, and would not be impounded nohow."

Mr. Lincoln once attended a lecture by Bishop Simpson. In the course of the talk, the Bishop told the story about an Englishman who asked a Kentuckian about the boundaries of the United States. The reply: "bounded on the East by the rising sun, on the West by the procession of the equinoxes, on the North by the Aurora Borealis, and on the South by the day of judgment." After the lecture, while discussing it, Mr. Lincoln remarked that the Kentuckian's description reminded him of the time John Bull met a North American Indian. Mr. Bull remarked: "the sun never sets on the English domain. Do you understand how that is?" "Oh yes," said the Indian, "that is because God is afraid to trust them in the dark."

In the law office, he would send the studying law students into laughter "with their hands on their sides, their heads thrown back, their mouths open, and the tears coursing down their cheeks, laughing as if they would die."

Mr. Lincoln walked up to a stage coach and asked a passenger inside if he'd take his overcoat to Springfield for him.

"Be glad to," the stranger said. "But how'll I know where

you'll be so as to get it to you?"

"Oh, that'll be easy," Lincoln replied, "since I'll be in it!"

In Quincy, Illinois, during a session of that circuit court, the lawyers were banded together, one evening, telling stories. Somehow the question of sorry horses came up and in the course of the story-telling session, one lawyer said he'd like to bet Lincoln that his horse was far sorrier than any Mr. Lincoln could ride. The bet was on! In the morning, the lawyer came down the street leading an ancient, sway-backed, spavined, blind, toothless nag that death, by a miracle, had by-passed. All waited for Lincoln to come on with his horse. Pretty soon he came down the street with his horse over his shoulder! It was a *sawhorse!* Lincoln sat on it and said, "this is the first time I've been beaten in a horse trade."

A statement was made by Judge Davis, in a Chicago restaurant, that he liked Chicago sausage because he figured that pork was safe to eat there because, in Chicago, hogs were cheaper than dogs. The notion put Lincoln in mind of a story.

"A grocer in Joliet was famous for the quality of his sausages, and supplied most of the town. But he got in a bitter argument with a customer who subsequently stamped out of the store in a furious rage. Soon he was back in the crowded grocery store carrying two huge but very dead cats. He swung them about by their tails, then planked them down on the butcher's counter. "There!" he said at the top of his voice, "This makes an even dozen today. I'll be around tomorrow to get paid for them."

In 1853, Philip Paxton described, in his "A Stray Yankee in Texas," story telling on the southern and western judicial circuits.

History has fortunately informed most of us of at least one great story teller of the frontier, Abraham Lincoln. The coonskin tales which he collected came to him everywhere he went, it seems, until he left Springfield — at Anderson Creek ferry, in the log store at New Salem, on a raft drifting down the great river, and in taverns at night when he foregathered with other lawyers in swings around the circuit. The lawyers, in particular, cherished good stories in which the vernacular figured prominently.

The origin and perpetuity of many of our queer and out-of-the-way phrases, may be traced to the semi-annual meetings of the gentlemen of the bar at the courts of our Southern and Western States.

These gentlemen, living as they do in the thinly inhabited portion of our land, and among a class of persons generally very far their inferiors in point of education, rarely enjoying anything that may deserve the name of intellectual society, are apt to seek for amusement in listening to the droll stories and odd things always to be heard at the country store or bar-room. Every new expression and queer tale is treasured up, and new ones manufactured against the happy time when they shall meet their *brothers-in-law* at the approaching term of the district court.

If ever pure fun, broad humor, and "Laughter holding both his sides," reign supreme, it is during the evening of these sessions. Each one empties and distributes his well filled budget of wit and oddities, receiving ample payment in like coin, which he pouches, to again disseminate at his earliest opportunity.

Billy Herndon, Lincoln's law partner for many years, was a heavy drinker. While on circuit one night, when all the circuit-riding lawyers were in a happy mood, they decided to break open a keg of oysters. Billy was about three sheets into the wind by this time. He ate the oysters and, shortly afterwards, began to feel sick. He rushed to the backyard of the tavern, hung on to a board fence, and vomited onto the other side which happened to be a pigpen. The hogs, of course, were delighted with Billy's leavings, and snorted and bellowed and generally made so much noise that Billy, drunk as he was, began to curse them in a loud voice, Lincoln heard the ruckus, came downstairs, and asked what the trouble was.

"Oh, not much," said one of his fellow lawyers. "Billy's drunk again, is all, and he got sick on the oysters or too much liquor, but that's him out there giving up of it all to the hogs, sort of divying up things with them, sharing, you might say."

Lincoln went to the door and called out to Herndon: "Billy come on back here. Don't stand out there arguing with those hogs. There's sure aplenty for all of you."

★   ★   ★   ★

A friend was looking at Mr. Lincoln's new coat. "Sure do like it, Abe. When did you get it?"

"Just got it. Brand new."

"But it appears to be a wee bit short."

"Perhaps. But it'll be long enough before I get another one."

★   ★   ★   ★

Of his speech delivered on 6 October 1854, the Illinois State Register — Springfield's Democratic newspaper — said that Mr. Lincoln began with jokes, "the character of which will be understood by all who know him by simply saying they were Lincolnisms."

★   ★   ★   ★

An opposing lawyer tried to convince a jury that precedent was superior to law, and ruled in all cases. Lincoln answered him this way: "Old Squire Bagley came to my office one day and said: 'Lincoln, I want your advice. Has a man who's got hisself elected Justice of the Peace the right to issue a marriage license?' I told him that he had not. Well, the old Squire got mad as all get out and said: 'Lincoln, I thought you was a lawyer. I had a bet on this proposition with Bob Thomas and both of us agreed to let you decide. But if you don't know no more'n that I sure did make a mistake. Hayall! I been Justice of the Peace heah fur eight long yars and I been marrying 'em all that time. An you tell me I ain't got the right? You don't know no more law less'n a gnat.'"

★   ★   ★   ★

A farmer came to Lincoln to ask his help in getting a divorce from his wife. The problem had surfaced because of their house . . . he wanted it painted brown and she wanted it white. The difference became so important that the wife had thrown crockery at the fellow, had used abusive language, and had poured scalding tea down his back. "I want a divorce!" the farmer demanded.

Lincoln suggested that the fellow go back and compromise. He suggested that they'd lived together a long time and could manage once again if both tried, if only for the sake of the children. He told the farmer to come back in four weeks.

In four weeks the farmer came back, saying "Lincoln, there's no need to start things against my wife. We've made up, a kind of compromise is how we did it."

"Compromise? Just how did you manage it?"

"Well," said the farmer, "we decided to paint the house white."

★   ★   ★   ★

"Although Illinois was conspicuous for the number of its story-tellers," said Joseph Gillespie, a fellow lawyer, "when Mr. Lincoln was about I never knew a man who would pretend to vie with him in entertaining a crowd."

★   ★   ★   ★

During a campaign against George Forquer, for the Legislature, Lincoln had just concluded a campaign speech. His opponent, Forquer, who had just built the grandest house in Springfield, and put up a thorough system of lightning-rod control, had made what even today is a blatant mistake: he had switched his political party from the Whigs, Mr. Lincoln's party, to the Democrats! And Lincoln took him to task.

"Mr. Forquer commenced his speech by announcing that 'the young man would have to be taken down; referring to me. It is for you fellow-citizens to say whether I am up or down. The gentleman has seen fit to allude to my being a young man; but he forgets that I am older in years than I am in the tricks and trades of politicians. I desire to live, and I desire place and distinction; but I would rather die now than, like the gentleman, live to see the day that I should change my politics for an office worth three thousand dollars a year, and then feel compelled to erect a lightning rod to protect a guilty conscience from an offended God.''

★   ★   ★   ★

In a discussion of the soul, Mr. Lincoln told the story of a Methodist minister in Kansas, living on a small salary paid quarterly, with his last payment distressingly delayed. He went to the trustees and asked for his pay since he was suffering from a lack of the most basic necessities of life.

"Money!" replied the trustees, "How distressing that you preach for money. It was our notion that you preached for the good of souls!''

"Souls!" exploded the minister. "I can't eat those. And if I could it would take a thousand such as yours to make a meal.''

★   ★   ★   ★

In his law office in Springfield, no matter how busy or how deeply engrossed in his work he might be, whenever anyone came in he would greet him with a pleasant or humorous remark, and before he left would inevitably tell a joke or anecdote.

★   ★   ★   ★

The fire brigade of Springfield was in need of new supplies. They mounted a fund-raiser, and one member went to Lincoln's office to solicit him for $20. Lincoln was most interested, listened carefully, then said: "Well, I'll tell you what I'll do, I'll go home to supper — Mrs. Lincoln is generally good-natured after supper — and I'll tell her I've been thinking of giving $40 to the fire brigade. And she'll say: 'Abe, will you never have any sense? Twenty dollars is quite enough.' So tomorrow, my boy, you come around and get your $20.'' And that's just what the solicitor did.

★   ★   ★   ★

When the Lincolns had their first baby, Mr. Lincoln remarked to a friend who had inquired about mother and child: "Doing just fine. But I was sure worried. You know how tiny Mary is? Well, I was worried that the baby'd have one leg short as Mary's, and one long as mine."

★   ★   ★   ★

Lincoln, one day, seemed to be having trouble quieting his two sons, Tad and Willy, who were trying to get at each other to fight. They were yelling like wildcats, and Lincoln had difficulty controlling them.

"What's the trouble, Mr. Lincoln?" a neighbor asked.

"Same old trouble since the world began," he replied. "I have three walnuts in my pocket and each of the boys want two."

★   ★   ★   ★

"I once had an Uncle," Lincoln said, "who was the most polite gentleman in the world. He was making a trip up the Mississippi when boat sank. He got his head above water for a moment, just long enough to take off his hat and say: 'Ladies and gentlemen, will you please excuse?' and down he went."

★   ★   ★   ★

Professor Charles Strozier quotes a contemporary describing Lincoln when telling a story: "Mirth seemed to diffuse all over him like a spontaneous tickle."

★   ★   ★   ★

Lincoln ran for Congress in 1846 against Peter Cartwright, a fire-and-brimstone Methodist circuit-rider who combined his campaigning with religious revivals.

One Sunday evening, he was exhorting his audience in church. He happened to see Lincoln in the back of the congregation. Lincoln had come to hear Cartwright so as to get his measure, to learn more about him. At the end of the sermon, Cartwright exhorted: "All who desire to lead a new life, to give their hearts to God and to go to heaven, will stand." Quite a few stood.

Cartwright went on: "All who do not wish to go to hell will stand." Now the entire audience was standing, all except Lincoln.

"I want you to observe," Cartwright continued, "that all of my congregation are standing, some on the first question as to their going to heaven, and some on the second question standing to show they do not want to go to hell. Only Mr. Lincoln, back there, remains seated, responding to neither invitation. Just where, Mr. Lincoln, do you think you are going?"

Lincoln stood slowly, cleared his throat, seemed to pause as if to collect his thoughts, then said, "Why Reverend Cartwright, I think the people will decide that for me. I'm going to Congress!"

★   ★   ★   ★

Billy Herndon said that "Mr. Lincoln was often perplexed to give expression to his ideas . . . He was frequently at a loss for a word, and hence was compelled to resort to stories, maxims, and jokes to embody his idea."

★   ★   ★   ★

The Final Years

John F. Farnsworth, an Illinois friend, said that the President told him: "Some of the stories are not so nice as they might be, but I tell you the truth when I say that a funny story, if it has the element of genuine wit, has the same effect on me that I suppose a good square drink of whiskey has on an old toper; it puts new life into me."

★   ★   ★   ★

During the Civil War a conference was held at Hampton Roads to seek means of ending the war. The President refused to enter into any agreement with persons in arms against the government, insisting that the surrender and the laying down of arms had to come before any talk of peace. One of the Confederate commissioners explained that there was precedent for such an agreement as the Confederacy was proposing, short of laying down arms, and that Charles I had several times made such agreements with those in arms against him. "I do not profess to be posted in history," the President replied. "All I distinctly remember about the case of Charles I is that he lost his head."

★   ★   ★   ★

Office seekers in large numbers plagued President Lincoln. One day he told a group of them this story:

"Once there was a great king who, in preparation for a long journey, asked his chief minister what the weather would be like. The minister said that the weather would be clear. On this advice, the king departed but when half way to his destination, a beggar on a donkey warned him: 'turn back, turn back! A bad storm is coming!' But the king believed his minister and drove on only to be met by a terrible storm that almost destroyed him. Returning to the palace, the king fired his minister and sent word to the beggar to come to see him. When he arrived the king, because of the beggar's wisdom — proved by predicting the storm — made him his chief minister. 'But I can't accept,' said the beggar, " 'twasn't I but my mule who predicted it. When he raises his ears, that means stormy weather. And his were raised way up!'' So the king made the mule his chief minister. "And ever since then" the President said, "every jackass wants a government job!''

★   ★   ★   ★

In a discussion with Massachusetts' Senator Chauncey Depew, Mr. Lincoln said:

"I have found, in the course of a long experience, that common people, take them as they run, are more easily influenced and informed through the medium of a story than in any other way."

★   ★   ★   ★

An Army officer, imbued with the notion that his troops should all have religion inspired in them, said to one of his teamsters. "My friend, do you know you are in a very dangerous business? You have a family at home, and you could be killed. Is it not proper that you give some thought to the salvation of your soul?"

"Yep. I shore have done a swarm of thinkin' about that," the soldier replied. "Shore have. But then if I gets to thinkin' too much about hit, who in the hell is agoin' to drive these hyar mules?"

★   ★   ★   ★

Mr. Lincoln could tell a whopper as well as the next man. When a lady asked if it was very hot in the South, he replied: "It sure is. Why, I saw a woman do her ironing with no way of heating her irons other than the sunshine, and as I came away, there she was putting her kettle in the window to get her tea water hot."

★   ★   ★   ★

One day while Mr. Lincoln was walking with Secretary Seward, the latter called his attention to a sign bearing the name: *T. R. Strong*. "Well," said the President, grinning, "It may be that T. R. Strong. But coffee are stronger."

★   ★   ★   ★

An anti-slavery group, many of them preachers, came to the White House to plump for a ban on slavery. Reverend Charles A. _____, made a long and impassioned appeal, quoting sources, to back his words, from both Old and New Testaments. Mr. Lincoln responded, at last, when the interminable words finally ended, with this: "Well, Gentlemen, it is not often one is favored with a delegation direct from the Almighty!"

★   ★   ★   ★

"You speak of Lincoln's stories," he said to a journalist, "but I don't think that is a correct phrase. I don't make the stories mine by telling them. I am only a retail dealer.''

The President was disgusted with military generals who made speeches, who bragged and claimed superhuman ability. He said they reminded him of a fellow back home who owned a dog that, the fellow said, was death on wolves, could kill a whole pack of them. So a wolf-hunting party was got up and started out. The man didn't much want to go, and kept his dog out of it as long as he could. But, at last, he had to go or lose face. So they went out in the woods where a pack of wolves was sighted. They turned the dog loose after them, and he disappeared. They looked everywhere but could not sight dog or wolves. Finally they met a farmer coming down the road in his wagon. They stopped him and asked if he'd seen anything of a dog chasing a pack of wolves. He said he had, awhile back, and 'the dog was a leetle ahead.' ''And that,'' said the President, ''is the position in which you find most of these braggert generals when they get into a fight with Johnny Reb. I don't like military orators.''

Henry C. Whitney, Mr. Lincoln's friend and fellow lawyer on the Circuit, reported him as saying: ''I laugh because I must not weep — that's all, that's all.''

The President's eye fell on a letter signed with such a flourish at the end of it that he could scarcely make out the name. ''That reminds me,'' he said, ''of the short-legged man who had a very long overcoat, so long that it wiped out his footprints in the snow.''

When he first entered the office, the President would go daily, first thing, to the drawer holding telegrams. He'd start at the top and read them until he got to the last one of the previous day, then he'd say, ''Well, boys I have got down to the raisins.''

The office help, after hearing him say this several times, once asked what the term 'raisins' meant. He told of a little girl celebrating her birthday who had eaten too freely of too many things. The last thing she gorged herself on was raisins, then she became deathly ill. When the doctor arrived, she was busy casting up accounts. The doctor, looking over the contents of the slop jar, remarked to the anxious parents that all danger was over since the child was 'down to raisins.' "So, when I reach the last message that I read on my last visit here, I know I need read no further, I'm 'down to raisins'."

★   ★   ★   ★

In 1862, President Lincoln received a long letter telling him how he should conduct his office. When asked how he would reply to the letter, he said: "I'll tell him the story of the Irishman whose horse got rambunctious, kicked and caught it's hoof in the stirrup. 'Begorra,' said the Irishman, 'and if its you wantin' to get on, I'll jest be gettin' off.' "

★   ★   ★   ★

Again talking of McClellan, whose excuse for not fighting the enemy was that he did not have enough troops, the President shook his head and said: "If I gave McClellan all the men he asks for, they couldn't find room to lie down, but would have to sleep standing up."

★   ★   ★   ★

With gossip and reports pouring in that the Rebels were advancing on Washington, but that on the one hand all was safe, and on the other that the enemy was due to take the city in a few hours, and the timid McClellan nowhere in sight to defend the city, the President murmured: "I wonder whether McClellan plans to use his army for anything. If not, I'd like to borrow it from him for a day or two."

★   ★   ★   ★

General McClellan seemed to be making no effort to move ahead. The popular cry was "on to Richmond," but Little Mac seemed in no hurry to get there. The President said McClellan's inactivity put him in mind of an incident that had happened to him back home. "I once wanted to get to a political convention, so I went to a livery stable and rented a horse. They gave me a slow one since they were on the other side — I think my opponent owned the stable — hoping that I'd not get there in time to speak. But I did, and when I returned, I said to the man: 'You keep this horse for funerals, don't you?' 'Oh no,' he replied. 'Well,' I said to him, 'I'm sure glad of that for if you did, this horse would never make it to the cemetary in time for the resurrection."

★   ★   ★   ★

McClellan, angered at Lincoln's steady request for reports so that he might know what was going on with the army, began to report every trivial detail, such as: *We have captured six cows. What shall we do with them? George B. McClellan.*

The answer came quickly: *As to the six cows captured — milk them. A. Lincoln.*

★   ★   ★   ★

Mr. Lincoln spotted an elderly Negro on the deck of a gunboat and asked about him. He discovered that he had been in the Ninth Illinois Infantry at Fort Donelson. The President began to question him:

"Were you in the fight?"

"Had a taste of it, suh."

"Stood your ground all right?"

"No suh, I run."

"Run at the first fire?"

"Yes suh, and would hab run soona had I knowed it war comin' "

"Why, that wasn't very commendable as to courage."

"Dat isn't in mah line, suh. Cookin's mah perfession."

"Sure, but what about your reputation?"

"Reputation don't mean much to me alongside ob mah life."

"Do you figure your life worth more than others?"

"Shore wuth more to me, suh."

"Then you must value it plenty high."

"Yes, suh, I does, more dan all dis wuld, more dan a million ob dollars, suh, for whut would dat be wuth to a man wid de bref out ob him? Self-preserbation am de furst law wid me."

"But why should you act on a different rule than other men?"

"Different men set different value on der lives. Mah life she ain't in de market."

"But if you lost it, you'd have the glory of knowing you died for your country."

"Dat ain't no satisfaction when der ain't no feelins."

"Then patriotism and honor are nothing to you?"

"Nuffin atall, suh — I figers them is among the vanities."

"If our soldiers all thought like you, we'd have lost the war"

"Yes, suh: and they ain't no help fur dat. Don't do no good to put up my life fer the gobernment cause no gobernment kin replace de loss to me."

"Do you think your outfit would have missed you if you'd been killed?"

"Maybe an maybe no, suh. A ded white man ain't much use to dese sojers, let along a dead nigga — but I'd a missed mahsef, and dat was de hull point wid me."

★   ★   ★   ★

At one of the hospitals, Mr. Lincoln walked beside a young lady who was bringing comfort to the soldiers. "My dear fellow," she asked one bedfast soldier. "Where were you hit!"

"At Antietam."

"Yes, but where did the bullet strike you?"

"At Antietam, ma'am."

The young lady dropped the conversation and moved on. She asked the President to continue the conversation with the injured soldier and find out where he was hit. He nodded and lingered behind to speak to the soldier, while the girl moved on. President Lincoln soon caught up with her. "And did you find out where that soldier was hit?" she asked.

"My dear girl," the President replied soberly, "Had you been in that soldier's place, the ball that hit him would have missed you . . ."

The President's humor was not always pure and "clean." Nathaniel Hawthorne visited Washington in 1862 and commented on the President's stories:

"A good many of them [the stories for which the President was 'so celebrated'] are afloat upon the common talk of Washington and certainly are the aptest, pithiest and funniest little things imaginable; though, to be sure, they smack of frontier freedoms and would not always bear repetition in the dining room, or on the immaculate pages of the Atlantic."

Before Jeff Davis's capture, General Sherman had asked President Lincoln whether he wanted him to capture Davis or let him escape. Mr. Lincoln answered him with a story. "Back in Sangamon County where I practiced law," President Lincoln began, "There was a temperance lecturer who was most strict in the doctrine of total abstinence. One very hot day the lecturer stopped at a friend's house and asked for a glass of lemonade. His friend asked if it wouldn't help things 'a leetle bit' to put a drop of something stronger in the drink. 'No,' the lecturer replied. 'I couldn't think of it. That'd be against my belief in abstinence.' At the same time he looked longingly at the black bottle that his friend was holding out to him. 'But,' he went on, 'if you could jest manage to put in a wee drop without my knowing it, well, I suppose it wouldn't be hurting me any.' And that's my position exactly, General Sherman," Lincoln went on. "I must oppose any escape of Jeff Davis; but if you could somehow let him slip away 'without my knowing it,' well, what would be the harm of that?"

And General Sherman had his answer!

In another similar case involving an important rebel official, when Mr. Lincoln was asked whether the man should be arrested as soon as he was sighted, Mr. Lincoln replied. "Better not. When you have got an elephant on your hands, and he wants to run away, you'd better let him."

★   ★   ★   ★

A delegation of clergymen called on the President to ask him to be more careful appointing chaplains to the army. Mr. Lincoln told them that he ahd no part in that chore, that chaplains were *elected* by the units they would serve. Persisting, the clergymen demanded that the President affect a change in the system.

The President heard them out, then asked them to listen to a story. "Back in Springfield," he began, "I was coming home from the office one day when I saw a little black boy I knew busily digging with his toe in a mud puddle. I asked him what he was doing. 'Makin' a church,' he told me. "A church? Well, maybe you'd best show me." And he did. 'Can't you see it?' the boy asked, pointing to an edifice entirely in his imagination. 'There's the steps to the door, and the pews where everybody sits, and there's the pulpit and above that the organ. Can't you see all that?' Yes I can, plain as day, I told him. But why don't you make a minister to go behind the pulpit? 'Mister Lincoln, suh,' the boy said, 'I ain't got enough mud for that.' "

★   ★   ★   ★

Linton Park, a painter and decorator now in the Union Army, was a vegetarian who needed special treatment. He went to see the President about the matter, explaining that he could not forget "the leeks and onions" he used to get back in Indiana County.

"You want me to turn you out to graze like Nebuchadnezzar?" Lincoln asked.

"That'd be a derned sight better than salt pork," Park replied. The President wrote out an order: "The bearer, Linton Park, is herewith granted permission to browse in whichever pasture suits him."

★   ★   ★   ★

General McClellan's foot-dragging in the war had exasperated President Lincoln almost beyond control. One day he remarked: "I wish McClellan would go at the enemy with something; I don't care what. General McClellan is a good and decent gentleman, all right, and a very good engineer. However, I fear his engineering talent is confined to stationary engines!"

★   ★   ★   ★

"He could rake a sophism out of its hole better than all the trained logicians of all schools," wrote John Hay, his secretary in the White House.

★   ★   ★   ★

The President had an argument with Secretaries Seward and Stanton, over the attitude to take against England and France who seemed close to declaring war on the United States because of the way the Civil War was going. Both secretaries advocated strong stands, declaring that honor was at stake and the opprobrious term of coward would be theirs if any less belligerent attitude were adopted. The President replied: "Why run such a large risk when we can take a smaller one? The less risk the better for us. There's the story of a soldier in the thick of a battle where bullets were flying thick as fleas. Finally his courage gave up, and he threw down his gun and fled for his life. As he was running away, an officer drew his revolver and yelled, 'Go back to your regiment or I'll shoot you!'

" 'Shoot and be hanged!' the soldier yelled back. 'What's one bullet to a whole hatful?' "

★   ★   ★   ★

Just after the President of the Confederacy, Jeff Davis, was captured, Mr. Lincoln had a visitor who demanded to know what he was going to do with his captive.

Lincoln studied the question a moment, then replied: "That reminds me of a story about a boy, way out in Illinois, who had caught and tamed a raccoon. But the critter caused so much trouble around the house that the mother demanded that he take it away and not come home until he'd disposed of it. The boy went to town with his 'coon tied to a strong piece of twine. A kind-hearted gentleman found him there, sitting on the curb, the 'coon attached to the twine, and the boy crying his eyes out. 'What's the matter sonny? Can I do anything to help?' the man asked. 'Matter!', the boy sobbed. 'Here I sit with this dern 'coon that I can't sell, I can't kill, and my Ma won't let me take it home, and you ask me what's the matter!'

"Well," said Mr. Lincoln, "That's the fix I'm in. I can't sell Davis, can't kill him, and I can't take him home."

★   ★   ★   ★

During the New York riots of the Civil War, Governor Seymour wired President Lincoln that he was jailing too many citizens, and was acting too harshly. President Lincoln replied: "We believe to the contrary. We'll not rest content until we see more (Seymour) there."

★   ★   ★   ★

Once the President was asked how large the Confederate Army was. "I reckon it at just about a million two hundred thousand," he answered. "And how do you figure it to be so large as that?" his questioner asked, entirely surprised at the magnitude of the figure. "Easy," President Lincoln replied. "Every time one of our generals gets whipped in action, he sends me a dispatch saying he was outnumbered three to one. Since we have 400,000 men, well, you can see the rebels must have at least that many men."

★   ★   ★   ★

President Lincoln signed a commission for Brigadier-General Alexander Schimmelpfennig. "There," he said, ending his signature on the form, "if the rebels ever capture that fellow, it'll take to the end of the war for them to learn how to pronounce his name."

★   ★   ★   ★

It was reported to President Lincoln that General Robert C.

Schenck had captured thirty or forty prisoners, all armed with
Colt's revolvers. Disturbed at the exaggeration of newspapers in
reporting on the war, Mr. Lincoln remarked that when they
found out about the capture, the pistols would appear in print,
the next day, not as Colts, but as Horse pistols.

When asked if he created the many stories he told, the President replied that he did not . . . that he was the performer rather
than the playwright of the thing.

★   ★   ★   ★

A gunboat contractor was trying to sell his product to the
Union forces and Mr. Lincoln was in on the interview. The contractor was stretching things a bit, wildly extolling his gunboat,
until the President remarked sarcastically: "Oh, yes. Sure.
There's no doubt that it'll run anywhere the ground's a leetle
moist."

★   ★   ★   ★

When a former Congressman, James Ashley, came to see him
to demand the Union armies moved faster and more decisively,
and to complain about General McClellan who commanded the
armies, the President began to tell a story. Ashley interrupted,
saying, "Mr. President, I beg your pardon but I didn't come
here this morning to hear a story."

"Ashley, I have great confidence in you," the President
replied, "and great respect for you, and I know how sincere you
are. But if I didn't tell these stories, I would die. Now sit down!"

★   ★   ★   ★

A new gun of great promise was proposed for the Union Army
and Mr. Lincoln formed a committee to report back on its true
value. When it did, the report was so voluminous that the president threw it aside in disgust, having no time to wade through it.
"When I send a man to buy a horse for me," he said, "I expect
him to come back and tell me his points — and not how many
hairs there are in his tail."

★   ★   ★   ★

A domineering woman marched into the President's office and demanded a commission for her son, declaring that her grandfather had fought at Lexington. Further, she said her Uncle was the only man not to flee Blandensburg, and that her father had fought at New Orleans. Going on, she added: "And my husband was killed at Monterey."

"I guess, Madam," said the President wryly, "that your family has done more than enough for the country. Let us give somebody else a chance!"

★   ★   ★   ★

The President enjoyed a story about himself, told by two Quakers. The one said he thought that the South would win the war because Jefferson Davis was a praying man. "But so is Abraham a praying man," responded the other.

"Yes, but the Lord will think Abraham is only joking." replied the first Quaker.

★   ★   ★   ★

Two hatters arrived at the White House, each with his gift of a hat for the President. After the presentation, both hatters stood back eager to hear the comment. Lincoln carefully examined the hats, then remarked solemnly: "Gentlemen, they mutually excel each other."

★   ★   ★   ★

Speaking of a lawyer in Washington, Mr. Lincoln said: "He's the biggest liar in town. And that reminds me of an old fisherman who had a great reputation for exaggerating the size of his catch. So he got a pair of scales and demanded that each fish he caught be weighed on that scale, and before witnesses. One day another fisherman borrowed the scale to weigh his newborn baby. That baby weighed forty-seven pounds!"

★   ★   ★   ★

An officer told the President that the Irish in his regiment caused him more trouble than any other group. "I believe it," said the President. "And our enemies make the same complaint."

As we have seen in a previous chapter, Mr. Lincoln read to his cabinet Artemus Ward's "High-handed Outrage at Utica." But his cabinet officers were not amused. "Why don't you laugh," the President begged of them. "With the fearful strain that is upon me day and night, if I did not laugh occasionally I should die, and you need this medicine as much as I do."

One time a crowd called Mr. Lincoln to his balcony where he stood with his tiny wife. His brief remarks were: "Here I am, and here is Mrs. Lincoln. That's the long and short of it."

President Lincoln pardoned a Union Army deserter, then told a story to suggest the proper course the deserter should take. "There was once a case in Illinois," the President said, "of hog theft. My friend Usher Linder defended the accused whom, before trial, he advised to get a drink of water . . . But, Linder advised his client, the water was a whole lot healthier for him in Tennessee than in Illinois!"

A similar tale of his that reveals his enjoyment in shooting the "bull" is illustrated with an Irish joke (the Irish were the butt, the "Polish jokes" of that day). This Irishman feared that he could not get his new boots on until he had worn them a few days "so's to stretch them!"

The President's skill at managing the difficult group of Cabinet officers, men like the "testy" Stanton and the "pompous" Chase, was wonderfully illustrated when he sent a delegation to Stanton with orders to grant their request. Stanton not only refused the President's order but called him "a fool."

"Did Stanton call me a fool?" the President asked the returned and disappointed delegation. "Well, I guess I had better go over and see Stanton about this. Stanton is usually right."

A delegation came to the President with a request that he appoint their man to be Commissioner of the Hawaiian Islands, stressing the fact that their man was ill, weak, and needed the climate for his health. "Gentlemen," President Lincoln replied, "there are eight other applicants for that position and every last one of 'em is sicker'n your man."

In the White House, the same sound sense of humor carried President Lincoln through some of the darkest days ever known in that august office. As his friend and law associate, Ward Lamon, said of those gruesome times in President Lincoln's life: "He lived by his humor, and would have died without it."

Petroleum V. Nasby was visiting President Lincoln and they were discussing the death of a well-known Illinois politican-soldier who was distinguished by his elephantine conceit, his enormous ego. A huge crowd had, surprisingly, shown up to attend the funeral. "If General _____ had known how big a funeral he would have had," said President Lincoln, "he'd have died years ago."

When it was mentioned that a certain river in Nebraska was named Weeping Water, the President remarked: "I suppose the Indians out there call it Minneboohoo, don't they? Since Laughing Water is Minnehaha in their language."

At dinner the discussion was about the elusive Confederate soldiers from Louisiana. "You can't catch those fellows," someone remarked. "Whip 'em and they retreat to the swamps and bayous where we can't follow 'em. It'd take fish nets to catch 'em back in those awful swamps, and we haven't got any."

"But we do have them," the President said, "built especially for such traitors whether in the bayous of Louisiana or anywhere."

"And just what kind of nets are you talking about, Mr. President?"

"Bayou nets!" the President said as he savagely speared a fishball!

★   ★   ★   ★

In the White House the President had to patiently listen to a caller brag about the virtues of his early American ancestors. "I don't worry much about the reputation of my father and grandfather," the President said, "I'm more concerned with the reputation of their sons and grandsons."

★   ★   ★   ★

Perhaps the most famous Lincoln joke was the rejoinder he made to a temperance delegation in his office to complain about General U.S. Grant's tendency to drink too much whiskey. They thought so intemperate an officer ought not have such a command, and that the President should fire him. President Lincoln responded that if he knew the brand of whiskey that a fighting general like Grant drank, he'd order a barrel of it sent to his other generals!

★   ★   ★   ★

The Marquis De Chambrun, a welcome visitor in the White House, made this observation: "He willingly laughed either at what was being said or at what he himself was saying. Then, suddenly, he would retire himself and close his eyes, while his face expressed a melancholy as indescribable as it was deep. After a few moments, as though by an effort of the will, he would shake off his mysterious weight and his generous and open disposition again reasserted itself. I have counted in one evening, more than twenty of such alterations of mood."

★   ★   ★   ★

"I am glad to take the hand of the man, who, with the help of the Almighty God will put down this rebellion," said a stranger at a reception.

"You are more than half right, sir," came the President's reply.

★   ★   ★   ★

Charles Sumner said of Lincoln's stories: "His ideas moved as the beasts entered Noah's ark, in pairs."

★   ★   ★   ★

The President liked to tell the story of two southerners, one the huge Robert Toombs, the other the pint-sized Alexander Stephens. Toombs got angry at Stephens and bellowed: "Why I could button your ears back and swallow you whole!"

Alexander Stephens retorted: "And if you did, you would have more brains in your stomach than you ever had in your head."

★   ★   ★   ★

And of course Mr. Lincoln liked the ever-popular tall tale. He told of a soprano who sang so high that to top her voice another singer needed a ladder.

★   ★   ★   ★

"I hate to sign these orders to shoot deserters," the President said, "because when they hear about it, it'll scare the poor devils to death."

★   ★   ★   ★

Judge Holt, who handled President Lincoln's reprieves of soldiers otherwise imprisoned or shot, said of him: "Without exception the most tender-hearted man I ever knew."

★   ★   ★   ★

President Lincoln liked nothing better than to share with others the delightful things he read and heard. John Hay, his secretary in the White House tells about this wonderful characteristic when he tells how, one night while writing in his "diary," the President came bursting into his room: ". . . to show Nicolay and me the little caricature, 'an Unfortunate Bee-ing,' seemingly utterly unconscious that he, with his short shirt hanging about his long legs, and setting out behind like the tail feathers of an enormous ostrich was infinitely funnier than anything in the book he was laughing at. What a man it is! Occupied all day with matters of vast moment, deeply anxious about the fate of the greatest army in the world, with his own fame and future hanging upon the events of the passing hour, he has yet such a wealth of simple bonhomie and good fellowship, that he gets out of bed and perambulates the house in his shirt, to find us that we may share with him the fun of Hood's poor little conceits."

★   ★   ★   ★

Clement Vallandigham was an Ohio politican who had been sent out of the country for disloyalty. But he was a candidate for Governor of his native state, Ohio. His wife left to join him in Canada, saying that she would not return except as the wife of the Governor of Ohio. President Lincoln heard this and told about an Illinoisan who was running for County Supervisor. On the morning of the election he left home saying to his wife: "Wife, tonight you shall sleep with the Supervisor of this county."

The man lost the election. That evening his wife was dressed and waiting for him at the door. "Wife, where are you going at this time of night," the man asked as he came up to his door.

"Going?" she replied, "why, you told me this morning that tonight I should sleep with the Supervisor of this county, and as Mr. P_____ is elected instead of yourself, I was going to his house."

★   ★   ★   ★

Noah Brooks, a trusted wartime reporter, said: "Probably many people who heard him, during the war, repeat long passages from stories, or comical articles, which he had seen in print, wondered how he ever found time to commit such trifles to memory. The truth was that anything that he heard or read fastened itself into his mind, if it tickled his fancy." Today, we would say that Mr. Lincoln had a photographic memory for stories that pleased him.

★   ★   ★   ★

At a most nerve-racking time during the Battle of the Wilderness, the President could get no word from General Grant who was at the busines of attacking General Lee's force of 65,000 men. It was a nerve-racking wait. To allay the tension, the President finally announced that: "Grant has gone into the Wilderness, crawled in, drawn up the ladder, and pulled in the hole after him."

★   ★   ★   ★

Benjamin P. Thomas, great biographer of Abraham Lincoln, wrote: "Lincoln's humor, in its unrestraint, its unconventionality, its use of back-country vernacular, its willingness to see things as they were, its shrewd comments in homely, earthy phrase, its contentment with externals, typified the American humor of his time. Two strains — pioneer exaggeration and Yankee laconicism — met in him. In his humor as in his rise from obscurity to fame and in his simple, democratic faith and thought, he epitomized the American ideal."

★   ★   ★   ★

Even in laughter the heart acheth;
And the end of mirth is heaviness.

Proverbs, 14:13

Chapter VII
Humor After the Civil War

*T*he humor of this period, from 1865 to about 1910 — from Abraham Lincoln through Mark Twain — has been labeled "Local Color" because it celebrated the enormously varied humor coming from widespread areas offering incredibly different conditions of life within the same nation. It was a situation never before encountered by mankind, and Americans were curious to know about these differences among their fellow citizens — differences in dialect, customs, dress, occupation, environment, and so on. The humorous writings of this period offered verbal pictures of the vastly different kinds of Americans, and of their ways lived in the disparate sections of the nation . . . even to Chicago! "Everybody writes local stories nowadays; it is as natural as whooping cough . . ." wrote one critic in 1894.

But "Local Color" humor was not appreciated by all Americans. The "better sort" among us looked down its snobbish nose at rib-tickling, plebian kinds of writing and continued to turn to Europe, particularly England, for the genteel laughter it thought appropriate. The critical judgments of expatriates like Henry James fed this snobbish tendency that adored a sly kind of wit with its genteel and gentlemanly chuckle, and lady-like smile, rather than the knee-slapping, gut-busting guffaw at a joke made by outlandish figures in coarse situations and with wacky viewpoints — all approaches that lay at the heart of our best, earlier humor. Even Mark Twain had to be "approved" by our English cousins at Oxford, England, before more elevated Americans would allow themselves to enjoy his wit and to consider him the genius he was.

Presented here is a selection of humorous local color writers who wrote in the several sections of the nation. They wrote in that almost peaceful period — excepting our Cuban excitement — from the Civil War to World War I. By then the period of eye-gouging fights, of wrasslin' with bears, of those wild and chest-beating boasts of the ring-tailed roarers, and of stories written in *busted English and fractured grammer had ended. Those times closed with the Civil War and the slavery that had helped to bring it on. The frontier was fast disappearing, and the United States had entered into a long period of nation-building that would allow it to take its place as the leader of the free world, and the exemplar of how people could and should live together. The nation's humor reflected the gravity of this new position that brought ironic laughter, although somewhat bemused, at the notion that we were assuming world leadership. It is the humor of a people creating something noble out of itself, and having a good laugh at the astonishing things that were happening to it in the process.*

★   ★   ★   ★

If Ben Franklin was a "harmonious multitude," Mark Twain was certainly a literary galaxy. He is our best known and most respected literary figure, of whose death it was said that it "caused more universal regret . . . than that of any other American man of letters."

Born in Missouri, he grew up in Hannibal, with the Mississippi River for his playground and principal source of education. As has been said, the river was his "University."

He quit school when twelve because his father could not quite provide for the family. The father's several "ships," hopefully launched, never quite made it back to port with a payload! Apprenticed to a printer, young Sam Clemens learned the trade that provided him a living in Missouri and the several states through which he early traveled on his way to becoming the "literary galaxy" he was.

Infected by his father's notion of quick, easy money, and sure that the printers' trade was no way to make it, he started down the Mississippi River headed for the Amazon and its cocoa, hoping to export the brown bean to America where, once made into the famous brown drink, it would make his fortune. But the river seduced him! He apprenticed himself to a sailboat captain for 1½ years, got his pilot's license and sailed the river as Cap-

tain Clemens for 3½ years more, until the Civil War made river traffic impossible and ended his nautical career. His climb up the literary ladder to fame was rapid from that point.

His assumed name, Mark Twain, was adapted from the sounding of "mark twain," a unit of measurement announcing that the steamboat was passing through water two fathoms (twelve feet) deep. This was altogether appropriate and significant because the river had formed the character, viewpoint, and the very being of Sam Clemens/Mark Twain. The river had given him the background for his work, the most renowned and reflective of the American frontier. And there was something of general appeal in his literary art, something that touched the hearts of people all over the world, a universal touch that gave his readers a timeless vision, an insight to the condition of all mankind, everywhere.

Born 26 years after Abraham Lincoln, there was a bit of the Lincolnesque about Mark Twain, a way with words, with humor, and a kind of biblical grandeur about his judgment of man, his vision of what a man should be. And like the Prophets of the Bible, he was disappointed with the reality. He seems to have been more severe than Psalm 8, believing that man was a good deal lower than the angels and not about to raise himself much higher. And yet one senses that Mark Twain, like Abraham Lincoln, never altogether relinquished his frontier belief that in spite of it all, man was worth all the anguish inflicted in the governing of him, and in the writing about him.

One would like to have been a friend of Mark Twain. He was an exceedingly good man.

Many critics consider the following story to be the wittiest that Mark Twain wrote, and his wisest. In the manner of Aesop, the bluejay is used to portray an aspect of mankind's condition. We have all known in our generation — and in every generation — the single-minded, pig-headed folks afflicted with "tunnel vision," who are so industrious and determined in their ways, refusing to change — or to admit they are wrong — that they end

*by bringing themselves and their associates to grief. Sometimes,
happily, they can see the humor in their stubborn wrong-
headedness, as the bluejays saw it in this great story, and then it
all ends in a rib-tickling laugh.*

JIM BAKER'S BLUE-JAY YARN

Animals talk to each other, of course. There can be no question about that; but I suppose there are very few people who can
understand them. I never knew but one man who could. I knew
he could, however, because he told me so himself. He was a
middle-aged, simple-hearted miner, who had lived in a lonely
corner of California, among the woods and mountains, a good
many years, and had studied the ways of his only neighbors, the
beasts and the birds, until he believed he could accurately
translate any remark which they made. This was Jim Baker. According to Jim Baker, some animals have only a limited education and use only very simple words, and scarcely ever a comparison or a flowery figure; whereas, certain other animals have
a large vocabulary, a fine command of language and a ready and
fluent delivery; consequently this latter talk a great deal; they
like it; they are conscious of their talent, and they enjoy "showing off." Baker said that, after long and careful observation, he
had come to the conclusion that the blue-jays were the best
talkers he had found among birds and beasts. Said he:

"There's more *to* a blue-jay than any other creature. He has
got more moods and more different kinds of feelings than other
creatures; and, mind you, whatever a blue-jay feels, he can put
into language. And no mere commonplace language, either, but
rattling, out-and-out book-talk — and bristling with metaphor
too — just bristling! And as for command of language — why,
you never see a blue-jay get stuck for a word. No man ever did.
They just boil out of him! And another thing: I've noticed a
good deal, and there's no bird, or cow, or anything that uses as
good grammar as a blue-jay. You may say a cat uses good grammar. Well, a cat does — but you let a cat get excited, once; you
let a cat get to pulling fur with another cat on a shed, nights, and
you'll hear grammar that will give you the lockjaw. Ignorant

people think it's the *noise* which fighting cats make that is so aggravating, but it ain't so; it's the sickening grammar they use. Now I've never heard a jay use bad grammar but very seldom; and when they do, they are as ashamed as a human; they shut right down and leave.

"You may call a jay a bird. Well, so he is, in a measure — because he's got feathers on him, and don't belong to no church, perhaps; but otherwise he is just as much a human as you be. And I'll tell you for why. A jay's gifts, and instincts, and feelings, and interests cover the whole ground. A jay hasn't got any more principle than a Congressman. A jay will lie, a jay will steal, a jay will deceive, a jay will betray; and four times out of five, a jay will go back on his solemnest promise. The sacredness of an obligation is a thing which you can't cram into no blue-jay's head. Now, on top of all this, there's another thing: a jay can out-swear any gentleman in the mines. You think a cat can swear. Well, a cat can; but you give a blue-jay a subject that calls for his reserve powers, and where is your cat? Don't talk to *me*—I know too much about this thing. And there's yet another thing: in the one little particular of scolding—just good, clean, out-and-out scolding—a blue jay can lay over anything, human or divine. Yes, sir, a jay is everything that a man is. A jay can cry, a jay can laugh, a jay can feel shame, a jay can reason and plan and discuss, a jay likes gossip and scandal, a jay has got a sense of humor, a jay knows when he is an ass just as well as you do—maybe better. If a jay ain't human, he better take in his sign, that's all. Now I am going to tell you a perfectly true fact about some blue-jays.

"When I first begun to understand jay language correctly, there was a little incident happened here. Seven years ago, the last man in this region but me moved away. There stands his house—been empty ever since; a log house, with a plank roof—just one big room, and no more; no ceiling—nothing between the rafters and the floor. Well, one Sunday morning I was sitting out here in front of my cabin with my cat, taking the sun, and looking at the blue hills, and listening to the leaves rustling so

lonely in the trees, and thinking of the home away yonder in the
States, that I hadn't heard from in thirteen years, when a blue-
jay lit on that house, with an acorn in his mouth, and says,
'Hello, I reckon I've struck something!' When he spoke, the
acorn fell out of his mouth and rolled down the roof, of course,
but he didn't care; his mind was all on the thing he had struck.
It was a knot-hole in the roof. He cocked his head to one side,
shut one eye and put the other one to the hole, like a 'possum
looking down a jug; then he glanced up with his bright eyes,
gave a wink or two with his wings—which signifies gratification,
you understand—and says, 'It looks like a hole, it's located like
a hole—blamed if I don't believe it *is* a hole!

"Then he cocked his head down and took another look; he
glances up perfectly joyful this time; winks his wings and his tail
both, and says, 'Oh, no, this ain't no fat thing, I reckon! If I
ain't in luck!—why, its a perfectly elegant hole!' So he flew
down and got that acorn, and fetched it up and dropped it in,
and was just tilting his head back with the heavenliest smile on
his face, when all of a sudden he was paralyzed into a listening
attitude, and that smile faded gradually out of his countenance
like breath off'n a razor, and the queerest look of surprise took
its place. Then he says, 'Why, I didn't hear it fall!' He cocked
his eye at the hole again and took a long look; raised up and
shook his head; stepped around to the other side of the hole, and
took another look from that side; shook his head again. He
studied a while, then he just went in the *de*tails—walked round
and round the hole, and spied into it from every point of the
compass. No use. Now he took a thinking attitude on the comb
of the roof, and scratched the back of his head with his right foot
a minute, and finally says, 'Well, it's too many for *me*, that's
certain; must be a mighty long hole; however, I ain't got no time
to fool around here; I got to 'tend to business; I reckon it's all
right—chance it anyway!'

"So he flew off and fetched another acorn and dropped it in,
and tried to flirt his eye to the hole quick enough to see what
become of it, but he was too late. He held his eye there as much

as a minute; then he raised up and sighed, and says, 'Consound it, I don't seem to understand this thing, no way; however, I'll tackle her again.' He fetched another acorn, and done his level best to see what become of it, but he couldn't. He says, 'Well, *I* never struck no such hole as this before; I'm of the opinion it's a totally new kind of a hole.' Then he begun to get mad. He held in for a spell, walking up and down the comb of the roof, and shaking his head and muttering to himself; but his feelings got the upper hand of him presently, and he broke loose and cussed himself black in the face. I never see a bird take on so about a little thing. When he got through, he walks to the hole and looks in again for a half a minute; then he says, 'Well, you're a long hole, and a deep hole, and a mighty singular hole altogether—but I've started to fill you, and I'm d——d if I *don't* fill you, if it takes a hundred years!'

"And with that, away he went. You never see a bird work so since you was born. He laid into his work like a nigger, and the way he hove acorns into the hole for about two hours and a half was one of the most exciting and astonishing spectacles I ever struck. He never stopped to take a look any more—he just hove 'em in, and went for more. Well, at last he could hardly flop his wings, he was so tuckered out. He comes a drooping down, once more, sweating like an ice-pitcher, drops his acorn in and says, '*Now* I guess I've got the bulge on you by this time!" So he bent down for a look. If you'll believe me, when his head come up again he was just pale with rage. He says, 'I shoveled acorns enough in there to keep the family thirty years, and if I can see a sign of one of 'em, I wish I may land in a museum with a belly full of sawdust in two minutes!'

"He had just strength enough to crawl up on to the comb and lean back agin the chimbly, and then he collected his impressions and begun to free his mind. I see in a second that what I had mistook for profanity in the mines was only just the rudiments, as you may say.

"Another jay was going by, and heard him doing his devotions, and stops to inquire what was up. The sufferer told him the whole circumstances, and says, 'Now yonder's the hole, and if you don't believe me, go and look for yourself.' So this fellow went and looked, and comes back and says, 'How many did you say you put in there? 'Not any less than two tons,' says the sufferer. The other jay went and looked again. He couldn't seem to make it out, so he raised a yell, and three more jays come. They all examined the hole, they all made the sufferer tell it over again, then they all discussed it, and got off as many leather-headed opinions about it as an average crowd of humans could have done.

"They did call in more jays; then more and more, till pretty soon this whole region 'peared to have a blue flush about it. There must have been five thousand of them; and such another jawing and disputing and ripping and cussing, you never heard. Every jay in the whole lot put his eye to the hole, and delivered a more chuckle-headed opinion about the mystery than the jay that went before him. They examined the house all over, too. The door was standing half-open, and at last one old jay happened to go and light on it and look in. Of course, that knocked the mystery gallery-west in a second. There lay the acorns, scattered all over the floor. He flopped his wings and raised a whoop. 'Come here!' he says, 'Come here, everybody; hang'd if this fool hasn't been trying to fill up a house with acorns!' They all came a-swooping down like a blue cloud, and as each fellow lit on the door and took a glance, the whole absurdity of the contract that that first jay had tackled hit him home, and he fell over backwards suffocating with laughter, and the next jay took his place and done the same.

"Well, sir, they roosted around here on the house-top and the trees for an hour, and guffawed over that thing like human beings. It ain't no use to tell me a blue-jay hasn't got a sense of humor, because I know better. And memory too. They brought jays here from all over the United States to look down that hole, every summer for three years. Other birds too. And they could all see the point, except an owl that come from Nova Scotia to visit the Yo Semite, and he took this thing in on his way back.

He said he couldn't see anything funny in it. But then, he was a good deal disappointed about Yo Semite, too.

★   ★   ★   ★

Mark Twain left in his estate many unpublished works, among them: LETTERS FROM THE EARTH. The following piece, LETTER VIII, is from that marvelous collection of them, edited by Bernard De Voto and published in 1974 by Harper & Row.

LETTER VIII

Man is without any doubt the most interesting fool there is. Also the most eccentric. He hasn't a single written law, in his Bible or out of it, which has any but just one purpose and intention—to *limit or defeat a law of God.*

He can seldom take a plain fact and get any but a wrong meaning out of it. He cannot help this; it is the way the confusion he calls his mind is constructed. Consider the things he concedes, and the curious conclusions he draws from them.

For instance, he concedes that God made man. Made him without man's desire or privity.

This seems to plainly and indisputedly make God, and God alone, responsible for man's acts. But man denies this.

He concedes that God has made angels perfect, without blemish, and immune from pain and death, and that he could have been similarly kind to man if he had wanted to, but denies that he was under any moral obligation to do it.

He concedes that man has no moral right to visit the child of his begetting with wanton cruelties, painful diseases and death, but refuses to limit God's privileges in this sort with the children of his begetting.

The Bible and man's statutes forbid murder, adultery, fornication, lying, treachery, robbery, oppression and other crimes, but contend that God is free of these laws and has a right to break them when he will.

He concedes that God gives to each man his temperament, his disposition, at birth; he concedes that man cannot by any process change this temperament, but must remain always under its domination. Yet if it be full of dreadful passions, in one man's case, and barren of them in anothers man's, it is right and rational to punish the one for his crimes, and reward the other for abstaining from crime.

There—let us consider these curiosities.

Temperament (Disposition)

Take two extremes of temperament—the goat and the tortoise.

Neither of these creatures makes its own temperament, but is born with it, like man, and can no more change it than can man.

Temperament is the law of God written in the heart of every creature by God's own hand, and *must* be obeyed, and will be obeyed in spite of all restricting or forbidding statues, let them emanate whence they may.

Very well, lust is the dominant feature of the goat's temperament, the law of God in its heart, and it must obey it and *will* obey it the whole day long in the rutting season, without stopping to eat or drink. If the Bible said to the goat, "Thou shalt not fornicate, thou shalt not commit adultery," even Man—sap-headed man—would recognize the foolishness of the prohibition, and would grant that the goat ought not to be punished for obeying the law of his Maker. Yet he thinks it right and just that man should be put under the prohibition. All men. All alike.

On its face this is stupid, for, by temperament, which is the *real law* of God, many men are goats and can't help committing adultery when they get a chance; whereas there are numbers of men who, by temperament, can keep their purity and let an opportunity go by if the woman lacks in attractiveness. But the Bible doesn't allow adultery at all, whether a person can help it or not. It allows no distinction between goat and tortoise—the excitable goat, the emotional goat, that has to have some adultery every day or fade and die; and the tortoise, that cold calm puritan, that takes a treat only once in two years and then goes to sleep in the midst of it and doesn't wake up for sixty days. No lady goat is safe from criminal assault, even on the Sabbath Day, when there is a gentleman goat within three miles to leeward of her and nothing in the way but a fence fourteen feet high, whereas neither the gentleman tortoise nor the lady tortoise is ever hungry enough for the solemn joys of fornication to be willing to break the Sabbath to get them. Now according to man's curious reasoning, the goat has earned punishment, and the tortoise praise.

"Thou shalt not commit adultery" is a command which makes no distinction between the following persons. They are required to obey it:

Children at birth
Children in the cradle.
School children.
Youths and maidens.
Fresh adults.
Older ones.
Men and women of 40.
Of 50.
Of 60.
Of 70.
Of 80.
Of 90.
Of 100.

The command does not distribute its burden equally, and cannot.

It is not hard upon the three sets of children.

It is hard—harder—still harder upon the next three sets—cruelly hard.

It is blessedly softened to the next three sets.

It has now done all the damage it can, and might as well be put out of commission. Yet with comical imbecility it is continued, and the four remaining estates are put under its crushing ban. Poor old wrecks, they couldn't disobey if they tried. And think—because they holily refrain from adulterating each other, they get praise for it! Which is nonsense; for even the Bible knows enough to know that if the oldest veteran there could get

his lost heyday back again for an hour he would cast that commandment to the winds and ruin the first woman he came
across, even though she were an entire stranger

It is as I have said: every statute in the Bible and in the
lawbooks is an attempt to defeat a law of God—in other words
an unalterable and indestructible law of nature. These people's
God has shown them by a million acts that he respects none of
the Bible's statutes. He breaks every one of them himself,
adultery and all.

The law of God, as quite plainly expressed in woman's construction, is this: There shall be no limit put upon your inter-
course with the other sex sexually, at any time of life.

The law of God, as quite plainly expressed in man's construction, is this: During your entire life you shall be under inflexible
limits and restrictions, sexually.

During twenty-three days in every month (in the absence of
pregnancy) from the time a woman is seven years old till she dies
of old age, she is ready for action, and *competent*. As competent
as the candlestick to receive the candle. Competent every day,
competent every night. Also, she *wants* that candle—yearns for
it, longs for it, hankers after it, as commanded by the law of God
in her heart.

But man is only briefly competent; and only then in the
moderate measure applicable to the word in *his* sex's case. He is
competent from the age of sixteen or seventeen thenceforward
for thirty-five years. After fifty his performance is of poor quality, the intervals between are wide, and its satisfactions of no
great value to either party; whereas his great-grandmother is as
good as new. There is nothing the matter with her plant. Her
candlestick is as firm as ever, whereas his candle is increasingly
softened and weakened by the weather of age, as the years go by,
until at last it can no longer stand, and is mournfully laid to rest
in the hope of a blessed resurrection which is never to come.

By the woman's make, her plant has to be out of service three
days in the month and during part of her pregnancy. These are
times of discomfort, often suffering. For fair and just compensa-

tion she has the high privilege of unlimited adultery all the other days of her life.

That is the law of God, as revealed in her make. What becomes of this high privilege? Does she live in the free enjoyment of it? No. Nowhere in the whole world. She is robbed of it everywhere. Who does this? Man. Man's statutes—if the Bible *is* the word of God.

Now there you have a sample of man's "reasoning powers," as he calls them. He observes certain facts. For instance, that in all his life he never sees the day that he can satisfy one woman; also, that no woman ever sees the day that she can't overwork, and defeat, and put out of commission any ten masculine plants that can be put to bed to her.* He puts those strikingly suggestive and luminous facts together, and from them draws this astonishing conclusion: The Creator intended the woman to be restricted to one man.

So he concretes that singular conclusion into a *law*, for good and all.

And he does it without consulting the woman, although she has a thousand times more at stake in the matter than he has. His procreative competency is limited to an average of a hundred exercises per year for fifty years, hers is good for three thousand a year for the whole time—and as many years longer as she may live. Thus his life interest in the matter is five thousand refreshments, while hers is a hundred and fifty thousand; yet instead of fairly and honorably leaving the making of the law to the person who has an overwhelming interest at stake in it, this immeasurable hog, who has nothing at stake in it worth considering, makes it himself!

You have heretofore found out, by my teachings, that man is a

* In the Sandwich Islands in 1866 a buxom royal princess died. Occupying a place of distinguished honor at her funeral were thirty-six splendidly built young native men. In a laudatory song which celebrated the various merits, achievements, and accomplishments of the late princess those thirty-six stallions were called her *harem*, and the song said it had been her pride and boast that she kept the whole of them busy, and that several times it had happened that more than one of them had been able to charge overtime. [M.T.]

fool; you are now aware that woman is a damned fool.

Now if you or any other really intelligent person were arranging the fairnesses and justices between man and woman, you would give the man a one-fiftieth interest in the woman, and the woman a harem. Now wouldn't you? Necessarily. I give you my word, this creature with the decrepit candle has arranged it exactly the other way. Solomon, who was one of the Deity's favorites, had a copulation cabinet composed of seven hundred wives and three hundred concubines. To save his life he could not have kept two of those young creatures satisfactorily refreshed, even if he had had fifteen experts to help him. Necessarily almost the entire thousands had to go hungry years and years on a stretch. Conceive of a man hardhearted enough to look daily upon all that suffering and not be moved to mitigate it. He even wantonly added a sharp pang to that pathetic misery; for he kept within those women's sight, always, stalwart watchmen whose splendid masculine forms made the poor lassie's mouths water but who hadn't anything to solace a candlestick with, these gentry being eunuchs. A eunuch is a person whose candle has been put out. By art.

From time to time, as I go along, I will take up a Biblical statute and show you that it always violates a law of God, and then is imported into the lawbooks of the nations, where it continues its violation. But those things will keep; there is no hurry.

★   ★   ★   ★

When he first came to Nevada, during the Civil War, Mark Twain was green as grass about the "anything goes" life out there. But he wanted to be known as a true westerner—one of the boys—as soon as possible. Quickly he learned that peer acceptance comes only with experience gained the hard way. . .as this superb story shows.

A GENUINE MEXICAN PLUG

I resolved to have a horse to ride. I had never seen such wild, free, magnificent horsemanship outside of a circus as these picturesquely clad Mexicans, Californians and Mexicanized

Americans displayed in Carson streets every day. How they rode! Leaning just gently forward out of the perpendicular, easy and nonchalant, with broad slouch-brim blown square up in front, and long *riata* swinging above the head, they swept through the town like the wind! The next minute they were only a sailing puff of dust on the far desert. If they trotted, they sat up gallantly and gracefully, and seemed part of the horse; did not go jiggering up and down after the silly Miss Nancy fashion of the riding schools. I had quickly learned to tell a horse from a cow, and was full of anxiety to learn more. I was resolved to buy a horse.

While the thought was rankling in my mind, the auctioneer came skurrying through the plaza on a black beast that had as many humps and corners on him as a dromedary, and was necessarily uncomely; but he was "going, going, at twenty-two!—horse, saddle and bridle at twenty-two dollars, gentlemen!" and I could hardly resist.

A man whom I did not know (he turned out to be the auctioneer's brother) noticed the wistful look in my eye, and observed that that was a very remarkable horse to be going at such a price; and added that the saddle alone was worth the money. It was a Spanish saddle, with ponderous *tapidaros*, and furnished with the ungainly sole-leather covering with the unspellable name. I said I had half a notion to bid. Then this keen-eyed person appeared to me to be "taking my measure"; but I dismissed the suspicion when he spoke, for his manner was full of guileless candor and truthfulness. Said he: "I know that horse—know him well. You are a stranger, I take it, and so you might think he was an American horse, maybe, but I assure you he is not. He is nothing of the kind; but—excuse my speaking in a low voice, other people being near—he is, without the shadow of a doubt, a Genuine Mexican Plug!"

I did not know what a Genuine Plug was, but there was something about this man's way of saying it that made me swear inwardly that I would own a Genuine Mexican Plug or die.

"Has he any other—er advantages?" I inquired, suppressing

what eagerness I could.

He hooked his forefinger in the pocket of my army-shirt, led me to one side, and breathed in my ear impressively these words:

"He can out-buck anything in America!"

"Going, going, going—at *twenty*-four dollars and a half, gen—'

"Twenty-seven!" I shouted, in a frenzy.

"And sold!" said the auctioneer, and passed over the Genuine Mexican Plug to me.

I could scarcely contain my exultation. I paid the money, and put the animal in a neighboring livery-stable to dine and rest himself.

In the afternoon I brought the creature into the plaza, and certain citizens held him by the head, and others by the tail, while I mounted him. As soon as they let go, he placed all his feet in a bunch together, lowered his back, and then suddenly arched it upward, and shot me straight into the air a matter of three or four feet! I came as straight down again, lit in the saddle, went instantly up again, came down almost on the high pommel, shot up again, and came down on the horse's neck—all in the space of three or four seconds. Then he rose and stood almost straight up on his hind feet, and I, clasping to his lean neck desperately, slid back into the saddle, and held on. He came down, and immediately hoisted his heels into the air, delivering a vicious kick at the sky, and stood on his forefeet. And then down he came once more, and began the original exercise of shooting me straight up again. The third time I went up I heard a stranger say:

"Oh, *don't* he buck, though!"

While I was up, somebody struck the horse a sounding thwack with a leathern strap, and when I arrived again the Genuine Mexican Plug was not there. A California youth chased him up and caught him, and asked if he might have a ride. I granted him that luxury. He mounted the Genuine, got lifted into the air once, but sent his spurs home as he descended, and the horse darted away like a telegram. He soared over three fences like a bird, and disappeared down the road toward the Washoe Valley.

I sat down on a stone with a sigh, and by a natural impulse one of my hands sought my forehead, and the other the base of my stomach. I believe I never appreciated, till then, the poverty of the human machinery—for I still needed a hand or two to place elsewhere. Pen cannot describe how I was jolted up. Imagination cannot conceive how disjointed I was—how internally, externally and universally I was unsettled, mixed up and ruptured. There was a sympathetic crowd around me, though.

One elderly looking comforter said:

"Stranger, you've been taken in. Everybody in this camp knows that horse. Any child, any Injun, could have told you that he'd buck; He is the very worst devil to buck on the continent of America. You hear *me*. I'm Curry. *Old* Curry. Old *Abe* Curry. And moreover, he is a simon-pure, out-and-out, genuine d——d Mexican plug, and an uncommon mean one at that, too. Why, you turnip, if you had laid low and kept dark, there's chances to buy an *American* horse for mightly little more than you paid for that bloody old foreign relic."

I gave no sign; but I made up my mind that if the auctioneer's brother's funeral took place while I was in the Territory I would postpone all other recreations and attend it.

After a gallop of sixteen miles the Californian youth and the Genuine Mexican Plug came tearing into town again, shedding foam-flakes like the spume-spray that drives before a typhoon, and, with one final skip over a wheelbarrow and a Chinaman, cast anchor in front of the "ranch."

Such panting and blowing! Such spreading and contracting of the red equine nostrils, and glaring of the wild equine eye! But was the imperial beast subjugated? Indeed he was not. His lordship the Speaker of the House thought he was, and mounted him to go down to the Capitol; but the first dash the creature made was over a pile of telegraph poles half as high as a church; and his time to the Capitol—one mile and three-quarters—remains unbeaten to this day. But then he took an advantage—he left out the mile, and only did three-quarters. That is to say, he made a straight cut across-lots, preferring fences and ditches to a crooked road; and when the Speaker got to the Capitol he said he had been in the air so much he felt as if he had made the trip on a comet.

In the evening the Speaker came home afoot for exercise, and got the Genuine towed back behind a quartz wagon. The next day I loaned the animal to the Clerk of the House to go down to the Dana silver mine, six miles, and *he* walked back for the exercise, and got the horse towed. Everybody I loaned him to always walked back; they never could get enough exercise any other way. Still, I continued to loan him to anybody who was willing to borrow him, my idea being to get him crippled, and throw him on the borrower's hands, or killed, and make the borrower pay for him. But somehow nothing ever happened to him. He took chances that no other horse ever took and survived, but he always came out safe. It was his daily habit to try experiments that had always before been considered impossible, but he always got through. Of course I had tried to sell him; but that was a stretch of simplicity which met little sympathy. The auctioneer stormed up and down the street on him for four days, dispersing the populace, interrupting business, and destroying children, and never got a bid—at least never any but the eighteen dollar one he hired a notoriously substanceless bummer to make. The people only smiled pleasantly, and restrained their desire to buy, if they had any. Then the auctioneer brought his bill, and I withdrew the horse from the market. We tried to trade him off at private vendue next, offering him at a sacrifice for second-hand tombstones, old iron, temperance tracts—any kind of property. But holders were stiff, and we retired from the market again. I never tried to ride the horse any more. Walking was good enough exercise for a man like me, that had nothing the matter with him except ruptures, internal injuries, and such things. Finally I tried to *give* him away. But it was a failure. Parties said earthquakes were handy enough on the Pacific coast—they did not wish to own one. As a last resort I offered him to the Governor for the use of the "Brigade." His face lit up eagerly at first, but toned down again, and he said the thing would be too palpable.

Just then the livery-stable man brought in his bill for six weeks' keeping—stall-room for the horse, fifteen dollars; hay for the horse, two hundred and fifty! The Genuine Mexican Plug had eaten a ton of the article, and the man said he would have eaten a hundred if he had let him.

I will remark here, in all seriousness, that the regular price of hay during that year and a part of the next was really two hundred and fifty dollars a ton. During a part of the previous year it had sold at five hundred a ton, in gold, and during the winter before that, there was such a scarcity of the article that in several instances small quantities had brought eight hundred dollars a ton in coin! The consequence might be guessed without my telling it: People turned their stock loose to starve, and before the spring arrived Carson and Eagle valleys were almost literally carpeted with their carcases! Any old settler there will verify these statements.

I managed to pay the livery bill, and the same day I gave the Genuine Mexican Plug to a passing Arkansas emigrant whom fortune delivered into my hand. If this ever meets his eye, he will doubtless remember the donation.

Now whoever has had the luck to ride a real Mexican plug will recognize the animal depicted in the chapter, and hardly consider him exaggerated—but the uninitiated will feel justified in regarding his protrait as a fancy sketch, perhaps.

★   ★   ★   ★

Mark Twain loved cats and often wrote about them. Several cats were tended in the several homes he owned, and their names were most remarkable: Stray Cat, Abner, Motley, Fraeulein, Lazy, Buffalo Bill, Soapy Sall, Cleveland, Sour Mash, Pestilence and Famine. And Tom Quartz, the subject cat of the following story, a fictional feline loser.

DICK BAKER'S CAT

One of my comrades there—another of those victims of eighteen years of unrequited toil and blighted hopes—was one of the gentlest spirits that ever bore its patient cross in a weary exile: grave and simple Dick Baker, pocket-miner of Dead House Gulch. He was forty-six, gray as a rat, earnest, thoughtful, slenderly educated, slouchily dressed and clay-soiled, but his heart was finer metal than any gold his shovel ever brought to light—than any, indeed, that ever was mined or minted.

Whenever he was out of luck and a little down-hearted, he would fall to mourning over the loss of a wonderful cat he used to own (for where women and children are not, men of kindly impulses take up with pets, for they must love something). And he always spoke of the strange sagacity of that cat with the air of a man who believed in his secret heart that there was something human about it—maybe even supernatural.

I heard him talking about this animal once. He said:

"Gentlemen, I used to have a cat here by the name of Tom Quartz, which you'd a took an interest in I reckon—most any body would. I had him here eight years—and he was the remarkablest cat *I* ever see. He was a large gray one of the Tom specie, an' he had more hard natchral sense than any man in this camp—'n' a *power* of dignity—he wouldn't let the Gov'ner of Californy be familiar with him. He never ketched a rat in his life—'peared to be above it. He never cared for nothing but mining. He knowed more about mining, that cat did, than any man *I* ever, ever see. You couldn't tell *him* noth'n' 'bout placer diggin'—'n' as for pocket-mining, why he was just born for it. He would dig out after me an' Jim when we went over the hills prospect'n', and he would trot along behind us for as much as five mile, if we went so fur. An' he had the best judgment about mining ground—why you never see anything like it. When we went to work, he'd scatter a glance around, 'n' if he didn't think much of the indications, he would give a look as much to say, 'Well, I'll have to get you to excuse *me*,' 'n' without another word he'd hyste his nose into the air 'n' shove for home. But if the ground suited him, he would lay low 'n' keep dark till the first pan was washed, 'n' then he would sidle up 'n' take a look, an' if there was about six or seven grains of gold *he* was satisfied—he didn't want no better prospect 'n' that—'n' then he would lay down on our coats and snore like a steamboat till we'd struck the pocket, an' then get up 'n' superintend. He was nearly lightenin' on superintending.

"Well, bye an' bye, up comes this yer quartz excitement. Everybody was into it—everybody was pick'n' 'n' blast'n' instead of shovelin' dirt on the hill-side—everybody was put'n' down a shaft instead of scrapin' the surface. Noth'n' would do Jim but *we* must tackle the ledges, too, 'n' so we did. We commenced put'n' down a shaft, 'n' Tom Quartz he begin to wonder what in the dickens it was all about. *He* hadn't ever seen any mining like that before, 'n' he was all upset, as you may say—he couldn't come to a right understanding of it no way—it was too many for *him*. He was down on it, too, you bet you—he was down on it powerful—'n' always appeared to consider it the cussedest foolishness out. But that cat, you know, was *always* agin new-fangled arrangements—somehow he never could abide 'em. *You* know how it is with old habits. But bye an' bye Tom Quartz begin to git sort of reconciled a little, though he never *could* altogether understand the eternal sinkin' of a shaft an' never pannin' out anything. At last he got to comin' down in the shaft hisself, to try to cipher it out. An' when he'd git the blues, 'n' feel kind o' scruffy, 'n' aggravated 'n' disgusted—knowin', as he did, that the bills was runnin' up all the time an' we warn't makin' a cent—he would curl up on a gunny sack in the corner an' go to sleep. Well, one day when the shaft was down about eight foot, the rock got so hard that we had to put in a blast—the first blast'n' we'd ever done since Tom Quartz was born. An' then we lit the fuse 'n' clumb out 'n' got off 'bout fifty yards—'n' forgot 'n' left Tom Quartz sound asleep on the gunny sack. In 'bout a minute we seen a puff of smoke bust up out of the hole, 'n' then everything let go with an awful crash, 'n' about four million tons of rocks 'n' dirt 'n' smoke 'n' splinters shot up 'bout a mile an' a half into the air, an' by George, right in the dead centre of it was old Tom Quartz a goin' end over end, an' a snortin' an' a sneezin', an' a clawin' an' a reachin' for things like all possessed. But it warn't no use, you know, it warn't no use. An' that was the last we see of *him* for about two minutes 'n' a half, an' then all of a sudden it begins to rain rocks and rubbage, an' directly he come down ker-whop about ten foot off f'm where we stood. Well, I reckon he was p'raps the orneriest lookin' beast you ever see. One ear was sot back on his neck, 'n' his tail was stove up, 'n' his eye-winkers was swinged off, 'n' he was all blacked up with powder an' smoke, an' all sloppy with mud 'n' slush f'm one end to the other. Well, sir, it warn't no use to try to apologize—we couldn't say a word. He took a sort of a disgusted look at hisself, 'n' then he looked at us—an' it was just exactly the same as if he had said—'Gents, maybe *you* think it's smart to take advantage of a cat that 'ain't had no experience of quartz minin', but *I* think *different*'—an' then he turned on his heel 'n' marched off home without evr saying another word.

"That was jest his style. An' maybe you won't believe it, but after that you never see a cat so prejudiced agin quartz mining as what he was. An' bye an' bye when he *did* get to goin' down in the shaft agin, you'd 'a been astonished at his sagacity. The minute we'd tetch off a blast 'n' the fuse'd begin to sizzle, he'd give a look as much as to say: 'Well, I'll have to git you to ex-cuse *me*,' an' it was surpris'n' the way he'd shin out of that hole 'n' go f'r a tree. Sagacity? It ain't no name for it. 'Twas *inspiration!*"

I said, "Well, Mr. Baker, his prejudice against quartz mining *was* remarkable, considering how he came by it. Couldn't you ever cure him of it?"

"*Cure him!* No! When Tom Quartz was sot once, he was *always* sot—and you might a blowed him up as much as three million times, 'n' you'd never a broken of his cussed prejudice agin quartz mining."

★   ★   ★   ★
A TEXAS MUSTANG

This example of local color American humor comes from the book, TEXAS SIFTINGS, by Sweet and Knott, published in 1882. It was a compilation of articles included in their "weekly illustrated journal" costing $2.00 a year, and "sold by all newsdealers in installments of 5 cents, payable weekly."

When the foreigner pictures a Texas mustang in his mind's eye, he thinks of a noble jet black horse, small and compactly built, with an arched neck, a flowing mane, and a prodigal wealth of tail. He gets his idea from reading the Mayne Reid class of illustrated lies of border life, where the "noble courser of the prairies" is represented as performing extraordinary feats in carrying his rider beyond the reach of a band of pursuing savages, who are left behind on the frontier of the picture. In the illustrations the mustang has a flashing eye, a distended nostril, a 1:39-¾ gait, and a tail that reaches to the southwestern corner of the chromo. These pictures, and the ghastly realities that exist on the Texas prairies, remind one of the gigantic pomological specimens, rich in color and juicy looking, that are painted on the outside of a can of preserved strawberries, and of the poor little pale, dwarfed berries inside.

The mustang is a species of horse, angular as a rail fence and without a pedigree. A difference of opinion exists as to his origin. Some say that he is of Spanish origin—descended from the horses brought from Spain by Cortez during the conquest of Mexico—while others are strongly of opinion that the original father of the race was a clothes-horse, and the female "fons et origo" a nightmare. From the fact that the mustang is destitute of blood, and taking into account his architectural construction, we are inclined to believe that the latter conjecture is the correct one.

He averages about fourteen hands in height. He has large ears, a long head, short mane, and burrs in his tail. He is seldom fat, has a protracted body, thin shoulders and hams, and looks not unlike a section of railroad trestle. In a late paper we read a description of a Texas mustang, by Rev. W.H. Murray, the celebrated Boston preacher. Brother Murray's mustang is the kind that thrives only in the "Frontier Scout" class of literature. When the preacher wrote the description referred to, he took such a grip on the truth, and stretched it so far, that away off here in Austin we heard it crack.

The genuine Texas mustang is a parody of the horse, but he is a very useful animal, nevertheless. In driving cattle he is more active and valuable than a large horse would be; and in the matter of shaking up the liver of an invalid, who has been ordered to take horseback exercise for his health, the Texas mustang is a triumph—and success.

★　　★　　★　　★

THE HODJA'S DONKEY ON HIS VERACITY

BY S. S. COX

A friend calls on Narr-ed-din to borrow his donkey.

"Very sorry," says the Hodja, who does not want to lend the animal, "but the donkey is not here; I have hired him out for the day."

Unfortunately, just at that moment the donkey begins to bray loudly, thus giving the direct lie to the Hodja.

"How is this, Hodja?" says his friend; "you say the donkey is away, and here he is braying in the stable!"

The Hodja, nothing daunted, replies in a grave manner:

"My dear sir, please do not demean youself so low as to believe that donkey rather than myself—a fellow-man and a venerable Hodja with a long gray beard."

The moral of the last fable some people never perceive. It is this:

An ass will always reveal himself by some inappropriate remark. Asses should seldom be seen, and never heard. The wise man hideth his ass when the borrower cometh around.

★　　★　　★　　★

John Kendrick Bangs (1862-1922)

Bangs was part of the literary establishment which wrote and

edited for the "better sort" of American, the well-educated and
refined types who were Victorian in outlook and manners.
Bangs described the humor he liked when he wrote praising
those "whose humor has been of the purest, sweetest sort...it is
not necessary nowadays to be vulgar to be amusing." American
humor had swung from the "vulgar" frontier to the "refined"
urban milieu, and Bangs is typical of the change.

In the following selection, from Bang's "A Houseboat on the
River Styx," great characters of the past are seen in a houseboat
on that river in Hades! They discuss the authorship of the works
of William Shakespeare, i.e., who really wrote them.

"How are you, Charon?" said Shakespeare, as the Janitor
assisted him on board. "Anyone here to-night?"

"Yes, sir," said Charon. "Lord Bacon is up in the library, and
Doctor Johnson is down in the billiard-room, playing pool with
Nero."

"Ha-ha!" laughed Shakespeare. "Pool, eh? Does Nero play
pool?"

"Not as well as he does the fiddle, sir," said the Janitor, with a
twinkle in his eye.

Shakespeare entered the house and tossed up an obolus.
"Heads—Bacon; tails—pool with Nero and Johnson," he said.

The coin came down heads up, and Shakespeare went into the
pool-room, just to show the Fates that he didn't care a tuppence
for their verdict as registered through the obolus. It was a
peculiar custom of Shakespeare's to toss up a coin to decide
questions of little consequence, and then do the thing the coin
decided he should not do. It showed, in Shakespeare's estima-
tion, his entire independence of those dull persons who supposed
that in them was entered the destiny of all mankind. The Fates,
however, only smiled at these little acts of rebellion, and it was
common gossip in Erebus that one of the trio had told the Furies
that they had observed Shakespeare's tendency to kick over the
traces, and always acted accordingly. They never let the coin fall
so as to decide a question the way they wanted it, so that unwit-
tingly the great dramatist did their will after all. It was part of

their plan that upon this occasion Shakespeare should play pool with Doctor Johnson and the Emperor Nero, and hence it was that the coin bade him to repair to the library and chat with Lord Bacon.

"Hullo, William," said the Doctor, pocketing three balls on the break. "How's our little Swanlet of Avon this afternoon?"

"Worn out," Shakespeare replied. "I've been hard at work on a play this morning, and I'm tired."

"All work and no play makes Jack a dull boy," said Nero, grinning broadly.

"You are a bright spirit," said Shakespeare, with a sigh. "I wish I had thought to work you up into a tragedy."

"I've often wondered why you didn't," said Doctor Johnson. "He'd have made a superb tragedy, Nero would. I don't believe there was any kind of crime he left uncommitted. Was there, Emperor?"

"Yes, I never wrote an English dictionary," returned the Emperor, dryly. "I've murdered everything but English, though."

"I could have made a fine tragedy out of you," said Shakespeare. "Just think what a dreadful climax for a tragedy it would be, Johnson, to have Nero, as the curtain fell, playing a violin solo."

"Pretty good," returned the Doctor. "But what's the use of killing off your audience that way. It's better business to let' em live, I say. Suppose Nero gave a London audience that little musicale he provided at Queen Elizabeth's Wednesday night. How many purely mortal beings, do you think, would have come out alive?"

"Not one," said Shakespeare. "I was mighty glad that night that we were an immortal band. If it had been possible to kill us we'd have died then and there."

"That's all right," said Nero, with a significant shake of his head. "As my friend Bacon makes Iago say, 'Beware, my lord, of jealousy.' You never could play a garden hose, much less a fiddle."

"What do you mean by attributing those words to Bacon?" demanded Shakespeare, getting red in the face.

"Oh, come now, William," remonstrated Nero. "It's all right to pull the wool over the eyes of the mortals. That's what they're there for; but as for us—we're all in the secret here. What's the use of putting on nonsense with us?"

"We'll see in a minute what the use is," retorted the Avonian. "We'll have Bacon down here." Here he touched an electric button, and Charon came in answer.

"Charon, bring Doctor Johnson the usual glass of ale. Get some ice for the Emperor, and ask Lord Bacon to step down here a minute."

"I don't want any ice," said Nero.

"Not now," retorted Shakespeare, "but you will in a few minutes. When we have finished with you, you'll want an iceberg. I'm getting tired of this idiotic talk about not having written my own words. There's one thing about Nero's music that I've never said, because I haven't wanted to hurt his feelings, but since he has chosen to cast aspersions upon my honesty I haven't any hesitation on saying it now. I believe it was one of his fiddlings that sent Nature into convulsions and caused the destruction of Pompeii—so there! Put that on your music rack and fiddle it, my little Emperor."

Nero's face grew purple with anger, and if Shakespeare had been anything but a shade he would have fared ill, for the enraged Roman, poising his cue on high as though it were a lance, hurled it at the impertinent dramatist with all his strength, and with such accuracy of aim withal that it pierced the spot beneath which in life the heart of Shakespeare used to beat.

"Good shot," said Doctor Johnson, nonchalantly. "If you had been a mortal, William, it would have been the end of you."

"You can't kill me," said Shakespeare, shrugging his shoulders. "I know seven dozen actors in the United States who are trying to do it, but they can't. I wish they'd try to kill a critic once in a while instead of me, though," he added. "I went over to Boston one night last week, and, unknown to anybody, I waylaid a fellow who was to play Hamlet that night. I drugged him, and went to the theatre and played the part myself. It was the coldest house you ever saw in your life. When the audience did applaud, it sounded like an iceman chopping up ice with a small pick. Several times I looked up at the galleries to see if there were not icicles growing on them, it was so cold. Well, I did the best I could with the part, and the next morning watched curiously for the criticisms.''

"Favorable?'' asked the Doctor.

"They all dismissed me with a line,'' said the dramatist. "Said my conception of the part was not Shakespearean. And that's criticism!''

"No,'' said the shade of Emerson, which had strolled in while Shakespeare was talking, "that isn't criticism; that's Boston.''

"Who discovered Boston, anyhow?'' asked Doctor Johnson. "It wasn't Columbus, was it?''

"Oh no,'' said Emerson. "Old Governor Winthrop is to blame for that. When he settled at Charlestown he saw the old Indian town of Shawmut across the Charles.''

"And Shawmut was the Boston microbe, was it?'' asked Johnson.

"Yes,'' said Emerson.

"Spelt with a P, I suppose?'' said Shakespeare. "P-S-H-A-W, Pshaw, M-U-T, mut, Pshawmut, so called because the inhabitants are always muttering pshaw. Eh?''

"Pretty good,'' said Johnson. "I wish I'd said that.''

"Well, tell Boswell,'' said Shakespeare. "He'll make you say it, and it'll be all the same in a hundred years.''

Lord Bacon, accompanied by Charon and the ice for Nero and the ale for Doctor Johnson, appeared as Shakespeare spoke. The philosopher bowed stiffly at Doctor Johnson, as though he hardly approved of him, extended his left hand to Shakespeare, and stared coldly at Nero.

"Did you send for me, William?'' he asked, languidly.

"I did,'' said Shakespeare. "I sent for you because this imperial violinist here says that you wrote *Othello*.''

"What nonsense," said Bacon. "The only plays of yours I wrote were *Ham—*"

"Sh!" said Shakespeare, shaking his head madly. "Hush. Nobody's said anything about that. This is purely a discussion of *Othello*."

"The fiddling ex-Emperor Nero," said Bacon loudly enough to be heard all about the room, "is mistaken when he attributes *Othello* to me."

"Aha, Master Nero!" cried Shakespeare, triumphantly. "What did I tell you?"

"Then I erred, that is all," said Nero. "And I apologize. But really, my Lord," he added, addressing Bacon, "I fancied I detected your fine Italian hand in that."

"No, I had nothing to do with the *Othello*," said Bacon. "I never really knew who wrote it."

"Never mind about that," whispered Shakespeare. "You've said enough."

"That's good too," said Nero, with a chuckle. "Shakespeare here claims it as his own."

Bacon smiled and nodded approvingly at the blushing Avonian.

"Will always was having his little jokes," he said. "Eh, Will? How we fooled 'em on *Hamlet*, eh, my boy? Ha-ha-ha! It was the greatest joke of the century."

"Well, the laugh is on you," said Doctor Johnson. "If you wrote *Hamlet* and didn't have the sense to acknowledge it, you present to my mind a closer resemblance to Simple Simon than to Socrates. For my part, I don't believe you did write it, and I do believe that Shakespeare did. I can tell that by the spelling in the original edition."

"Shakespeare was my stenographer, gentlemen," said Lord Bacon. "If you want to know the whole truth, he did write *Hamlet*, literally. But it was at my dictation."

"I deny it," said Shakespeare. "I admit you gave me a suggestion now and then so as to keep it dull and heavy in spots, so that it would seem more like a real tragedy than a comedy punctuated with deaths, but beyond that you had nothing to do with it."

"I side with Shakespeare," put in Emerson. "I've seen his autographs, and no sane person would employ a man who wrote such a villanously bad hand as an amanuensis. It's no use, Bacon, we know a thing or two. I'm a New-Englander, I am."

"Well," said Bacon, shrugging his shoulders as though the results of the controversy were immaterial to him, "have it so if you please. There isn't any money in Shakespeare these days, so what's the use of quarrelling? I wrote *Hamlet*, and Shakespeare knows it. Others know it. Ah, here comes Sir Walter Raleigh. We'll leave it to him. He was cognizant of the whole affair."

"I'll leave it to nobody," said Shakespeare, sulkily.

"What's the trouble?" asked Raleigh, sauntering up and taking a chair under the cue rack. "Talking politics?"

"Not we," said Bacon. "It's the old question about the authorship of *Hamlet*. Will, as usual, claims it for himself. He'll be saying he wrote Genesis next."

"Well, what if he does?" laughed Raleigh. "We all know Will and his droll ways."

"No doubt," put in Nero. "But the question of *Hamlet* always excites him so that we'd like to have it settled once and for all as to who wrote it. Bacon says you know."

"I do," said Raleigh.

"Then settle it once and for all," said Bacon. "I'm rather tired of the discussion myself."

"Shall I tell 'em, Shakespeare?" asked Raleigh.

"It's immaterial to me," said Shakespeare, airily. "If you wish—only tell the truth."

"Very well," said Raleigh, lighting a cigar. "I'm not ashamed of it. I wrote the thing myself."

There was a roar of laughter which, when it subsided, found Shakespeare rapidly disappearing through the door, while all the others in the room ordered various beverages at the expense of Lord Bacon.

★   ★   ★   ★

George William Peck (1840-1916)

*George W. Peck was a success story in the American Tradi-
tion. He was raised on a hardscrabble Wisconsin farm and in
small towns of that state. At fifteen he was apprenticed to a
printer and followed the newspaper business successfully. His
weekly newspaper,* The Sun, *published in Milwaukee, sold
80,000 copies a week across the nation, and helped to twice
elect him Governor of Wisconsin.*

*But Peck's lasting fame was his development of a fictional
young teen-ager known as Peck's Bad Boy, a term still with us
100 years after the publication of the books that immortalized
the boy. Peck's Bad Boy was a master of the practical joke, one
upmanship, and the dirty trick. His incorrigibly mischievous
ways gave our language the term we use until today to describe
an aggravating, mischievous boy.*

The following selection is taken from The Grocer Man and
Peck's Bad Boy, *published in 1883. Here the Bad Boy cures his
Daddy of a bad drinking habit...the hard way!*

PECK'S BAD BOY

"Come in," said the grocery man to the bad boy, as the youth
stood on the steps in an uncertain sort of way, as though he did
not know whether he would be welcome or not. "I tell you, boy,
I pity you. I understand your Pa has got to drinking again. It is
too bad. I can't think of anything that humiliates a boy, and
makes him so ashamed, as to have a father that is in the habit of
hoisting in too much benzine. A boy feels as though everybody
was down on him, and I don't wonder that such boys often turn
out bad. What started your Pa to drinking again?"

"O, Ma thinks it was losing money on the Chicago races. You
see, Pa is great on pointers. He don't usually bet unless he has
got a sure thing, but when he gets what they call a pointer, that
is, somebody tells hin a certain horse is sure to win, because the
other horses are to be pulled back, he thinks a job had been put
up, and if he thinks he is on the inside of the ring he will bet. He

says it does not do any hurt to bet, if you win, and he argues that a man who wins lots of money can do a great deal of good with it. But he had to walk home from the Chicago races all the same, and he has been steaming ever since. Pa can't stand adversity. But I guess we have got him all right now. He is the scartest man you ever saw," and the boy took a can opener and began to cut the zinc under the stove, just to see if it would work as well on zinc as on tin.

"What, you haven't been dissecting him again, have you?" said the grocery man, as he pulled a stool up beside the boy to hear the news. "How did you bring him to his senses?"

"Well, Ma tried having the minister talk to Pa, but Pa talked Bible, about taking a little wine for the stomach's sake, and gave illustrations about Noah getting full, so the minister couldn't brace him up, and then Ma had some of the sisters come and talk to him, but he broke them all up by talking about what an appetite they had for champagne punch when they were out in camp last summer, and they couldn't have any affect on him, and so Ma said she guessed I would have to exercise my ingenuity on Pa again. Ma has an idea that I have got some sense yet, so I told her that if she would do just as I said, me and my chum would scare Pa so he would swear off. She said she would, and we went to work. First I took Pa's spectacles down to an optician, Saturday night, and had the glasses taken out and a pair put in their place that would magnify, and I took them home and put them in Pa's spectacle case. Then I got a suit of clothes from my chum's uncle's trunk, about half the size of Pa's clothes. My chum's uncle is a very small man, and Pa is corpulent. I got a plug hat three sizes smaller than Pa's hat, and the name out of Pa's hat and put it in the small hat. I got a shirt about half big enough for Pa, and put his initials on the thing under the bosom, and got a number fourteen collar. Pa wears seventeen. Pa had promised to brace up and go to church Sunday morning, and Ma put these small clothes where Pa could put them on. I told Ma, when Pa woke up, to tell him he looked awfully bloated, and excite his curiosity, and then send for me."

"You didn't play such a trick as that on a poor old man, did you?" said the grocery man, as a smile came over his face.

"You bet. Desperate dieases require desperate remedies. Well, Ma told Pa he looked awfully bloated, and that his dissipation was killing him, as well as all the rest of the family. Pa said he guessed he wasn't bloated very much, but he got up and put on his spectacles and looked at himself in the glass. You'd a dide to see him look at himself. His face looked as big as two faces, through the glass, and his nose was a sight. Pa looked scared, and then he held up his hand and looked at that. His hand looked like a ham. Just then I came in, and I turned pale, with some chalk on my face, and I begun to cry, and I said, 'Oh, Pa, what ails you? You are so swelled up I hardly knew you.' Pa looked sick to his stomach, and then he tried to get on his pants. O, my, it was all I could do to keep from laughing to see him pull them pants on. He could just get his legs in, and when I got a shoe horn and gave it to him, he was mad. He said it was a mean boy that would give his Pa a shoe horn to put on his pants with. The pants wouldn't come around Pa into ten inches, and Pa said he must have eat something that disagreed with him, and he laid it to watermelon. Ma stuffed her hankerchief in her mouth to keep from laffing, when she see Pa look at hisself. The legs of the pants were so tight Pa could hardly breathe and he turned pale, and said, "Hennery, your Pa is a mighty sick man,' and then Ma and me both laughed, and he said we wanted him to die so we could spend his life insurance in riotous living. But when Pa put on that condensed shirt, Ma she laid down on the lounge and fairly yelled, and I laughed till my sides ached. Pa got it over his head, and got his hands in the sleeves, and couldn't get it either way, and he couldn't see us laugh, but he could hear us, and he said, 'It's darned funny, ain't it, to have a parent swelled up this way. If I bust you will both be sorry.' Well, Ma took hold of one side of the shirt, and I took hold of the other, and we pulled it on, and when Pa's head came through the collar, his face was blue. Ma told him she was afraid he would have a stroke of apoplexy before he got his clothes on, and I guess Pa thought so too. He tried to get the collar on, but it wouldn't go half way around his neck, and he looked in the glass and cried, he looked so. He sat down in a chair and panted, he was so out of breath, and the shirt and pants ripped, and Pa said there was no use living if he was going to be a rival to a fat woman in the side show. Just then I put the plug hat on Pa's head, and it was so small it was going to roll off, when Pa tried to fit it on his head, and then he took it off and looked inside of it, to see if it was his hat, and when he found his name in it, he said, 'Take it away. My head is all wrong too.' Then he told me to go for the doctor, mighty quick. I got the doctor and told him what we were trying to do with Pa, and he said he would finish the job. So the Doc. came in, and Pa was on the lounge, and when the Doc. saw him, he said it was lucky he was called just as he was, or we would have required an undertaker. He put some pounded ice on Pa's head the first thing, ordered the shirt cut open, and we got the pants off. Then he gave Pa an emetic, and had his feet soaked, and Pa said, 'Doc., if you will bring me out of this I will never drink another drop.' The Doc. told Pa that his life was not worth a button if he ever drank again, and left about half a pint of sugar pills to be fired into Pa every five minutes. Ma and me sat up with Pa all day Sunday, and Monday morning I changed the spectacles, and took the clothes home, and along about noon Pa said he felt as though he could get up. Well, you never see a tickleder man than he was when he found the swelling had gone down so he could get his pants and shirt on, and he says that doctor is the best in this town. Ma says I am a smart boy, and Pa has taken the pledge, and we were all right. Say, you don't think there is anything wrong in a boy playing it on his Pa once in a while, do you?"

"Not much. You have very likely saved your Pa's life. No, sir, joking is all right when by so doing you can break a person of a bad habit," and the grocery man cut a chew of tobacco off a piece of plug that was on the counter, which the boy had soaked in kerosene, and before he had fairly got it rolled in his cheek he spit it out and bagan to gag, and as the boy started leisurely out the door the grocery man said, "Lookahere, condemn you, don't you ever tamper with my tobacco again, or by thunder I'll maul you," and he followed the boy to the door, spitting cotton all the way; and, as the boy went around the corner, the grocery man thought how different a joke seemed when it was on somebody else. And then he turned to go in and rinse the kerosene out of his mouth, and found a sign on a box of new, green apples, as follows:—

COLIC OR CHOLERA INFANTUM
YOU PAYS YOUR MONEY
AND TAKES YOUR CHOICE

★   ★   ★   ★

Edgar W. (Bill) Nye (1850-1896)

Born in Maine, Nye was raised in St. Croix County, Wisconsin, and gave his background as follows: "I traced our people back to the European police courts and even beyond that, discovering, at last, in France, our Coat of Alms." A witty satirist, Nye was enormously popular and a prolific writer, turning out 30,000 words a week along with some 50 letters! Philosopher John Dewey called him a "great satirist," writing: "few Americans have done more to expose pretense and superstition."

THE OPIUM HABIT

I have always had a horror of opiates of all kinds. They are so seductive and so still in their operations. They steal through the blood like a wolf on the trail, and they seize upon the heart at last with their white fangs till it is still forever.

Up the Laramie there is a cluster of ranches at the base of the Medicine Bow, near the north end of Sheep Mountain, and in sight of the glittering, eternal frost of the snowy range. These ranches are the homes of the young men from Massachusetts, Pennsylvania and Ohio, and now there are several "younger sons" of Old England, with herds of horses, steers and sheep, worth millions of dollars. These young men are not the kind of whom the metropolitan ass writes as saying "youbetcherlife," and calling everybody "pardner." They are many of them college graduates, who can brand a wild Maverick or furnish the easy gestures for a Strauss waltz.

They wear human clothes, talk in the United States language, and have a bank account. This spring they may be wearing chaparajos and swinging a quirt through the thin air, and in July they may be at Long Branch, or coloring a meerschaum pipe among the Alps.

Well, a young man whom we will call Curtis lived at one of these ranches years ago, and, though a quiet, mind-your-own-business fellow, who had absolutely no enemies among his companions, he had the misfortune to incur the wrath of a tramp sheep-herder, who waylaid Curtis one afternoon and shot him dead as he sat in his buggy. Curtis wasn't armed. He didn't dream of trouble till he drove home from town, and, as he passed through the gates of a corral, saw the-hairy face of the herder, and at the same moment the flash of a Winchester rifle. That was all.

A rancher came into town and telegraphed to Curtis's father, and then a half dozen citizens went out to help capture the herder, who had fled to the sagebrush of the foothills.

They didn't get back till toward daybreak, but they brought the herder with them. I saw him in the gray of the morning, lying in a coarse gray blanket, on the floor of the engine house. He was dead.

I asked, as a reporter, how he came to his death, and they told me—opium! I said, did I understand you to say "ropium?" They said no, it was opium. The murderer had taken poison when he found that escape was impossible.

I was present at the inquest, so that I could report the case. There was very little testimony, but all the evidence seemed to point to the face that life was extinct, and a verdict of death by his own hand was rendered.

It was the first opium work I had ever seen, and it aroused my curiosity. Death by opium, it seems, leaves a dark purple ring around the neck. I did not know this before. People who die by opium also tie their hands together before they die. This is one of the eccentricities of opium poisoning that I have never seen laid down in the books. I bequeath it to medical science. Whenever I run up against a new scientific discovery, I just hand it right over to the public without cost.

Ever since the above incident, I have been very apprehensive about people who seem to be likely to form the opium habit. It is one of the most deadly of narcotics, especially in a new country. High up in the pure mountain atmosphere, this man could not secure enough air to prolong life, and he expired. In a land where clear, crisp air and delightful scenery are abundant, he turned his back upon them both and passed away. Is it not sad to contemplate?

LIFE INSURANCE AS A HEALTH RESTORER

BY BILL NYE

Life insurance is a great thing. I would not be without it. My health is greatly improved since I got my new policy. Formerly I used to have a seal-brown taste in my mouth when I arose in the morning, but that has entirely disappeared. I am more hopeful and happy, and my hair is getting thicker on top. I would not try to keep house without life insurance. Last September I was caught in one of the most destructive cyclones that ever visited a republican form of government. A great deal of property was destroyed and many lives were lost. People who had no insurance were mowed down on every hand, but aside from a broken leg I was entirely unharmed.

I look upon life insurance as a great comfort, not only to the beneficiary, but to the insured, who very rarely lives to realize anything pecuniarily from his venture. Twice I have almost raised my wife to affluence and cast a gloom over the community in which I lived, but something happened to the physician for a few days so that he could not attend to me, and I recovered. For nearly two years I was under the doctor's care. He had his finger on my pulse or in my pocket all the time. He was a young western physician, who attended me on Tuesdays and Fridays. The rest of the week he devoted his medical skill to horses that were mentally broken down. He said he attended me largely for my society. I felt flattered to know that he enjoyed my society after he had been among horses all the week that had much greater advantages than I.

My wife objected seriously to an insurance on my life, and said she would never, never touch a dollar of the money if I were to die, but after I had been sick nearly two years, and my disposition had suffered a good deal, she said that I need not delay the obsequies on that account. But the life insurance slipped through my fingers somehow, and I recovered.

In these days of dynamite and roller rinks, and the gory meat-ax of a new administration, we ought to make some provisions for the future.

★   ★   ★   ★

Charles Dudley Warner (1829-1900)

Warner was a lawyer, practicing in Chicago. He was a prolific writer who worked.with Mark Twain on The Gilded Age, *as well as publishing ten travel books of his own, and a wealth of newspaper articles.*

The work habits of plumbers are changeless, from generation to generation...it seems.

PLUMBERS

Speaking of the philsophical temper, there is no class of men whose society is more to be desired for this quality than that of plumbers. They are the most agreeable men I know; and the boys in the business begin to be agreeable very early. I suspect the secret of it is, that they are agreeable by the hour. In the dryest of days my fountain became disabled: the pipe was stopped up. A couple of plumbers, with the implements of their craft, came out to view the situation. There was a good deal of dif-ference of opinion about where the stoppage was. I found the plumbers perfectly willing to sit down and talk about it—talk by the hour. Some of their guesses and remarks were exceedingly ingenious; and their general observations on other subjects were excellent in their way, and could hardly have been better if they had been made by the job. The work dragged a little—as it is apt to do by the hour. The plumbers had occasion to make me several visits. Sometimes they would find, upon arrival, that they had forgotten some indispensable tool, and one would go back to the shop, a mile and a half, after it, and his companion would await his return with the most exemplary patience, and sit down and talk—always by the hour. I do not know but it is a habit to have something wanted at the shop. They seemed to me very good workmen, and always willing to stop and talk about the job, or anything else, when I went near them. Nor had they any of the impetuous hurry that is said to be the bane of our American civilization. To their credit be it said, that I never observed anything of it in them. They can afford to wait. Two of them will sometimes wait nearly half a day while a comrade goes for a tool. They are patient and philosophical. It is a great pleasure to meet such men. One only wishes there was some work he could do for *them* by the hour. There ought to be reciprocity. I think they have nearly solved the problem of life: it is to work for other people, never for yourself, and get your pay by the hour. You then have no anxiety, and little work. If you do things by the job you are perpetually driven: the hours are scourges. If you work by the hour, you gently sail on the stream of Time, which is always bearing you on to the haven of Pay, whether you make any effort or not. Working by the hour tends to make one moral. A plumber working by the job, trying to unscrew a rusty, refractory nut in a cramped position, where the tongs continually slipped off, would swear; but I never heard one of them swear, or exhibit the least impatience at such a vexation, working by the hour. Nothing can move a man who is paid by the hour. How sweet the flight of time seems to his calm mind!

★   ★   ★   ★

James M. Bailey (The Danbury News Man) (1841-1894)

Bailey was a newspaper owner-writer in Danbury, Conn. His humorous newspaper "colyum" was a forerunner of today's popular and syndicated newspaper columnists like Art Buchwald, Erma Bombeck, and Russell Baker. Bailey was popular nationally, his first book selling 33,000 copies in eleven weeks!

WHAT HE WANTED IT FOR

Those who attended the sale of animals from Barnum's hippodrome in Bridgeport, the other day, report the following occurence. A tiger was being offered. The bid run up to forty-five hundred dollars. This was made by a man who was a stranger, and to him it was knocked down. Barnum, who had been eyeing the stranger uneasily during the bidding, now went up to him, and said:

"Pardon me for asking the question; but will you tell me where you are from?"

"Down South a bit," responded the man.

"Are you connected with any show?"

"No."

"And are you buying this animal for yourself?"

"Yes."

Barnum shifted about uneasily for a moment, looking alternately at the man and the tiger, and evidently trying his best to reconcile the two together.

"Now, young man," he finally said, "you need not take this animal unless you want to; for there are those here who will take it off your hands."

"I don't want to sell," was the quiet reply.

Then Barnum said, in his desperation:

"What on earth are you going to do with such an ugly beast, if you have no show of your own, and are not buying for some one who is a showman?"

"Well, I'll tell you," said the purchaser. "My wife died about three weeks ago. We lived together for ten years, and—and I miss her." He paused to wipe his eyes, and steady his voice, and then added: "So I've bought this tiger."

"I understand you," said the great showman in a husky voice.

★   ★   ★   ★

Finley P. Dunne (1868-1936)

Dunne, a Chicago journalist, wrote under the pen name of Martin Dooley, or Mr. Dooley, and used Irish dialect to enhance his humor. He was a remarkable writer who gave laughter to millions of Americans with the odd situations he got Mr. Dooley into and out of. And Dooley represented the solipsistic, "I'm gonna get mine!" philosophy of his time (and perhaps all times) when he made such classic remarks as these: "Trust everybody...but cut the cards." And, "tis the wise man that goes through life thinkin' of himself, fills his own stomach and takes away what he can't eat in his pocket."

The first story is a tall tale, a whopper of the kind that so delighted Americans of that time...and this.

THE GREAT HOT SPELL

It was sultry everywhere, but particularly in Archey Road; for in summer Archey Road is a tunnel for the south-west wind, which refreshes itself at the rolling-mill blasts, and spills its wrath upon the just and unjust alike. Wherefore Mr. Dooley and Mr. McKenna were both steaming, as they sat at either side of the door of Mr. Dooley's place, with their chairs tilted back against the posts.

"Hot," said Mr. McKenna.

"Warrum," said Mr. Dooley.

"I think this is the hottest September that ever was," said Mr. McKenna.

"So ye say," said Mr. Dooley. "An' that's because ye're a young man, a kid. If ye was my age, ye'd know bether. How d'ye do, Mrs. Murphy? Go in, an' fill it ye'ersilf. Ye'll find th' funnel undher th' see-gar case.—Ye'd know bether thin that.

Th' Siptimber iv th' year eighteen sixty-eight was so much hotter
thin this that, if ye wint fr'm wan to th' other, ye'd take
noomoney iv th' lungs,—ye wud so. 'Twas a remarkable summer, takin' it all in all. On th' Foorth of July they was a fut of
ice in Haley's slough, an' I was near flooded out be th' wather
pipe bustin'. A man be th' name of Maloney froze his hand settin' off a Roman candle near Main Sthreet, an'—Tin cints,
please, ma'am. Thank ye kindly. How's th' good man?—As I
said, it was a remarkable summer. It rained all August, an' th'
boys wint about on rafts; an'a sthreet-car got lost fr'm th' road,
an' I dhrove into th' canal, an' all on boord— 'Avnin', Mike.
Ah-ha, 'twas a great fight. An' Buck got his eye did he? A good
man.

"Well, Jawn, along come Siptimber. It begun fairly warrum,
wan hundherd or so in th' shade; but no wan minded that. Thin
it got hotter an' hotter, an' people begun to complain a little.
They was sthrong in thim days,—not like th' doods they raise
now,—an' a little heat more or less didn't kill thim. But afther a
while it was more thin most of thim wanted. The sthreet-car
thracks got so soft they spread all over th' street, an' th' river
run dhry. Afther boilin' f'r five days like a— How are ye, Demp-
sey? Ye don't tell me? Now th' likes of him runnin' f'r aldherman! I'd as lave vote f'r th' tillygraph pole. Well, be good to
ye'resilf. Folks all well? Thanks be.—They shut off th' furnaces
out at th' mills, an' melted th' iron be puttin' it out in th' sun.
Th' puddlers wurruked in iron cases, an' was kept alive be men
playin' a hose on thim fr'm th' packin' house refrigerator. Wan
of thim poked his head out to light his pipe, an' he was— Well,
well, Timothy, ye are quite a sthranger. Ah, dear oh me, that's
too ba-ad, too ba-ad. I'll tell ye what ye do. Ye rub th' hand in
half of a potato, an' say tin paters an' ave's over it ivry day fir tin
days. 'Tis a sure cure. I had wan wanst. Th' kids are thrivin', I
dinnaw? That's good. Better to hear thim yellin' in th' sthreet
thin th' sound of th' docthor's gig at th' dure."

"Well, Jawn, things wint fr'm bad to worse. All th' beer in th'
house was mulled; an' Mrs. Dinny Hogan—her that was Odelia

O'Brien—burned her face atin' ice-crame down be th' Italyan man's place, on Halsthed Sthreet. 'Twas not sthrange sight to see an ice-wagon goin' along th' sthreet on fire— McCarthy! Mc-Carthy! come over here! Sure , ye're gettin' proud, passin' by ye'er ol' frinds. How's thricks in th' Ninth? D'ye think he will? Well, I've heerd that, too; but they was a man in here to-day that says the Boohemians is out f'r him with axes. Good-night. Don't forget th' number.''

"They was a man be th' name of Daheny, Jawn, a cousin of th' wan ye know, that started to walk up th' r-road fr'm th' bridge. Befure he got to Halsthed Sthreet, his shoes was on fire. He turned in an alarm; but th' fire departmint was all down on Mitchigan Avnoo, puttin' out th' lake, an' ''—

"Puttin' out what?'' demanded Mr. McKenna.

"Puttin' out th' lake,'' replied Mr. Dooley, stolidly. "They was no insurance— A good avnin' to ye, Mrs. Doyle. Ye're goin' over, thin? I was there las' night, an' a finer wake I niver see. They do nawthin' be halves. How was himsilf? As natural as life? Yes, ma'am, rayqueem high mass, be carredges to Calv'ry.''

"On th' twinty-fifth of Siptimber a change come. It was very sudden; an', steppin' out of th' ice-box where I slept in th' mornin', I got a chill. I wint for me flannels, an' stopped to look at th' thermomether. It was four hundherd an' sixty-five.''

"How much?'' asked Mr. McKenna.

"Four hundherd an' sixty-five.''

"Fahrenheit?''

"No, it belonged to Dorsey. Ah! well, well, an' here's Cassidy. Come in, frind, an' have a shell of beer. I've been tellin' Jawnny about th' big thaw of eighteen sixty-eight. Feel th' wind, man alive. 'Tis turnin' cool, an' we'll sleep to-night.''

★   ★   ★   ★

ON REFORM CANDIDATES

"That frind of ye'ers, Dugan, is an intilligent man,'' said Mr. Dooley. "All he needs is an index an' a few illusthrations to make him a bicyclopedja of useless information.''

"Well," said Mr. Hennessy, judiciously, "he ain't no Socrates an' he ain't no answers-to-questions colum; but he's a good man that goes to his jooty, an' as handy with a pick as some people are with a cocktail spoon. What's he been doin' again ye?"

"Nawthin'," said Mr. Dooley, "but he was in here Choosday. 'Did ye vote?' says I. 'I did,' says he. 'Which wan of th' distinguished bunko steerers got ye'er invalu'ble suffrage?' says I. 'I didn't have none with me,' says he, 'but I voted f'r Chester Haitch,' says he. 'I've been with him in six ilictions,' says he, 'an' he's a good man,' he says. 'D'ye think ye're votin'f'r th' best?' says I. 'Why, man alive,' I says, 'Chester Haitch was assassinated three years ago,' I says. 'Was he?' says Dugan. 'Ah, well, he's lived that down be this time. He was a good man,' he says.

"Ye see, that's what thim rayform lads wint up again. If I liked rayformers, Hinnissy, an' wanted f'r to see thim win out wanst in their lifetime, I'd buy thim each a suit of chilled steel, ar-rm thim with raypeatin' rifles, an' take thim east of State Sthreet an' south of Jackson Bullyvard. At prisint th' opinion that pre-vails in th' ranks of th' gloryous ar-rmy of ray-form is that there ain't annything worth seein' in this lar-rge and commodyous desert but th' pest-house an' the bridewell. Me frind Willum J. O'Brien is no rayformer. But Willum J. undherstands that ther's a few hundherds of thousands of people livin' in a part of th' town that looks like nawthin' but smoke fr'm th' roof of th' Onion League Club that have on'y two pleasures in life, to wur-ruk an' to vote, both of which they do at th' uniform rate of wan dollar an' a half a day. That's why Willum J. O'Brien is now a sinitor an' will be an aldherman afther next Thursdah, an' it's why other people are sindin' him flowers."

"This is th' way a rayform candydate is ilicted. Th' boys down town has heerd that things ain't goin' r-right somehow. Franchises is bein' handed out to none of thim; an' wanst in a while a mimber of th' club, comin' home a little late an' thryin' to riconcile a pair of r-round feet with an embroidered sidewalk, meets a sthrong ar-rm boy that pushes in his face an' takes away all his marbles. It begins to be talked that th' time has come f'r good citizens f'r to brace up an' do somethin', an' they agree to nomynate a candydate f'r aldherman. 'Who'll we put up?' says they. 'How's Clarence Doolittle?' says wan. 'He's laid up with a coupon thumb, an' can't r-run.' 'An' how about Arthur Doheny?' 'I swore an oath whin I came out of colledge I'd niver vote f'r a man that wore a made tie.' 'Well, thin, let's thry Willie Boye.' 'Good,' says th' comity. 'He's jus' th' man f'r our money.' An' Willie Boye, after thinkin' it over, goes to his tailor an' ordhers three dozen pairs of pants, an' decides f'r to be th' sthandard-bearer of th' people. Musin' over his fried eyesthers an' asparagus an' his champagne, he bets a polo pony again a box of golf-balls he'll be ilicted unanimous; an' all th' good citizens make a vow f'r to set th' alar-rm clock f'r half-past three on th' afthernoon of iliction day, so's to be up in time to vote f'r th' riprisintitive of pure gover'mint."

"'Tis some time befure they comprehind that there ar-re other candydates in th' field. But th' other candydates know it. Th' sthrongest of thim—his name in Flannigan, an' he's a re-tail dealer in wines an' liquors, an' he lives over his establishment. Flannigan was nomynated enthusyastically at a prim'ry held in his bar-rn; an' befure Willie Boye had picked out pants that wud match th' color of th' Austhreelyan ballot this here Flannigan had put a man on th' day watch, tol' him to speak gently to anny raygistered voters that wint to sleep behind th' sthove, an' was out that night visitin' his frinds. Who was it judged the cake walk? Flannigan. Who was it carrid th' pall? Flannigan. Who was it sthud up at th' christening? Flannigan. Whose ca-ards did th' grievin' widow, th' blushin' bridegroom, or th' happy father find in th' hack? Flannigan's. Ye bet ye'er life. Ye see Flannigan wasn't out f'r th' good of th' community. Flannigan was out f'r Flannigan an' th' stuff.

"Well, iliction day come around; an' all th' imminent frinds of good gover'mint had special wires sthrung into th' club, an' waited f'r th' returns. Th' first precin't showed 28 votes f'r Willie Boye to 14 f'r Flannigan. 'That's my precin't,' says

Willie. 'I wondher who voted thim fourteen?' 'Coachmen,' says
Clarence Doolittle. 'There are thirty-five precin'ts in this ward,'
says th' leader of th' rayform ilimint. 'At this rate, I'm sure of
440 meejority. Gossoon,' he says, ' put a keg of sherry wine on
th' ice,' he says. 'Well,' he says, 'at last th' community is relieved fr'm misrule,' he says. 'To-morrah I will start in arrangin'
amindmints to th' tariff schedool an' th' ar-bitration threety,' he
says. 'We must be up an' doin',' he says. 'Hol' on there,' says
one of th' comity. 'There must be some mistake in this fr'm th'
sixth precin't,' he says. 'Where's the sixth precin't?' says
Clarence. 'Over be th' dumps,' says Willie. 'I told me futman to
see to that. He lives at th' cor-ner of Desplaines an' Bloo Island
Av'noo on Goose's Island,' he says. 'What does it show?' 'Flannigan, three hundherd an' eight-five; Hansen, forty-eight;
Schwartz, twinty; O'Malley, sivinteen; Casey, ten; O'Day, eight;
Larsen, five; O'Rourke three; Mulcahy, two, Schmitt, two;
Moloney, two; Riordon, two; O'Malley, two; Willie Boye, wan.'
'Gentlemin,' says Willie Boye, arisin' with a stern look in his
eyes, th' rascal has bethrayed me. Waither, take th' sherry wine
off th' ice. They'se no hope f'r sound financial legislation this
year. I'm goin' home.'

"An', as he goes down th' sthreet, he hears a band play an'
sees a procission headed be a calceem light; an', in a carredge,
with his plug hat in his hand an' his di'mond makin' th' calceem
look like a piece of punk in a smoke-house, is Flannigan, payin'
his first visit this side of th' thracks.''

★   ★   ★   ★

A. H. Lewis (1855-1914)

A. H. Lewis was born in Cleveland, Ohio and followed many
varied jobs during his life: he was a lawyer, wandering cowboy,
journalist, correspondent and editor. He is remembered as the
writer of some of the wackiest cowboy stories ever written.

In the following selection from his book, WOLFVILLE
DAYS (1902), the scene is set between the rival cowtowns of
Wolfville and Red Dog, Arizona. The Wolfville cowboys assem-

*ble to hear Wolfville's sage, the Old Cattleman, tell the story of
the first newspapers to come to the rival towns. He describes the
efforts of the two editors to bring on a gunfight, a battle occasioned by the nasty editorials that each has printed against the
other in* The Stingin' Lizard, *the newspaper of the "inferior"
town of Red Dog, and* The Coyote, *the newspaper of that "exalted and refined" town of Wolfville—where the Old Cattleman,
the storyteller, resides.*

*His story may reveal the oddest gunfight in history, described
in the funniest cowboy lingo of all time.*

THE WOLFVILLE DAILY COYOTE

"It's ever been a subject of dissensions between Colonel
Sterett an' myse'f as to where impartial jestice should lay the
blame of that Red Dog paper's failure. Colonel Sterett charges it
onto the editor; but it's my beliefs, an' I'm j'ined tharin by
Boggs an' Texas Thompson, that no editor could flourish an' no
paper survive in surroundin's so plumb venomous an' p'isen as
Red Dog. Moreover, I holds that Colonel Sterett, onintentional
no doubt, takes a ja'ndiced view of that brother publisher. But I
rides ahead of my tale.

"Thar comes a day when Old Man Enright heads into the Red
Light, where we-all is discussin' of episodes, an' he packs a letter
in his hand.

" 'Here's a matter,' he says, 'of public concern, an' I asks for
a full expression of the camp for answer. Here's a sharp by the
name of Colonel William Greene Sterett, who writes me as
how's he's sufferin' to let go all holts in the States an' start a
paper in Wolfville. It shall be, he says, a progressif an'
enlightened journal, devoted to the moral, mental an' material
upheaval of this here commoonity, an' he aims to learn our
views. Do I hear any remarks on this litteratoor's prop'sition?'

" 'Tell him to come a-runnin', Enright,' says Jack Moore; 'an'
draw it strong. If thar's one want which is slowly but shorely
crowdin' Wolfville to the wall, it's a dearth of literatoor; here's
our chance, an' we plays it quick and high.'

" 'I ain't so gala confident of all this,' says Dan Boggs. 'I'm sort o' allowin' this hamlet's too feeble yet for a paper. Startin' a paper in a small camp this a-way is like givin' a six-shooter to a boy; most likely he shoots himse'f, or mebby busts the neighbor, tharwith.'

" 'Oh, I don't know,' says Doc Peets, who, I wants to say, is as sudden a white man, mental, as I ever sees; 'my notion is to bring him along. The mere idee of a paper'll do a heap for the town.'

" 'I'm entertainin' sentiments sim'lar,' says Enright; 'an' I guess I'll write this Colonel Sterett that we'll go him once if we lose. I'm assisted to this concloosion by hearin', the last time I'm in Tucson, that Red Dog, which is our rival, is out to start a paper, in which event it behooves Wolfville to split even with 'em at the least.'

" 'That's whatever!' says Moore. 'If we allows Red Dog to put it onto us that a-way we might jest as well dissolve Wolfville as a camp, an' reepair to the woods in a body.'

"Enright sends Colonel Sterett word, an' in four weeks he comes packin' in his layout an' opens up his game. Colonel Sterett, personal, is a broad, thick, fine-seemin' gent, with a smooth, high for'ead, grey eyes, an' a long, honest face like a hoss. The Colonel has a far-off look in his eyes, like he's dreamin' of things sublime, which Doc Peets says is the common look of lit'rary gents that a-way. Texas Thompson, however, allows he witnesses the same distant expression in the eyes of a foogitive from jestice.

"Colonel Sterett makes a good impression. He evolves his journal an' names it the *Coyote*, a name applauded by us all.

" 'This yere imprint, the *Coyote*,' says Jack Moore, 'is a howlin' triumph, an' any gent disposed can go an' make a swell bet on it with every certainty of a-killin'. Also, I remember yereafter about them bullets.'

"Meanwhile, like I states prior, Red Dog has its editor, who whirls loose a paper which he calls the *Stingin' Lizard*. The Red Dog sheet ain't a marker to Colonel Sterett's *Coyote*, an' it's the

yooniversal idee in Wolfville, after ca'mly comparin' the two
papers, that Colonel Sterett as a editor can simply back that Red
Dog person plumb off the ground.

"It ain't no time before Colonel Sterett an' the Red Dog
editor takes a cirklin' for trouble, an' the frightful names they
applies to each other in their respectif journals, an' the accoosa-
tions an' them epithets they hurls, would shore curdle the blood
of a grizzly b'ar.

"An' as if to complicate the sitooation for that onhappy sport
who's gettin' out the Red Dog *Stingin' Lizard*, he begins to have
trouble local. Thar's a chuck-shop at Red Dog—it's a plumb
low j'int; I never knows it to have any grub better that beans,
salt pig an' airtights,—which is called the ABE LINCOLN
HOUSE, an' is kept by a party named Pete Bland. Which this
yere Bland also owns a goat, the same bein' a gift of a Mexican
who's got in the hole to Bland an' squar's accounts that a-way.

"This goat is jest a simple-minded, every-day, common kind of
a goat; but he's mighty thorough in his way, allers on the hustle,
an' if he ever overlooks a play, no one don't know it. One day,
when the Red Dog editor is printin' off his papers, up comes the
goat, an' diskyardin' of the tin-can which he's chewin', he begins
debauchin' of himse'f with this yere edition of the *Stingin'
Lizard*. It's mighty soon when the editor discovers it an' lays for
the goat permiscus; he goes to chuckin' of him up a whole lot.
The goat's game an' declar's himse'f, an' thar starts a altera-
tion with the editor an' the goat, of which thar's no tellin' the
wind-up, an' which ends only when this yere Bland cuts in, an'
the goat's drug home. The paper is stopped an' the editor puts
in this:

"Our presses are stopped to-day to say that if the weakminded person who
maintains the large, black goat which infests our streets, does not kill the
beast, we will. To-day, while engaged in working off our mammoth edition
out back of our building, the thievish creature approached unnoticed and
consumed seventeen copies of the *Stingin' Lizard*.

"Which this yere Bland gets incensed at this, an' puts it up the
editor can't eat with him no more. But better counsel smooths it

over, an' at last this Bland forgives the editor, an' all is forgot.
The goat, however, never does; an' he stamps his foot an' prowls
'round for a fracas every time him an' that editor meets.

"All this yere time Colonel Sterett an' this same Red Dog
editor maintains them hostilities. The way they lams loose at
each other in their papers is a terror. I allers reckons Colonel
Sterett gets a heap the best of this yere mane-chewin'; we-all so
regyards it, an' so does he; an' he keeps his end up with great
sperit and voylence.

"These yere ink-riots don't go on more'n two months,
however, when Colonel Sterett decides that the o'casion calls for
somethin' more explicit. As he says, 'Patience ceases to be
trumps,' an' so he saddles up a whole lot an' rides over to Red
Dog, personal. Colonel Sterett don't impart them plans of his to
no one; he simply descends on his foe, sole an' alone, like that
game an' chivalrous gent of bell letters which he shorely is; an',
son, Colonel Sterett makes a example of that slander-mongerin'
Red Dog editor.

"It's about the last drink time in the mornin', an' a passel of
the Red Dog sports is convened in front of the Tub of Blood
s'loon, when they-all hears a crash an' looks up, an' thar's their
editor a-soarin' out of his second-story window. Of sourse, in a
second or so, he hits the ground, an' them Red Dog folks goes
over to get the rights of this yere phenomenon. He ain't hurt so
but what he gets up an' limps 'round, an' he tells 'em it's the
Wolfville editor does it. Next time the *Stingin' Lizard* come out,
we read about it:

"The gasconading reptile who is responsible for the slimy life of that
prurient sheet, the *Coyote*, paid a sneaking visit Saturday. If he had given us
notice of his intentions, we would have prepared ourselves and torn his
leprous hide from his debauched and whiskey-poisoned frame, and polluted
our fence with it, but he did not. True to his low, currish nature, he crept
upon us unawares. Our back was toward him as he entered, perceiving which
the cowardly poltroon seized us and threw us through our own window. Having accomplished his fiendish work, the miscreant left, justly fearing our
wrath. The *Stingin' Lizard's* exposure of this scoundrel as a drunkard,
embezzler, wife-beater, jail-bird, thief, and general all-round blackleg promp-
ted this outrage. Never mind, the creature will here from us.

" 'Which this newspaper business is shorely gettin' some bilious, not to say hectic, a whole lot,' says Dan Boggs, as we read this. 'I wonder if these yere folks means fight?'

" 'Why,' says Enright, 'I don't know as they'd fight none if we-all lets 'em alone, but I don't see how we can. This sort of racket goes on for years in the East, but Wolfville can't stand it. Sech talk as this means blood in Arizona, an' we insists on them traditions that a-way bein' respected. Besides, we owes somethin' to Colonel Sterett.'

"So Enright an' Cherokee hunts up our editor an' asks him whatever he aims to do, an' tells him he's aroused public sentiments to sech heights thar'll be a pop'lar disapp'intment if he don't challenge the Red Dog editor an' beef him. Colonel Sterett allows he's crazy to do it, an' that the Wolfville public can gamble he'll go the distance. So Cherokee an' Jack Moore puts on their guns an' goes over to Red Dog to fix time an' place. The Red Dog editor says he's with 'em, an' they shakes dice for place, an' Cherokee an' Moore wins.

" 'Which as evidence of good faith,' says Cherokee, 'we picks Red Dog. We pull this thing off on the very scene of the vict'ry of Colonel Sterett when he hurls your editor through his window that time. I holds the same to be a mighty proper scheme.'

" 'You-all needn't be timid none to come,' says the Red Dog sports. 'You gets a squar' deal from a straight deck; you can gamble on that.'

" 'Oh, we ain't apprehensif none,' says Cherokee an' Jack; 'you can shorely look for us.'

"Well, the day's come, an' all Wolfville an' Red Dog turns out to see the trouble. Jack Moore an' Cherokee Hall represents for our editor, an' a brace of Red Dog people shows down for the *Stingin' Lizard* man. To prevent accidents, Enright an' the Red Dog chief makes every gent but them I names, leave their weapons some'ers else, wherefore thar ain't a gun in what you-all might call the hands of the pop'laces.

"But thar comes a interruption. Jest as them dooelists gets placed, thar's a stoopendous commotion, an' chargin' through the crowd comes that abandoned goat. The presence of so many folks seems like it makes him onusual hostile. Without waitin' to catch his breath even, he lays for the Red Dog editor, who, seein' him comin', bangs away with his '45 an' misses. The goat hits that author in the tail of his coat, an' over he goes; but he keeps on slammin' away with the '45 jest the same.

"Which nacherally everybody scatters for cover at the first shot, 'cause the editor ain't carin' where he p'ints, an' in a second nobody's in sight but them two journalists an' that goat. I'll say right yere, son, Colonel Sterett an' his fellow editor an' the goat wages the awfullest battle which I ever beholds. Which you shorely oughter heard their expressions. Each of 'em lets go every load he's got, but the goat don't get hit onct.

"When we-all counts twelve shots—six apiece—we goes out an' subdoos the goat by the power of numbers. Of course, the dooel's ended. The Red Dog folks borries a wagon an' takes away their man, who's suffered a heap; an' Peets, he stays over thar an' fusses 'round all night savin' of him. The goat's all right an' goes back to the ABE LINCOLN HOUSE, where this yere Pete Bland is onreasonable enough to back that shockin' conduct of his'n.

"Which it's the last of the Red Dog *Stingin' Lizard*. That editor allows he won't stay, an' Bland, still adherin' to his goat, allows he won't feed him none if he does. The next issue of the *Stingin' Lizard* contains this:

"We bid adieu to Red Dog. We will hereafter publish a paper in Tucson; and if we have been weak and mendacious enough to speak in favor of a party of the name of Bland, who misconducts a low beanery which insults an honourable man by stealing his name—we refer to that feed-trough called the ABE LINCOLN HOUSE—we will correct ourselves in its columns. This person harbours a vile goat, for whose death we will pay $5, and give besides a life-long subscription to our new paper. Last week this mad animal made an unprovoked assault upon us and a professional brother, and beat, butted, wounded, bruised and ill-treated us until we suffer in our whole person. We give notice as we depart, that under no circumstances will we return until this goat is extinct.

"Followin' the onexpected an' thrillin' finish of Colonel

Sterett's dooel with the Red Dog editor, an' from which Colonel Sterett emerges onscathed, an' leavin' Peets with his new patient, we-all returns in a body to Wolfville. After refreshments in the Red Light, Enright gives his views.

" 'Ondoubted,' observes Enright, 'our gent, Colonel Sterett, conducts himse'f in them painful scenes between him an' the goat an' that Red Dog editor in a manner to command respects, an' he returns with honors from them perils. This Red Dog editor's done put himse'f outside the pale of any high-sperited gent's consideration by them actions, an' can claim no further notice. Gents, in the name of Wolfville, I tenders congrat'lations to Colonel Sterett on the way in which he meets the dangers of his p'sition, an' the sooperb fashion in which he places before us one of the greatest journals of our times. Gents, we drinks to Colonel William Greene Sterett an' the *Coyote*.' "

★   ★   ★   ★

Marcus Mills Pomeroy (1833-1896)

"Brick" Pomeroy was a Douglas democrat and bitterly opposed to Abraham Lincoln, as evidenced in his vitriolic newspaper articles against him. Pomeroy was a remarkable man of the American tradition, who spent much of his life as a newspaper editor, then quit that vocation to conceive, organize, and project a five-mile railroad tunnel through the Rocky Mountains some sixty miles west of Denver!

WONDERFUL HAIR—REPRODUCER

Dr. ——, of New York, sent us a cake of his Onguent, with the modest request to "puff it, and send the bill."

Venerable and far-sighted capillary producer! We do, and more too. Your Onguent is a big thing. Although in small cakes, it is neverthe less a colossal item. We tried it. Following the printed directions given, we made a lather and applied the brush. The lather was mixed in a glass dish, and in four minutes a beautiful hair, all shades of color, had started from the dish. We applied some to our face, and it took four swift-working barbers to cut down and mow away as fast as the beard grew. We put a little on the toe of each boot, and in an hour they looked like Zouave mustaches. We put some on a crowbar, and it is covered with long, curly hair like a buffalo, and in the coldest weather it can be used without mittens. A little on the carriage-pole started the hair on it like moss. We dropped some on the stove, and as the fire was kindled the hair started, and the hotter the stove became, the faster grew the hair, till the smell of burnt hair became so powerful as to drive all from the room. The stove was set in the barn, and it can't be seen now, as the hair is literally stacked upon it. Only one application. A little applied in a wagon-tire has in five days started a vigorous crop, and now the wagon can be driven over a plank-road and not make the least noise, so well are the wheels covered with soft hair. Only one application—dollar a cake. We skinned a goose, put on some of the Onguent, and in two hours the feather-grower was enveloped in hair like a squirrel, and was seen this morning trying to climb a shagbark hickory in the backyard. A little applied to the inkstand has given it a coat of bristles, making a splendid pen-wiper at little cost. We applied the lather to a tenpenny nail, and the nail is now the handsomest lather-brush you ever saw, with a beautiful growth of soft hair at the end of it, some five or six feet in length. Only a dollar a cake! Applied to door stones, it does away with the use of a mat. Applied to a floor, it will cause to grow therefrom hair sufficient for a Brussels carpet. A little of this Onguent lather was accidently dropped on the head of our cane, which has been perfectly bald for over ten years, and immediately a thick growth of hair formed, completely covering it, compelling us to shave the head twice a week. Only a dollar a bottle—directions thrown in. A little weak lather sprinkled over a barn makes it impervious to wind, rain, or cold. It is good to put inside of children's cradles—sprinkle on sidewalks, anything, where luxuriant grass is wanted for use or ornament. We put a little on the head of navigation, and a beautiful hair covered it. A little on the mouth of Mississippi river started hair there resembling the finest red-top grass, in which cows, sheep, pigs, snipes, woodcock, and young ducks graze with keen relish. Only a dollar a cake. Sent by mail to any address. One application will grow a luxuriant mustache for a boy. One dollar a cake. Samson used it.

★   ★   ★   ★

George T. Lanigan (1845-1886)

Lanigan was a newspaperman all of his life. Born in Canada, he worked mainly on American newspapers, and as a kind of roving reporter for out-of-state news wanted by big city newspapers. He, like Ambrose Bierce, contributed "Fables" with a nom de plume—G. Washington Aesop—and they were very popular with Americans.

THE MERCHANT OF VENICE

A Venetian merchant, who was lolling in the lap of luxury, was accosted upon the Rialto by a Friend who had not seen him for many months. "How is this?" cried the latter; "when I last saw you your Gaberdine was out at elbows, and now you sail in your own Gondola!" "True," replied the Merchant, "but since then I have met with serious losses, and been obliged to compound with my Creditors for ten Cents on the Dollar.

Moral.—Composition is the Life of Trade.

★   ★   ★   ★

THE GOOD SAMARITAN

A certain man went from Jerusalem to Jericho, and fell among Thieves, who beat him and stripped him and left him for dead. A Good Samaritan, seeing this, clapped Spurs to his Ass and galloped away, lest he should be sent to the House of Detention as a Witness, while the Robbers were released on Bail.

Moral.—The Perceiver is worse than the Thief.

★   ★   ★   ★

Robert J. Burdette (1844-1914)

Burdette was editor of the Burlington, Iowa newspaper, the Hawkeye, *and his work was syndicated and distributed across the nation.*

PREACHING v. PRACTICE

A Sea Cliff, L.I., audience was dreadfully shocked last Sunday night. Just as a local temperance leader was about to begin his address, he leaned too closely over the candle and his breath caught fire. He afterwards explained, however, that he had been using camphor for the toothache. The amendment was accepted, and the talk went on.

★   ★   ★   ★

Ambrose Bierce (1842-1913)

Ambrose Bierce was the kind of person and writer "who could," in the words of Prof. Walter Blair of the University of Chicago, "persuade practically anyone to cross the street to avoid him." Why? Because he was an unrelieved bundle of clear-eyed pessimism who saw the dark side of life as the only true, real side of it...and his writing reflects that outlook.

Bierce was prolific, writing for newspapers and magazines, living on the east coast in New York, then on the west coast in San Francisco—where he did his most enduring writing—and in England. Elegant in person, literate and learned, he was temperate in all but his satirical, invective-filled writing. But his biographer, Prof. Earnest Jerome Hopkins, said in his defense: "Whatever Ambrose Bierce satirized most vigorously was, when analyzed, something...calculated to undermine the dignity and true fulfillment of human life."

Dead ends, hurts, failures and tragedies marked his life. A decorated, brave, admired officer (Brevet Major) in the Civil War, he suffered a terrible head wound that may be a factor leading to understanding his outlook on life. His older son was killed in a gun-fight, the younger boy died an alcoholic, and his wife of thirty-three years divorced him. Alone, in 1913, Bierce went to Mexico and simply disappeared, never to be heard from. He was 71. It was an appropriate conclusion to the life of a man who was unrelenting in his harsh, unloving but witty observations on the human condition.

A MATTER OF METHOD

A Philosopher seeing a Fool beating his Donkey, said:

"Abstain, my son, abstain, I implore. Those who resort to violence shall suffer from violence."

"That," said the Fool, diligently belabouring the animal, "is what I'm trying to teach this beast—which has kicked me."

"Doubtless," said the Philosopher to himself, as he walked away, "the wisdom of fools is no deeper nor truer that ours, but they really do seem to have a more impressive way of imparting it."

★　　★　　★　　★

A rich man wanted to tell a lie, but the lie was of such monstrous size that it stuck in his throat; so he employed an editor to write it out and publish it in his paper as an editorial. But when the Editor presented his bill the Rich Man said:

"Be content—is it nothing that I refrained from advising you about investments?"

★　　★　　★　　★

LEGISLATOR AND SOAP

A member of the Kansas Legislature meeting a Cake of Soap was passing it by without recognition, but the Cake of Soap insisted on stopping and shaking hands. Thinking it might possibly be in the enjoyment of the elective franchise, he gave it a cordial and earnest grasp. On letting it go he observed that a part of it adhered to his fingers, and running to a brook in great alarm, proceeded to wash it off. In doing so he necessarily got some on the other hand, and when he had finished washing, both were so white that he went to bed and sent for a physician.

★　　★　　★　　★

THE CAT AND THE BIRDS

Hearing that the birds in an aviary were ill, a Cat went to them and said that he was a physician, and would cure them if they would let him in.

"To what school of medicine do you belong?" asked the

Birds.

"I am a Miaulopathist," said the Cat.

"Did you ever practice Gohomoeopathy?" the Birds inquired, winking faintly.

The Cat took the hint and his leave.

★   ★   ★   ★

THE FISHER AND THE FISHED

A Fisherman who had caught a very small Fish was putting it in his basket when it said:

"I pray you put me back into the stream, for I can be of no use to you; the gods do not eat fish."

"But I am no god," said the Fisherman.

"True," said the Fish, "but as soon as Jupiter has heard of your exploit, he will elevate you to the deitage. You are the only man that ever caught a small fish."

★   ★   ★   ★

THE WOLF AND THE FEEDING GOAT

A Wolf saw a Goat feeding at the summit of a rock, where he could not get at her.

"Why do you stay up there in that sterile place and go hungry?" said the Wolf. "Down here where I am the broken-bottle vine cometh up as a flower, the celluloid collar blossoms as the rose, and the tin-can tree brings forth after its kind."

"That is true, no doubt," said the Goat, "but how about the circus-poster crop? I hear that it failed this year down there."

The Wolf, perceiving that he was being chaffed, went away and resumed his duties at the doors of the poor.

★   ★   ★   ★

THE CRAB AND HIS SON

A Logical Crab said to his Son, "Why do you not walk straight forward? Your sidelong gait is singularly ungraceful."

"Why don't you walk straight forward yourself," said the Son.

"Erring youth," replied the Logical Crab, "you are introducing new and irrelevant matter."

★   ★   ★   ★

THE EXPATRIATED BOSS

A Boss who had gone to Canada was taunted by a Citizen of Montreal with having fled to avoid prosecution.

"You do me a grave injustice," said the Boss, parting with a pair of tears. "I came to Canada solely because of its political attractions; its Government is the most corrupt in the world."

"Pray forgive me," said the Citizen of Montreal.

They fell upon each other's neck, and at the conclusion of that touching rite the Boss had two watches.

★   ★   ★   ★

THREE RECRUITS

A Farmer, an Artisan, and a Labourer went to the King of their country and complained that they were compelled to support a large standing army of mere consumers, who did nothing for their keep.

"Very well," said the King, "my subjects' wishes are the highest law."

So he disbanded his army and the consumers became producers also. The sale of their products so brought down the prices that farming was ruined, and their skilled and unskilled labour drove the artisans and labourers into the almshouses and highways. In a few years the national distress was so great that the Farmer, the Artisan, and the Labourer petitioned the King to reorganize the standing army.

"What!" said the King; "you wish to support those idle consumers again?"

"No, your Majesty," they replied—"we wish to enlist."

★   ★   ★   ★

THE MAN AND THE BIRD

A Man with a Shotgun said to a Bird:

"It is all nonsense, you know, about shooting being a cruel sport. I put my skill against your cunning—that is all there is of it. It is a fair game."

"True," said the Bird, "but I don't wish to play."

"Why not?" inquired the Man with a Shotgun.

"The game," the Bird replied, "is fair as you say; the chances are about even; but consider the stake. I am in it for you, but what is there in it for me?"

Not being prepared with an answer to the question, the Man with a Shotgun sagaciously removed the propounder.

★   ★   ★   ★

FORTUNE AND THE FABULIST

A Writer of Fables was passing through a lonely forest when he met a Fortune. Greatly alarmed, he tried to climb a tree, but the Fortune pulled him down and bestowed itself upon him with cruel persistence.

"Why did you try to run away?" said the Fortune, when his struggles had ceased and his screams were stilled. "Why do you glare at me so inhospitably?"

"I don't know what you are," replied the Writer of Fables, deeply disturbed.

"I am wealth; I am respectability," the Fortune explained; "I am elegant houses, a yacht, and a clean shirt every day. I am leisure, I am travel, wine, a shiny hat, and an unshiny coat. I am enough to eat."

"All right," said the Writer of Fables, in a whisper; "but for goodness' sake speak lower."

"Why so?" the Fortune asked, in surprise.

"So as not to wake me," replied the Writer of Fables, a holy calm brooding upon his beautiful face.

★   ★   ★   ★

THE FOGY AND THE SHEIK

A Fogy who lived in a cave near a great caravan route returned to his home one day and saw, near by, a great concourse of men and animals, and in their midst a tower, at the foot of which something with wheels smoked and panted like an exhausted horse. He sought the Sheik of the Outfit.

"What sin art thou committing now, O son of a Christian dog?" said the Fogy, with a truly Oriental politeness.

"Boring for water, you black-and-tan galoot!" replied the Sheik of the Outfit, with that ready repartee which distinguishes the Unbeliever.

"Knowest thou not, thou whelp of darkness and father of disordered livers," cried the Fogy, "that water will cause grass to spring up here, and trees, and possibly even flowers? Knowest thou not, that thou art, in truth, producing an oasis?"

"And don't you know," said the Sheik of the Outfit, "that caravans will then stop here for rest and refreshments, giving you a chance to steal the camels, the horses, and the goods?"

"May the wild hog defile my grave, but thou speakest wisdom!" the Fogy replied, with the dignity of his race, extending his hand. "Sheik."

They shook.

★   ★   ★   ★

THE TREASURY AND THE ARMS

A Public Treasury, feeling Two Arms lifting out it contents, exclaimed:

"Mr. Shareman, I move for a division."

"You seem to know something about parliamentary forms of speech," said the Two Arms.

"Yes," replied the Public Treasury, "I am familiar with the hauls of legislation."

★   ★   ★   ★

THE DECEASED AND HIS HEIRS

A Man died leaving a large estate and many sorrowful relations who claimed it. After some years, when all but one had had judgment given against them, that one was awarded the estate, which he asked his Attorney to have appraised.

"There is nothing to appraise," said the Attorney, pocketing his last fee.

"Then," said the Successful Claimant, "what good has all this litigation done me?"

"You have been a good client to me," the Attorney replied, gathering up his books and papers, "but I must say you betray a surprising ignorance of the purpose of litigation.

★   ★   ★   ★

American enterprise helped to make this country great. But in our long commercial history, we've had some mighty weird business enterprises and entrepeneurs! Ambrose Bierce illustrates with an example.

THE FAILURE OF HOPE & WANDEL

From M. Jabez Hope, in Chicago, to Mr. Pike Wandel, of New Orleans, December 2, 1877.

I will not bore you, my dear fellow, with a narrative of my journey from New Orleans to this polar region. It is cold in Chicago, believe me, and the Southron who comes here, as I did, without a relay of noses and ears will have reason to regret his mistaken economy in arranging his outfit.

To business. Lake Michigan is frozen stiff. Fancy, O child of a torrid clime, a sheet of anybody's ice, three hundred miles long, forty broad, and six feet thick! It sounds like a lie, Pikey dear, but your partner in the firm of Hope & Wandel, Wholesale Boots and Shoes, New Orleans, is never known to fib. My plan is to collar that ice. Wind up the present business and send on the money at once. I'll put up a warehouse as big as the Capitol at Washington, store it full and ship to your orders as the Southern market may require. I can send it in planks for skating floors, in statuettes for the mantel, in shavings for juleps, or in solution for ice cream and general purposes. It is a big thing!

I inclose a thin slip as a sample. Did you ever see such charming ice?

From Mr. Pike Wandel, of New Orleans, to Mr. Jabez Hope, in Chicago, December 24, 1877.

Your letter was so abominably defaced by blotting and blurring that it was entirely illegible. It must have come all the way by water. By the aid of chemicals and photography, however, I have made it out. But you forgot to inclose the sample of ice.

I have sold off everything (at an alarming sacrifice, I am sorry to say) and inclose draft for net amount. Shall begin to spar for orders at once. I trust everything to you—but, I say, has anybody tried to grow ice in *this* vicinity? There is Lake Ponchartrain, you know.

From Mr. Jabez Hope, in Chicago, to Mr. Pike Wandel, of New Orleans, February 27, 1878.

Wannie dear, it would do you good to see our new warehouse for the ice. Though made of boards, and run up rather hastily, it is as pretty as a picture, and cost a deal of money, though I pay no ground rent. It is about as big as the Capitol at Washington. Do you think it ought to have a steeple? I have it nearly filled—fifty men cutting and storing, day and night—awful cold work! By the way, the ice, which when I wrote you last was ten feet thick, is now thinner. But don't you worry; there is plenty.

Our warehouse is eight or ten miles out of town, so I am not much bothered by visitors, which is a relief. Such a giggling, sniggering lot you never saw!

It seems almost too absurdly incredible, Wannie, but do you know I believe this ice of ours gains in coldness as the warm weather comes on! I do, indeed, and you may mention the fact in the advertisements.

From Mr. Pike Wandel, of New Orleans, to Mr. Jabez Hope, in Chicago, March 7, 1878.

All goes well. I get hundreds of orders. We shall do a roaring trade as "The New Orleans and Chicago Semperfrigid Ice Company." But you have not told me whether the ice is fresh or salt. If it is fresh it won't do for cooking, and if it is salt it will spoil the mint juleps.

Is it as cold in the middle as the outside cuts are?

From Mr. Jabez Hope, From Chicago, to Mr. Pike Wandel, of New Orleans, April 3, 1878.

Navigation on the Lakes is now open, and ships are thick as ducks. I'm afloat, *en route* for Buffalo, with the assets of the New Orleans and Chicago Semperfrigid Ice Company in my vest pocket. We are busted out, my poor Pikey—we are to fortune and to fame unknown. Arrange a meeting of the creditors and don't attend.

Last night a schooner from Milwaukee was smashed into matchwood on an enormous mass of floating ice—the first berg ever seen in these waters. It is described by the survivors as being about as big as the Capitol at Washington. One-half of that iceberg belongs to you, Pikey.

The melancholy fact is, I built our warehouse on an unfavorable site, about a mile out from the shore (on the ice, you understand), and when the thaw came—O my God, Wannie, it was the saddest thing you ever saw in all your life! You will be *so* glad to know I was not in at the time.

What a ridiculous question you ask me. My poor partner, you don't seem to know very much about the ice business.

★   ★   ★   ★

In almost every generation, Americans have sought the advice of pundits, experts writing in local newspapers. And almost as often, satirists have poked fun at them in those same newspapers as, for example, in the following replies to correspondents.

Laura B. M., Kaufman: "I hear a great deal about a new fashionable folly—the decoration of plates by amateur artists. How is the thing done, and can you describe what the decorations consists of?"

We have had several plates decorated lately by female members of our family. The way they did it was after this fashion: They first warmed the plate, then they laid on it several slices of the breast of a turkey, a second joint, some cranberries, dressing (without onions), and a couple of boiled Irish potatoes. Try that sort of decoration, and your friends will appreciate your artistic ability.

J. P. C., Millican, Texas: "I want to learn to play on the flute. How would you advise me to go about it? Will I need a teacher?"

No; you do not need a teacher, but you had better borrow a flute. It would be well at first to select some retired spot where you can practice undisturbed. We would suggest that you hire or buy a ship and go out on the wild, tempestuous ocean—the ever changing sea—out amid the weird winds' wild roar, and the bilious billows' moan. There, far out of sight of land, with naught to distrub you but the voice of the cheerful sea gull as he skims the ocean blue and chants his merry lay, you can heave your top-gallan's'l, box your anchor, and toot and toot and flute till you can't rest. After you practice for a year or two amid those surroundings, we would advise that you go west and herd sheep for the balance of your days. If that does not effect a cure, your case is a hopeless one.

W. J. K., Palestine: "I am a young man of limited means; I have only been in the State a short time, and it doesn't suit me to stay here longer. Would you advise me to go to Mexico? Please advise me at length through the columns of your paper."

As you have not given us full particulars, we are hardly in a position to advise you understandingly. In a general way, however, we would suggest that if you have stolen a horse, the safest thing you could do would be to get over into Mexico as quickly as possible, even if you have to steal another horse to get there on; but if you have only killed an acquaintance, there is no reason why you should put yourself to the inconvenience of running off to Mexico. Stay where you are, prove insanity, self-defence, or an alibi, and become a leading citizen.

T.A.R., Cuero: "What can I do with a dog that is covered

with fleas?"

You can do several things. Soak the dog in coal oil; that will kill all the fleas—and the dog. You can take him out to the woods and saw his head off. If he is a white dog you can pick all the fleas off, dye him black, and sell him as a new dog. There is no limit as to the number of things you can do to a dog as we presume you own. If he was our property we think we would use him as a flea ranch. If properly cultivated he would yield fleas enough to supply all the demand for miles around, and you would have fleas left over to invest, give to the poor, and to use for seed. Ponder over this and don't be hasty about disposing of your dog. There may be millions in him.

Robert J., Brenham:

The "disunwellness" that you say you are suffering from can be cured.—Our Family Medicine Book says the following will do it: "Mix castor oil and brandy together—three ounces of oil to two ounces of brandy—and use until relieved." The Sifters have tried the ingredients named, but, owing probably to the fact that they modified the formula somewhat, one of them taking the oil and the other the brandy, there is a difference of opinion in this office as to the general effect of the medicine.

Chapter VIII
The Bawdy Part

*T**he material for this chapter was not easy to find, a reflection on earlier strictures against printing and distributing bawdy stories, jokes, and poems. The nineteenth and early twentieth century standards for literary morality assured that ribald material would be anonymously collected, secretly printed and closely held. Anonymity was required not only because of the law but because of the social stigma accompanying the printing, distribution and ownership of such material.*

As always, many Americans delighted in telling, hearing, and some in writing bawdy humor, despite public anathemas. Nevertheless, public and private disapproval assured the scarcity of bawdy writings. For example, only three copies of THE STAG PARTY, a ribald collection, published circa 1888, are known today—one in the Denver Public Library, one in the Beinecke Library at Yale University, and one from which some of the material for this chapter was taken, the copy in the library of The Kinsey Institute for Research in Sex, Gender, and Reproduction, at the University of Indiana. There may be more copies but, as Harry J. Mooney, Jr., of the Denver Public Library, said in 1980: "Where they are now seems to be a well-kept secret of private owners, booksellers, and nervous institutions[!]."

Other sources of material were as difficult to come upon, and most were authored by fictitious collectors who had them printed by nonesuch publishers. For example, "The Book of a Thousand Laughs" was authored by someone with the appropriate nom de plume of O.U. Schweinickle with no listed printer/publisher. Clearly, the penalties both legal and social were then so severe as to justify the careful anonymity of authors and printers.

To include this final chapter of bawdy writings, in the face of obvious caveats, represents a bold yet hopeful decision. Some people detest dirty stories! And yet those who enjoy them are legion. Both groups can agree that our history shows the bawdy story as an omnipresent aspect of American culture. To "excise" it as Billy Herndon was advised to do, and did, with Mr. Lincoln's bawdy stories—when Herndon wrote his great biography of Abraham Lincoln—would deprive the reader of an integral, vital, and joyous (to most) aspect of American humor and life in all its past generations.

And yet, aware of those who find bawdy tales repellent, there is the American option of defiance—and the closing of the book—just at this juncture. For others, let us paraphrase the earlier, noncommittal anecdote of Abraham Lincoln: "Well, for those who like that sort of thing I should think it is just the sort of thing they would like."

PISSING IN THE SNOW*

Told by Frank Hembree, Galena, Mo., April, 1945. He heard it in the late 1890s. J.L. Russell, Harrison, who spun me the same yarn in 1950, says it was told near Green Forest, Ark., about 1885.

One time there was two farmers that lived out on the road to Carico. They was always good friends, and Bill's oldest boy had been a-sparking one of Sam's daughters. Everything was going fine till the morning they met down by the creek, and Sam was pretty goddam mad. "Bill," says he, "from now on I don't want that boy of yours to set foot in my place."

"Why, what's he done?" asked the boy's daddy.

"He pissed in the snow, that's what he done, right in front of my house!"

"But surely, there ain't no great harm in that," Bill says.

"No harm!" hollered Sam. "Hell's fire, he pissed so it spelled Lucy's name, right there in the snow!"

*All stories with titles followed by an asterisk(*) are from *Pissing in the Snow*, Vance Randolph, 1976. University of Illinois Press, Champaign, Illinois. They are a collection of Ozark folk tales.

"The boy shouldn't have done that," says Bill. "But I don't see nothing so terrible bad about it."

"Well, by God, I do!" yelled Sam. "There was two sets of tracks! And besides, don't you think I know my own daughter's handwriting?"

★　　★　　★　　★

"NOT BUILT THAT WAY"

A boy will eat and a boy will drink,
　　And a boy will play all day;
But a boy won't work and a boy won't think,
　　Because he ain't built that way.

A girl will sing and a girl will dance,
　　And a girl will work crochet;
But she can't throw a stone and hit a church,
　　Because she ain't built that way.

A girl will flirt and a girl will mash,
　　And ne'er give herself away;
But she can't strike a match on the seat of her pants,
　　Because she ain't built that way.

She may perhaps ride straddle when a young and giddy gal,
　　And cut some naughty capers in her play;
But she cannot utilize a standing urinal,
　　Just because she ain't built that way.

★　　★　　★　　★

A WONDERFUL ORGAN.

To ★ ★ ★ ★ ★

The erection of an organ in any church circle is always desirable—it opens up a future, and occasionally a sister. The organ I propose to furnish you is one of the self-erecting kind, and therefore would be less expensive than the one you propose. It can be worked by hand, but not perfectly, the co-operation of the young sisters being necessary to complete ecstacy. If all the conditions are perfect, the sister completely resigned, then a complete state of beatitude follows, after which

"Not one wave of trouble rolls across my peaceful breast,"

is sung in a restful manner. It is needless to add that the organ is played out for that day, and if erected at all, it must stand on its head.

I do not recommend my organ solely on account of its size, and it is not claimed that it would do for a whole circuit or conference. I do claim, however, that it is just the size for a good-sized congregation. Neither do I think the size of the pipe is so important as the tone, and it is the latter that has given my organ such a reputation wherever I have introduced it. My organ has a bellows attachment adjusted to heat and cold, and chronometer balance. If touched by the delicate hand of a soulful sister, the response is instantaneous, and the vibrations at once permeate the whole spinal column. Temporary collapse follows, but *prolapsus uterus* never. When the organ is being operated well, a drooping of the eyelids, flushed cheek and "lolling" of the tongue supervenes. If the diagnosis is completed, the toes will be found in knots. Rest and fresh air will, however, restore the normal functions. All this I can promise for my organ, and have abundant testimony to prove it.

The organ heretofore used by the female portion of your church has undoubtedly been that old, collapsed, wind-broken, squeaky one, owned by the preacher, and used so extensively by Beecher in his Plymouth Church congregation. It was good in its day, but belongs to ancient history. The bellows hangs too low, and the pipe, though of large size, is leaky. Besides this, the cost of erection is enormous, and it is always liable to take the wrong shoot and miss a note. The most valuable use it can be put to is in taking it to church sociables and betting which way it will fall.

You are entirely mistaken about my organ being out of repair. It is in excellent working order. It has been used slightly this winter in the skating rinks, and has got a wee-waw and semi-rotary motion, which will be a new revelation in the rural districts, and very soothing to the bowels. I have sometimes thought the "peal" was affected, but that is superficial. I have known girls of thirteen to play it successfully, while to the wife and widow it fills a long felt want. There are no "aching voids" in the neighborhood where it resides. It is self-sustaining, and has a head of its own. It is a daisy. It will play simultaneously pianissimo, fortissimo, allegro, damfino and fisher's hornpipe in a way to astonish the congregation. All it wants is reciprocity on the part of a plump, tight-built sister and one who can take up her stock as she goes along. Wind may escape but water, never. After the tune is played out the musicians will be played out also, and both look and feel ashamed. No effort on the part of the operator is necessary to stop, for when the old thing is run down it stops itself. The impression at first will be, that while the operator may linger a week or two, that it is too dead to skin.

The value of such an instrument to a village choir is beyond calculation. It is better felt than described, and the smile of heavenly satisfaction that will settle on the face of the sister upon feeling the thrill of this organ, as it pours its sweet bliss into her soul, will make even heaven a howling wilderness.

★   ★   ★   ★

HE LOST HIS MEMORY*

One time there was a man named Jeff that was eighty-two years old, but mighty spry for his age. The young fellows was all surprised when they found out that Jeff still went a-hunting twice a week, and he could ride horses just as good as anybody. They was always joking about how Jeff run after the womenfolks, but nobody really believed it.

Some of the boys got to talking one day, and they all says it must be fine to be healthy like that, when a fellow is eighty-two years old. But Jeff just shook his head. "It ain't no fun to be old," he says, "because your memory always goes back on you." The boys just kind of kidded him along, and they says so long as a man can do a little fucking, it don't make no difference if he can remember things or not.

But old Jeff shook his head some more, and he says it makes a man look awful foolish. "Why, just last night I woke up with a hard-on," says he, "so I roused my wife to have a little fun. But Mary says for me to shut up, because we have already done it twice, not thirty minutes before. And there was two towels laying on the floor, so I knowed she was telling the truth." Jeff looked mighty gloomy. "It's kind of sad, when a man gets so old he can't remember things like that," says he.

Them young fellows just stared at Jeff goggle-eyed, but nobody said another word. The old man looked solemn, they didn't rightly know if he was kidding 'em or not. It stands to reason that he was, but you can't never tell for sure.

★   ★   ★   ★

THE DRUMMERS AND THE FIFER

Down in the valley a small rivulet runs there,
A neat little cavern all covered with hair;
Two drummers and a fifer to this place did repair,
The fifer went in, the drummers stayed out—
Kept jostling, and joggling, and boggling about;
The fifer came out, he hung down his head,
"By gad," says the drummers,
"Our fifer is dead!"

★   ★   ★   ★

THE NEW HIRED MAN*

One time there was a young fellow come a-walking down the road, and it looked like he was about sixteen years old. He asked the farmer to hire him, and just then a bull topped a cow right by the barn. "What's that animal a-doing?" says the farmer, and the boy answered, "I reckon he's just a-r'aring up to see the grass." When the farmer heard that he says, "You are just the man I am looking for, because most of the farmhands talk so rough I won't have 'em in my house." So then he wants to know what the young man's name is, and the fellow says, "Just call me Fuckemboth."

When they got to the house the farmer says, "This is my daughter Nelly, and this is my wife." And then he pulled up

Nelly's dress to show her cunt, and he says, "That is the jail house." Next he pulled up his wife's dress to show her cunt, and he says, "That is the penitentiary." He give the fellow a hard look. "Them is two places a young man better keep away from," says he. And then the farmer walked out of the house.

Nelly and the old woman stood there a-looking at the young fellow. "So you are the new hired man," says Nelly, and then she wants to know what his name is. "Just call me Beans," says the boy. Nelly kind of giggled, and she says it's a funny name, but easy to remember. And the old woman says that reminds me, we have got beans in the pot right now. The farmer come back in the house then, and they all set down and eat their supper.

Pretty soon they went to bed, and it was not a very big house. Along in the night Nelly begun to grunt and fart pretty loud. The farmer roused up, and he says "Nelly, what's the matter?" The girl drawed a deep breath. "Beans is laying heavy on my stomach," she says, and the old man went back to sleep. After while Nelly begun to grunt and fart again, so the old woman got up and went over to see about it. She seen that Beans was laying on her daughter sure enough, and she begun to holler for the old man. The farmer was about half asleep, and he didn't understand all this hollering about beans. All of a sudden he thought of the new hired man, so he sung out "Fuckemboth! Fuckemboth!" The boy didn't return no answer, but the old woman sure was surprised to hear her husband a-talking like that. She just went back to bed, and never said another word. The farmer dropped off to sleep again, and the new hired man went right ahead with what he was a-doing.

When they got up next morning the young fellow walked over to the fireplace, with his pecker a-sticking out so you could have hung your hat on it. "Looks like a night in jail didn't do no good," says Nelly. The old woman just kind of giggled. "If he don't quieten down, I reckon we'll have to put him in the penitentiary," she says. The hired man didn't return no answer, but pretty soon he quit his job and walked on down the road. A

young fellow don't mind going to jail once in a while, but the
penitentiary is something else again.

★ ★ ★ ★

ANOTHER TRIUMPH FOR WOMENS' RIGHTS

Good old Ben Adams (may his tribe increase,
And may his days be long and end in peace!)
Had one fair daughter—Sally was her name—
Who at the village school led every game;
She'd run, jump, whistle,—anything in short,
Which boys or girls have e'er devised for sport;
In running races, many a lusty lout
Had vainly tried to tucker Sally out.
Full many a wrestling match did she contest,
And could cross buttocks with the very best;
She'd grasp her hips, bend back and touch the floor,
Or kick six feet high upon the school house door.
The village boys had tried for many a day
To think up some game Sally couldn't play;
But all in vain; whate'er their wits devise
Sally was sure to carry off the prize.
At length, one pleasant day in leafy June,
The boys were lying on the green at noon,
When, coming down the lane, with swinging stride,
And head erect, the maiden they espied.
Up jumped George Tompkins—"Boys, I have it now,
We'll beat Sal Adams this time, anyhow!"
"How?" cried each lad. Says George, "Out trickers all,
And see who'll piss the highest on the wall."
No sooner said than done; at it they went,
And 'gainst the school-house door many a stream they sent;
Some weak and puny, little rills,
Would scarce rise higher than the window sills;
While some, with greater head, their mark would score,
High on the clap-boards, half way up the door.
While thus engaged, the maid approached the group,

Who greeted her with many a lusty whoop.
George Tompkins, sending high his stream in air,
Cried, "There, Sal Adams, beat that if you dare!"
Then joined they all in one triumphant howl,
Thinking at last they'd got the champion foul.
Sal lowly muttered, "If I must, I must!"
Then cried, "Stand back! I'll beat it boys, or bust."
Well to the front, she ranged them all around,
Then bending, till her head 'most touched the ground,
And grasping 'twixt her finger and her thumb,
The muzzle of her young Tududelum,
And canting round her slender, supple wrist,
She gave the thing a sort of rifle twist.
And, tossing o'er her back her homespun skirt,
She braced herself for one almighty squirt;
High in the air her plump round butt she raised,
And at the school-house door full tilt she blazed.
Whir-r-ish-sh! it sounded like a rocket's flight,
Sent heavenward on some Fourth of July night.
Sal straightened up with triumph in her eye,
And cried, "George Tompkins, how is that for high?"
Then, with the air and carriage of a queen,
She dropped her skirts and strode across the green;
Up rushed the boys, the contest to decide,
And mark the effect of Sal's moist broadside.
They looked, and lo! the stream Sal Adams pissed
Was full three clapboards higher than all the rest.

★   ★   ★   ★

Here's to the tree of life
    That maidens love to span,
It stands between two stones
    Upon the Isle of Man.

Here's to the little bush
    That would that tree entwine

It blossms once in every month,
And bears its fruit in nine.

★   ★   ★   ★

Sunday-school class—Stupid boy; pretty girl teacher.

Teacher (to stupid boy)—How did Samson slay the Philistines?

Stupid boy don't know anything about it, but the bright boy behind him does, and leaning forward whispers the answer to stupid boy: "With the jaw-bone of an ass." Stupid boy repeats the answer as he catches it, thus: "He jawbed 'em in the ass."

★   ★   ★   ★

A RIDDLE

Letitia has a large one, and so has Cousin Luce;
Elizabeth has a small one, tho' large enough for use;
A child may have a little one enclosed within a clout;
In fact, all females have one—no girl is born without.

But men, nor boys, nor buck, nor bear, nor ram was ever known
To have one, either large or small, to rightly call his own.
All fowls have one, not cocks of course; and tho' prolific
     breeders,
The fact that fish have none is known to piscatorial readers.

Hermaphrodites have none; mermaids are minus too;
Nell Gwynne possessed a double share, we read, if books are
     true;
Lasciviousness there has its source; harlots their use apply;
Without it lust has never been, and even love would die.

'Tis used by all in nuptial bliss, in carnal pleasure found,
Destroy it, life becomes extinct, the world is but a sound.
Beneath a soft and glossy curl, each lass has one in front;
To find it on an animal, you at the stern must hunt.

Now, tell me what the object is, but pause before you guess it;
If you are mother, maid or man, I swear you don't possess it.

Answer: the letter "L".

★   ★   ★   ★

Last spring.
> A little horse-hair sofa
> In a parlor stood;
> A youth and maiden courting,
> So far—so good.

This spring.
> A little crib, with baby
> Making lots of bother,
> Stands in place of sofa,
> So far—no father.

★   ★   ★   ★

SNAKE ON THE BRIDGE*

One time there was two fellows going home from the tavern, and they was both pretty drunk. The fellow that led the way was six foot tall, and the little one carried a walking stick because his leg had got crippled. Just about midnight they come to the bridge, and the big fellow thought of an old saying about how it is healthy to piss in running water, so he started to take a leak.

The moon was a-shining, but it was pretty dark on the bridge, and the crippled fellow was about half blind anyhow. Soon as he seen the big man's tool a-flopping over the rail he hollered "Snake!" and whacked it with that there cane. The big man screeched like a wildcat, and grabbed his pecker with both hands. "Bust him again, Tom!" the big fellow yelled, "he's bit me!" They do say the big man never did know what really happened, because the crippled fellow was scared to speak up. There ain't no telling what that big drunk might do, if he found out somebody has hit his tally-whacker with a stick.

The boys around town thought it was a great joke, and for a long time after that they would holler "Snake!" at each other right on Main Street. Some other fellow would holler back, "Bust him again! He's bit me!" and then both of them would laugh. The womenfolks all heard the story, of course, but they had to act innocent like they didn't know what them boys meant. Probably that's why everybody thought it was so funny.

★   ★   ★   ★

A certain lady was asked if she had ever gone through bankruptcy. No, she replied, but I have been pushed for money.

★   ★   ★   ★

ON THE ROAD OF ANTHRACITE

> The porter sleeps, the drummer creeps,
> Into the berth where Phoebe sleeps.
> All through the night he holds her tight
> Upon the road of anthracite.
> The months roll by, and with a sigh
> Poor Phoebe says—Now I know why
> My corset's tight, it was that night,
> Upon the road of anthracite.
> The drummer too is feeling blue,
> And many a time that night did rue,
> Alas poor soul he burnt his pole
> Upon the road that burns hard coal.
> And as you see if you'd be free
> From ills that hurt you when you pee,
> Just travel right by day and night,
> Keep off the road of anthracite.

★   ★   ★   ★

"What's that, mam'selle?" the little boy questioned his governess, as he pointed at the penis of the elephont. The zoo's elephant was busy pissing. "You mean ze trunk?" asked the lady. "No," said the boy, that thing danging down in the middle." "Oh, you mean ze tail," the lady said. "No, no, that that thing there," the child insisted, pointed straight at it. "Oh, zat, zat is nothing," said the governess. A Frenchman who was standing nearby tipped his hat. "Mam'selle is blase," he said, lifting his eyebrows.

★　　★　　★　　★

A colored fellow was calling on his girl and she asked him, "Rastus, does you believe in a heahafter?" "I certainly does, Mandy," he answered, "take off your clothes, you know what I's heah after."

★　　★　　★　　★

Some snappy headings for newspaper stories. Couple eloped in airoplane...Hi-Diddle Diddle.

Married dentist named as co-respondent. Filled the wrong cavity.

Shit house turned over in storm with man inside. Interred but not dead.

★　　★　　★　　★

What is the difference between a boutonierre and a syringe?

One you put in your buttonhole and the other you put...well...hm-m-m...the other is made of rubber.

★　　★　　★　　★

WHANG

I will tell you a little story,
　　A story that I have heard,
You may think it's a fable,
　　But it's gospel, every word;
When the Lord made Father Adam,
　　They say he laughed and sang,
And he sewed him up the belly,
　　With a little piece of WHANG.

But when the Lord had finished,
　　He found He'd measured wrong,
For when the WHANG was knotted,
　　It was several inches long;
Said he, "Tis but eight inches,
　　So I guess I'll let it hang;"
So he left on Adams belly,

That little piece of WHANG.

But when the Lord made mother Eve,
    I imagine He did snort,
When He found that the WHANG HE sewed her with,
    Was several inches short;
"It leaves an awful gap," said He,
    "But I don't give a dang,
She can fight it out with Adam,
    For the little piece of WHANG.

So ever since the ancient days,
    When human life began,
There's been a constant wage and strife,
    Twixt the woman and the man,
The woman swear they'll have that piece,
    That on our bellies hang,
To fill that awful gap of theirs,
    Where the Lord ran out of WHANG.

So let us not be selfish boys,
    With what the woman lack,
But split "fifty-fifty" on the WHANG
    To fill the awful lack;
For the good Lord never intended,
    It should always idle hang.
When He left on Adam's belly
    That little piece of WHANG.

★   ★   ★   ★

THE ART OF MAKING SALTPETRE

To provide for making their gunpowder the Confederates had to resort to all sorts of devices, such as digging out and leaching the earth from all smokehouses, barns and caves, and making artificial beds of all sorts of nitrogenous refuse, having agents for this purpose in every town and city. The agent in Selma, Ala., who was particularly energetic and enthusiastic in his work, put the following advertisement in the newspapers:—

"The ladies of Selma are respectfully requested to preserve all chamber lye collected about their premises, for the purpose of making nitre. A barrel will be sent around daily to collect it.

> John Harrelson, Agent,
> Nitre and Min. Bureau, C.S.A.

This attracted the attention of the Army poets, and the first of two effusions resulted. It was copied and privately circulated all over the Confederacy, and finally crossing the line, an unknown Federal poet added "The Yankee View of It."

THE CONFEDERATE VIEW OF IT

John Harrelson, John Harrelson,
  You are a wretched creature;
You've added to this cruel war
  A new and useful feature.
You'd have us think while every man
  is bound to be a fighter,
The ladies—bless the pretty dears—
  Should save their pea for nitre.

John Harrelson, John Harrelson,
  Where did you get the notion
To send your barrel round the town,
  To gather up the lotion?
We thought the girls had work enough
  In making shirts and kissing,
But you have put the pretty dears
  To patriotic pissing.

John Harrelson, John Harrelson,
  Do pray invent a neater
And somewhat less immodest way
  Of making your saltpetre.
For 'tis an awful idea, John,
  Gunpowdery and cranky,
That when a lady lifts her skirts,
  She's killing of a Yankee.

THE YANKEE VIEW OF IT

John Harrelson, John Harrelson,
   We've read in song and story,
How women's tears, in all the years,
   Have moistened fields of glory;
But never was it told before,
   That mid such scenes of slaughter,
Your Southern beauties dried their tears,
And went to making water.

No wonder that your boys are brave!
   Who wouldn't be a fighter,
If every time he fired his gun,
   He used his sweetheart's nitre?
And vice versa, what could make
   A Yankee soldier sadder,
Than dodging bullets fired by
   A pretty woman's bladder?

They say there was a subtle smell,
   Which lingered in the powder,
And as the smoke grew thicker and
   The din of battle louder,
That there was found in this compound
   One serious objection;
No soldier boy could whiff of it,
   Without having an erection.

★   ★   ★   ★

Several officers in Paris were out with some French girls and it just happened that none of them were very tall. One of the girls remarked: "None of ze Americaine officers are very tall." "No," said one, "but we have large privates."

★   ★   ★   ★

FARM COMFORTS

While traveling through the country,
   Selling goods and looking wise,

We see some funny faces,
And we see some funny guys.
The big hotels are costly
Cozy, snug and warm,
But some way, they're not in it,
With the comforts of the farm.
Now, for instance, there's the s—house
As we used to say at home,
Looming up in the garden
Like a big cathedral dome.
It was not so very handsome,
But still it had its charm,
When I think of the happy moments
In the —house, on the farm.
A common old board structure,
Whitewashed and looking swell,
A soap box in the corner,
And a door that squeaked like Hell.
It had no chain, no bell, no strap,
No electric lights adorn,
Still I love that dear old s—house,
That s—house on the farm.
There's where I screwed the hired girl,
Well, sometimes, twice a day,
That's where I tried to smoke,
Dad's dear old pipe of clay.
There's where my mother spanked me,
Till she nearly broke her arm,
Because I stole a pie and ate it,
In the s--house on the farm.
There's where I hid my books and slate,
While hiding off from school,
There's where the old gent caught me,
While playing with my t——l.
There's where I used to sit and sleep,
So free from care and harm,

And I learned to pull my p——n,
In the s—house, on the farm.

★   ★   ★   ★

ANYWAY, HE SURE GOT HIM

Rats were very plentiful in the cellar. There was a bag of nuts
in one end of the cellar and a bag of apples in the other. John
placed a trap by the bag of apples and one by the bag of nuts.
That evening at supper a noise was heard in the cellar and John
hurried down. He shouted up to Mary: "I got him." And she
said: "Where, by the apples?" And he answered: "No."

★   ★   ★   ★

A traveling man who had occasion to stop off on business in
Palm Beach, after a hasty courtship, grabbed off the daughter of
a rich New Yorker, and married her. He sent a telegram to the
father as follows: Married your daughter this morning. Going to
Tampa with her tonight.

★   ★   ★   ★

AN AWKWARD MISTAKE

A young man who is engaged to a young lady wishes to buy
her a valentine remembrance. Not being able to decide for
himself he went shopping with his sister, she buying a pair of
drawers and he a pair of gloves for his lady friend. In sending,
the parcels got mixed and the drawers were sent to the lady
friend with the following note:
"Dear One:

I bought this little remembrance for you. Oh! how I wish no
hand would touch them after you put them on, but I know such
a wish is in vain. A thousand hands may touch them while I am
not at your side and other eyes than mine may see them on you
at parties. I bought the smallest size I could get and if they are
too large let them wrinkle down as a great many girls wear them
that way. Always wear them at parties as I want to see how they
fit. Some fellows may soil them but you can clean them with benzine if you leave them on to dry. I hope they are not too small.

Blow into them before you put them on.

"Ever Your Own"

CHARLEY

★   ★   ★   ★

SEMINOLE MEDICINE*

One time there was a boy got his leg broke, and two other fellows stuck around while somebody rode after the doctor. The whiskey was all gone, but they give the patient some Seminole medicine to cheer him up. "Do you know how they make that stuff?" says one. "Sure I do," the other man says, "you just mix grain alcohol and horse piss, with a chaw of tobacco for flavor."

The first fellow just nodded his head. "That's right," says he, "and it's the best tonic in the Territory. My little brother was weak as a cat, but we give him that Seminole remedy for six days, and it sure fixed him up. He walked into the pool-hall Saturday night, and smashed two balls together. Didn't leave nothing but a little pile of dust."

"Yeah, that's how it works," says the other fellow. "My brother-in-law got so puny, the hens thought he was a worm. But Sis fed him that medicine, and he sure mended fast. He whipped everybody on the place, and then grabbed our two big bulls, and swung 'em round his head. When they come together it shook the whole township, like a earthquake."

"What become of the critters?" asked the first man.

"We never did rightly know what went with them bulls," the other fellow answered. "There wasn't nothing left only a big pile of bull-shit."

Neither one of them story-tellers cracked a smile, but the boy on the ground laughed so hard that he forgot all about his leg. He was still a-laughing when the doctor come and took him off to the hospital.

★   ★   ★   ★

THE NEW IDEA

A chap who had slept with a girl all night, as he leaves her, hands her a $5.00 bill. It might be added, that he had used a condom. It'll be six dollars, said the young ladies. What's the idea, asked the chap. A dollar cover charge, old dear, was the reply.

★　　　★　　　★　　　★

What is the difference between a thrill and a scare? Twenty eight days.

★　　　★　　　★　　　★

A woman who had just moved to a new city wanted to get along socially and decided she would join some of the swell clubs. First she went to the riding club and because she had no horse they refused to let her join. Then she tried the Yacht Club and because she did not own a yacht she was refused admission there. A friend of her's asked her why she didn't try the Country club.

★　　　★　　　★　　　★

A man walking with his friend bowed to a girl and his companion asked, "Do you know her?" "Yes, she's my tailor's daughter and she's the only thing he ever made that fits me.

★　　　★　　　★　　　★

A lady goes into a bank in New York and lays down a Russian Ten Thousand Rouble note and asks the Cashier to please give her American money for it.

The Cashier hands her out seventy-nine cents.

Do you mean to tell me, that's all I get for that.

That is all it is worth, madam, answers the cashier.

The dirty Son of a Bitch, she says, and I gave him breakfast, too.

★　　　★　　　★　　　★

A traveling man was calling on his customer in Little Rock. Having sold him a nice bill of goods, he found by looking at his watch he had missed his train and would have to stay over until that night, having the entire afternoon with nothing to do. His customer, Mr. Smith, said, "I'll have my daughter take you out for a drive." The salesman figured she was probably homely as Hell but much to his surprise and delight when she arrived behind a spanking team of bays he found she was a very beautiful girl. After having driven for half an hour he started with a few feels, etc., etc., and before the afternoon was gone he had gotten what he wanted. When he arrived in St. Louis he found a letter with the address of Smith in the corner card and opening he found a small piece of a horse whip with the following in poetry:

> I'm sending you a token,
> Of a horse whip that is broken
> There were foot prints on my dashboard, upside down.
> There were grease stains on my cushion
> Which proved there had been pushin'
> And my little daughter Venus hasn't come around.

He answered as follows:

> I'm the guy that did the pushin'
> Put the grease stains on the cushion
> Put the foot-prints on the dashboard, upside down.
> But since I met your daughter, Venus
> I've had trouble with my penis,
> And I wish I hadn't made your God-damned town.

★　　　★　　　★　　　★

Shortly after the armistice, a lady walks into a Doctor's office and asks that he give her a thorough examination. I'm not feeling at all well, having just gotten over an operation.

"Major?" asks the Doctor.

"No, First Lieutenant," answers the lady.

★　　　★　　　★　　　★

A lady whose husband snored terribly, went to the Doctor and asked him if he could suggest a remedy. He told her it was a simple matter. All she had to do while he was asleep was to spread his legs apart gently without waking him. After a week she came back and said, Doctor, your advice was splendid, it worked like a charm. But tell me, I can not understand how such a simple thing would stop his snoring. Well you see, it's like this, said the Doctor, when you spread his legs apart, his testicles drop down over his air intake, shutting off the draft and he stops snoring immediately.

★   ★   ★   ★

AN EARLY ATTEMPT AT ERA

Speech made by Mrs. Parkhust on February 18, 1909, before Congress, pertaining to Woman Suffrage:

"We must have what the men have—It may not be much, but we must have it. If we cannot have it without friction, we will have it with friction. If we cannot have it through our organization, we will have it through our combination—or without, if necessary. We absolutely refuse to be packed in the gallery any longer but insist on being placed on the floor of the House. The drunken loafer at the other end of the house says: 'Down with the petticoats!' I say 'Up with the petticoats and down with the trousers, and then things will be visible in the true light."

★   ★   ★   ★

A tramp was leaning against a home
Close by a window frame,
Inside he heard voices,
Just then a woman exclaimed.

"You simply can't do it this way
Hurry don't you see I can't wait
You always let it wobble so,
You just can't keep it straight.

Now, let us try it this way,
But be careful of my dress,
If you let it slip out, you know
You'll make an awful mess.

If you can't do it this way
We can't do it at all,

I think that your's must be too big
Or mine must be too small.

Just have a little patience dear,
And you will surely win,
See now you've got it straight,
For God sake shove it in.''

By this time the tramp got excited
And for the window dove
And saw a woman and a man
Fitting stove pipe to a stove.

THE WAY IT STARTED

Pushing his way into a crowd on a corner, little Mose saw two colored brethern fighting to beat the band. Turning to one of the bystanders, he asked what the fight was about, and received the answer that they were fighting about an agreement.

"How come? How come? Explain dat all to me. I done heard tell of people fightin' 'bout a disagreement many times, but I done nebbah heard tell of two people fightin' 'bout an agreement.''

"Dat's where you is foolish. I explains dat to you all: De one fellah says to do odder, "My wife am de best piece ob ass in dis whole town.' And de odder fellah agreed with him. Den de fight started.''

An old man of 75, an oil millionaire, married a girl of about thirty. One of his best friends said to him, for heaven's sake, why did you do that. Don't you know that kid will run around with at least ten fellows, all of whom can give her what she wants and what you can't do. Say, he said, I'd rather have a ten per cent interest in a gusher than a 100 per cent interest in a dry hole.

Mr. Malone and her husband were always quarreling. It got on the nerves not only of themselves, but of the neighbors. One of these finally expostulated with Mrs. Malone. "Trate the man nice," she said. "Whin he comes home bring him his slippers, light his pipe fer him, wear a niglijay and sit on his lap. Make the ould man comfy." Mrs. Malone determined to try it. So that evening when Pat came hime he was greeted like a lover by his mistress. Mrs. Malone had turned the light low, and was in a transparent flimsy. She threw her arms about his neck and kissed him lusciously. Leading him to a soft chair she brought his slippers, filled his pipe and lit it for him. Then she cuddled up on his lap and began to fondle him. "Let's go to bed, dearie?" she whispered sweetly. "We might as well," said Pat. "I'll get hell when I get home anyway."

★   ★   ★   ★

THE SAILOR'S LANGUAGE*

One time there was a country boy that had joined the Navy, and he went a-swaggering around Little Rock. He looked pretty good in his uniform with the ribbons on it, and lots of people was a-buying him drinks. The boy got uncommon drunk, because he was not used to store-boughten liquor. A pretty girl says "Hello, sailor," and so they went up to her room in the hotel.

The pretty girl wanted her money before they done anything serious, and he give her two dollars. The sailor figured he was getting on fine, but the truth is he had drunk too much for that kind of business. After while he says, "How am I doin', Babe?" The pretty girl just kind of yawned, and she says, "Oh, about three knots."

Well, what she said is Navy talk, all right. But the sailor was kind of bothered. "What do you mean, three knots?" says he. The girl just yawned again. "Well," she says, "it's not hard, and it's not in, and you're not going to get your two dollars back."

★ ★ ★ ★

HELL

Just what is meant by this word "Hell"
They say sometimes, "It's cold as Hell,"
Sometimes they say, "It's hot as Hell,"
When it rains hard, "It's Hell," they cry
It's also "Hell" when it is dry.
They "hate like "Hell," to see it snow,
It's "A Hell of a wind," when it starts to blow,
Now "How in Hell' can anyone tell
"What in Hell' they mean by this word "Hell?'
This married life is "Hell' they say,
When he comes in late there's "Hell to Pay,"
When he starts to yell, it's "A Hell of a note."
It's "Hell" when the kid you have to tote,
It's "Hell" when the doctor sends his bills,
For a "Hell of a lot" of trips and pills,
When you get this you will know real well
Just what is meant by this word "Hell."
"Hell yes!" "Hell no!" and "Oh, Hell" too!
"The Hell you don't," "The Hell you do."
And "What in Hell!" and "The Hell it is,"
"The Hell with your" and "The Hell with his!"
Now, "Who in Hell" and "Oh, Hell, where?"
And "What the Hell do you think I care?"
But "The Hell of it is," "It's sure as Hell,"
We don't know "What in the Hell" is "Hell."

★ ★ ★ ★

THE OLD MAN'S LAMENT

At the close of our existence
When we've climbed life's golden stairs,
And the chilling winds of autumn
Kindly toss our silvered hairs,
When we feel our manhood ebbing
and we're up to life's last ditch,
And we find our faithful Peter

Soundly sleeping at the switch
Gosh, almighty, ain't it awful,
Don't it make us deathly sick,
When the hateful fact confronts us,
That we've got a lifeless Dick.
Ain't it sad for us to know,
When we take him down the street,
That he ne'er again will wrestle
With the pussies that we meet.
That he never again will bristle
On a wet and windy day,
When some maiden shows her stocking,
In that naughty, cunning way.

Oh, my poor old loyal King Pin,
How my heart goes out to you,
For I can not but remember,
All the stunts you used to do.
How you charmed the maids and maidens
And the dashing widows too,
How you had the whole bunch begging
for a little bit of you.
Do you think I have forgotten,
When each charming girl you tried,
I would never make you quit her,
till she sighed, I'm satisfied.
Do you think I'll now forget you,
Just because you are so dead,
And because when I command you,
You can't lift your pallid head?
No, indeed, my valiant comrade,
Naught shall rob you of your fame,
henceforth you shall be my Pisser,
And I'll love you just the same.

★   ★   ★   ★

The night after raid on an apartment house, with a questionable reputation, the Judge, looking over the women taken in the raid is horrified to see amongst those brought before him the wife of a very close acquaintance of his, a man high up in the financial and social world. He looks at her and says, "Mrs.——— I am inexpressibly shocked and astounded to find you amongst these other women. Do you mean to tell me that you are a professional Prostitute?" "No, Judge," she answers, smiling sweetly, "but a very enthusiastic Amateur."

A farmer once wrote to Sears Roebuck & Company to ask for the price of toilet paper. He received an answer directing him to look on page 507 of their catalogue. "If I had your catalogue," he wrote back, "would I ask you for the price of toilet paper?"

A girl bought a pair of stockings at Marshall Fields' and sent them back with a note saying they were not up to her expectation. They sent her another pair and sent her a little note saying, "We hope that these will tickle your fancy."

Mutt meets Jeff and says: "Jeff, I'm going to the breadery." "You mean, Mutt, you're going to the bakery." "No, I don't," is the answer. "When I want bread I go to the breadery and when I want grain I go to the granery." Jeff leaves him for awhile and comes back all dolled. "Where are you going, Jeff?" asks Mutt. "Oh, I'm going to the country."

A southern colonel, goes into one of the modern hotel toilets, where you drop a nickel into the slot in order to get into the private enclosure. When he comes out he hands the colored attendant a fifteen cent tip. "Thank you, Sah, thank you, Colonel, I's much obliged, indeed I is." "What's the matter?", asks the Colonel. "Isn't business good?" "Why, Colonel," says Sambo, "all day long it's been Piss, Piss, Piss, and you'se de first S—t dats been in here today."

★   ★   ★   ★

A week before the wedding the young girl came to her mother in tears. "I'm so afraid about getting married," she said. "I'm afraid I won't be able to please my sweetheart." Her mother, who wanted to make the girl's trials easier, undertook to explain to her the secrets of married life. With some hesitation, she began to explain to the girl what she would have to go through, "Oh, that doesn't bother me, mother," said the daughter, "I can fuck all right, but I can't cook."

★   ★   ★   ★

"You're asking am I a good cook?" said the wife of a travelling man to a friend. "Why, my Abie is just crazy for the pot roast I make. In fact, when he comes home from the road that's the second thing he asks for!"

★   ★   ★   ★

THE PREACHER AND THE LADY*

(This story was known in the 15th century.)

One time there was a widow-woman named Hale that lived up on Coon Creek, and the other women didn't like her, but the menfolks all thought she was wonderful. There was men right here in town that would sneak out and leave their wife pretty near every night, and old Jim Butterfield used to lock up his store and go see the widow in broad daylight. Them fellows burnt up the Coon Creek road all the time, and they didn't care who knowed it, neither.

The womenfolks all says the widow Hale ought to be throwed in jail, but the sheriff wouldn't do nothing, because he was pussy-simple too. So then a bunch of church people went to see the preacher, which his name was Wilkes. They wanted him to tell the widow-woman she better behave herself, or else move away. Because if she don't, the decent women is going to give the widow Hale a horse-whipping, and then run her out of the country. Old preacher Wilkes grumbled a good deal, but finally he says he'll go up on Coon Creek and see about it.

They didn't have no cars in them days, but young Park Chambers took the preacher out there in his new buggy. When they got to the widow Hale's cabin Park just waited outside, and old man Wilkes was gone a long time. Finally he come back out, a-shaking his head. "Mistress Hale is a good Christian woman," he says, "cultured and refined the best you ever seen! I don't understand why the ladies are telling all them bad stories about her!"

So then the preacher just stood there, a-looking back at the widow woman's house on Coon Creek. "All right, Reverend," says young Park Chambers. "Just button up your pants, and we'll get home in time for dinner."

★　　　★　　　★　　　★

A marriage-broker was trying to arrange a match between a business man and a beautiful young girl. But the business man was obdurate. "Before I buy goods from a mill I looked at swatches, and before I get married I must also have a sample," he said. "But, my God, you can't ask a virtuous, respectable girl for a thing like that," said the marriage-broker. "I'm a man from business," said the other, "and that's the way it will be done, or not at all." The broker went off in despair to talk with the girl. "I got for you a fine feller, with lots of money," he said. "He's a business man and his rating is O.K. But he's a little crazy. He says he's a good business man and wouldn't go into nothing blind. He must have a sample." "Listen," said the girl. "I'm so smart a business man as he is. Sample I wouldn't give him. References...yes!"

★　　　★　　　★　　　★

HE TRIED

He tried her on the sofa,
　　He tried her on the chair,
He tried her on the window-seat
　　But he couldn't get it there.
He tried her sitting on his lap

And lying on the floor,
He tried her up against the wall
And against the parlor-door.
He tried her this way and that way
And how it made her laugh
To see the different ways he tried
To take her photograph.

★   ★   ★   ★

A professor of botany was lecturing to a girl's class. "This twig you will notice," said he, "is composed of bark, hardwood, and pith. Of course you know what pith is." The class stared at him blankly. "Don't you know what pith is?" the professor repreated. "You, Miss Brown, you know what pith is, do you not?" "Yeth, thir," said Miss Brown.

★   ★   ★   ★

The Dinktown band was doing its best when someone called the piccolo player a son of a bitch. The leader's baton beat a tatoo on his music stand, and the players became silent. He turned to his audience. "Who called my piccolo player a son of a bitch?" he demanded. A voice in the rear of the theatre yelled back: "Who called that son of a bitch a piccolo player?"

★   ★   ★   ★

ANY CONNECTION?

Old Man Grim glanced up from his plate of beans and corn-bread; his son Johnny closed the door and turned a dejected face toward the elder.

'What's the matter of yuh?" grunted his father. "I thought yuh was as good as hired."

"I was—'ntil he made me do a bunch of writin'—then he said he couldn't keep me."

"Why?"

"He said I—I—was ill—ill—illiterate."

"It's a domm dirty lie," screamed the Old Man. "I married yer mother six weeks afore yew was born."

★ ★ ★ ★

It was a foggy morning, and the fishing smacks off Gloucester nosed their way out of the harbor. Suddenly a sailor in one hailed another: "Hello, John, I have news for you." "What is it?" "Wife had a baby, a boy." "What'd he weigh?" the other voice called. "Four pounds," came the reply, thru the fog. "Hell, you hardly got your bait back!"

★ ★ ★ ★

Mandy:—Ah'd like a little vacation, Missus. Ah wants to go home and see mah chillun.
Mistress:—Well, Mandy, I didn't know you were married.
Mandy:—Ah ain't, Missus. But ah ain't been neglected.

★ ★ ★ ★

Before the races Alexander took his girl around to the stables to look over the horses to see if they couldn't pick a winner. The first stall they looked into was that of a young stallion with a good record. The beast was in fine fettle, evidently, the way he was waving the distinguished mark of his horsehood. Pearl considered it a while with sufficient interest. Then drawing her boyfriend away, she said, "Don't bet on him, Alec. Dat hoss dere ain't gonna win. He ain't got his mind on his business."

★ ★ ★ ★

The twins were having a bath and both parents watched, fondly. Suddenly Mary began to cry. "Mamma," I want one of those things that's hanging from Bobby," pointing to his little pecker..."Quiet, now, quiet," mother said. "If you're a good little girl you'll get one of them." "And if you're a bad little girl," said father, "you'll get a lot of them."

★ ★ ★ ★

A young student was undressing in his bedroom, when he discovered, you may imagine with what joy, that a girl just across the alley was also undressing. They reached a state of nudity together and then she noticed him. He motioned her to join him, but she shook her head. The young man raised his window a trifle, and she hers. "Come on over," he whispered. "How?" the girl asked. "Walk over on this," the youth said, laying his stiff prick on the sill. "Yes," said the cautious girl, "But how'll I get back?"

★   ★   ★   ★

Abrams frantically dashed up the stairs of his home. "Sarah," he panted, "we got to move out of here right away. I just found out the most terrible thing. I just learned that the janitor from this house screwed every woman in it but one." "Yeh, I know," said Sarah, "that's that stuck up thing on the third floor."

★   ★   ★   ★

IN SCHOOL

A teacher asks her class of boys to compose a sentence with the word "pistol" in it. One little boy gets up and says, his brother was in the war and brought him back a German pistol. Another little boy gets up and says that his father belongs to the militia and goes once a week for pistol practice. Little Abe Cohen gets up and says, "Last Sunday my sister Beckie went to a picnic and she drank so much ginger ale she pissed till Tuesday."

★   ★   ★   ★

A swimming meet was being held in the East and one girl who no one seemed to know beat every one with the greatest ease and won the prize. The instructor and referee, who had been there a good many years went up to her and said, "lady, I have been here a good many years and refereed a great many matches, but I never saw any one win with such consummate ease, and tell me, where did you learn that wonderful rhythm that you have in the water?" Oh, she answered, "I used to be a street walker in Venice."

★   ★   ★   ★

The train came to a halt with a sudden jar. Two men sprang

into the aisles, one tall man, the other short. Both brandished guns. "Hands up everybody," yelled the tall man. "You men line up on this side, women on the other. Now we ain't going to hurt nobody that behaves. Gents, shell out your dough and jewelry. All the men are going to be robbed and then we'll fuck all the women." "Easy now, easy," protested the smaller robber, "never mind that last. We'll just cop the dough and beat it." "You mind your own business," spoke up an old maid. "Who's robbing this train, I'd like to know."

★   ★   ★   ★

Senator Hoare of Massachusetts was one day delivering a long speech against a certain bill for which Senator Roscoe Conkling stood sponsor. As he outlined his points against the bill Senator Hoare kept first his right hand, and then his left in his trousers' pockets. Senator Conkling, who was a noted wit, rose to remark that "the Senator from Massachusetts seems to be leaving no stone unturned to prevent the passage of his bill."

★   ★   ★   ★

All the dinner guests were assembled, having given up expecting Dr. Blank, a well known surgeon, who was late, to say the least. However, he arrived at just that moment, breathless. Making his apologies to the hostess he explained that he had been hurriedly summoned to the hospital to perform an operation. Instantly the guests were eager to learn what the operation was, et cetera, et cetera. But the surgeon said the subject was a delicate one, what with the presence of so many ladies. This objection was quickly over-ruled by the ladies themselves, who pointed out that since all present were married folk there should be no undue modesty. "Well, then" said the doctor, "we cut through the penis of the patient, who was suffering from..." "Pardon me," interrupted the hostess, "did you have to saw through the bone?" As one person the assembled company rose and bowed elaborately to the host!

★   ★   ★   ★

The minister of a Methodist church in a little Illinois town was speaking a few words on proper conduct to the Sunday school. "Now, children, before I close the lesson, I want to ask you a few questions on the things I have been talking about. Willie," he said to a model little boy in the front row, "tell me, do you know where little boys and girls go when they do bad things?" "Sure," piped up the town terror, whose name also was Willie, and who had for the first time been lured into the church. "Back of the churchyard."

★   ★   ★   ★

KITCHEN AND TABLE LANGUAGE AND ETIQUETTE
Why did the salt shaker?
Because he saw the spoon holder, the potato masher, the egg beater, the lemon squeezer, the can opener, the nut cracker, but when he saw the CORK SCREWER!—IT WAS ALL OFF."

★   ★   ★   ★

Every Sabbath morning when the auld folks had gone to the kirk Annie would be visited by her lover, Jock, and they would use the service hours as opportunity for screwing. One bright Sabbath day Jock arrived just after auld folks had departed, and whistling a bonnie air leaped up the steps three at a time to Annie's bedroom. The lass was removing her waist when Jock burst in, puffing the final bars of Annie Laurie. His sweetheart gave him a disapproving look. Jock apparently didn't notice this, for, putting his arms around Annie he began another tune. The lass tore herself from his arms and began to redress. "Why, what is it, Annie?" asked Jock. "Have I done aught to offend ye?" "Stop it, stop it," said the girl. "Ye were whistlin' and I will no fornicate wi' a man who whistles on Sunday."

★   ★   ★   ★

A fellow takes his girl home and stays a long time in the vestibule. Coming down and jumping into the taxi, he suddenly tells the taxi driver, "for God's sake drive to a doctor. I am bent double and can't straighten up." Coming into the doctor's office, he tells the doctor what the trouble is and the doctor says, "no wonder, you can't straighten up! Your pants button is buttoned to your vest."

★   ★   ★   ★

THE FOLKS ON RUMPUS RIDGE*

One time there was an old couple that lived on Rumpus Ridge, and they had a terrible pretty daughter. It was just about dark when a stranger come along, and he says, "I have got lost, and will you let me stay all night?" They give him the spare room, and he watched careful to see where the pretty girl's bed was. After everybody had went to sleep, the town fellow sneaked over there. But the girl and her mother had traded places, so she got screwed by mistake. The old woman giggled, and the stranger was pretty mad, but there wasn't nothing he could do about it.

Pretty soon somebody come walking past in their bare feet, and the town fellow knowed the pretty girl had went back to her own bed. After awhile he slipped over there again, and crawled in with the pretty girl. She was glad of it, and you never seen such a shagging match. The stranger stayed there a long time, and it was pretty near daylight when he got back to the spare room.

Next morning the old man just set in the kitchen, with a shotgun right by his chair. There wasn't much said, but the town fellow felt kind of uneasy. He eat some breakfast though, and got ready to leave. "How much do I owe you?" says he. The old farmer just looked at him. "I don't charge nobody for bed and victuals," says he, "but this here breaking up people's family is a bad business." The town fellow was shaking like holly in a high wind. "I don't care about the old woman," says the farmer, "because she's limbered enough pricks to build a bridge over James River. But Lucy is just a innocent child, and never screwed nobody but me in her whole life." With that the old man picked up the shotgun, and he cocked both hammers.

The town fellow stood there with his mouth open, and he didn't know whether to shit or go blind. But finally he says, "Well, I am always willing to do the right thing." The old farmer studied awhile, and then he let one hammer of the shotgun down easy. "Stranger," says he, "do you think three dollars is too much?" The town fellow give him the money, and then the old man let the other hammer down easy.

The pretty girl was hanging some clothes out behind the house, and she waved at the town fellow when he walked on down the road. But the town fellow never looked back. "I don't care about the money," says he, "it's the principle of the thing." And nobody likes to be scared out of a year's growth with a shotgun, neither.

★   ★   ★   ★

A couple of bookies, standing in front of the Hotel Taft turned to look after a "Follies" girl who passed. "Gee," said one, "I feel like screwing that dame again." "What!" said the other, "you mean to tell me you screwed that swell dame?" "No," was the answer, "but once before I felt like it."

★   ★   ★   ★

Brown brought home a parrot that he said he had bought at auction, and which was supposed to be a wonderful bird. But for over two months neither Jones nor his wife, who had at first objected to Polly, could make the pet talk. They tried everything from "Polly wants a cracker," to "Hello, Polly, pretty Polly" but with no results. They concluded the bird was deaf and dumb. One afternoon, while the head of the house was in his office Mrs. Jones invited the ladies of the sewing circle to her home. One of them interrupted the gossip to state that she had secured a fine pair of hose at Gimbles, and lifted her skirt to show them. Another showed a marvelous corset she had purchased at Bests. A third showed a neat silk petticoat. Mrs. Jones lifted her skirt and said: "Look at these wonderful bloomers, all silk, that I bought at Altmans." The parrot, who had cocked his head from one to the other of the ladies now chirped up: "Ah, home at last. Could one of you whores give me a cigarette?"

★   ★   ★   ★

Mr. Cohen writes to his former friend Mr. Goldberg as follows: Dear Sir: I wish you to be in my office tomorrow morning at ten o'clock sharp. I understand you have been making love to my wife. He received a letter from Goldberg, which started as follows: Dear Mr. Cohen. Your circular letter received. I will be at the mass meeting.

★   ★   ★   ★

A large cowboy, who, troubled by a horny feeling which he had no immediate prospect of relieving, went to a pharmacist to get something for it, in the way of a bromide. He was somewhat embarrassed when he found a woman in attendance. "Pardon me," he said, "but I'd like to see the boss." "Why, I'm the boss," said the woman. "Well then, a-er, man clerk," said the Westerner. "We haven't any," the owner replied, "you tell me what you want. I won't be embarrassed." "Well," said the stranger, "I've got a terrible erection that won't go down. What can you give me for it?" "Just a minute," said the woman, and went to the back of the drug store. In a few minutes she returned. "I've just been talking to my sister, who makes up the prescriptions, and who is my partner in this store," she said," and the best we can do is offer you the store and five hundred dollars."

★   ★   ★   ★

THE REASON WHY

The dogs once held a meeting,
They came from far and near,
Some came in automobiles
With loud hurrah and cheers.
But before inside the hall,
They were allowed to take a look,
They had to take their ass-holes,
And hang them on a hook.

Then to the hall they went at once,
The Mother, Son and Sire
But hardly were they seated,
When someone hollered "Fire."
When out they ran all in a bunch,
They had no time to look,
And each one took at random,
An ass-hole from a hook.
They got their ass-holes all mixed up,
It made them awful sore,
To think they did not have the one
They always had before.
And that's the reason that you see
When you go down the street,
Each dog will stop to swap a smell
From every dog they meet.
And here's the reason that a dog
Will leave a nice fat bone
To go and smell an ass-hole
'Cause he hopes to find his own.

★   ★   ★   ★

In France a "safety" or condom is known as capote Anglaise, or "English cap." A gentleman once went into a French shop, intending to purchase a dark cap, to wear in mourning for his wife, who recently died. He knew the French word for cap was capote, so he asked for that. Several were shown him, but he wanted one English style, so he asked for a capote Anglaise. The clerk sent him to the drug department, where he repeated his request to the lady clerk. She arched her brows and asked him what color he wanted. "My wife has just died," he answered, "so I want a black one." "Such refined delicacy," said the clerk.

★　　★　　★　　★

THANK HEAVEN

Electrical appliances have superseded steam,
The old style sailing vessel is an antiquated dream,
We have our horseless vehicles, the bicycles and sich,
And women wear silk hosiery and never knit a stitch,
We've telegraph that's wireless, we talk through air and sea,
We play machine pianos and never touch a key,
The belly ache of old is called appendicitis now,
We're eating cheese and butter not the part of any cow,
We've machines to do our talk, singing, laughing, too, as well,
What next will be surplanted by machines is hard to tell.
Improvement is our motto, and what else may come to stay,
Thank God we'll make the babies in the same old fashioned
　　way.

★　　★　　★　　★

Teacher had asked her pupils to make rhymes of two lines
each. Many elegant specimens were submitted, until little
Johnny rose and offered:
　　"May Jane McKane, of Boston, Mass.
　　Went into the ocean up to her ankle."
"Why that doesn't rhyme," said the teacher. "It will," said
Johnny, "when the tide comes in."

★　　★　　★　　★

SO LONG, MR. PREACHER

Because of a disagreement with the Ladies' Aid Society,
Reverend Johnston, of the African Methodist Church, had been
asked to resign.
His Farewell address was, in part, as follows:—
　　"Brethern and Sisters: I received your request for my resigna-
tion, which I accept and I shall leave you all with no regrets
whatever. I shall not say goodby, nor shall I say farewell,
because those words do not express my feelings. Neither shall I
say "au revoir," but I simply want to call the attention of each

and everyone here, to the small bunch of Mistletoe pinned to my coat tail. Kindly do your duty as I pass down the aisle. Amen!''

★   ★   ★   ★

A bachelor girl is a woman who has never been married.

An old maid is a woman who has never been married nor anything!

★   ★   ★   ★

With fond regrets I now remember
Those happy days of youthful fun
When all my limbs were lithe and limber,
Did I say all? "Yes, all but one."
Those happy days have gone forever
Those happy days of youthful fun,
My limbs have all grown hard and stiffer,
Did I say all? "Yes, all but one."

★   ★   ★   ★

An Englishman was pacing up and down the corridor of the hospital, waiting while his wife was being confined. Suddenly the doctor emerges from the room and says, "I have to congratulate you. You are the father of a fine seven pound boy." "Oh, I say," said the Englishman, "that's ripping, doctor, ripping." The doctor disappears into the room again and after a few minutes the Englishman sees a nurse run hurriedly in. Ten minutes later the doctor comes out again and says, "Sir, I have to congratulate you again. You are the father of another fine six pound boy." "Oh, my royal aunt," ejaculates the Englishman, "that's quite wonderful." A short time later, the doctor again emerges, with his bag and putting his gloves. "I say, doctor," said the new father, "would you mind doing me a favor?" "If I can," says the doctor, "certainly." "Well, just go back and have another look around. You see, my wife she's such a roomy old bitch!"

★   ★   ★   ★

An Englishman returned home suddenly one day from a

meeting in the House and directed that his wife be sent to him. "Madame is in her boudoir," the butler replied. "Very well, then I'll go to her," said m'Lord. "I'm afraid, Sir, she has company," suggested the servant. True enough when the M.P. softly opened the door of his wife's bedroom he saw her, or more properly her legs, high in the air, under the vigorous stroking of her lover. The Englishman seized his hunting rifle from a rack and levelled it on the offenders. "Remember, Sir, you're a sportsman," softly whispered the butler, "shoot him on the rise."

★　　★　　★　　★

THE CIRCUS COME TO TOWN*

One time there was a circus come to this town with elephants, and some of the folks got excited, because their horses broke loose, and also the people here hadn't never seen nothing like that before. Old man Massey thought the elephants must be a fake with leather on the outside, and never did believe it till he seen one of 'em shit right in front of the courthouse. Most of us knowed better, of course. But twenty years after the circus had come and went, the fellows around town was still cracking jokes about them elephants.

The boys used to tell how one of 'em got loose when the red wagons pulled into East Elsey. Next morning old Biddy Walters come to the sheriff's office. She says there is a tremendous big animal in her turnip patch, and it will have to be got rid of. The sheriff knowed what it was, but he asked the old woman a lot of questions just for fun, because there was some town folks a-listening. "What is the critter doing in your garden patch?" he says. "The goddam thing is a-walking backwards," says Biddy Walters, "pulling up turnips with his tail!"

The town folks laughed when they heard that, and Biddy begun to get mad. The sheriff just shook his head, and he says maybe Mistress Walters better go somewheres and lay down, because the hot sun don't agree with her. The old woman was so goddam mad she couldn't talk for a minute, so the sheriff says, "What else is the monster a-doing?" Biddy Walters just scowled at him. "You won't believe it," she says, "but I'm going to tell you, anyhow. The last I seen of the varmint, he was a-sticking my turnips up his ass!"

It don't look like anybody would be so ignorant as that, in this day and generation. But the folks that knowed Biddy Walters still tell the tale, and every one of 'em swears it is the God's truth.

★   ★   ★   ★

It seems a wealthy playboy out for the night, flirted with a lovely young girl at the bar, and at length, escorted her to his apartment. Instead of being a tramp, she was well-groomed, chic and apparently most intellectual. Thinking he must impress her to get anywhere, he exhibited a few etchings, old prints and first editions and finally produced some wine. He asked if she would prefer Port or Sherry.

'Oh, Sherry by all means,' she answered, "Sherry to me is just nectar of the Gods, just gazing at it in the crystal clear decanter fills me with anticipation of a strange and heavenly thrill, and as the stopper is lifted out, the gorgeous liquid slides, serpent-like, into the goblet, I inhale the exotic and tangy fumes, and am carried off on the soft wings of ecstasy. Furthermore, when actually sipping this tantalizing potion, my entire being simply glows, and while a thousand velvety violins throb in my ears, I am tenderly lifted into a new and more exquisitely beautiful world."

On the other hand she said, "Port makes me fart."

★   ★   ★   ★

MARKING 100%

A medical student who had been out on a big party until 5:00 A.M. sat in a class room trying to pass an exam. His head was still fairly buzzing with the hangover from the party and he could just about see the paper. The first question was:

"Name five reasons why mothers' milk is better for babies than cows' milk."

The student scratched his head and put down:

1. It's fresher.
2. It's cleaner.

Then he thought a while and wrote:

3. The cats can't get to it.
4. It's easier to take to a picnic.

Well pleased with the results he had so far achieved, he studied long on the last reason. He thought and thought, but could not remember what the last reason was. Finally he had an inspiration, and the next day the professor read as the fifth reason:

5. It comes in such cute containers.

★　　★　　★　　★

The president of the Insure 'Em All Life Insurance Company was speaking at a company dinner. He had been speaking over two hours, and it was near midnight. Yet none of his employees had dared leave the room. There was a long list of speakers to follow, and these impatiently waited for the president to stop speaking. But he just rambled on. Finally, however, he sat down, after introducing the next speaker, a visiting English insurance man. The latter rose and said: "The hour has grown so late, gentlemen, that I will not deliver my speech, but will instead tell you a little story: A wee bird was flying about one day, when it suddenly began to rain. The downpour drenched the bird and it fell to earth, where the rain beat on it ceaselessly. Finally, toward noon the sun came out and warmed the little bird, so that it beat its wings and fluttered about. A horse passed by and dropped some breakfast for the wee bird, and it ate, and it ate till it could eat no more. Then straight into the air flew the wee bird, and, in good spirits, began to chirp. And it chirped and it chirped till a hawk, flying high in the sky, heard it, and swooping down on the little bird, gobbled it up. "And the moral of this little story," concluded the Englishman, to the president's discomfiture, "is this: when you're full of horseshit, don't chirp too much!"

★   ★   ★   ★

An American who was attending a banquet in a London house given by Lady Brighton, felt quite embarrassed when the lady broke wind. One of the Englishmen rose immediately, said, "I beg you pardon," and sat down again. Once more the lady farted and another English guest rose and apologized. "What's the idea?" asked the American of his neighbor. "Why don't you know? That's the gentlemanly thing to do," said the other. Again her ladyship let go, but this time the American rose, restraining another Englishman who was about to get up. "I beg your pardon, sir," he said, "but allow ME! This one's on yours truly."

★   ★   ★   ★

A Hotel Astor hired a man to drive their bus and instructed him to meet incoming trains and to announce in a loud voice, "Free bus to Hotel Astor." On his way to the station on his first trip he kept repeating "Free bus to Hotel Astor" until he had it perfect. Arriving at the station he became confused at the noise and started spieling—"Free hotel to bust your Astor"—I mean, "Free ass at Hotel Buster"—I mean, "Freeze your bust at the Hotel Astor"—I mean, "Bust your ass at the Hotel Freezer—I mean, "Oh nuts!—Take a street car."

★   ★   ★   ★

EVOLUTION

An example in evolution with a moral. Man is born, lives, dies, his body is then interred, becomes fertilizer and helps make the grass grow fast and thick and green. Along comes a horse, eats the grass, digests it, and it then becomes a horseturd.

Moral: Don't kick a horseturd—it may be your Grandpa.

★   ★   ★   ★

This famous speech is reputed to have been delivered by Senator Cassius Johnson while speaking from the floor of the Arkansas Legislature, during Reconstruction Days following the Civil War. But there were other contemporaries who swore that

*it was not a matter of "reputed," that the good Senator actually
and truly did make this speech. Nobody is absolutely sure so
that in terms of history there is a reasonable doubt that Senator
Johnson did in fact make this speech. But in terms of humor, the
thousands of G.I.s who have heard it, the fraternity brothers,
barroom buddies, stag party participants, and others, in the
minds of all these bibulous folks who have heard and laughed
uproariously at it, there can be no doubt at all.*

ON CHANGING THE NAME OF ARKANSAS
TO AR-KANSAS

"Mr. Speaker. Mr. Speaker: For the last half an hour, I've
been trying to get the floor, and every time I catch your eye, you
wiggle and squirm like a mangy dog with a flea in his ass.

"Maybe you don't know who I am. I'm Senator Johnson from
Johnson county, Arkansas, where we raise men who are men,
and women who are glad of it. Why down in Johnson county a
man can't even stick his ass out the window to take a good country shit without getting his tail filled with buckshot. Down in
Johnson county we raise girls who, at the tender age of sixteen,
can throw their left tit over their right shoulder and wipe their
ass with the nipple thereof, or squirt milk up their asshole, as the
occasion demands. When I was a boy at the age of fourteen, I
had a prick the size of a roasting ear, the pride of Johnson county. Why I could piss halfway across the Oachita river. (The
Speaker: Out of order. Out of order.) You're Goddamned right
it was out of order; if it hadn't been I could have pissed clear
across the son-of-a-bitch.

"Now here is this narrow assed, long gutted, cross-eyed son of
a cross between a Missouri mule and a gorilla, who proposes
that the name of Arkansas be changed to Ar-Kansas. Why, Mr.
Speaker, to compare the fair state of Arkansas to that of Kansas
is to compare the light of the noonday sun in all its brilliance to
the feeble glow of a lightning bug's ass; or to compare the sweet
fragrance of an American Beauty rose to the foul quintessence of
a Mexican burro's fart. Why, to compare the great state of

Arkansas to that of Kansas is to compare the puny penis of a Peruvian prince and the tiny testicles of a Turkish tyrant to the bulky balls of a Roman gladiator.

"Yes, gentlemen, you may pluck the tail feathers of the American eagle. You may piss from the Washington monument. You may shit on the White House steps, and wipe your ass on the Declaration of Independence. Yes, you may even rape the Goddess of Liberty, but change the name of Arkansas, NO. Not only no, but hellfire and damnation, no!"

★   ★   ★   ★

LET'S PLAY WHAMMY! *

One time there was a fellow named Brooks that lived on the second floor of the hotel. He took a few drinks at the tavern, and a girl come along that was drinking gin, so pretty soon him and her got to talking. But she says it looks kind of vulgar for people to set around in taverns, so they bought another bottle and went up to his room at the hotel.

After awhile he says, "Let's play whammy," but the girl never heard of whammy, and she says how do you do it? "We just take off our clothes," says he, "and you stand at one side of the room, while I stand on the other side. Then we run towards each other fast, and meet in the middle." The girl says that sounds like a fine game, and we will try it once. But they had got pretty drunk by that time, so Brooks missed the girl and fell out of the window.

The fellow didn't get hurt much because he had fell in some bushes, but there wasn't no way to get back through the window because it is too high off the ground. So he went to the kitchen door, and told the porter to fetch him a raincoat or something. But the porter says there ain't no need of that. "Jesus Christ!" says Brooks, "you want me to walk through the hotel stark naked, with all them people a-looking at me?" The porter says it is all right, because nobody will see you.

So then he looked through the glass in the door, and sure enough the lobby was plumb empty, and nobody in the dining room neither. Brooks couldn't figure out what become of all the people, because it was only eight o'clock, so he asked the hotel clerk. "Oh, they're all upstairs," says the clerk, "a-watching the doctors trying to get some woman off a doorknob."

★　　★　　★　　★

AN ITALIAN TOURIST TOLD
THE FOLLOWING STORY

You know, I don' lak that Dallas worth a sheet...They don't got any hospitality. Thees morning I go to the coffee shop for my breakfast. I tol' the girl, "Lady, I want two peece toast."...Wat you teenk? She bring one peece toast. I say, "Lady, I want two peece." She say, "If you want to peece, go to toilet." I say, "Please, Lady you don' understand: I want to peece on my plate." She say, "Don' peece on your plate you son-of-a-beech." I no see that Lady before in all my life. I won't eat where they call me a son-of-a-beech...

I walk out.

I go Adolphus for my dinner, and the Lady bring me spoon, knife and napkin, but don' bring me the foork. I say, "Lady, I wanna foork."...She say, "What you talk? Everybody wanna foork."...I say, "You don' understand, I wanna foork on table."...She say, "You don' care where you foork, you son-of-a-beech," so I figure I don't eat...I go to my room to go to bed.

I go to my room...I no gotta sheet on my bed, so I phone manager that I wanna sheet, He say, "If you wanna sheet, you go to the bathroom...I tol' heem, "I don' wanna sheet in bathroom I wanna sheet on bed." He say, "Don' sheet on bed, you son-of-a-beech."...

I decide to check out.

I go down to check out and pay my bill and tell that Dallas man I gonna check out and go to Houston. He say, "Well, my fren, goodbye and peece on you."...I say, "Peece on you, you son-of-a-beech." Because I am so mad in my face I feel lak I can whip any man twice my heavy and two times my old.

★   ★   ★   ★

THE FAIR BATHER

I knew a young lady at Atlantic last year,
Whose hobby was swimming below the long pier,

Every morning she'd go, this trim little lass,
To give you the pleasure of seeing her

Antics in water, in surf or on sand—
The cutest of all, the belle of the strand.

Her robe of blue serge, the best of good fits,
Displaying her arms and the swell of her

Tidy contour from her head to her feet;
'Twas just the right thing—decidedly neat.

She was never late, always came to the scratch
To enjoy the delight of cooling her

Shapely body in water so blue, restless and salt,
If she missed any tricks, 'twas not her own fault.

She would float on her side and for shells she would hunt,
And go through the motions of washing her

Clothes out so tidy and wringing them dry,
And hanging them up with a tired-out sigh.

She could dive like a frog and swim like a duck,
And showed by her acts that she knew how to

Frolic in water, clear up to her chin
Without getting drowned, as so many have been.

Exhausted with swimming, for the shore she would start,
And enjoy the strange pleasure of letting a

Fresh wave roll over her and tickle her toes,
And wash out the sand from her bright-colored hose.

Good health, little maid; good cheer be your wont,
Be good to yourself; take care of your

Comely complexion, don't let the sun burn it
Nor anything else, for then all would spurn it.

★   ★   ★   ★

DO YOU KNOW YOUR OWN ASS?

Over in England there is a little island called "The Isle of Man" and a very peculiar thing about the people on this island is they don't believe in automobiles and the climate is such that they cannot keep horses, so they have a donkey; or what is commonly called an Ass. Now everyone, as I said, has an Ass. Some have just ordinary Asses; Asses that you wouldn't look twice at. Others have very extraordinary Asses.

The mayor, for instance, has an Ass that no one would look at twice, but the mayor's wife has a beautiful Ass; people who really know Asses say that she has one of the finest Asses that they have ever seen. Men often stop her as she goes through the marketplace, patting her Ass.

On Sunday they all go to church on their Asses. Of course, sometimes the girls ride on the boys' Asses. And sometimes the boys ride on the girls' Asses. Now, on this particular Sunday morning, the preacher had to leave immediately following the services, so he thought he had better have his Ass handy. He tied it just outside the window. During the services a fire broke out, and, of course, everyone ran to save their Asses.

The preacher jumped out the window expecting to land on his Ass, but there was a big hole there and he fell into the hole instead, which only goes to prove that even a preacher doesn't know his Ass from a hole in the ground.

★   ★   ★   ★

SAD BUT TRUE

From twenty to thirty if a man lives right,
It's once in the morning and once at night.
From thirty to forty if he still lives right,
He cuts out the morning or else at night.
From forty to fifty it's now and then,
From fifty to sixty it's God knows when.
From sixty to seventy if he still is inclined,
Don't let them kid you, it's still on his mind.

With women it's different, it's morning or
   night,
Regardless whether they live wrong or right.
Age cuts no figure. They are always inclined
Nothing to get ready not even their mind.
So after all is said and done,
A man of sixty has completed his run.
The women of sixty, if figures don't lie,
Can take the old root till her time comes to
   die.

★   ★   ★   ★

FOLLOW YOUR LEADER*

One time there was a farmer that give his boy hell, because the young fellow would go to town pretty near every night. "Pappy," says the boy, "you're just jealous because you have got old, and can't do no running around yourself." But Pappy says it is foolish to talk like that. "We'll both go to town," says he. "You just follow me, and do everything I do. I reckon that will show who's the best man!" So the young fellow says all right.

Soon as they got to town the old man tossed off a whole bottle of whiskey, with a horse-quart of beer for a chaser. The boy done his best, but he couldn't drink that much liquor. Next they went to the hotel, and the old man eat the biggest beefsteak you ever seen, with three orders of fried potatoes. The boy done pretty good, but he couldn't eat no such a bait as that. Finally the old man headed for the whore-house, and the boy says to himself "Here is one place I will beat the old booger easy, no matter what he does!"

When they got in the whore-house the old man started kidding the girls and giving them some money. Pretty soon he had four of 'em a-prancing around the room stark naked, while him and the young fellow just watched 'em. Finally the old man pulled out his big long tallywhacker, and tied it in a knot. "All right son," says he. "Let's see you do that!"

The boy just set there goggle-eyed, because he couldn't even bend his pecker, no matter if his life depends on it. So pretty soon they both went back home, and that is the end of the story. It just goes to show that one man's meat is another man's poison, as the fellow says.

A Selected List
for Further Reading

Chapter I
Tall Tales, Whoppers and Windies

Blair, Walter. *Tall Tale America*. Funk & Wagnalls. New York. 1931.

Botkin, B.A. ed. *A Treasury of American Folklore*. Crown Publ. New York. 1949.

Botkin, B.A. *A Treasury of Western Folklore*. Bonanza Books. New York. 1980.

Chittick, V.L.O. *Ring-Tailed Roarers: Tall Tales of the American Frontier, 1830-1860*. Paxton Printers. Idaho. 1946.

Dorson, Richard M. *Jonathan Draws the Longbow*. Cambridge. 1946.

DuMond, Frank L. *Tall Tales of the Catskills*. Atheneum. New York. 1908.

Masterson, James R. *Tall Tales of Arkansas*. Chapman & Grimes. Boston. 1943.

Meine, Franklin J., ed. *Tall Tales of the Southwest; An Anthology of Southern and Southwestern Humor, 1830-1860*. Knopf. New York. 1930.

Randolph, Vance. *Ozark Mountain Folk*. New York. 1932.

Thomas, Lowell. *Tall Stories*. Funk & Wagnalls Co. New York. 1931.

Chapter II
Jokes from 1842-1912

Avery, Samuel P. *The Harp of a Thousand Strings; Or, Laughter for a Lifetime*. Dick & Fitzgerald. New York. 1858.

Bayle, S. *Books of Anecdotes and Jokers' Knapsack*. John E. Potter & Co. Philadelphia. 1866.

Brown, Marshall. *Wit and Humor*. S.C. Griggs & Co. Chicago. 1881.

Burdette, Robert J. *Burdette's World of Humor.* Excelsior Publishing House. New York. 1886.

Byrn, M. Lafatte M.D. *The Repository of Wit and Humor.* Boston. 1857.

Clinton, T. *Pat Rooney's Quaint Conundrums and Funny Gags.* DeWitt Publ. New York. 1879.

Cox, Palmer. *Squibbs of California; or, Every-Day Life.* Mutual Publ. Co. Hartford. 1874.

Dumon, Frank. *Burnt Cork; or the Amateur Minstrel.* DeWitt. N.Y. 1881.

Evans, George E. *Book of Anecdotes and Budget of Fun.* 1859. *Diamonds Scintillating Jokes.* M.A. Honohue & Co. Chicago. 1912.

Kempt, Robert. *The American Joe Miller.* Adams & Francis. London. 1865.

Kenny, W. Howland. *Laughter in the Wilderness.* Kent State U. Press. Kent, Ohio. 1976.

Landon, Melville E. *Comical Hits by Famous Wits.* Thomas & Thomas. Chicago. 1900.

Shillaber, Benjamin P. *One Thousand Comical Stories.* Dick & Fitzgerald. Chicago. 1912.

Sinclair, W.D. *Chicago Jokes & Anecdotes.* 1866.

Williams, Gus. *World of Humor.* DeWitt Pub. Co. New York. 1880.

Chapter III
Colonial and Frontier Humor

Baldwin, Joseph G. *The Flush Times of Alabama and Mississippi.* D. Appleton & Co. New York. 1853.

Blair, Walter & Meine, Franklin. *Mike Fink, King of Mississippi Boatmen.* Henry Holt & Co. New York. 1933.

Crockett, David. *Narrative of the Life of David Crockett of West Tennessee.* Philadelphia, Baltimore, London. 1834. *Colonel Crockett's Exploits and Adventures in Texas.* Philadelphia. 1936. New York.

Life of Colonel Crockett. Philadelphia. 1860, [1865], [1882].

Life and Adventures of Davy Crockett. An Autobiography. New York. [1882], [1903].

An Autobiography of Davy Crockett, with an Introduction by Hamlin Garland. New York. 1923.

The Adventures of Davy Crockett; Told Mostly by Himself. New York. [1934].

Herzog, Peter. *Frontier Humor, or, A Few Belly Laughs From the Territorial Press, 1847-1887.* Press of the Territorian. Santa Fe. 1966.

Inge, M. Thomas, ed. *The Frontier Humorists.* Archon Books. Hamden. 1975.

Kenny, W. Howland. *Laughter in the Wilderness: Early American Humor to 1783.* Kent State University Press. Kent, Ohio. 1976.

A Legend of the Ohio. Cincinnati. 1848.

Mince Pie for the Millions. Philadelphia. 1846.

Nick of the Woods, or the Jibbernainosoay. Turner & Fisher. Philadelphia and New York. 1846.

Sloane, David E. *The Literary Humor of the Urban Northeast, 1830-1890.* Louisiana State University Press. Baton Rouge. 1983.

Twenty-Five Cents Worth of Nonsense: or The Treasure Box of Unconsidered Trifles. Fisher & Brothers. New York. 184-?.

Zall, P.M. *Ben Franklin Laughing.* University of California Press. Berkley. 1980.

Chapter IV
A Gallery of Fearsome Critters

Botkin, B.A. *A Treasury of New England Folklore.* Bonanza. 1965.

Cox, William T. *Fearsome Creatures of the Lumberwood.* Judd & Dutweiler, Inc. Washington. 1911.

Dorson, Richard M. *Man and Beast in American Comic Legend.*

Indiana University Press. Bloomington, Indiana. 1982.

Dorson, Richard. *Bloodstoppers and Bearwalks.* Harvard U. Press. Cambridge. 1952.

Kearney, Lake Shore. *The Hodag, and Other Tales of the Logging Camps.* Wausau, Wisconsin. 1928.

Schwartz, Alvin. *Kickle Snifters and Other Fearsome Critters, Collected from American Folklore.* J.B. Lippincott. New York. 1939.

Tyron, Henry H. *Fearsome Critters.* Idlewild Press. New York. 1939.

Chapter V
Oh, Those Phunny Phellows!

Bagby, George William. *The Letters of Mozis Addums to Billy Ivvins.* Richmond. 1862, 1878.

What I Did with My Fifty Millions. By Moses Addums. Philadelphia. 1874.

Meekins's Twinses, a Perduckshun uv Mozis Addums. Richmon. 1877.

A Week in Hepsidam. Richmond. 1879.

The Old Virginia Gentleman and Other Sketches. 2 vols. New York. 1910, 1911.

Browne, Charles Farrar. *Artemus Ward; His Book.* New York. 1862, 1863, 1864, 1865, 1867.

Artemus Ward; His Travels. New York. 1865, 1866.

Artemus Ward among the Mormons. London. 1865.

Artemus Ward. Grate Snaix. His Book. Montreal. 1866.

Artemus Ward in London. New York. 1867.

Artemus Ward's Lecture. London. 1869, 1882. New York.

Artemus Ward's Best Stories. Edited by Clifton Johnson, with an Introduction by William Dean Howells. New York. 1912.

Selected Works of Artemus Ward. New York. 1924.

Locke, David Ross. *The Nasby Papers.* Indianapolis. 1864.

Divers Opinions, and Prophecies of Yours Trooly, Petroleum

V. Nasby. New York. 1865.

Swingin' Round the Cirkle. By Petroleum V. Nasby. Boston.

Ekkoes from Kentucky. Boston. 1867.

The Impendin Crisis uv the Democracy. Toledo. 1868.

The Struggles (Social, Financial and Political) of Petroleum V. Nasby. Boston. 1872, 1888.

The Morals of Abou Ben Adhem. Boston. 1874, 1875.

Nasby in Exile; or, Six Months of Travel. Toledo, Boston. 1882.

The Nasby Letters. Toledo. 1893.

Newell, Robert Henry. *The Orpheus C. Kerr Papers.* New York. 1862, 1863, 1865, 1871.

Smoked Glass.

The Cloven Foot. New York. 1870.

Versatilities. Boston. 1871.

The Walking Doll. New York. 1872.

Pullen, John J. *Life and Laughter of Artemus Ward, 1834-1867.* Archon Books. Hamden. 1983.

Smith, Charles H. *Bill Arp, So-Called.* New York. 1866.

Bill Arp's Letters. New York. 1868.

Bill Arp's Peace Papers. New York. 1873.

Bill Arp's Scrap Book; Humor and Philosophy. Atlanta. 1884.

The Farm and the Fireside. Atlanta. 1891, 1892.

Chapter VI
Abraham Lincoln's Stories

Basler, Roy P., ed. *The Collected Works of Abraham Lincoln.* The Abraham Lincoln Association and Rutgers University Press. Springfield and New Brunswick. 1953.

Blair, Walter. *Horse Sense in American Humor.* U. of Chicago Press. Chicago. 1942.

Case, Carleton. *The Wit and Humor of Abraham Lincoln.* Shrewsbury. Chicago. 1916.

Conwell, Russell H. *Why Lincoln Laughed.* Harpers. New York. 1922.

Dawley, T.R. *Old Abe's Jokes, Fresh from Abraham's Bosom.* New York. 1864.

Feeks, J.F. *Lincolniana, or The Humor of Uncle Abe.* New York. 1864.

Gross, Anthony. *Lincoln's Own Stories.* Harpers. New York. 1912.

Hertz, Emmanuel. *Lincoln Talks.* Viking. New York. 1939.

Humorous and Pathetic Stories of Abraham Lincoln. Lincoln Publ. Co. Fort Wayne. (1894?)

Lincoln's Anecdotes. American News Co. New York. 1867.

McClure, J.B. *Anecdotes of Abraham Lincoln and Lincoln Stories.* Rhodes & McClure. Chicago. 1879.

Newman, Ralph J. *The Stories Lincoln Liked Best.* Chicago Sunday Tribune Magazine. Chicago. 1953.

Oates, Stephen B. *With Malice Towards None.* Harper and Row. New York. 1977.

Strozier, Charles B. *Lincoln's Life Preserver.* American Heritage. Feb./Mar. 1982.
   Lincoln's Quest for Union. Basic Books, Inc. New York. 1982.

Thomas, Benjamin P. *Portrait for Posterity.* Rutgers University Press. New Brunswick. 1947.

Whitney, Henry Clay. *Life on the Circuit with Lincoln.* Estes & Lauriat. Boston.

Williams, Henry L. *The Lincoln Story Book.* Dillingham. New York. 1907.

Chapter VII
Humor after the Civil War

Bailey, James Montgomery. *Danbury News Man's Almanac.* Boston. 1873.
   Life in Danbury. Boston. 1873.
   They All Do It. Boston 1877.
   The Danbury Boom. Boston. 1880.

Bangs, John Kendrick. *Three Weeks in Politics.* New York. 1894.

The Idiot. New York. 1895.

Mr. Bonaparte of Corsica. New York. 1895.

Houseboat on the Styx. New York. 1895.

Paste Jewels. New York. 1896.

Pursuit of the Houseboat. New York. 1897.

Bierce, Ambrose. *The Friend's Delight.* London. 1872.

Nuggets and Dust Panned Out in California. London. 1873.

Tales of Soldiers and Civilians. San Francisco. 1891.

Black Beetles in Amber. San Francisco. 1892.

Shapes of Clay. San Francisco. 1893.

Fantastic Fables. New York. 1899.

The Cynic's Word Book. New York. 1906.

The Collected Works of Ambrose Bierce. Citadel Press. Secaucus. New York. 1946.

Burdette, Robert Jones. *Hawkeyetems.* Burlington. 1877.

The Rise and Fall of the Moustache and Other "Hawkeyetems." Burlington. 1877.

Hawkeyes. New York. 1879. Republished as *Innach Garden and Other Sketches.* New York. 1886.

Samuel L. Clemens (Mark Twain). *The Celebrated Jumping Frog of Caleveras County and Other Sketches.* New York. 1867.

The Innocents Abroad. Hartford. 1869.

Mark Twain's Burlesque Autobiography and First Romance. New York. 1871.

Roughing It. Hartford. 1872.

The Gilded Age. (Written in collaboration with C.D. Warner.) Hartford. 1874.

Mark Twain's Sketches, New and Old. Hartford. 1875.

The Adventures of Tom Sawyer. Hartford. 1876.

A Tramp Abroad. Hartford. 1880.

Life on the Mississippi. Boston. 1883.

Adventures of Huckleberry Finn. New York. 1884.

A Connecticut Yankee in King Arthur's Court. New York. 1889.

The American Claimant. New York. 1892.

Tom Sawyer Abroad. New York. 1894.

The Tragedy of Pudd'nhead Wilson. Hartford. 1894.

Following the Equator. Hartford. 1897.

The Collected Works of Mark Twain. Bonanza. New York. 1919.

Dunne, Finley Peter. *Mr. Dooley in Peace and War.* Boston. 1898, 1899.

Mr. Dooley in the Hearts of His Countrymen. Boston. 1899.

What Mr. Dooley Says. Chicago. 1899.

Mr. Dooley's Philosophy. New York. 1900.

The Life and Adventures of Private Miles O'Reilly. New York. 1864. Tarrytown. 1926.

Baked Meats of the Funeral. New York. 1866.

Lanigan, George Thomas. *Fables of G. Washington Aesop.* New York. 1878.

Nye, Edgar Wilson. *Bill Nye and Boomerang.* Chicago. 1881, 1885, 1887, 1889, 1890, 1894, 1901.

Forty Liars and Other Lies. Chicago. 1882, 1884, 1887, 1893, 1894, 1901.

Baled Hay. New York. 1884, 1887. Chicago.

Bill Nye's Blossom Book. Chicago. 1885.

Remarks. Chicago. 1887, 1893, 1896, 1901.

Bill Nye's Chestnuts, Old and New. Chicago. 1887, 1894.

Bill Nye's Cordwood. Chicago. 1887.

Bill Nye's Thinks. Chicago. 1888, 1889.

Bill Nye's History of the United States. Philadelphia. 1894, 1895, 1896. Chicago. 1905.

Peck, George W. *Peck's Sunshine.* Chicago. 1882, 1887, 1900.

Peck's Bad Boy and His Pa. Chicago. 1883, 1887, 1893, 1900.

Peck's Bad Boy and His Pa, No. 2. The Grocery Man and Peck's Bad Boy. Chicago. 1883, 1887, 1893, [1894], 1900.

How Private George W. Peck Put Down the Rebellion. Chicago. 1887.

Peck's Uncle Ike and the Red-Headed Boy. Chicago. 1899.

Pomeroy, Marcus Mills. *Sense, or Saturday-Night Musings and*

Thoughtful Papers. New York. 1868.
Nonsense, etc. by "Brick" Pomeroy. New York. 1868.
Our Saturday Nights. New York. 1871.
Gold-Dust. New York. 1871.

Chapter VIII
The Bawdy Part

Aurand, A. Monroe. *Two-in-a-Bed*. (?)
Faro, William. *Anecdota Americana*. New York. (?) 1933.
Randolph, Vance. *Pissing in the Snow*. U. of Illinois Press. Champaign. 1976.
Schweinickle, O.U. (?). *The Book of a Thousand Laughs. Stag Party*. 1888.

General Reading

Blair, Walter. *Native American Humor, 1800-1900*. Am. Book Co. 1937.
Blair, Walter & Hill, Hamlin. *America's Humor*. Oxford U. Press. 1980.
Blair, Walter & McDavid, Raven I., Jr. *The Mirth of a Nation*. U. of Minnesota Press. Minneapolis. 1983.
Botkin, B.A. *A Treasury of American Folklore*. Bonanza. New York. 195–.
Eastman, Max. *The Enjoyment of Laughter*. Simon & Schuster. New York. 1936.
Hall, Wade. *The Smiling Phoenix*. U. of Flo. Press. Gainesville. 1965.
Meine, Franklin J. *Tall Tales of the Southwest*. Alfred A. Knopf. New York. 1930.
Rourke, Constance. *American Humor, A Study of the National Character*. Harcourt Brace & Co. New York. 1935.
Rubin, Louis D., Jr., ed. *The Comic Imagination in American Literature*. Rutgers U. Press. New Brunswick. 1973, 1983.
Tandy, Jessica. *Crackerbox Philosophers in American Humor and Satire*. New York. 1925.
Wells, Carolyn, ed. *An Outline of Humor*. G.P. Putnam's Sons. New York. 1932.